FLORIDA STATE
UNIVERSITY LIBRARIES

MAY 24 2001

TALLAHASSEE, FLORIDA

ON THE FOUNDATIONS OF MONOPOLISTIC COMPETITION AND ECONOMIC GEOGRAPHY

ECONOMISTS OF THE TWENTIETH CENTURY

General Editors: Mark Perlman, *University Professor of Economics, Emeritus, University of Pittsburgh* and Mark Blaug, *Professor Emeritus, University of London, Professor Emeritus, University of Buckingham and Visiting Professor, University of Exeter*

This innovative series comprises specially invited collections of articles and papers by economists whose work has made an important contribution to economics in the late twentieth century.

The proliferation of new journals and the ever-increasing number of new articles make it difficult for even the most assiduous economist to keep track of all the important recent advances. By focusing on those economists whose work is generally recognized to be at the forefront of the discipline, the series will be an essential reference point for the different specialisms included. Wherever possible, the articles in these volumes have been reproduced as originally published using facsimile reproduction, inclusive of footnotes and pagination to facilitate ease of reference.

A list of published and future titles in this series is printed at the end of this volume.

On the Foundations of Monopolistic Competition and Economic Geography

The Selected Essays of B. Curtis Eaton and Richard G. Lipsey

B. Curtis Eaton

Professor of Economics, Simon Fraser University, Canada

Richard G. Lipsey

Fellow, Canadian Institute for Advanced Research, and Professor of Economics, Simon Fraser University, Canada

ECONOMISTS OF THE TWENTIETH CENTURY SERIES

Edward Elgar
Cheltenham, UK • Lyme, US

© B. Curtis Eaton and Richard G. Lipsey 1997

All rights reserved. No part of this publication may be reproduced, stored in a retrieval system, or transmitted in any form or by any means, electronic, mechanical, photocopying, recording, or otherwise without the prior permission of the publisher.

Published by
Edward Elgar Publishing Limited
8 Lansdown Place
Cheltenham
Glos GL50 2HU
UK

Edward Elgar Publishing, Inc
1 Pinnacle Hill Road
Lyme
NH 03768
US

A catalogue record for this book is available from the British Library

Library of Congress Cataloging-in-Publication Data

Eaton, Buford Curtis, 1943–
  On the foundations of monopolistic competition and economic geography : the selected essays of B. Curtis Eaton and Richard G. Lipsey.
    (Economists of the twentieth century)
  Includes bibliographical references.
  1. Space in economics. 2. Industrial location. 3. Economic geography. 4. Competition. I. Lipsey, Richard G., 1928– .
  II. Title. III. Series.
  HB 199.E273 1997
  338.6'042–dc21   96–48051
                                                                    CIP

ISBN 1 85898 536 6

Printed and bound in Great Britain by
Biddles Limited, Guildford and King's Lynn

Contents

Acknowledgements		vii
Introduction: Beyond Neoclassical Competitive Economics		ix
1	'The Principle of Minimum Differentiation Reconsidered: Some New Developments in the Theory of Spatial Competition', *Review of Economic Studies*, **XLII** (1), January 1975, 27–49.	1
2	'The Non-Uniqueness of Equilibrium in the Löschian Location Model', *American Economic Review*, **66** (1), March 1976, 77–93.	24
3	'The Introduction of Space into the Neoclassical Model of Value Theory' in *Studies in Modern Economic Analysis*, (eds M.J. Artis and A.R. Nobay), Basil Blackwell, 1977, 59–96.	41
4	'Spatial Monopoly, Natural Monopoly, Pure Profits, and Land Rents', Queen's University Discussion Paper No. 265, June 1977.	68
5	'A Comment on Location and Industrial Efficiency with Free Entry', Queen's University Discussion Paper No. 269, June 1977.	86
6	'Freedom of Entry and the Existence of Pure Profit', *The Economic Journal*, **88**, September 1978, 455–69.	94
7	'The Theory of Market Pre-emption: The Persistence of Excess Capacity and Monopoly in Growing Spatial Markets', *Economica*, **46**, May 1979, 149–58.	109
8	'Comparison Shopping and the Clustering of Homogeneous Firms', *Journal of Regional Science*, **19** (4), 1979, 421–35.	119
9	'The Block Metric and the Law of Markets', *Journal of Urban Economics*, **7**, 1980, 337–47.	134
10	'Exit Barriers are Entry Barriers: The Durability of Capital as a Barrier to Entry', *The Bell Journal of Economics*, **11** (2), Autumn 1980, 721–9.	145
11	'Capital, Commitment, and Entry Equilibrium', *The Bell Journal of Economics*, **12** (2), Autumn 1981, 593–604.	154
12	'An Economic Theory of Central Places', *The Economic Journal*, **92**, March 1982, 56–72.	166
13	'Address Models of Value Theory' (with G.C. Archibald) in *New Developments in the Analysis of Market Structure*, (eds J.E. Stiglitz and G.F. Mathewson), Macmillan Press, 1986, 3–47.	183
14	'Product Differentiation' in *Handbook of Industrial Organization Volume One*, (eds R. Schmalensee and R.D. Willig), North-Holland 1989, 725–68.	228
15	'The Theory of Multinational Plant Location: Agglomerations and Disagglomerations' (with A.E. Safarian) in *Multinationals in North America*, (ed. L. Eden), University of Calgary Press, 1994, 79–102.	272

vi *On the Foundations of Monopolistic Competition and Economic Geography*

16 'Increasing Returns, Indivisibility and All That', Simon Fraser
    University Discussion Paper, June 1993.   296

Name index   313

Acknowledgements

The author and publishers wish to thank the following who have kindly given permission for the use of copyright material.

Academic Press for article: 'The Block Metric and the Law of Markets', *Journal of Urban Economics*, **7**, 1980, 337–47.

American Economics Association for article: 'The Non-Uniqueness of Equilibrium in the Löschian Location Model', *American Economic Review*, **66** (1), March 1976, 77–93.

Basil Blackwell Ltd for articles: 'The Introduction of Space into the Neoclassical Model of Value Theory' in *Studies in Modern Economic Analysis*, (eds M.J. Artis and A.R. Nobay), 1977, 59–96; 'Freedom of Entry and the Existence of Pure Profit', *The Economic Journal*, **88**, September 1978, 455–69; 'The Theory of Market Pre-emption: The Persistence of Excess Capacity and Monopoly in Growing Spatial Markets', *Economica*, **46**, May 1979, 149–58; 'An Economic Theory of Central Places', *The Economic Journal*, **92**, March 1982, 56–72.

Elsevier Science Publishers b.v. for article: 'Product Differentiation' in *Handbook of Industrial Organization Volume One*, (eds R. Schmalensee and R.D. Willig), North-Holland 1989, 725–68.

Journal of Regional Science for article: 'Comparison Shopping and the Clustering of Homogeneous Firms', **19** (4), 1979, 421–35.

Macmillan Press and C.G. Archibald for article: 'Address Models of Value Theory' in *New Developments in the Analysis of Market Structure*, (eds J.E. Stiglitz and G.F. Mathewson), 1986, 3–47.

Rand for articles: 'Exit Barriers are Entry Barriers: The Durability of Capital as a Barrier to Entry', *The Bell Journal of Economics*, **11** (2), Autumn 1980, 721–9; 'Capital, Commitment, and Entry Equilibrium', *The Bell Journal of Economics*, **12** (2), Autumn 1981, 593–604.

Review of Economic Studies Ltd for article: 'The Principle of Minimum Differentiation Reconsidered: Some New Developments in the Theory of Spatial Competition', **XLII** (1), January 1975, 27–49.

University of Calgary Press and A.E. Safarian for article: 'The Theory of Multinational Plant Location: Agglomerations and Disagglomerations' in (ed. L. Eden), 1994, 79–102.

Every effort has been made to trace all the copyright holders but if any have been inadvertently overlooked the publishers will be pleased to make the necessary arrangements at the first opportunity.

Introduction: Beyond Neoclassical Competitive Economics

B. Curtis Eaton and Richard G. Lipsey

This volume contains our joint papers on address models of value theory and related issues. This introductory essay provides an overview of our work in the form of the vision of the economy that we have developed. We begin with a few methodological remarks.

From the very beginning of our collaboration, our objective has been to develop a deeper understanding of product differentiation, including spatial differentiation, and the industrial structures that give rise to this phenomenon. As such, our work is grounded on what we see as the important facts regarding product differentiation, while, in theorizing, our purpose has been to provide an explanation for these awkward facts. In this methodological approach, awkward facts are to be welcomed because they serve to constrain the theory. Although it may be impossible to explain everything that is known about the issue in question, our objective has been to explain some significant subset of the awkward facts using theories that are not obviously inconsistent with the remaining observations. Although we did not start out to develop a critique of the standard neoclassical competitive vision of the economy, in which market power is either ignored entirely or treated as an annoying side issue, we found that accommodating the salient awkward facts forced us to abandon this vision.

In section I of this essay, we discuss our reasons for rejecting the neoclassical, competitive vision of the economy. In sections II and III, we discuss the address models that have been instrumental in developing our own vision of the economy. Finally, in Part IV, we outline our world view and contrast it with other competing visions of the economy. The elements of our own view are developed in more detail in the research papers included in this volume.[1]

I. Rejecting the neoclassical vision

It is impossible to observe the world without some preconceptions, and we began with neoclassical preconceptions. Slowly, however, we came to appreciate the ubiquity of three phenomena that are not easily accommodated in the neoclassical framework – lumpiness, specificity, and diversity – and eventually we came to see the ways in which these phenomena undermine the neoclassical, competitive vision of the world.

Lumpiness

In neoclassical theory, all inputs are perfectly divisible. When we look at the world, however, we see lumpiness everywhere. We have come to see lumpy knowledge, lumpy capital goods, and the associated scale effects as fundamental.

Knowledge is costly to acquire and it is non-rivalrous. Hence, once a particular bit of knowledge is produced, it can potentially provide an infinite quantity of services. From an economic perspective, a particular piece of knowledge can be thought of as a capital good with an infinite lump of embodied services. Product-development capital – the knowledge associated with the design and engineering of products, production facilities and marketing plans – has played a central role in much of our work. Many of the costs associated with product development are completely unrelated to output, and none of them are proportionate to output. Hence, when the resources devoted to product development are taken into account, the technology for producing the product is non-convex, and average costs of production decline over some initial range of total output.

More generally, we would argue that since changing knowledge lies at the heart of technological change, which in turn lies at the heart of economic growth, the non-convexities that arise from the once-and-for-all, non-rivalrous nature of knowledge are pervasive and important. As the following example illustrates, one clear implication of this non-convexity is that history matters. In the late 1970s and early 1980s very high, short-term real interest rates induced firms to learn how to economize on transactions balances and to further develop an infrastructure of worldwide, short-term lending markets to facilitate their efforts. When interest rates fell back again to historically more normal levels, this knowledge was not lost and the infrastructure did not spontaneously decay. As a result of this massive but short-lived upward blip in interest rates, the demand function for transactions balances shifted permanently. In this sort of situation, history matters in the sense that economic behaviour at any point in time is determined by the current and past values of the relevant economic variables.

If a particular bit of knowledge is a capital good with an infinite lump of embodied services, a particular piece of physical capital is a capital good with a strictly positive (but usually not infinite) lump of embodied services. As we argue in Chapter 16 just as knowledge entails an underlying non-convexity, the lumpiness of physical capital goods is a manifestation of an underlying non-convexity in the technology of producing capital goods. Roughly, the argument is the following. Consider some real capital good. If the technology for producing the capital good was convex, half the services of the capital good could be embodied in a smaller capital good at no more than half the cost. Then, given a positive interest rate, it would be cheaper to produce two of the smaller capital goods, in sequence as needed, since sequential production involves less costly waiting. Carried to its logical extreme, the argument says that if the technology for producing capital goods – goods with a lump of embodied services – was convex, then cost minimizing firms would never produce them, opting instead to produce disembodied flows of services. Hence, the fact that we do see capital goods is an indication of an underlying non-convexity. This non-convexity, of course, implies that the average costs of producing the services that are embodied in capital goods are declining over some initial range of total services. By extension, if the capital good in question is firm specific, the argument implies declining average cost over some initial range of the firm's output.

The lumpiness of knowledge and physical capital goods is mirrored in other aspects of economic activity. Economic activity is extremely lumpy in geographic space. Production is not spread evenly across the globe as butter is spread over bread. Instead, it is concentrated in particular geographic areas and, within those areas, in specific sites. Consumption activity is also clustered geographically, and subject to important indivisibilities that are associated with transport facilities and personal shopping trips. Similarly, the products that firms choose to make are spread lumpily in characteristic space. Existing products represent a small number of points in the space of imaginable products, and, for every product that is made, consumers can be found who would prefer some other product with a slightly different bundle of characteristics but that is not made.

Specificity
In the neoclassical production function, all inputs are non-specific. Labour, physical capital and human capital can all be used to produce any product and transferred from one production activity to another. When we look at the world, however, we see that both physical and human capital is to a great extent activity-specific. A dam cannot be used to assemble motor cars, nor can an auto assembly plant be used to produce auto parts, let alone bread. A well-trained engineer can be used in a number of activities but not (without further training) to teach sociology, nor to analyse national accounts data, nor to edit a set of rushes into a marketable movie.

Lumpiness plus specificity
Though lumpiness and specificity are ordinarily not part of the neoclassical, competitive vision, in isolation neither lumpiness nor specificity is destructive of the vision. Assume that the technology for producing some new asset (either a machine or some useful piece of knowledge) is non-convex as described above. Then, the average cost per unit of service will decline over some initial range of total services embodied in the good. If the asset is non-specific in the sense that it can be used in all lines of productive activity, its lumpiness does not matter since the asset can be spread over many uses. Next, consider an asset that is specific in the sense that it can be used in just one productive activity. If it is not lumpy (that is, if its technology is convex), it can be made to embody an infinitesimal amount of services at no cost penalty, and its specificity does not matter.

It is the combination of lumpiness and specificity that first caused us to question the neoclassical, competitive vision of the economy. If a capital asset is both product-specific and lumpy, the non-convexity in the asset's technology will be mirrored in the technology of production of the good that it helps to make. In particular, average costs of producing the good will be declining over some initial range of output, and minimum efficient scale will be strictly positive. In this case, if industry output is small relative to minimum efficient scale, neoclassical, competitive results are not possible. Still, it might be the case that in the vast majority of industries total output is large relative to minimum efficient scale; from the perspective of the neoclassical vision, market power and market failure would then be annoying side issues necessitating appropriate footnotes and qualifications, but the vision itself would survive.

Diversity

We see revealed diversity of tastes in individuals' decisions. Consumers in similar economic situations make different consumption decisions. Workers in similar economic situations make different career choices, and, within any one career, they make different subsidiary choices such as avoiding or accepting specific risks. Such choices reveal people to have different tastes and different preferences. Current psychological knowledge tells us that these taste differences are rooted partly in different genetic makeups and partly in different past experiences. With the exception of identical siblings, each person's genetic make-up is unique; so too, each person's past experience is unique. And it is our view that their preferences are also unique.

We also see revealed diversity in production decisions. For example, Toyota produces several models of car, and within each model, hundreds of variants. Dozens, perhaps hundreds, of ready-to-eat cereals, each available in two or three different sized packages are available at the typical supermarket. A teenager shopping for basketball shoes can choose among 20 or 30 different designs, and perhaps ten different sizes of each design. Despite the impressive array of available goods, another fact that strikes us is the paucity of goods relative to the diversity of tastes over individuals. From any particular individual's point of view, it would be possible to design a car, or a ready-to-eat cereal, or a basketball shoe that was more desirable than the ones currently available. This observation leads to the question: Why do most of us buy off-the-shelf, rather than tailor-made products? It is not any physical inability to produce more products that explains this fact. Instead, it is the combination of non-convexity and specificity as outlined above.

Another fact that strikes us is that we do not see, or see only rarely, a number of firms producing identical consumers' goods and services. Honda, and Volkswagen, and Ford all produce a range of cars, but with rare exceptions, they do not produce the same cars. Why? Because, given the diversity of tastes, when a firm contemplates the creation of a new product it is almost always more profitable to create a niche for the new product rather than clone an existing product exactly, thereby exposing itself to the risk of ruinous competition that is inherent with identical products and non-convex technologies.

Clearly, the neoclassical model can incorporate diversity of tastes. But, as we shall argue below, what it cannot incorporate is the infinite potential diversity of products that is central to our vision. If that is built into a neoclassical type model the result bears no relation to the competitive model which is the basis for most neoclassical welfare and policy conclusions.

Lumpiness plus specificity plus diversity

If the combination of lumpiness and specificity causes us to question the neoclassical vision of the economy, the combination of lumpiness, specificity, and diversity causes us to reject it. Just imagine what the economy as outlined above would look like in an equilibrium in which no firm found it attractive to develop any new product. Necessarily for each good, total output would be large relative to minimum efficient scale, otherwise some firm would find it profitable to enter at a nearby point in the product characteristic space. Then, far from being annoying side issues, market power and 'market failure' are seen to be ubiquitous phenomena, and the neoclassical, competitive vision is seen to be entirely inadequate.

II. Basic assumptions

Our work started with two basic observations. First, as students of Industrial Organization, it was apparent to us that perfect competition was seldom if ever found in the manufacturing and service industries which account for the bulk of economic activity in a modern economy. Products in both of these industries are typically differentiated but natural monopolies are rare, making some version of 'imperfect competition' the relevant market structure. Second, production and consumption are seen to be distributed unevenly in both geographic and characteristic space and this seems to have important implications for economic activity that are not caught in the neoclassical spaceless economy.

Geographic space and product-characteristic space

When we deal with geographic space, the major choice is one of dimensionality. Will we analyse spaces of one, two or three dimensions, which are the only ones relevant to our experience on the planet on which we live? In the model of geographic space, goods are naturally described by their locations in the space, that is, by their addresses.

When we deal with product differentiation, we face a more fundamental choice. Will we adopt a goods-are-goods model or an address model in which goods are described by their addresses in a product characteristic space? In the former, the set of all possible goods is specified by an exogenously given list or range; in the latter, the set is characterized by a continuous space whose dimensions stand for product characteristics. We chose the address model, first, because it neatly incorporated the awkward fact that goods have well-defined descriptions in a continuum of possible products, and second, because it conformed with our judgement that an important part of inter-firm competition is choice of which goods in the continuum to develop and produce. Our reasons for choosing the address model rather than the goods-are-goods model are discussed in more detail in Chapters 13 and 14.

As anyone familiar with this literature will know, there is a close analogy between the address model of product characteristics and the address model of geographic space in the sense that many of the insights of the product-characteristic model can be carried over to a model of geographic space, and vice versa. In most of what follows, we will argue in terms of a generic model that bears either interpretation.

As it turned out, this model could explain the following awkward facts, discussed in more detail in Chapter 14, some of which are inconsistent with the goods-are-goods version of monopolistic competition which is commonly used today to deal with issues involving product differentiation.

1. In many industries, a large number of differentiated products is produced.
2. In many industries, two or more different firms rarely produce the same product.
3. The set of products that are actually produced is a small subset of the set of possible products.

4. In many industries, each firm produces a range of differentiated products.
5. Any one consumer purchases only a small subset of the available products.
6. Consumers perceive the differences among differentiated products to be real and are often in close agreement on which products are the closest substitutes for each other. That is, consumers perceive products as points in characteristic space.
7. Tastes are revealed to differ across consumers.

Exogenous and endogenous variables
We have argued in Section I that specificity, lumpiness and diversity are important phenomena which we cannot avoid when we come to study the observed diversities of product characteristics and industrial locations. To theorize about the relations between these two sets of observations, we need to decide how much of the observed specificity, lumpiness and diversity is endogenous and how much exogenous.

Diversity requires the least discussion. We take the observed diversities of tastes, of potential geographic locations, and of potential product characteristics as exogenous.

Although some degree of specificity seems to be a universal feature of physical goods, the observed degrees of specificity of physical capital (and human capital and software) seem also to be endogenous. On the human capital side, one can choose the degree to which one specializes, and for any degree of specialization of individual A's human capital, it is always possible to imagine individuals B and C who have expertise in the same area as A but whose knowledge is respectively more and less specialized than A's. Similar considerations apply to physical capital. The degree to which machinery and tools are specialized is a choice variable for their producers. For any tool or machine, A, it is always possible to design two other tools: tool B which does only some of the things A does, and tool C which does all of the things A does and some other things as well.

Thirdly, consider the lumpiness which we observe in both labour and capital. Clearly, the lumpiness of people is exogenous. People are also activity- and place-specific which is also exogenous in the sense that physical laws ensure that they can only be in one place and do one thing at a time.[2] In contrast the observed lumpiness of capital goods seems endogenous in the sense that one could always design a product-specific capital good with less embodied services (less durability) than the one currently in use.

Where lumpiness and specificity are endogenous, they need to be explained. For example, we cannot produce a continuum of goods because there are significant costs of developing (and marketing) a product to occupy any one point in characteristic space and because of the lumpiness of many of the capital goods needed in production. In Chapter 16 we consider the lumpiness of these capital goods. As we have noted above, we argue that the only reason for choosing more capital-good lumpiness than the minimum that is physically possible, is a non-convexity in embodying services in capital goods. Durability requires waiting to extract the valuable services contained in a capital good, and with a positive interest rate, waiting is costly. If half the services could be embodied in some less durable capital good at half the cost, it would pay to utilize successively two units of the less durable good since this plan involves less waiting than using one unit of the more durable good. So capital goods are typically made more durable than is necessary because there is a non-convexity in embodying capital services in a produced capital good. Without such a non-convexity in the production of capital goods, all such goods would be observed to be of the minimum possible durability thus involving the minimum of embodied services and hence the minimum interest costs of waiting for those services to be extracted.

The above arguments lead us to the general conclusion that the very existence of endogenous lumpiness and specificity are manifestations of underlying non-convexities in some relevant technology. Of course, these technologically driven non-convexities change as technology changes. For example, recent developments in computer assisted production have greatly increased the range of economically feasible product variety by making it possible to vary the characteristics of some generic products more or less continuously using the same (lumpy) capital goods. In such cases, the lumpinesses of the capital good determines the minimum economic volume of production of the whole group of differentiated products but not of any one of them. So long as there are enough batches, different goods can efficiently be produced in small batches, often even on a one-off basis. The point here is that the underlying technology of production dictates the menu of specificity in the capital goods and hence the amount of diversity that is economically feasible, but (into the foreseeable future at least) does not permit a continuum of production that covers all of the relevant characteristic space.

III. Implications

In our work we have tried to construct models that incorporate lumpiness, specificity, and diversity in empirically relevant ways, and then to explore their many interesting implications. Some of the most important of these implications are outlined in what follows. We give intuitive explanations and provide references to the more formal derivations in our other writings.

Balkanization of markets

The nearly ubiquitous presence of product differentiation in goods and service production requires that we depart from perfect competition, something that Industrial Organization theorists have accepted for generations. The Chamberlinian version of the departure is one in which all differentiated versions of one generic product line are in symmetrical competition with each other. This is implied by Chamberlin's famous symmetry assumption: the entry of a new product reduces in equal proportion the demand for all existing differentiated goods produced in that industry. Soon after the publication of Chamberlin's classic, Nicholas Kaldor pointed out that this assumption did not conform with the awkward facts. He argued, for example, that the entry of a new small car into the car market would greatly affect the demands for existing small cars, moderately affect the demands for middle-sized cars and only slightly affect the demands for large luxury cars. (Of course, the relations are more complex than suggested above since cars compete with each other in many more dimensions than mere size.)

Our vision agrees with Kaldor's. When we study the underlying sources of product diversity by modelling product characteristics in an address model, we find that, within one industry, each product typically does not compete with equal intensity with all other products. Figure 1 illustrates this point in the simplest case of a one-dimensional, bounded linear market in which all existing products, located at $d_1, d_2, \ldots d_n$, have a common price. There is a continuum of customers located along the market, and given a common price for the available products, all customers buy the nearest product. (In geographic space, each customer's location is where he or she resides; in characteristic space, the definition of a customer's location requires some care, but it may be loosely thought of as the point that the customer would select if offered the choice of any point on the continuum at some common price.) In this simple version, each product has only two competitors. If the price of one of the products was lowered slightly, the market for that product would grow, and the markets of the two neighbouring products would shrink, but the markets of more distant firms would be unaffected. No matter how densely the space is packed with products, this market balkanization persists: each firm stubbornly continues to have only two competitors. Clearly, this is a model of overlapping oligopolies, not one of symmetrical competition among all firms and products.[3]

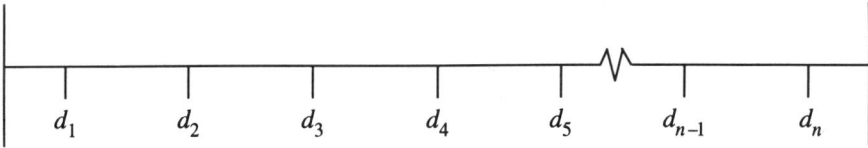

Figure 1

Lumpiness plus specificity plus diversity once again
If all individuals were identical and preferred one point in characteristic space over all others, only one generic type of each product would be produced. The communist planners would have got it right! Instead, free markets generate a remarkable plethora of differentiated products. The problem is to explain diversity not conformity. In the Chamberlinian version of monopolistic competition, as formalized by Dixit and Stiglitz for example, diversity is explained by the tastes of a single representative consumer whose utility rises the more differentiated versions of each single generic product she consumes. In our version, the diversity is driven by differing tastes among individuals so that, at the same prices and incomes, some prefer small cars, some middle-sized cars and some large ones. We believe this catches the awkward facts better than the alternative Chamberlinian version.

Given a convex technology and diverse tastes, a continuum of differentiated versions of each generic product would be produced. In fact, only a small number of points in any product-characteristic space are occupied by produced products. The factors that explain the absence of a continuum of product characteristics are non-convexities associated with lumpinesses and specificity in production. So diversity of tastes drives product diversity, while non-convexities and specificities in production limit that diversity.

Pure profits in address models
We can use the following simple cost function, which incorporates non-convexities due to product development, to make what we think are fundamental points about the potential for pure profit and the nature of competition in address models, as compared to non-address models:

$$C(Q_x) = K + cQ_x$$

where Q_x is quantity produced of good x, K is a fixed cost associated with product development, and c is a constant marginal cost of production. Importantly, since product development is product specific, K is also a sunk cost.

In the neoclassical model, fixed costs for the firm create the so-called integer problem. Fixed costs imply that entry and exit alter capacity in finite amounts. As a result, there will typically be some number of firms, n, such that those firms can make profits while $n + 1$ make losses. The integer problem of lumpy entry with fixed costs can account for substantial pure profits in equilibrium when demand is only sufficient to support a few firms. However, for any given amount of lumpiness, as the market demand expands, the amount of profits that can be explained by this phenomenon quickly diminishes. For example, if profits can be earned by 100 identical firms who sell a homogenous product and assume that they are price takers, while 101 such firms just fail to cover full costs, the amount of pure profits that each of the 100 can earn is extremely small. One way to grasp this result is to observe that the $(n + 1)st$ new entrant increases the capacity that serves the single homogenous market by $(100/n)$ per cent. Another way is to hold price fixed, and to observe that, post-entry, the entrant sells a quantity that is $n/(n + 1)$ times the quantity sold by an established firm pre-entry. (See Chapter 14 pp. 252–3 for a fuller discussion.)

The story is virtually the same in the Chamberlinian, non-address model of product differentiation. As in the neoclassical model, the potential for profit vanishes as the number of firms increases. In fact, in this literature the integer problem is usually completely ignored, and the number of products is determined by a zero-profit condition.

In an address model, lumpiness and specificity also gives rise to pure profits in entry equilibrium but these profits do not vanish as the demand, and hence the number of products, increases over any given market space. We have argued this fundamental point in a number of different ways. (See, for example, Chapters 6 and 14 and Eaton and Wooders (1985).) Here we provide an illustration using a very simple, quite restrictive model.

Consider the address model pictured in Figure 2, where products and consumers are located along the perimeter of a circle with circumference equal to one. Suppose that the density of consumers is uniform (and equal to D) and that established products are evenly spaced along the circle, at $d_1, d_2, ..., d_n$. Assume also that all products have the same, exogenous price p ($p > c$), and that consumers buy from the nearest firm. Then, the distance between adjacent products and the size of each established product's market are both of length $1/n$. Because the sunk cost K is a product development cost, it is location specific, so product locations are fixed.

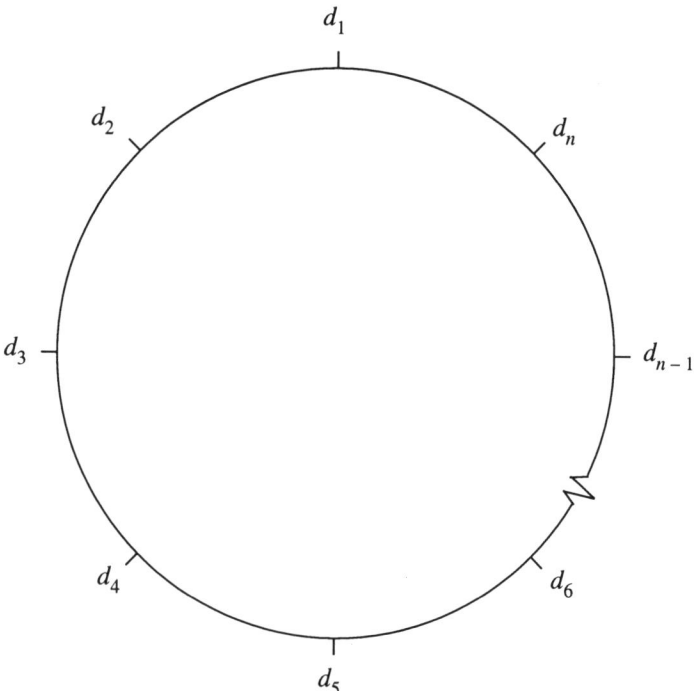

Figure 2

Hence, an entrant must pick a niche, and any niche is as good as any other. The entrant's market will be exactly half the size of the niche it enters; that is, the size of its market will be $1/2n$. The entrant's revenues net of marginal costs are then $(p - c)D/2n$, and the no-entry condition is

$$(p - c)D/2n < K \text{ or } n > (p - c)D/2K$$

The profit of an established firm prior to entry is, of course,

$$\pi = [(p - c)D/n] - K$$

Since the established firm's market is twice as large as the entrant's, it is readily apparent that $\pi > 0$ does not necessarily violate the no-entry condition. What may not be apparent is that the potential for pure profit does not vanish, or even diminish, as the density of demand and hence the number of products grows.

To assess the potential magnitude of pure profit in entry equilibrium, we must minimize n, subject to the no-entry condition. The solution to this problem is $n^* = (p - c)D/2K$, supposing for simplicity that $(p - c)D/2K$ is an integer. Then, evaluating the profit of an established product at n^*, we get an upper limit on the profit of an established product in entry-equilibrium:

$$\pi^* = K$$

The corresponding lower limit on the number of firms is, of course,

$$n^* = (p - c)D/2K$$

Notice, although n^* increases linearly with D, π^* is independent of D. In other words, in this address model the potential for pure profit does not vanish, or even diminish, as the market grows. (As shown in Eaton and Wooders (1985), this property of address models is not dependent on the assumption that prices are exogenous. Indeed, in their model, the potential for profit increases when prices are endogenized.)

We conclude that, in sharp contrast to models of undifferentiated oligopoly and non-address or Chamberlinian models of product differentiation, address models are stubbornly, indeed, fundamentally oligopolistic.

Non uniqueness

As is apparent from our analysis of profit in no-entry equilibrium, in address models many configurations of existing firms are consistent with the conditions that no new firm wishes to enter and that no existing firm wishes to exit. These conditions merely put limits on the minimum and maximum distances that can separate existing firms. At one extreme, no firm may be so close to its neighbours that it fails to cover its full long run costs. At the other extreme, no firm can be far enough away from one of its neighbours so as to present a niche that offers non-negative profits to a new firm entering that niche.

In such situations, history matters. In contrast where equilibrium is unique, the long run configuration of firms is a function solely of the current pattern of demand and costs. Since equilibrium is not unique in address models of free entry, the current configuration is a function of, among other things, the demands and expectations at those past times when existing firms entered. Thus, the present constellation of firms cannot be explained without knowing the conditions of the market when entry occurred.

In response to theorizing on characteristic and geographic differentiation, including our piece which established non-uniqueness of free-entry equilibrium (Chapter 1), Prescott and Visscher (1977) produced an elegant model in which free entry produces a unique equilibrium. A virgin market appears spontaneously with a given customer density function and firms enter in an orderly, sequential fashion. By backward induction, each firm arrives at its optimal location, given the locations of previous entrants and the optimal behaviour of subsequent entrants. Uniqueness is preserved! However, only in a model that conflicts with all the known facts about the evolution of new product technologies. Radical new products, such as aircraft, lasers, and computers, typically begin life in crude forms and then go through a process of evolution, often lasting decades, and involving the characteristics of the product, its range of applications, and the experience gained by users and hence their demand for it.(For a fuller discussion see, for example, Lipsey and Bekar (1995)). This was the kind of evolutionary process we had in mind when we originally argued that non-uniqueness made the present allocation of products and/or firms in the market path dependent. Given entry under one set of conditions for technology of the product its production process and the market demand for it, the alteration of those conditions (as the product and its production processes evolve) will not produce a unique response – indeed there may be no response at all for some quite large alterations in the market conditions. So the present distribution of products in characteristic space will not depend on current demand and technology alone, but on how that demand and technology has evolved over time.[4]

Non-optimality
Non-optimality of free-entry equilibrium follows from the non-uniqueness of equilibrium in the one-dimensional markets that we have considered so far. When we came to consider two-dimensional markets, we found an even more surprising result. The optimal configuration of firms in a two-dimensional space is well known to be a hexagonal lattice. In much work in locational economics, this configuration is imposed as an equilibrium condition. However, what is interesting is whether or not this result will emerge from primitive behavioural assumptions rather than as an imposed assumption. To study this issue, we built a computer model of entry into a two-dimensional space. We found to our surprise that entry would never create a hexagonal lattice and, when we imposed such a configuration and then allowed entry to occur at the most profitable locations in response to increasing customer density, that hexagonal lattice was broken up immediately. Entry created rectangular lattices but never hexagonal ones. The optimality that Lösch analysed, and that many investigators have assumed would be created by the price system, is neither created nor sustained under free entry into an expanding two-dimensional spatial market (Chapter 2).

Rent dissipation
Those raised in the neoclassical tradition are likely to argue at this point that landlords or property owners will appropriate the pure profits due to location. In an unpublished paper now printed in this collection, we argue that this is not so (Chapter 4). Instead of being transferred to other categories in the functional distribution of income, the profit generated in address models provides an incentive for rivalrous behaviour among existing firms that dissipates some of the profit. Among these are pre-emptive entry (Chapter 7) and early replacement of capital (Chapter 10).

Clustering
The phenomenon of clustering has long interested economists: firms cluster, activities cluster and products cluster. There are many reasons for this phenomenon. We first investigated the reason suggested in Hotelling's seminal 1929 article. We found that the Hotelling-type, wasteful, competitive clustering is a phenomenon of market boundaries. In address models of the type considered by Hotelling, wasteful clustering is only necessary where the market boundary of a firm coincides with the boundary of the whole market. Such a firm has an incentive to locate close to its

nearest neighbour. It has little or nothing to lose by moving away from the market boundary since there are no competitors between it and that boundary. When there are only two firms in the market, both firms have one of their own market boundaries coincident with the boundary of the whole market and so, in this special case, all firms cluster. For n firms, only the two outside pairs must cluster, while the rest may be evenly spaced throughout the market.[5]

We then went on, following leads first pointed to by Christaller, to study other reasons for clustering – reasons which were not socially wasteful as is Hotelling's competitive clustering. In Chapter 8 we showed that comparison shopping, combined with a non-convexity due to the indivisibility of shopping trips, leads firms to desire to locate close to at least one competitor. This kind of clustering, which is found for example when a department store in a shopping mall encourages competing speciality stores to locate nearby, is not necessarily socially wasteful since it reduces the costs of desirable comparison shopping.

In Chapter 12 we investigated the clustering of outlets selling different commodities, which is the basis of central place theory. We created a simple model in which two types of commodities were purchased at different intervals and, in contrast to Lösch's original treatment, firms were motivated by profit maximization in choosing their locations. By allowing the population density to increase, we found a number of interesting things about the evolution of central places:

> the demand externalities created by multipurpose shopping ... give rise to higher order central places, and equilibrium satisfies a hierarchical principle. The model ... yields insights into the phenomenon of excess capacity in retailing, into the dynamic process of expansion of the retail sector in a growing market, and into the role played by, and the motivation behind, shopping centres.

Once again, the whole process is quite non-neoclassical, being driven this time by the non-convexities arising from the fixed costs of shopping trips.

IV. Alternative visions

In this section, we suggest some competing visions of the economy ending with our own.

The neoclassical world of 'as if perfect competition'

One vision is the neoclassical world of perfect competition. Both the assumptions and the predictions of perfect competition are violated by so many common observations that the belief that it still catches enough aspects of reality to make it useful seems to us to be nothing more than an act of faith in the face of strongly contradictory evidence. Perfect competition is inconsistent with a wide range of observations of the modern economy, including product differentiation, economies of large scale production, oligopoly, active rivalrous behaviour and almost universal price setting (rather than price taking) in manufacturing and service industries. It is hard to imagine, therefore, what evidence would conflict with the quasi-religious belief that in the long run the economy behaves as if it were perfectly competitive even though many of the micro predictions of perfect competition are refuted by common observations.

A current variant of this view is that perfect competition, plus transactions costs, can explain everything we see so that more complex industrial structures are not required in order to predict the economy's long-run behaviour. While we accept that transactions cost analysis is highly valuable in many contexts, we argue that the assumption that transactions costs are measured by any residual behaviour not explained by perfect competition turns the model's predictions into tautologies consistent with all possible observations – and, of course, a theory that is consistent with all possible observations explains none of them. The survival of the belief that perfect competition is a useful predictive theory of the economy's long-run behaviour seems to us to be symptomatic of many economists' urge to have positive 'results', which usually means obtaining conclusions about welfare with implied policy prescriptions, even though the conclusions are derived from a model which is no more than an elaborate fiction couched in highly complex mathematical language.

Modern monopolistic competition
The late 1970s and early 1980s witnessed an active research programme directed at formalizing the Chamberlinian vision in terms that could be handled mathematically, both in partial models of single industries and, more importantly, in general equilibrium models of the whole economy.

The Dixit–Stiglitz version of this model (as described in Chapter 14) did the job and is today used as the model of product differentiation in many fields, including many endogenous micro-based growth models. (See, for example, Grossman and Helpman (1991).) These models are essentially spaceless in the sense that each product is equally substitutable for all other products and hence equally close to all other products in whatever the relevant space that defines them.[6] The set of all possible goods is either countably infinite, such as the set of all positive integers (Dixit–Stiglitz), or a continuum, such as the positive half of the real line (Grossman and Helpman). In Dixit–Stiglitz, the set of produced goods is a finite subset of the set of possible goods and is produced by a finite number of firms. In Grossman–Helpman, the set of produced goods is a continuum over some range running from 0 to n^* and is produced by a continuum of firms. Both the continuous and discrete versions explain diversity in terms of the taste function of a single representative consumer who uses some of each and every product (every brand of toothpaste, every type of car, etc.) and who has equal elasticity of substitution between all differentiated versions of each single generic product. This is the equivalent of Chamberlin's symmetry assumption. It makes every brand of cigarettes or type of car equally substitutable for every other brand or type and it implies that the entry of a new cigarette or car takes demand equally from every existing brand. Furthermore, the assumption of a single representative consumer allows welfare statements to be made since he or she has a well-behaved utility function – and so, by simple aggregation, does the community which he or she represents.

There is no way that the consumer behaviour assumed in this model, and the firm behaviour predicted by it, can be derived from a world in which individual differentiated products have locations in either (or both of) characteristic or geographic space so that each has closer and more distant competitors. Indeed, this model violates so many of the awkward facts that we believe its survival can best be understood in terms of the same forces that held perfect competition in the forefront for so long (and still does in some circles). Some of the awkward facts that are inconsistent with the Dixit–Stiglitz model are those numbered 5, 6 and 7 above. The address model accommodates these facts by assuming that different consumers have different taste functions defined over characteristic space. The Dixit–Stiglitz version must treat the representative consumer either as an acknowledged fiction used because it generates 'results' and policy prescriptions in spite of the absence of any empirical basis, or as potentially capable of being aggregated from individuals with different tastes. There is good reason to believe, however, that this aggregation would be impossible, since it is easy to generate market behaviour in address models that is inconsistent with the choices that would be made by any Dixit–Stiglitz representative consumer.

One common defence of the use of this model is that, until it can be replaced by a tractable general equilibrium model of the behaviour of overlapping oligopolies, it is the best that can be developed in the present state of the art. The problem with this defence is that it provides no reason for using a model that conflicts with so many of the awkward facts to derive confident conclusions about welfare and policy. Be that as it may, the acceptance of the model seems to provide another example of the propensity of many economists to prefer fictional 'results' to messy reality. If the world is one of overlapping oligopolies which make ambiguous the welfare effects of many changes that would have determinate effects in the Dixit-Stiglitz model, we wonder about the value of pretending otherwise – of pretending, that is, that the world is something that it obviously is not just because that something is more tractable than models which seem to catch the awkward facts.

Our vision
When we look at the world we are impressed with the diversity that we see, some of which is exogenous and some endogenous to economic signals. People are genetically diverse in both their talents and their tastes. For example, a genetic disease influences one's taste for certain drugs. Just as skills are partly endogenous because they are learned in response to economic incentives, so are tastes partly endogenous to economic and social signals. For example, the different tastes for pork among Christians, Moslems and Jews are clearly not genetic. This is not, however, a theme which we have chosen to take up in our work, although it would be a natural part of our world view if we developed it fully. The diversity of firms is driven more by endogenous forces than by the diversity of the tastes of firms (if firms can be said to have tastes). Goods and services are also diverse. They are, however, much less diverse than tastes – as is revealed by the concentration of production in both geographic and characteristic spaces. (*Ceteris paribus* we would prefer a good produced at our consumption point rather than at the nearest shopping outlet and most of us would prefer a product with some bundle of characteristics intermediate between the characteristics of each existing differentiated product.)

The world is also characterized by pervasive lumpiness and specificity, some of which is exogenous and some endogenous. Product development, capital goods, learning, and marketing campaigns are examples of things that are in some degree both lumpy and specific. The degree of specificity of capital goods and software is endogenous although some specificity would seem to be a universal characteristic of all lumpy goods. Both lumpiness and specificity are manifestations of an underlying non-convexity in some relevant technology.

While lumpiness and specificity cause nothing but trouble to economists in the neoclassical tradition, they are key parts of our vision of the economy, at least when they work in combination with each other. For example, product differentiation is driven by differences in tastes and is limited by the non-convexities associated with lumpiness and specificity (which explains why product diversity is so much less than taste diversity). Spatial differentiation is driven by differences in customer locations and limited by non-convexities associated with production, including those arising from the lumpiness of capital.

This interpretation of reality has many implications. Lumpy capital creates a discreteness of entry into markets extended in geographic and characteristic space which means that new entrants into a given market typically expect smaller markets and profits than those of established products and firms. This implies that established products and firms can earn substantial pure profits without attracting entry. The existence of pure profits in free entry equilibrium implies that the equilibrium configuration of existing firms and products is not unique.

The result of all this, as Nicholas Kaldor long ago pointed out, is a world of pervasive, overlapping oligopolies, with persistent pockets of pure profits. Neither perfect competition nor Chamberlinian monopolistic competition (in its original or its new Dixit–Stiglitz guise) captures the characteristics of such a world.

The pure profits that typically exist in free-entry equilibrium cannot be appropriated by landlords (Chapter 8) nor competed away by the spatial relocation of firms or products (Chapter 13). They therefore create an incentive for strategic rent-seeking behaviour which will erode some of them in ways that may or may not be socially unproductive. Pre-emptive entry into a growing market, predatory entry into some market situations, early replacement of capital to hold a minimum commitment in the market, are all forms of rivalrous behaviour which are financed by pure profits and which dissipate some of them. Some of these forms of behaviour such as early replacement of capital are inconsistent with the minimization of production costs. This tells us that, in contrast to the models of perfect and monopolistic competition, cost minimization is not an implication of profit maximization in address models. This is because costs of specific lumpy capital create a commitment to the market that can protect locational profits. All of these forms of behaviour rely on the partial property rights created by the location of lumpy specific capital in some market (Chapter 11). If there were no lumpiness and no product specificity, contestability would eliminate the profits. As it is, these pervasive phenomena preclude the operation of the forces analysed in the contestability literature.

The non-convexities that we have emphasized also drive much of the clustering that we see. Comparison and multipurpose shopping, combined with indivisibilities of people and automobile trips, explains the clustering of retail establishments – both those that sell similar and different goods. It also explains the bundles of goods sold by supermarkets and department stores. Externalities in product development combined with lumpiness of capital goods drive the clustering of goods in characteristic space. Lumpiness and specificity of capital combined with other non-convexities drive agglomerations of production activities. (Although we deal with this issue only briefly in Chapter 15, this clearly is in the spirit of our work.)

All of the above holds in a relatively well-behaved world of exogenous customer density functions, well-defined distance functions and equilibria that exist. However, none of these conditions can be assumed to hold in general. In what follows, we consider dropping each of these conditions in turn.

In practice, the location of buyers and sellers is mutually interdependent. This can lead to a wider range of possible equilibrium positions as shown by the property that the two different configurations that are obtained first by holding customer density constant and allowing firms to adjust and second by holding firms constant and allowing customers to adjust may both be free-entry equilibria. (Although we did not follow this line of reasoning very far, it is discussed in Chapter 3 and in our unpublished paper on endogenous customer density that is discussed in Lipsey (1981).)

In our simple models, distance is well defined as the length of the straight line joining any two points. In geographic space, however, urban travel is usually along roads set out at right angles to each other which implies that distance is often better measured by a block rather than a Cartesian metric. The block metric leads to some quite odd looking market boundaries and to large discrete shifts of demand from one location to another in response to marginal shifts in price or in the firm's location around some critical values (Chapter 9). This, in turn, can lead to some bizarre looking demand functions exhibiting, among other things, large discontinuities.

The conclusion of almost everything we have said so far is that history matters in a way that it does not in neoclassical theory (a proposition we first put forward in Chapter 3). This leads us to reject the neoclassical vision of equilibria that are independent of the path by which they are approached and of an economy with no arrow of time. Instead, the current state of the system is seen to be path dependent. Where we now are depends on where we were in the past, and on what forces have operated between then and now.

It follows that there is no grand invisible hand, inevitably leading the economy through the operation of the price system to an optimum allocation of resources that cannot be improved upon. There are, however, some rather pretty 'little hands'. For example, perfect price discrimination (delivered pricing) when individual demand is characterized by a reservation price for one unit of the product, results in complete static optimality. (See Chapter 14 and Eaton and Schmitt (1995).)

Given the pervasive market power and the absence of unique equilibria that is contained in our vision, piecemeal welfare economics seems unlikely to be of much assistance in improving matters. Typically, when we move resources into one of our markets, they are coming from another non-perfectly competitive market. Further, piecemeal welfare economics necessitates the solution of a nasty preference recovery problem (as discussed in Chapter 14). In our world, firms have several strategic variables at their command: price, diversity of location in product and characteristic space, degree of lumpiness and specificity of capital. All of these endogenous variables would have optimal values in the first-best equilibrium. Since they act as strategic variables in firm competition, there is no presumption that the unhindered price system will produce optimal values of any of them, nor is it clear how any one of them should be changed if piecemeal alterations of the existing configuration are possible.

We hasten to add that our position does not conflict with the argument that the price system is better than known alternatives although it does conflict with the proposition that the price system ensures optimality. One of us has written frequently about the contrast between the informal and the formal defences of the price system. (See in particular Lipsey (1994).) The formal defence relies on the mathematical proof of the optimality of a perfectly competitive economy. The informal defence argues in non-mathematical terms that the price system is better than any known alternative. We accept the strength of the informal defence: the price system is better than any known alternative. We reject the formal defence that the price system produces optimality as being inconsistent with the model of the economy that we have developed to explain the awkward facts that we have enumerated.

Notes

1. We have written several papers which have some aspects of surveys (see Chapters 3, 14 and 15 this volume) and Lipsey (1981). To avoid unnecessary duplication, we briefly recapitulate what is needed here and give cross references to the more detailed treatments to be found elsewhere.
2. Some readers have objected that people often do 'two things at a time'. What this means, however, is that they are able to switch back and forth between doing elements of two activities, one at a time, in such a way that both activities are completed (read 'done') at the same time.
3. It might seem at first sight that as the dimensionality of the product characteristic space is increased, this balkanization would quickly diminish. This does not, however, seem to be the case for quite a large number of dimensions, although what happens when the dimensionality is increased without limit, is unclear. For further discussion, see Chapter 13.
4. Our experience suggests that the Prescott–Visscher article is often the only one on this whole subject to which students are exposed. This gives them the impression that uniqueness is the norm under free entry and gives us the impression that many people are more concerned with saving the appearance of uniqueness than with discovering the consequences of entry under conditions that actually seem to prevail in newly developing markets.
5. This is fully analysed in Chapter 1. Some further conditions are needed to get full clustering of the outside pairs. How close the outside firm comes to its inside neighbour depends on demand conditions. With point demand, the outside firm will wish to pair with its neighbour; if there is some elasticity of demand, the firm will come closer than it would if it had a competitor between it and the market boundary, but will not necessarily pair with its neighbour (that is, will not come as close as possible).
6. Mark Blaug (1978) has discussed the lack of attention paid to spatial economics by Anglo-Saxon, neoclassical economists. He suggests that both this lack, and the attention paid to it in the German literature may have been historical accidents. Although historical accident is a possible explanation, there were also good doctrinal reasons why the economists who were outside of the mainstream of Anglo-Saxon neoclassicism would be the ones to produce economic theories that were hard to incorporate into the orthodox system. Furthermore, such theories often had unorthodox implications, such as the rejection of the universal superiority of free trade or the non-convexities that are a necessary ingredient of spatial models.

References

Blaug, M. (1978), *Economic Theory in Retrospect*, 3rd edition, (Cambridge: Cambridge University Press).

Chamberlin, E. (1965), *The Theory on Monopolistic Competition*, 8th edition, (Cambridge: Harvard University Press).

Eaton, B.C. and N. Schmitt (1995), 'Flexible Manufacturing and Market Structure', *American Economic Review*, **84** (4), September, 875–88.

Eaton, B.C. and M. Wooders (1985), 'Sophisticated Entry in a Model of Spatial Competition', *Rand Journal of Economics*, **16** (2), Summer, 282–97.

Grossman, G. and E. Helpman (1991), *Innovation and Growth in the Global Economy*, (Cambridge: MIT Press).

Hotelling, H. (1929), 'Stability in Competition', *Economic Journal*, **39**, March, 41–57.

Kaldor, N. (1935), 'Market Imperfection and Excess Capacity', *Economica*, 33–50.

Lipsey, R.G. (1981), 'Space Capital and Value', a public lecture given at Queen's University, reprinted in *Selected Essays of R.G. Lipsey, Volume I, Microeconomics, Growth and Political Economy*, (Cheltenham: Edward Elgar) forthcoming 1997.

Lipsey, R.G. (1994), 'Markets, Technological Change and Economic Growth', Quaid-I-Azam Invited Lecture, in *Pakistan Development Review*, **33** (4), Winter, 327–52.

Lipsey, R.G. and C. Bekar (1995), 'A Structuralist View of Technical Change and Economic Growth' in *Bell Canada Papers on Economic and Public Policy Vol. 3*, Proceedings of the Bell Canada Conference at Queen's University, November 1994, (Kingston: John Deutsch Institute).

Prescott, E.C. and M. Visscher (1977), 'Sequential Location Among Firms with Foresight', *Bell Journal of Economics*, **8**, 378–93.

[1]

The Principle of Minimum Differentiation Reconsidered: Some New Developments in the Theory of Spatial Competition[1,2]

B. CURTIS EATON
University of British Columbia

and

RICHARD G. LIPSEY
Queen's University

I. INTRODUCTION

In his famous 1929 paper, [14], Hotelling presented a model of two firms competing to sell a homogeneous product to customers spread evenly along a linear market. In equilibrium the duopolists are located at the centre of the market rather than being in the locations that would minimize transport costs. Hotelling originally suggested that his model explained a wide variety of social phenomena.

Boulding, who appears to have been the originator of the term *principle of minimum differentiation* (called MD hereafter) to describe Hotelling's result, is even more extravagant in his suggestions as to the range of phenomena that are explained by the model. He writes [5, p. 484]:

> This is a principle of the utmost generality. It explains why all the dime stores are usually clustered together, often next door to each other; why certain towns attract large numbers of firms of one kind; why an industry, such as the garment industry, will concentrate in one quarter of a city. It is a principle which can be carried over into other " differences " than spatial differences. The general rule for any new manufacturer coming into an industry is " make your product as like the existing products as you can without destroying the differences ". It explains why all automobiles are so much alike and why no manufacturer dares make a car in which a tall hat can be worn comfortably. It even explains why Methodists, Baptists, and even Quakers are so much alike, and tend to get even more alike.

Hotelling's model has been criticized and extended in the 40-odd years since its publication. It has also been applied to a number of specific cases (see e.g. [25]). In the present paper we have set ourselves the tasks of examining, in a more systematic fashion than has been done to date, the cases to which MD applies and of discovering other principles applicable to small-group competition. We consider how robust is the tendency

---
[1] *First version received February* 1972; *final version accepted December* 1973 (*Eds.*).
[2] We are indebted to many colleagues for comments and suggestions. We are also indebted to the Queen's Institute for Economic Research for generous support over a two year period.

toward MD in the face of changes in the specification of the model. Five assumptions seem critical: (a) the nature of the consumers' demand (either one unit per period at a parametric price or completely inelastic); (b) the number of firms is restricted to two; (c) each firm adopts zero conjectural variation (called ZCV hereafter) with respect to the behaviour of the other firm; (d) the firms compete in a linear market that has boundaries; and (e) the customers are evenly spread throughout the market. We do not study variations in assumption (a) because they have been dealt with extensively elsewhere.

Although the analysis is in terms of location theory, many of the results generalize to other forms of differentiation, and the conditions under which they do are mentioned briefly in footnote 3, p. 46.

The paper is divided into two parts: one-dimensional markets and two-dimensional markets. Within each we distinguish (a) bounded, (b) unbounded but finite, and (c) unbounded, infinite spaces. Among other things, we show: in one dimension the nature of the space is not, as many investigators have thought, critical; in two dimensions, however, the very existence of equilibrium may depend upon the nature of the space; the commonly-used rectangular customer density function [1] yields results that do not generalize to any other density function; multiple equilibria occur in many simple models; and MD occurs only when the number of firms is restricted to two.

The assumptions of our basic model are as follows:

(i) Customers are distributed throughout the market according to a customer density function which is integrable and once differentiable.
(ii) Each customer purchases one unit of the product per unit of time.
(iii) Transport costs are an increasing function of distance.
(iv) Customers always buy from the firm that quotes the lowest delivered price (mill price plus transport cost).
(v) All firms charge the same parametric mill price.
(vi) Production is at constant marginal cost which is less than the mill price.
(vii) There are no costs of relocation. Presented with the chance of changing its location to change its market from M_1 to M_2, the firm will move if M_2 is preferred to M_1; it will remain where it is if M_1 is the same as or preferred to M_2.
(viii) No more than one firm can occupy a given location.
(ix) In choosing its location, the ith firm conjectures either (a) that all other firms will leave their own location unaltered (ZCV) [2]; or (b) that some other firm, j, will change its location in a way that causes the maximum possible loss of market to i.
(x) Firms seek to maximize their profits subject to their conjectural variation.

In Section IV we discuss the consequences of altering assumptions (ii), (iv), (v) and (vi).

A few terms that are used throughout the paper need to be defined.

The ith Firm's Market Boundary. (a) An interior boundary is the locus of points that are equidistant from the ith firm and one other firm, and not closer either to any other firm or to some portion of the market boundary; (b) an exterior boundary is that portion of the market boundary that is closer to the ith firm than to any other firm.

An Interior Firm. A firm whose entire market boundary is an interior boundary.

A Peripheral Firm. A firm whose market boundary is an exterior boundary over some of its range.

---

[1] The density function most commonly encountered in the literature is rectangular (see e.g. [3] [6], [9], [14], [17], [18], [24], [27] and [28]).

[2] Although not applicable in all situations, ZCV is a reasonable assumption, either where the equilibrium is approached very rapidly so that firms do not have time to learn their opponents' reactions, or where relocation occurs with a long time lag (because, e.g., relocation is very costly) as with many locational problems.

Paired Firms. Two firms are said to be paired when the distance between them is as small as is permitted. The minimum permitted distance, δ, is arbitrary and its size is unimportant as long as it is " small " in relation to the overall size of the market.

Minimum Differentiation. This is said to occur when all firms in the market are separated from their neighbours by the distance δ.

Equilibrium. The ith firm is in equilibrium when there is no location that is preferred to its present location. The whole market is in equilibrium whenever all n firms are individually in equilibrium.

II. ONE-DIMENSIONAL MARKETS

In one-dimensional markets the location of the ith firm divides its market segment into two sides. Where the two sides are unequal they are referred to as *the long and short sides of the* firm's market. Each side is also referred to as a *half-market* (whether or not the sides are of equal length).

Assumption (iv) implies that if the ith firm is an interior firm, its market extends half the distance to its two neighbours. *The length of an interior firm's market is thus half the length of the interval between its two neighbours wherever the firm locates within that interval.* If it is a peripheral firm, its market extends all the way to the market boundary in one direction and half way to its one neighbour in the other direction.

When two firms are paired, the short side of each of their markets is $\delta/2$. It is assumed for ease of analysis that the short side of the market is zero for paired firms (actually it goes to zero as $\delta \to 0$).

FIGURE 1

Firms are indicated by numbers and the boundaries of the firms' markets by broken lines.

Model 1. The assumptions that distinguish this model are ZCV and a rectangular customer density function (i.e. the customers are evenly spread along the line).

We first apply Model 1 to a line of finite length which gives us Hotelling's model. The length of the market is taken as unity, and its boundaries are at 0 and 1. We refer to this type of market as a *bounded one-dimensional* (B, 1-D) market.

Figure 1 illustrates our definitions. Firms 1 and 2 are paired; 1 is a peripheral firm and 2 an interior firm. The boundary between 1 and 2 is located at a point Y distance from the market boundary. The long side of 1's market is Y (equals 1's whole market). Firm 3 is located at $3Y$. The boundary between 2 and 3 is at $2Y$. Firm 2's long side is thus Y (equals its whole market) while the left hand side of 3's market is also Y (its right hand size is not determined until firm 4 is located).

The necessary and sufficient conditions for equilibrium are: (1.i) no firm's whole market is smaller than any other firm's half market; (1.ii) the two peripheral firms are paired.[1]

Any firm can capture a market equal in length to either half market of any other firm by pairing with it. Thus condition (1.i) is necessary. An unpaired *peripheral firm* can always increase its market by moving towards its neighbour. Thus condition (1.ii) is necessary. The proof of sufficiency is omitted for brevity but it can be found in [11, p. 9].

The application of these equilibrium conditions to various situations distinguished by the number of firms in the market is tricky. It is necessary to consider some of the cases individually.

[1] Chamberlin [6, Appendix C] appears to have missed this critical condition.

One Firm. The location of one firm is indeterminate since it captures the whole market wherever it goes.

Two Firms. Both are peripheral firms and, therefore, by condition (1.ii) they must be paired. Condition (1.i) dictates that they be paired at the market's centre. This is Hotelling's *MD* result.

Three Firms. It is impossible to satisfy the equilibrium conditions when there are three firms in the market. The only way to satisfy (1.ii) is for both peripheral firms to be paired with the interior firm. But this leaves the interior firm with a market area of virtually zero—a violation of (1.i).[1]

Four Firms. Condition (1.ii) requires that the peripheral firms be paired and (1.i) is satisfied only if the pairs are located at the first and third quartiles.

Five Firms. The only possible equilibrium pattern for five firms is obtained by making firms 3 and $n-2$ in Figure 1 coincident—i.e. they are the same firm. The peripheral pairs are located at 1/6 and 5/6, and firm 3 is in the centre of the market.

Six Firms. With six firms the equilibrium configuration ceases to be unique. Two limiting cases are shown in Figure 2, (*a*) and (*b*). Both of these exhibit the necessary

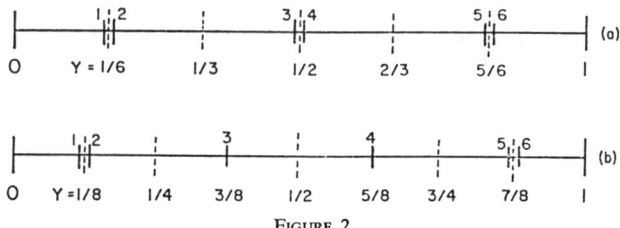

FIGURE 2

symmetry shown in Figure 1. The first case, however, *minimizes* the distance between the third and fourth firms and thereby *maximizes* the market lengths of the four firms in the peripheral pairs. The second case *maximizes* the distance between 3 and 4 and thereby minimizes the equal market lengths for peripheral pairs. In the first case, all six firms have equal markets and in the second case the four firms in the peripheral pairs have markets of 1/8 while the inner two firms have markets of 1/4.

In equilibrium, firms 3 and 4 can be separated by any distance between the extremes of δ and 1/4.[2] Firms 3 and 4 must both be separated from their neighbouring peripheral pair by the distance $2Y$, but they can be separated from each other by any distance up to $2Y$. This means that firms 3 and 4 can have any market [3] between 1/6 and 1/4. The reader can easily demonstrate for himself that there is an infinite number of equilibria for each $n>5$.

---

[1] Lerner and Singer [16] have noted the continuance of oscillations when three firms move according to Hotelling's rules. The above treatment establishes the non-existence of equilibrium. Both Lerner and Singer and Chamberlin appear reluctant to accept this instability. Chamberlin [6] implies that two firms will be located at one quartile and the third firm at the other quartile. Equilibrium cannot, of course, exist unless the assumptions of the model are changed.

[2] This is the critical result missed by Lerner and Singer [16, p. 181] in their otherwise complete analysis of this model. They do discover the extreme cases (and analyse these in detail for eight firms) but they wrongly assert that there is not a continuous range between these extremes over which the markets of the firms can vary in equilibrium. Lösch [18, p. 74], following Chamberlin [6], makes the stronger (and incorrect) assertion that " the intermediate firms are all equally spaced from each other ".

[3] The range of possible locations with respect to their own market boundaries is not independent of the size of their market. If they have a market of 1/4 they must be located at its mid-point. If they have a market of only 1/6, they must be paired and hence located at one of the ends of their market. If they are separated by a distance d, such that $1/6 < d < 1/4$ they can be located over a range within their markets.

To complete the analysis of six or more firms, three questions need to be answered. First, what is the range of possible market lengths for the various firms that is compatible with equilibrium? Second, what are the equilibrium configurations that minimize, and that maximize transport costs? Third, how do total transport costs compare with the transport costs in the socially optimal configuration?

Two propositions concerning relative market sizes follow immediately from the equilibrium conditions: (1) no firm can have a market more than twice as large as any other firm's market; and (2) no firm can have a market smaller than Y—the market length of the firms in the peripheral pairs. The minimum and the maximum possible sizes for an individual firm's market depend upon the number of firms in the market, and upon whether or not the firm is a member of a peripheral pair. The bounds are [1]

$$1/(2n-4) \leq L_p \leq 1/n \text{ and } 1/(2n-6) \leq L_i \leq 2/(n+1)$$

where L_p is the length of the market of each of the firms in the peripheral pairs and L_i is the length of the market of any other firm.[2] The configuration that minimizes transport cost for n firms has all firms spread out along the line serving equal markets of length $1/n$ divided into equal half markets of $1/2n$. This socially optimal configuration is, however, not an equilibrium one because the peripheral firms must be paired in equilibrium. The equilibrium configuration with the lowest transport costs has two firms paired at each end of the market and all other firms spread evenly throughout the market. This configuration "wastes" the transport-cost-reducing potential of one of the two firms in each of the peripheral pairs.

The equilibrium configuration that maximizes transport costs has all firms paired (or all but one if n is odd). This configuration "wastes" the cost-reducing potential of every other firm and gives transport costs that are exactly double (n even) those resulting from the socially-optimal configuration.

We now test the basic conjecture that the behaviour of this model depends critically on the nature of the space by transferring Model 1 to a circle whose circumference is unity. This is a one-dimensional space, but if we continue to move along it in one direction or the other we do not encounter a boundary but instead return to our starting place. We refer to this market as being unbounded, finite, one-dimensional (U, F, 1-D). Because there are no boundaries, there are only interior firms. Condition (1.i) is now the necessary and sufficient condition for equilibrium.

One Firm. As in the line, the location of one firm is indeterminate.

Two Firms. No matter where the second firm locates it gets half the circle as its market. Thus in contrast to (B, 1-D) space, any configuration is an equilibrium one.

Three Firms. There are an infinite number of equilibria. (Contrast this with (B, 1-D) space for $n = 3$.) To see this locate firms 1 and 2 arbitrarily and then draw a diameter

---

[1] These bounds are established as follows. *Lower bound on L_p*: The four peripheral firms have Y each, the remaining $n-4$ firms have markets of $2Y$ (divided into half-markets of Y) giving $Y = 1/(2(n-4)+4)$. *Upper bound on L_p*: Since no market can be smaller than Y, its value is maximized by giving all firms a market of Y. Given the configuration at the outer part of the line in Figure 1 we need to pair all firms if n is even and all but one if n is odd. With n even this gives $Y = 1/n$ and with n odd $Y = 1/(n+1)$ since the unpaired firm must have a market of $2Y$. (If it had less, at least one of its neighbours would have a market of less than Y.) *Lower bound on L_i*: The location of the peripheral pairs and their neighbours (as in Figure 1) determines ten half-markets (four of which are zero) and uses a distance of $6Y$. Now let one interior firm have a market of only Y. To do this we must use another $2Y$ of the line and four more half-markets (two for the firm in question and one for each of its neighbours). This determines 14 half-markets (of Y or zero) and uses $8Y$ and leaves $1-8Y$ to be divided between the remaining $2n-14$ half markets. To minimize Y we maximize the markets of the other firms by giving each of them two equal half-markets of Y. Thus $Y = (1-8Y)/(2n-14) = 1/(2n-6)$. *Upper bound on L_i*: If n is odd, pair all but one firm giving $n+1$ non-zero half markets of which the firm in question has two, giving it a market of $2/(n+1)$. When n is even, pair all but two firms leaving $n+2$ non-zero half-markets, of which the non-paired firms have two each, giving them markets of $2/(n+2)$.

[2] Having established that one or more equilibria exist (for $n \neq 3$), it is of interest to know whether or not the dynamic process implied by our model is convergent. This problem is considered at length in [11, footnote 16].

through 1 and 2 (see Figure 3) to intersect the circle at C' and C''. Any location for firm 3 in the arc $C'C''$ produces an equilibrium configuration. Any other location puts one of the firms into disequilibrium.[1]

The multiplicity of equilibria persists as n is increased and all we can do is to place some limits on the size of the firm's market. These bounds are $1/2(n-1) \leq L \leq 2/(n+1)$, where L is the length of the market arc for a single firm.[2]

On the circle, unlike the line, the socially-optimal configuration is compatible with equilibrium: all firms are equally spaced at a distance $1/n$ apart. The cost-maximizing equilibrium configuration is the same as on the line: all firms are paired (n even) so that transport costs are twice what they need to be for any given n.

The conclusions reached in our analysis of Model 1 suggest rejection of two conjectures that are commonly found in the literature. First, the nature of the space is not critical to the behaviour of the model [3]: as n increases beyond 5 the behaviour on the line becomes increasingly similar to that on the circle. Second, MD is not a characteristic configuration of the linear model for $n > 2$.[4]

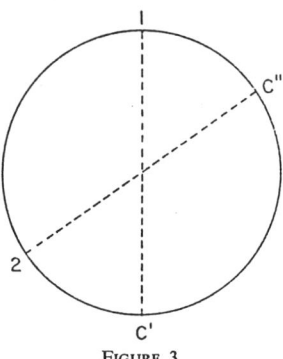

FIGURE 3

Model 2. This is the same as Model 1—a bounded linear market with a rectangular customer density function—except that the firms do not make a ZCV assumption. Instead, when any firm i chooses its location it conjectures that another firm j will relocate in such a way as to cause the maximum loss of market to i—firm j does this by pairing with i on the long side of i's market. Firm i thus adopts a minimax strategy (MM) of choosing the location that minimizes the damage that j can do to it—i.e. it maximizes the short side of its market. The firm maximizes its short side by locating in the middle of its own market

[1] We are indebted to Professor D. Winch of McMaster University for pointing out an error in our original treatment of this problem and for suggesting this demonstration.

[2] These bounds are established as follows. *Lower bound on L*: Make firm 1's market X by locating 2 and 3 on either side of 1. This determines four half-markets and uses $2X$. Divide the remaining $1-2X$ of the market into $(2n-4)$ equal half markets. Since the smallest possible whole market for 1 is one of the half markets of any of the other firms we have $X = (1-2X)/(2n-4) = 1/2(n-1)$. *Upper bound on L*: This is the same as on the line.

[3] Lösch [18, p. 75] for example, conjectures that it is.

[4] Linear models of competition have frequently been applied to politics. Hotelling used his model to explain the similarity of the Democratic and Republican parties. Smithies motivates the introduction of downward-sloping demand curves into Hotelling's model to explain dissimilarities between parties due to concern over loss of voters at the peripheries. If the Smithies' model is extended beyond two parties, however, the implication is that the extreme parties will be the largest and all other parties will be of equal size, see [9]. To the extent that Hotelling's model (our model 1) is applicable, a variety of party sizes is possible and the extreme parties will be the smallest ones. The less extreme parties can co-exist with substantial differences in their sizes and the central party need not be the largest. In neither model will all the parties be clustered at the centre. Perhaps the most explicit development of a linear model of politics is due to Anthony Downs [8]. For a critical appraisal of such models see Donald Stokes [26].

and this implies that interior firms locate at the mid point between their two neighbours and that peripheral firms locate one-third of the distance from the market boundary to their one neighbour.

This single proposition determines the unique equilibrium configuration for any n. The firms will be spaced along the line so as to have equal market areas of $1/n$ and equal half markets of $1/2n$. Thus (with one exception) [1] a minimax strategy leads the firms to locate in the socially-optimal configuration; this configuration occurs whether the firms are guarding against the damage that could be done by a new entrant or by a move from one of the existing firms.[2] It is worth noting that MM is the entry minimising strategy: if i maximizes the market left to it after j's entry, this minimizes the market available to the new entrant j.

Two firms, j and k, can always pair on either side of a third firm, i, thus reducing i's market to virtually zero. For this reason any MM model becomes completely indeterminate where $n > 2$ and where firm i looks ahead to the maximally-damaging moves to be taken by two other firms.

Now transfer Model 2 to the $(U, F, 1-D)$ market of the circumference of a circle. Since peripheral firms are not paired on the bounded line, the removal of the boundaries has little effect on the behaviour of the model. There are a few differences, however, when $n = 1$ or 2. Unlike the line, when $n = 1$ the location of the firm is not determined on the circle. As with the line, the location of the two firms is determined, and is socially optimal, when they are guarding against entry by a third firm.[3]

In summary, MM produces the socially-optimal configuration.[4] There is no absence of equilibrium for $n = 3$, nor any special cases for $n > 2$. Also the conjecture that the nature of the space critically affects the behaviour of a linear model with a MM strategy must be rejected.

Model 3. This is Model 1—ZCV in a $(B, 1-D)$ market—but with customer density functions that are not rectangular. We denote the customer-density function as $c(X)$ where X is distance measured from the arbitrary origin. The firm is, of course, interested in the number of its customers rather than in the physical size of its market. In Models 1 and 2 number of customers is exactly proportional to market size. In Models 3 and 4 this is not so and the terms " size of whole market " and of " size of half market " refer to the *number of customers* in the relevant segments. Similarly the terms " long side " and " short side " refer not to physical length but the sides of the market containing *more* and *less customers*.

The necessary and sufficient conditions for equilibrium in Model 3 are:

(3.i)   no firm's whole market is less than another's long-side market;
(3.ii)   peripheral firms are paired;

---

[1] The case of two firms where the firms know there is no possibility of a third entrant provides the only exception to this rule. By locating at the centre of the market the firm ensures that it will have half of the market if its opponent pairs with it and more than half if its opponent does anything else. If one firm locates anywhere else it will have a market of less than 1/2 after the other firm has paired with it on the side that faces the centre of the whole market. If, however, the two firms are guarding against losses caused by a third firm newly entering the market, they will be driven to locate at the first and third quartiles. This gives them markets of 1/2 and they stand to have their market reduced to 1/4 by the new entrant. This distinction between a new entrant and a move by an existing firm is only relevant for two firms.

[2] Michael Tietz [27] has considered a variant of Hotelling's model in which firms pursue a minimax strategy and firm 1 has n_1 plants and firm 2 has n_2, $(n_1 > n_2)$. If firm 1 locates first it can obtain more than $n_1/(n_1+n_2)$ of the market. This solution is not socially optimal and is in apparent contradiction to our results. Tietz' solution is, however, not an MM equilibrium since after firm 2 enters firm 1 is not in its MM equilibrium. If both firms are free to move and both are minimaxing, the equilibrium is socially optimal with each plant serving $1/(n_1+n_2)$ of the market.

[3] If the two firms know they are playing a two-person game and are thus guarding against a move only by the other firm, their locations are indeterminate since wherever either locates, they share the market equally between themselves.

[4] Samuelson [21] suggests that the socially-optimal configuration will occur on the circle only for $n = 2, 4, 8, 16$, etc. This is only true for Model 2 if the existing firms are not allowed to relocate after the entry of a new firm. Steven Grace [13] in reply to Samuelson, suggests a plausible dynamic of entry which implies that the number of firms in the market grow as 2, 4, 8, 16, etc.

(3.iii) if i is an unpaired interior firm $c(B_L) = c(B_R)$;
(3.iv) if i is a paired firm $c(B_{SS}) \geq c(B_{LS})$;

where B_L and B_R denote the ith firm's left-hand and right-hand boundaries, and B_{SS} and B_{LS} denote its short-side and long-side boundaries.

Proof. Since we only need the necessity of these conditions for our subsequent analysis, we omit the proof of their sufficiency. The arguments for the necessity of (3.i) and (3.ii) are analogous to those given for Model 1. To establish the necessity of (3.iii), form the expression for the ith firm's market (M_i): when the ith firm is located at X_i

$$M_i = \int_{B_L}^{X_i} c(X)dX + \int_{X_i}^{B_R} c(X)dX = C(B_R) - C(B_L) \qquad \ldots(1)$$

where $C(X) = \int c(X)dX$. We know that $B_L = (X_{i-1} + X_i)/2$ and $B_R = (X_{i+1} + X_i)/2$. Differentiating M_i with respect to X_i:

$$\frac{\partial M_i}{\partial X_i} = \tfrac{1}{2}c(B_L) - \tfrac{1}{2}c(B_R).$$

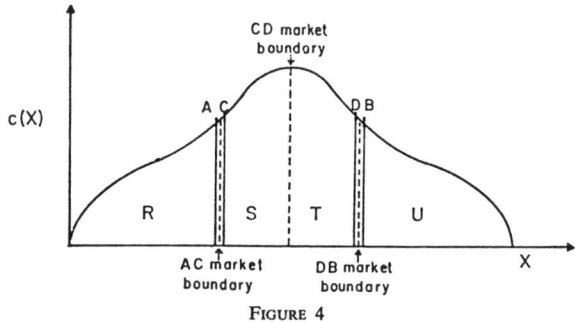

FIGURE 4

The first-order condition for a maximum is then $c(B_L) = c(B_R)$ which establishes the necessity of (3.iii). To establish the necessity of (3.iv) let a paired firm consider moving away from its immediate neighbours. (By assumption it cannot move closer to the firm with which it is paired.) By the argument immediately above the rate of change of its market is

$$\frac{\partial M_i}{\partial X_i} = \tfrac{1}{2}c(B_{LS}) - \tfrac{1}{2}c(B_{SS}).$$

If the inequality in (3.iv) holds then $\partial M_i/\partial X_i < 0$ for movements away from the firm with which i is paired, and if the inequality does not hold $\partial M_i/\partial X_i > 0$ for such movements.

Now consider possible equilibrium configurations. Whatever the shape of the customer-density function, there is always an equilibrium for $n = 2$: the two firms are paired at the median of the density function. Also, there is never an equilibrium for $n = 3$ since the pairing of both peripheral firms violates condition (3.i) for the interior firm.

There are no equilibria for *any* $n > 3$ on a customer density function that is strictly monotonic increasing from each market boundary to a single mode! It may be helpful to consider the example of four firms locating on a symmetric uni-modal customer density function. The only configuration that satisfies (3.i) and (3.ii) has the firms paired at the quartiles of the density function. This is illustrated in Figure 4 where the areas R, S, T and U are equal. But this configuration leaves condition (3.iv) unsatisfied for the two interior firms. Hence there is no equilibrium configuration. (The dynamic behaviour is discussed in [11], p. 20.)

We now consider variable density functions more generally and begin by establishing the following theorem.

Theorem. *With a variable customer density function that is not rectangular over any finite range of X, a necessary condition for equilibrium is that the number of firms does not exceed twice the number of modes.*

Proof. (1) Equilibrium condition (3.iii) implies that the market interval of any unpaired firm must contain at least one turning point as an interior point in the interval. Furthermore, the turning point must be a maximum (since if it were a minimum and condition (3.iii) were satisfied, the firm's market would be at a local minimum). (2) Equilibrium condition (3.iv) implies that any paired firm whose customer density is increasing away from the firm in the direction of its long-side market boundary must have a maximum point in the customer density function as an interior point in that firm's market. Since it must

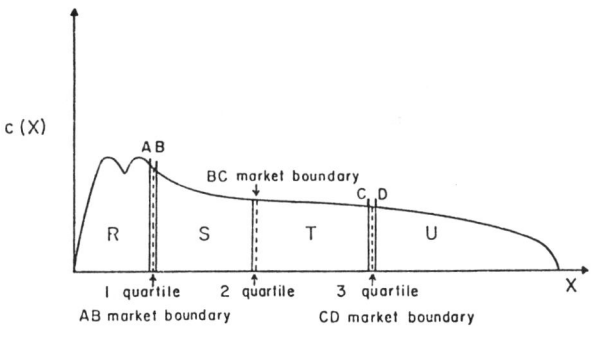

FIGURE 5(a)

always be true for *one* of any pair of firms, not located at a mode, that $c(X)$ is increasing for a movement away from the firm's location towards its long-side boundary, the long side of the market of one of the firms in each pair must include a mode. (3) Since every unpaired firm and one member of every paired firm must have a market that includes the mode as an interior point (or as a short-side boundary if the firms are paired *at* the mode) it is impossible to fulfil the necessary conditions with $n > 2M$.

$n \geq 2M$ is only a necessary condition. For density functions with $M > 1$ there may or may not be stable equilibrium configurations even if $4 \leq n \leq 2M$.[1] A complete taxonomy would be tedious but two examples of the absence of equilibrium in bimodal distributions with $n = 4$ are illustrated in Figure 5. In each case, the firms are shown paired at the quartiles of the density function (the areas R, S, T, and U are equal). In Figure 5(a) condition (3.iv) is not satisfied for firm C, while in Figure 5(b) condition (3.iv) is not satisfied for either firms B or C.

A further point, relating to the dynamics of disequilibrium systems, is worth noting. If a firm enters the market, or considers moving, and its market is not to include the mode as an interior point it will always wish to pair with another firm. When the system is necessarily in disequilibrium ($n > 2M$) some firms must always be unable to include the

---

[1] Downs [8] implies that a stable multi-party system requires a multi-modal distribution of voters. Our results indicate that such a system can exist with a rectangular distribution of voters, and that the number of parties that can exist in an equilibrium configuration is limited only when the distribution is non-rectangular.

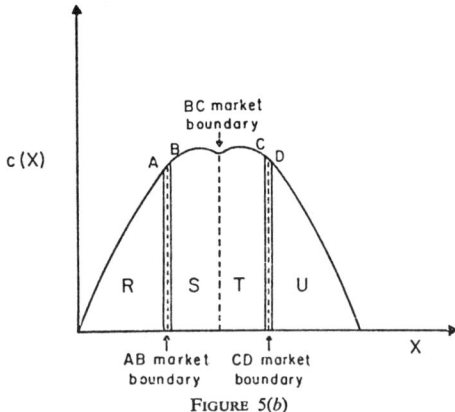

FIGURE 5(b)

mode in their markets and so will always seek to pair with another firm (who will then wish to move away from that firm). This phenomenon of pairing in disequilibrium situations is so pervasive, especially in 2-D markets, that it seems reasonable to refer to a *principle of pairing* as a basic characteristic of disequilibrium models.

When the number of firms is $2M$, conditions (3.iii) and (3.iv) require that the firms all be paired. Thus transport costs are *necessarily* twice their socially-optimal level. When $n<2M$, there is some indeterminancy in the location of the firms (at least for some density functions) and a full taxonomy of locations and transport costs does not seem worth while.

Now transfer Model 3 from the bounded line to the circumference of the circle. Conditions (3.i), (3.iii) and (3.iv)—but not (3.ii)—are the necessary and sufficient conditions for equilibrium on the circle. Since the proof that $n \leq 2M$ is a necessary condition for equilibrium does not employ condition (3.ii), this result generalizes immediately to the circle. Thus the change from bounded to unbounded finite space in no way affects the behaviour of the model with ZCV and a variable customer density function. The variable customer density function does, however, produce results that differ significantly from those obtained for the rectangular density function (which can now be regarded as a special case of the variable density function in which the number of modes is infinite).

Model 4. Model 4 combines the MM strategy with a variable customer density function and is applied first to the bounded linear market. We must distinguish between a local equilibrium (no move in the neighbourhood of the firm's present location will increase its short side market) and a global equilibrium (*no* move will increase the firm's short side market.) There are two distinct possibilities for local equilibrium of an individual firm.

Type I local equilibrium conditions. The ith firm is located at X_i such that

(4.i) $\qquad \int_{B_L}^{X_i} c(X)dX = \int_{X_i}^{B_R} c(X)dX.$

For interior firms

(4.ii.a) $\qquad 2c(X_i) \geq c(B_L), c(B_R)$ or $2c(X_i) \leq c(B_L), c(B_R)$.

For a left-hand peripheral firm

(4.ii.b) $\qquad 2c(X_i) \geq c(B_R).$

For a right-hand peripheral firm

(4.ii.c) $\quad 2c(X_i) \geqq c(B_L)$.

(1) If condition (4.i) does not hold, but condition (4.ii) does, the firm cannot be in equilibrium since it can always increase either one of its market sides (and hence its small side) by moving towards the boundary of the other of its market sides. (2) If condition (4.i) does hold but (4.ii) does not, the firm can increase *both* sides of its market by moving *towards* the boundary for which $c(B) > 2c(X_i)$. (This result follows immediately from the fact that as a firm moves to the right, its right-hand market changes at the rate of $\tfrac{1}{2}c(B_R) - c(X_i)$ and its left-hand market changes at the rate of $c(X_i) - \tfrac{1}{2}c(B_L)$.)

Notice that Type I equilibrium locates the firm in the centre of its market—i.e. at the median of the customer density function. (This is consistent with our results for a rectangular density function.) If (4.ii) does not hold when the firm is at the centre of its market (because the density function is " too steep ") the firm is not in MM equilibrium. This possibility gives rise to Type II equilibrium in which the firm does not locate at the centre of its market.

Type II local equilibrium conditions. An interior firm, i, must satisfy either

(4.iii.a) $\quad c(X_i) = \tfrac{1}{2}c(B_R)$ and $c(X_i) \leqq \tfrac{1}{2}c(B_L)$

or

(4.iii.b) $\quad c(X_i) = \tfrac{1}{2}c(B_L)$ and $c(X_i) \leqq \tfrac{1}{2}c(B_R)$.

A right-hand peripheral firm must satisfy

(4.iv.a) $\quad c(X_i) = \tfrac{1}{2}c(B_L)$.

A left-hand peripheral firm must satisfy

(4.iv.b) $\quad c(X_i) = \tfrac{1}{2}c(B_R)$.

Once these conditions hold, the firm can no longer increase its short side market by moving toward that boundary, because it is no longer true that $c(B_S) > 2c(X_i)$.

Now consider the existence of global equilibria. Such equilibria can be shown to exist for some density functions. An example can be obtained from Figure 6 by cutting

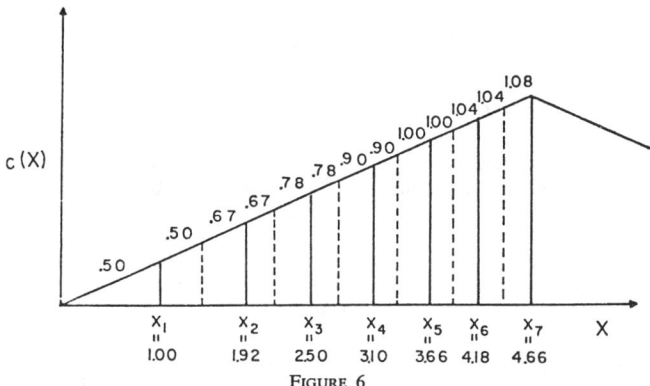

FIGURE 6

off at X_5 and assuming that 3·66 is the modal point of a symmetrical distribution whose left-hand side is shown by the figure over the range $[0, X_5]$. Each firm is in type I local equilibrium. For example, firm 2's half markets are each 0·67 and firm 3's are 0·78.

Global equilibrium configurations do not always exist for any n on any density function. Figure 6 provides an example. Seven firms are located in the left-hand side of a particular symmetrical density function in the unique configuration that satisfies the local equilibrium conditions. (The seventh firm is at the mode and the remaining six firms are not shown.) Although the local equilibrium conditions are everywhere satisfied, firm 1 is not in global equilibrium at X_1 since its two equal half-markets (of 0·50) are less than the two equal half markets it could obtain by locating between firms 6 and 7.[1]

Finally, we turn to the relationship between the *MM* equilibria and the transport-cost minimizing configuration.

Theorem. *The MM equilibrium minimizes transport costs if and only if each firm is in Type I local equilibrium.*[2]

Proof. Letting transport costs be one per unit of commodity per unit of distance, total transport costs for n firms are:

$$TC = \sum_{i=1}^{n} \left\{ \int_{B_L}^{X_i} c(X)(X_i - X)dX + \int_{X_i}^{B_R} c(X)(X - X_i)dX \right\}. \quad \ldots(2)$$

There are n necessary conditions for minimizing transport costs involving n unknowns, $X_i, (i = 1, \ldots, n)$ that can be generated from (2):

$$\frac{\partial TC}{\partial X_i} = 0, \quad (i = 1, \ldots, n).$$

For i, an interior firm, collect the terms involving i in equation (2). Letting

$$G(X) = \int Xc(X)dX \text{ and } C(X) = \int c(X)dX$$

and evaluating the integrals the terms can be reduced to

$$-X_{i-1}C\left(\frac{X_i + X_{i-1}}{2}\right) + 2X_iC(X_i) - 2G(X_i)$$

$$-X_iC\left(\frac{X_i + X_{i-1}}{2}\right) - X_iC\left(\frac{X_i + X_{i+1}}{2}\right) + 2G\left(\frac{X_i + X_{i-1}}{2}\right) + 2G\left(\frac{X_i + X_{i+1}}{2}\right)$$

$$-X_{i-1}C\left(\frac{X_i + X_{i+1}}{2}\right).$$

Differentiating with respect to X_i and simplifying, we obtain the ith transport minimizing condition:

$$C(X_i) - C\left(\frac{X_i + X_{i-1}}{2}\right) = C\left(\frac{X_i + X_{i-1}}{2}\right) - C(X_i). \quad \ldots(3)$$

(3) is immediately seen to be equivalent to condition (4.i).[3] Thus if all firms are in Type I equilibrium, transport-costs are minimized. If Type II equilibrium prevails for any firm, however, that firms' half-markets are not equal. Hence the configuration is not transport-cost minimizing.

We have thus shown that for a given n and a given density function, the minimax strategy may or may not lead to an equilibrium configuration, and, if it does, the configuration may or may not be transport-cost minimizing.

[1] These examples lead to the conjecture that for any density function there is a maximum number of firms that is consistent with equilibrium. The conjecture is strengthened, at least for uni-modal functions, by the observation that as one moves towards higher values of $c(X)$ the number of customers served by successive firms increases—since the boundary between firms i and $i+1$ must bisect the distance between them, firm i must have fewer customers in each of its half markets than firm $i+1$.

[2] It is well known (see e.g. [1]) that, assuming transport costs are a linear function of distance, the transport cost-minimizing location for a single firm is at the median of the density function. Our analysis generalizes this result to n firms.

[3] The demonstration that the first and nth transport-cost minimizing conditions are equivalent to the Type I minimax equilibrium conditions is similar to the demonstration for the ith interior firm, and is omitted.

Model 4 can be transferred to a circle without changing any of the results that we have reached for the line: global equilibria are possible (assume for example, that Figure 6 depicts one-half of a symmetrical density function on a circle with a minimum at $X = 0$ and a maximum at $X = 3.66$ and that there are nine firms in the market); global equilibrium may not exist (assume, for example, that Figure 6 depicts one-half of a circle that goes as far as 4.66 on either side of the minimum at $X = 0$ before reaching its single maximum point, and that there are 13 firms in the market).[1]

Conclusions for one-dimensional space

(1) The wide range of generalizations of the Hotelling model suggested by Boulding and others appears suspect. The results are very sensitive to changes in the number of firms, to changes in conjectural variation, and to changes in the distribution of customers throughout the market. Surprisingly, however, only a few of the results appear sensitive to the existence or non-existence of market boundaries.

(2) Genuine MD appears to be a very special case in the linear model, existing only for $n = 2$. This suggests that a critical step is to test the conjecture that MD will reassert itself when the market is extended to a two-dimensional space.[2]

(3) With a rectangular density function, ZCV produces multiple equilibria. The equilibrium set includes the socially-optimal configuration on the circle but does not on the line. With a rectangular density function, MM produces a unique equilibrium which is the socially-optimal configuration.

(4) The most surprising set of conclusions relates to the effects of abandoning the rectangular customer density function. We originally conjectured, falsely as it turned out, that the assumption of a rectangular density function was not critical on the arguments that local clusters could always be created by making the non-rectangular density function multi-modal and that, while a non-rectangular uni-modal function might pull the firms in towards the centre, it would not seriously upset any configuration established for a rectangular function. The general acceptance of some such conjecture seems necessary to explain the considerable attention that continues to be paid to rectangular customer density functions. In the ZCV models, however, equilibrium cannot exist if the number of firms exceeds twice the number of modes in the density function. Under MM, equilibrium does not necessarily exist, nor where it exists, is it necessarily socially-optimal.

III. TWO-DIMENSIONAL MARKETS

Our objectives are, of necessity, much less ambitious in 2-D space than in 1-D space both because the literature in 1-D space is more extensive and because the location problem is much simpler in 1-D space. Our two-dimensional work is limited to the effects of transferring Model 1—ZCV and a constant customer density function [$c(X, Y) = K$]—to a bounded 2-D space. We investigate the questions of existence and uniqueness of equilibrium in a space bounded by a circle, a disc.

An implication of our assumption that consumers buy from the nearest firm is that the boundary between two firms is the locus of points that are equi-distant from the two firms, and this is given by the perpendicular bisector of the line joining them.

One Firm. As with the 1-D markets, a single firm captures the whole market wherever it locates in the disc and is thus in equilibrium anywhere.

Two Firms. There is a unique equilibrium with two firms: they are paired in the centre of the market. To see this assume that firm 1 is located anywhere other than at the market centre and draw a diameter through 1. If firm 2 now enters the market and

---

[1] A third type of 1-D space is the unbounded infinitely extensible space of the real line. A great deal of attention has been paid to such space in 2-D but not in 1-D models. We argue on p. 29 of [11] that Models 1 through 4 extend to this space with little change in their properties.

[2] For an example of this conjecture see Lösch [18, p. 75] and Lipsey [17, p. 255-256].

pairs with 1 locating on the diameter and just closer to the centre than 1, firm 2 then captures more than half of the entire market. It now pays 1 to relocate on the same diameter but just inside 2, thus capturing more than half the market. If both firms are free to move they continue to "leapfrog" inwards along the diameter until they are located at the centre. At this point they split the market equally between themselves and no relocation can increase either firm's market area.

Thus two firms in the disc exactly reproduce the Hotelling result: 2's entry creates MD even if no relocation is possible, and the equilibrium with relocation produces MD with both firms located at the centre of the market.[1]

Three or more Firms. If a third firm, 3, enters, when 1 and 2 are in equilibrium at the centre of the market, 3 will pair with either of the two existing firms. The firm that is paired with both of the other firms now has virtually no market and it will pay it to relocate outside of one of the other two firms. This could produce a leapfrogging outwards along a diameter that is exactly analogous to what happens with three firms in the $(B, 1-D)$ market. In the 2-D market, however, the firms are not constrained to remain on a single diameter. Thus it is not obvious how three or more firms will behave in the disc, and using conventional analytical techniques the problem is very complex, perhaps intractable. Further analysis requires that we use a simulation technique; we conjecture an equilibrium configuration, determine its exact location, and then test the conjecture numerically.

Three configurations seemed worth investigation as candidates for equilibrium. *Configuration I*: All firms are evenly spaced around a circle whose radius is less than unity. *Configuration II*: this is the same as Configuration I except that there is an additional firm located at the centre of the disc. *Configuration III*: those configurations that give equilibrium in an infinitely extensible plane, i.e. a Löschian space. Elsewhere we have shown that the socially-optimal hexagonal configuration of firms is not a unique equilibrium configuration in this space (see [12]). Indeed many other configurations which give firms identical (but not necessarily regular) hexagonal, rectangular or square market areas can be equilibrium configurations in Löschian space.

Configuration I. We conjecture that the firms will be regularly spaced around a circle, concentric with the market boundary. The firms thus lie at the tips of a regular, n-sided polygon and their market areas are pieces of pie all meeting at the centre of the market. To set the firms in this configuration and check the conjecture, we need to discover the radius, r, of their circle of location. This is done as follows.

Equilibrium in any configuration requires that if any firm is free to move it will choose not to move. If Configuration I is to be an equilibrium, then if $n-1$ of the firms are located at the tips of an n-sided regular polygon, defined by the circle of radius r, the nth will choose to locate at the vacant tip of the polygon. r is obtained by relying on this property of equilibrium. Let n firms be so located. Rotate the axis so that the nth firm is located on the Y axis, and let this firm consider relocation, *but constrain it to locate somewhere on the Y axis*. Along the Y axis the nth firm's market area MA, is a function of only

---

[1] Nicos Devletoglou [7] develops a duopoly model in 2-D space which does not exhibit MD; in fact, it exhibits more than socially-optimal differentiation. His duopolists serve a bounded, two-dimensional market area. Each consumer is assumed to minimize travelling costs subject to the condition that he is indifferent between the two firms if the absolute value of the difference between the distances he has to travel to them is less than some critical value. This " minimum sensible " condition, or zone of indifference when combined with a " fashion " or " imitation " effect on the part of " indifferent " consumers, gives rise to uncertainty as to quantity demanded from a particular firm in a particular period, and the uncertainty implies inventory costs. This effect prevents MD because the number of such indifferent consumers (and hence inventory costs) increases as the duopolists move toward each other. It is Devletoglou's dynamic assumption, however, that is critical to the location of the duopolists. He constrains the duopolists to locate symmetrically on any diameter of the circle and effectively assumes that a move by one firm toward (away from) the centre of the market is matched by an exactly symmetrical move by the opposing duopolist, and these symmetrical reactions are anticipated. Provided demand is not completely inelastic, such a dynamic will produce the joint-profit maximizing configuration in the absence of " minimum sensible " (see [24], p. 123). In addition, the inventory costs implied by the " minimum sensible " and the fashion effect produce a dispersion of the duopolists even greater than the quartiles of the diameter.

three variables: the radius of location of the other $n-1$ firms; n, the number of firms; and Z, the distance along the Y axis at which the nth firm chooses to locate.

If our original conjecture is correct, the nth firm will want to be the same distance, r, away from the origin as the other firms, provided that r is at its equilibrium value. If so we will have $r = Z$ in equilibrium. Substituting this equality into the first order condition for a maximum of MA with respect to Z gives

$$r = \tfrac{1}{2}\sqrt{\left(1+\sin\left(\frac{\pi}{2}-\frac{2\pi}{n}\right)/2\right)}. \qquad \ldots(4)$$

If r is set at any value other than that given by the above expression, then $\partial MA/\partial Z \neq 0$ evaluated at $Z = r$, and *any* firm would wish to move. (The details of this derivation appear in Appendix B of [11].)

To determine if the configuration is an equilibrium one with respect to a small movement of the firm in *any* direction is an almost impossible task using analytical methods, and in any case much more is required to establish global equilibrium.[1] We therefore use a simulation approach. We locate n firms on a circle of radius r. We then allow one firm to consider a large number of alternative locations and numerically calculate its market area for each of these.

The problem that must be solved in order to use a simulation approach to location on the disc can be simply stated: given the location of n existing firms at points $P_i(X_i, Y_i)$, $i = 1, ..., n$, what size market area can a new entrant expect to have if he locates at an arbitrarily chosen point $P_0(X_0, Y_0)$? Our approach is to trace out the various segments of the firm's market boundary, calculating increments to the firm's market area as we proceed around the boundary. The steps required to implement this approach are detailed in Appendix A of [11].

The market area maps produced by this technique reveal that although any firm is in a local equilibrium in Configuration I, it is not in global equilibrium. The four firm case is illustrated in Figure 7. Three firms are located on a circle of radius 0·354. The numbers in the diagram give firm 4's market area for each indicated location. (Since the disc is of unit radius, its area is π.) The diagram shows that the point (0, 0·354) is a local maximum but that it is not a global maximum. Global maxima occur at two points very close to the firm's neighbours. From $n = 3$ to at least 17 the same result occurs: if the firms are located on a circle of radius r and any one is free to move, it will wish to relocate next to either one of its neighbouring firms.

Thus if we impose the circular configuration, it immediately breaks up. The way in which it breaks up suggests a principle of pairing similar to that found in (1-D) markets. The sub-optimal differentiation is a disequilibrium phenomenon since the other paired firm will immediately wish to shift its location.

Configuration II. One firm is located in the centre of the circle, the remaining firms are regularly spaced out around a circle of radius r'. A procedure analogous to that outlined above was used to determine r'. We checked this configuration for up to 17 firms and the results are as follows.

[1] To determine if the point $(0, r)$ is a local equilibrium for the nth firm form the analytical expression for its MA when both the X and the Y co-ordinates can vary. Differentiate it with respect to X and Y and see if these expressions are zero evaluated at $(0, r)$. Check the second order condition to see if this is a maximum for movements that leave the firm's neighbours unchanged, discover all (X, Y) combinations that satisfy the maximum conditions. For different locations, however, the firm will have different neighbours. The MA must have at least two boundaries and it can have as many as $n+1$ (one each with the $n-1$ other firms and two with the boundary of the disc). This implies there are

$$_{(n+1)}C_2 + {_{(n+1)}C_3} + \ldots + {_{(n+1)}C_{(n+1)}} = M$$

possible sets of potential boundaries, B_i. For each B_i identify the set of points $S_i(X_i, Y_i)(i = 1, ..., M)$ for which B_i is the relevant boundary. Eliminate all B_i for which S_i is the null set and for each of the remaining B_i form the expression for market area. Find the particular point within each S_i which maximizes the market area. From the set of local maximum market areas pick the largest. This yields the global maximum for one firm for given locations of the other $n-1$ firms.

(1) The firm in the central location is not even at a local maximum for $n = 3$. For $3 < n < 9$ the central firm is at a local maximum but not at a global maximum: its market is maximized by moving just outside of one of the firms on the circle. For $n > 8$ the central firm is in a global maximum.

(2) The $n-1$ firms located symmetrically on the circle are always at a local maximum but never at a global maximum for any n up to 17. (It did not seem worth while checking for larger values of n.) Any of the $n-1$ firms maximizes its market by relocating very close to either of its neighbours.

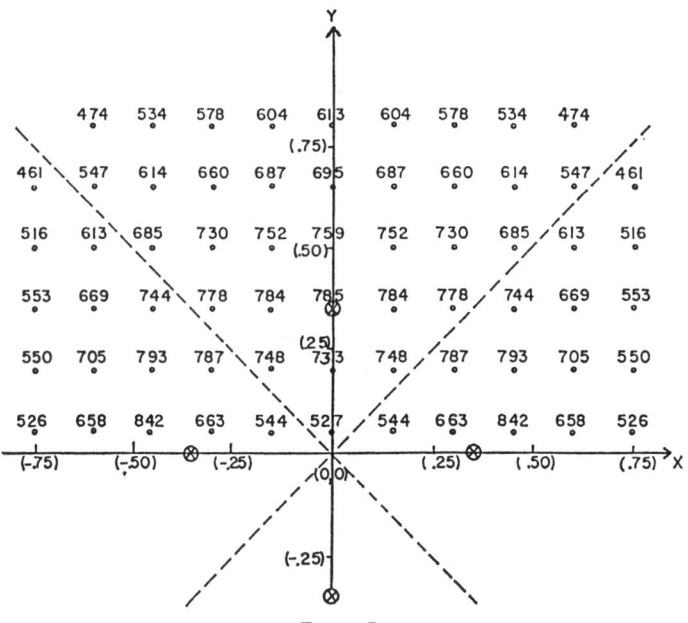

FIGURE 7

Market areas for alternative locations of one firm when three other firms are placed on a circle of radius 0·354 (only the relevant portion of the disc is shown).

Configuration III. The regular hexagonal configuration (which provides the most familiar equilibrium configuration in Löschian space) is adapted to the disc in the following way. Populate an infinitely extensible 2-D space with firms in a hexagonal configuration. Drop a circle centred on one firm. The firms left outside of this circle cease to exist.

The first five configurations that are obtained in this manner are of 1, 7, 11, 15 and 19 firms. One firm is in equilibrium anywhere in the disc but none of the configurations for $n > 1$ are equilibrium configurations. For $n = 7$ configurations II and III are identical. Figure 8 illustrates the absence of equilibrium for $n = 19$. It shows the initial pattern and the configuration after one round of relocations. Clearly, the hexagonal pattern has broken up completely: there are four closely grouped pairs of firms, two groups of three, and five firms are without close neighbours. The importance of the result of this one round of relocations is that it forces us to reject the conjecture that the Löschian pattern would be only slightly distorted near the boundaries as peripheral firms squeezed in to pick up some market from their interior neighbours. This conjecture leads to only a mild distortion, but not a break-up, of the hexagonal pattern of market boundaries.

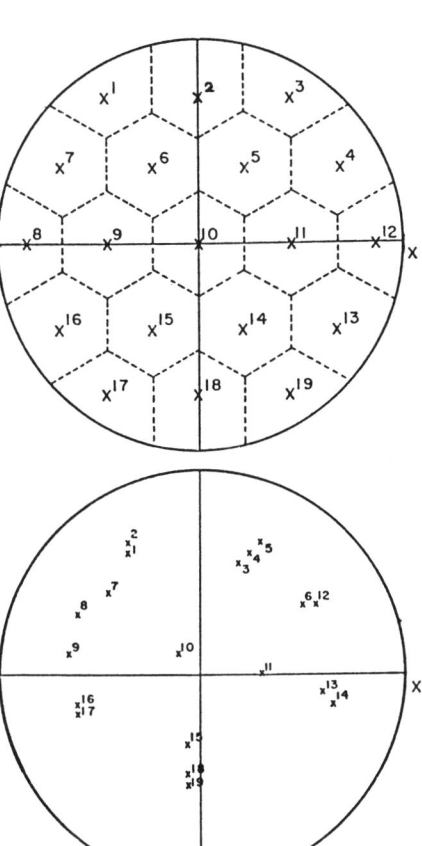

FIGURE 8

We have also transferred other patterns, such as squares and rectangles, that give equilibrium configurations in Löschian space on to the disc. The patterns always break up and the reason is always the same: firms on the periphery will prefer to pair with a neighbour rather than stay where they are.

The number of real cases for which the infinitely extensible plane is the correct analogue must be rather small and the great interest in the hexagonal configuration can only be explained by the assumption, sometimes made explicitly but more often implicitly that the results obtained from Löschian space transfer to a bounded, 2-D space.[1] This assumption

---

[1] Edward Leamer [15] has used simulation techniques to investigate in some detail the question of socially-optimal location patterns in (B, 2-D) space. He discovers that the socially-optimal pattern corresponds closely to the hexagonal configuration, and he presents a behavioural model of the firm which he asserts does converge to the optimal configuration. He is, however, not satisfied with his behavioural model and suggests that the model under investigation here, ZCV with respect to location, would be more appropriate. He *wrongly* asserts, however, that the ZCV model would also converge to the socially-optimal configuration [15, p. 242]. Beckman clearly implies that the hexagonal pattern is the equilibrium pattern for (B, 2-D) space when n is large [4, p. 41]. Samuelson seems tempted to apply the results from unbounded markets to bounded markets although he seems undecided between the square and hexagonal patterns [22, pp. 343-344].

is mistaken. The existence of boundaries to the market is critical to the behaviour of the model in 2-D space (although not in 1-D space).

All three conjectured equilibrium configurations have been rejected and we advance the hypothesis that there is no equilibrium configuration for Model 1 on the disc for $n > 2$.[1] It is now necessary to study the dynamic behaviour of the model. We do this for two reasons: (1) there may be equilibrium configurations, the nature of which we have not guessed, but to which our dynamic model might quickly converge; (2) if we discover a pattern of perpetually recurring oscillations, we will have disproved the existence of an equilibrium configuration that is obtainable independently of initial conditions. Indeed, if our starting configuration is not just chosen haphazardly, but is in some sense a likely configuration, we will have thrown strong doubt on the possibility of ever attaining an equilibrium.

The procedure for studying the dynamic behaviour is as follows. The first firm is placed in the centre of the market and the second firm is allowed to pair with it. Each additional firm is then allowed to enter the market one at a time in its market-maximizing location. After all n firms have entered, the existing firms are allowed to relocate in the sequence in which they entered.

Briefly our results are as follows. For $n = 3$ all three firms begin on a diameter through the origin which we take as the X axis. They then leap-frog outwards exactly as in 1-D space. The outward movement continues to a point where it finally pays one firm to depart slightly from the X axis. It then pays the next firm also to depart from the X axis. The third firm then finds it most profitable to return to the centre of the disc. The other two firms immediately follow recreating the MD grouping at the centre. The outward leapfrogging then begins again and the pattern repeats endlessly.

The four-firm case is shown in Figure 9. The firms enter so as to create an MD configuration which may be referred to as a " main-street ". They then leapfrog out along the diameter, but the pattern soon breaks up into apparent confusion (but the principle of pairing remains clearly observable). Soon, however, it pays someone to move near the centre of the circle and the others immediately follow. They line up on a new " main-street " and the outward leapfrogging begins again. The figure shows one such sequence. After four such sequences, however, they line up in a " main-street " that exactly reproduces the initial main street.

Five firms are even more complex and we have taken the model through 70 individual moves. The firms leapfrog outwards, break up into apparent confusion, and finally regroup in a main-street near the origin. This sequence continues with each main-street configuration being near the origin but in a slightly different location than the previous one. We have not carried the dynamic model beyond $n = 5$.[2]

We strongly suspect, but as yet cannot prove, the non-existence of any equilibrium configurations in the disc beyond $n = 2$. Certainly, for up to $n = 17$ none of the three configurations that seemed likely to produce equilibrium actually did so. Also up to $n = 5$ there appear to be regular, cyclic oscillations.

During the whole disequilibrium process the firms tend to be clustered into several unstable groupings and all of the firms are well within the circle of location which would

---

[1] In a paper published in this issue Mr Shaked of Nuffield College, Oxford proves the non-existence of equilibrium for three firms on the disc.
[2] This is suggestive of some urban phenomena and to study the behaviour of Model 1 with larger n we allowed 23 firms to enter the market one at a time in their ZCV locations (setting δ at 0·05). The resulting configuration had 19 firms grouped in a main-street along the X axis extending from $-0·45$ to $+0·45$ and two groups of two firms on the Y axis, one at 0·40 and 0·45, and the other at $-0·40$ and $-0·45$. When relocation was allowed, the firms near the origin moved to pair with the peripheral firms on both extremes of the X and Y axes. The resulting configuration left no firms in the centre of the market and four local clusterings of firms well out on the positive and negative portions of the two axes. Further study of this suggestive dynamic behaviour requires the development of more sophisticated models.

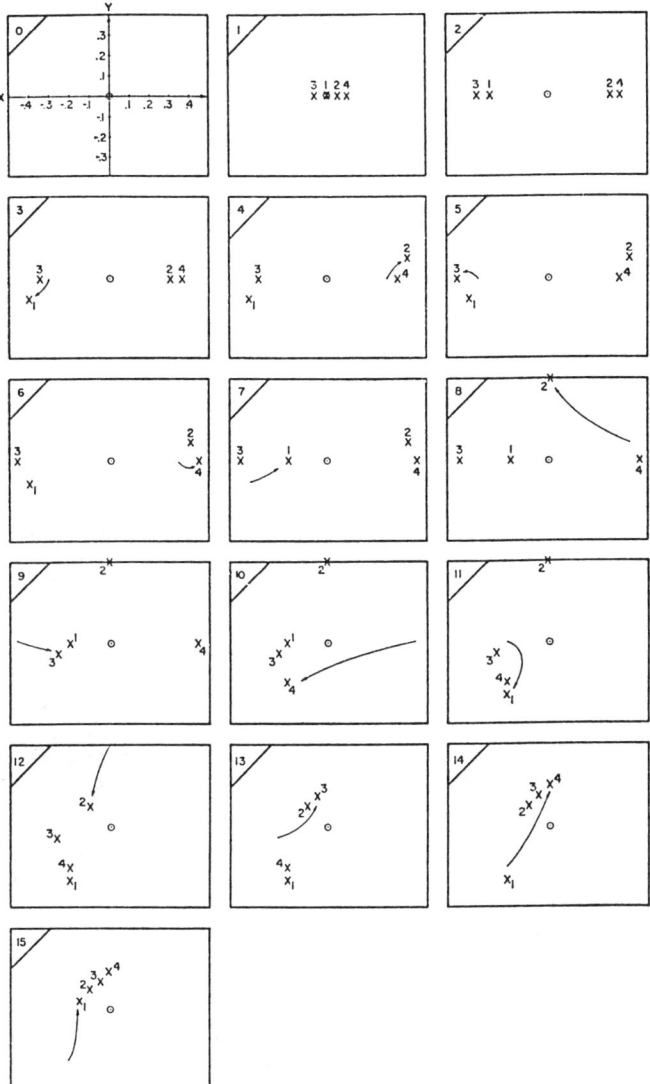

FIGURE 9

The Four-firm Dynamics

The market area is a disc but only the relevant central portion is shown. The X and Y axes and the scale are shown in cell (0). In the subsequent cells only the origin is indicated by $\odot$.

(1) The initial position after entry.
(2) The position reached after a series of outward jumps along the X axis.
(3)-(15) Successive positions reached by a single relocation of one firm. The movement of the firm in question is shown by an arrow.

minimize the costs of transport.[1] This reinforces the conjecture that the principle of pairing (or possibly a more general principle of " local clustering ")[2] should replace the principle of minimum differentiation. It also suggests the further conjectures that the absence of equilibrium may be important in many locational contexts, and that suboptimal locations may be a persistent result through all of the dynamic fluctuations in locational patterns.

IV. CONCLUSIONS

Minimum Differentiation. Of the models that we have studied, minimum differentiation is a property only of those in which firms pursue a strategy of zero conjectural variation (ZCV) and where the number of firms is restricted to two.

Principle of Local Clustering. When a new firm enters a market, or when an existing firm relocates, there is a strong tendency for that firm to locate as close as possible to another firm. This behaviour tends to create local clusters of firms in many equilibrium and disequilibrium situations. The principle of minimum differentiation is a special case of the principle of local clustering when the number of firms in the market is restricted to two.

Multiple Equilibria. Under ZCV with a rectangular distribution of customers, an infinite number of equilibria exists in unbounded, one-dimensional space for any n, and in bounded one-dimensional space when $n>5$. (We showed in [12] that multiple equilibria also exist in infinitely extensible 2-D space.)

The Non-existence of Equilibrium. For $n>2$ in a bounded two-dimensional market under ZCV and an even distribution of customers there do not appear to be any equilibrium configurations. If firms adopt a ZCV strategy in a one-dimensional market, the maximum number of firms consistent with equilibrium is twice the number of modes in the density function. Even under the minimax strategy, equilibrium does not exist for some n and some non-rectangular density functions.[3]

In conclusion brief attention may be given to the sensitivity of our results to variations in those of our assumptions that may seem most restrictive.

Assumption (iv): It has seemed intuitively appealing to many readers of earlier drafts of this paper that Hotelling's minimum-differentiation result would reassert itself for $n>2$ if we assumed that customers were indifferent between two firms, whenever their delivered prices differed by less than some arbitrary amount, Δ. We may briefly study this conjecture in the bounded, linear market.

Assume that firms obtain equal shares of customers who are indifferent between them and let a be the cost of transporting a unit of the commodity over the whole (unit) range of the market. If all firms locate within $\Delta/2a$ of the centre of the market we will have a sort of minimum differentiation and the firms will each have $1/n$ of the total market. But unless Δ/a is large in relation to the total market this central grouping will not be an equilibrium configuration.

[1] The radius of location that minimizes transport costs is 0·49, 0·56 and 0·63 for $n = 3$, 4 and 5. The maximum distance from the centre of the disc reached by any of the firms during the dynamic adjustment process is 0·42, 0·45 and 0·47 for $n = 3$, 4 and 5.

[2] Baumol reaches a similar conclusion in a different context [2]. He considers the problem of entry in a 2-D, Lancaster type, characteristics space. When two firms are present, a third will choose to produce a product which is very similar to that produced by one of the already existing firms. For a discussion of the limitations of Baumol's approach see [23].

[3] The conditions under which our results generalize to non-spatial forms of differentiation (product characteristics) are of some interest. Let the bounded line represent a continuum of some non-spatial characteristic, colour for example—and let the Cartesian co-ordinates of any point on the disc represents a combination of two characteristics, smoothness and alcoholic content of whisky, for example. Then let the customer density function describe the distribution of customer's most preferred points through the appropriate space. A firm's location is also described by the characteristic(s) of the product it produces. For our results to generalize we require that consumers buy from the firm that is nearest to their most-preferred point in the characteristic(s) space. In one-dimension this requirement is easily understood, and in two the requirement implies that a monotonic transformation of the scales on either or both of the axes can be found such than an individual's indifference curves are circular around his most preferred point.

The case of $n = 3$: Locate firm 1 at $1/2 - \Delta/2a$, firm 2 at $1/2$ and firm 3 at $1/2 + \Delta/2a$. Let firm 1 consider moving. If it goes to $1/2 - \Delta/a$ it gains exclusive control of a peripheral market of $1/2 - \Delta/a$ and a half share of an interior market of Δ/a. It will make this move if $1/2 - \Delta/a + \Delta/2a > 1/3$, i.e., if $\Delta/a < 1/3$. (If this condition holds it is easy to show that there is no equilibrium for $n = 3$.)

The case of $n > 3$: Locate the peripheral firms at $1/2 - \Delta/2a$ and $1/2 + \Delta/2a$ and let one interior firm consider relocating to become a peripheral firm. If it locates Δ/a away from its nearest neighbour it obtains a peripheral market of $1/2 - \Delta/2a - \Delta/a$ and some part of a shared interior market of Δ/a. The firm will certainly move if $1/2 - \Delta/2a - \Delta/a > 1/n$, i.e. $\Delta/a < (n-2)/3n$.

Thus if Δ/a is large enough a sort of minimum differentiation may result although there will be a wide range ($1/2 - \Delta/2a$ to $1/2 + \Delta/2a$) over which the firms may be haphazardly located; but if Δ/a is not " too large " our results hold.

Assumption (v): It has been alleged that our model is uninteresting because we abstract from price competition. The allegation implies that if we incorporated price competition into the model, virtually all of our results would not hold. Of course there are situations in which price competition has no meaning (e.g. political behaviour). It is clear that, where price competition is relevant, at least some of our results do continue to hold. For example, the important result that peripheral firms tend to pair is not dependent upon the assumption of a parametric price (see [10] and [24].) This shows that the introduction of price competition into our models is not sufficient to establish that the socially-optimal distribution of firms is an equilibrium configuration. Precisely which of the results in this paper require alteration under price competition is difficult to establish and is the subject of further research.

Assumption (ii): Our demand assumption may seem unduly restrictive. However, many of our results are clearly not dependent upon this assumption. We have shown elsewhere [12] that the existence of multiple equilibria in unbounded 2-*D* space is not dependent upon the inelasticity of demand. It is well known that the tendency toward *MD* under duopoly remains when demand is less than perfectly elastic [24]. It is also true that the tendency toward pairing of peripheral firms survives the introduction of downward sloping demand (see [9] and [10]).

Assumption (vi): We have not explicitly considered entry equilibrium. Our cost assumption implies that free entry would result in one firm per customer and zero transport costs. To consider free entry we must alter the assumption to avoid this result. One common assumption is to assume that each firm has the same fixed cost of production in addition to its constant marginal cost (see [3], [9], [19] and [28]). By selecting a suitable value for the fixed costs any equilibrium configuration determined in this paper, for an arbitrary n, can be made a free-entry equilibrium in the sense that existing firms are at least covering costs while a new entrant does not expect to do so. Thus any equilibrium in this paper remains a possible equilibrium given free entry.

The wide variety of theoretical results that we have obtained suggests that careful, detailed specification of the behaviour of firms, of the nature of the space, and of the distribution of customers is essential. Contrary to conjectures commonly found in the literature many of the results obtained from one model do not generalize to other models.

REFERENCES

[1] Alonso, W. " Location Theory ", in *Regional Development and Planning*, J. Friedmann and W. Alonso, eds. (Cambridge: The MIT Press, 1964).

[2] Baumol, W. " Calculation of Optimal Product and Retailer Characteristics: The Abstract Product Approach ", *Journal of Political Economy*, **75** (October 1967), pp. 674-685.

[3] Beckmann, M. "Equilibrium Versus Optimum: Spacing of Firms and Patterns of Market Areas", *Northeast Regional Science Review*, **1** (1971), pp. 1-20.

[4] Beckmann, M. *Location Theory* (New York: Random House, 1968).

[5] Boulding, K. *Economic Analysis*; Vol. I, *Microeconomics*, 4th Ed. (New York: Harpers, 1966).

[6] Chamberlin, E. *The Theory of Monopolistic Competition* (Cambridge: Harvard Univ. Press, 1932), Appendix C.

[7] Devletoglou, N. "A Dissenting View of Duopoly and Spatial Competition", *Economica* (May 1965), pp. 140-160.

[8] Downs, A. "An Economic Theory of Political Action in a Democracy", *Journal of Political Economy*, **65** (April, 1957), pp. 135-150.

[9] Eaton, B. "One-Dimensional Market Models and Monopolistic Competitive Theory", UBC Discussion Paper No. 70 (1972).

[10] Eaton, B. "Spatial Competition Revisited", *Canadian Journal of Economics*, **5** (May 1972), pp. 268-277.

[11] Eaton, B. and Lipsey, R. G. "The Principle of Minimum Differentiation Reconsidered: Some New Developments in the Theory of Spatial Competition", Queen's Institute for Economic Research, Discussion Paper No. 87 (1972).

[12] Eaton, B. and Lipsey, R. G. "Unsuspected Perversities in the Theory of Location", Queen's Institute for Economic Research, Discussion Paper No. 88 (1972).

[13] Grace, S. "Professor Samuelson on Free Enterprise and Economic Efficiency: A Comment", *Quarterly Journal of Economics*, **81** (May 1970), pp. 337-340.

[14] Hotelling, H. "Stability in Competition", *Economic Journal*, **39** (March 1929), pp. 41-57.

[15] Leamer, E. "Locational Equilibria", *Journal of Regional Science*, **8** (No. 2, 1968), pp. 229-242.

[16] Lerner, A. and Singer, H. "Some Notes on Duopoly and Spatial Competition", *Journal of Political Economy*, **45** (February 1941), pp. 423-439.

[17] Lipsey, R. G. *An Introduction to Positive Economics*, First Edition (London: Weidenfeld & Nicholson, 1963).

[18] Lösch, A. *The Economics of Location* (New Haven: Yale University Press, 1954).

[19] Mills, E. and Lav, M. "A Model of Market Areas with Free Entry", *Journal of Political Economy* (June 1964), pp. 278-288.

[20] Neutze, G. "Major Determinants of Location Patterns", *Land Economics*, **43** (May 1967), pp. 227-232.

[21] Samuelson, P. "The Monopolistic Competition Revolution", in *Monopolistic Competitive Theory: Studies in Impact*, R. Kuenne, ed. (New York: Wiley & Sons, 1967).

[22] Samuelson, P. "Reply", *Quarterly Journal of Economics*, **81** (May 1970), pp. 341-345.

[23] Schuster, H. "Further Remarks on the Theory of Product Differentiation", *Journal of Political Economy*, **77** (September-October 1969), pp. 828-833.

[24] Smithies, A. "Optimum Location in Spatial Competition", *Journal of Political Economy*, **49** (June 1941), pp. 423-439.

[25] Steiner, P. " Monopoly and Competition in Television: Some Policy Issues ", *Manchester School*, **29** (May 1961), pp. 107-131.

[26] Stokes, D. " Spatial Models of Party Competition ", *American Political Science Review*, **57** (1963), pp. 368-377.

[27] Teitz, M. " Locational Strategies for Competitive Systems ", *Journal of Regional Science*, **8** (No. 2, 1968), pp. 135-148.

[28] Telser, L. " On the Regulation of Industry : A Note ", *Journal of Political Economy*, **77** (December 1969), pp. 937-952.

[29] Zeuthen, F. " Theoretical Remarks on Price Policy: Hotelling's Case with Variations ", *Quarterly Journal of Economics*, **49** (February 1933), pp. 231-253.

[2]

The Non-Uniqueness of Equilibrium in the Löschian Location Model

By B. Curtis Eaton and Richard G. Lipsey*

The great emphasis placed on regular hexagonal market networks in location theory suggests a presumption that: 1) this network is the unique equilibrium configuration when the number of firms in the market is given, and 2) free entry will cause this network to prevail. These presumptions have been prevalent in the literature since the monumental work of August Lösch. In this paper we argue that both presumptions are wrong: the regular hexagonal lattice is only one of a large number of equilibrium configurations, and free entry does not necessarily produce regular hexagons.

It is well known that (subject to the condition that every point in the space be served) the hexagonal network of market boundaries would be the planner's solution.[1] This result is not at issue here. The question that we consider is whether or not free competition, with each firm seeking to maximize its own profits, will bring about the hexagonal configuration of firms. If this question is to be studied satisfactorily, it is important not to assume the answer at the outset, but rather to make behavioral assumptions suitable to the decisions of independent firms and households and then to determine whether or not the hexagonal configuration will result from the assumed behavior.

In Section I of this paper we analyze a simple model designed to deal with this question. In Section II we relax some of the model's more restrictive assumptions. In the concluding section we discuss the reasons why our results differ from those that appear to follow from Lösch's famous treatment of the same problem.

I. The Analysis of the Simple Model

A. *The Model*

We begin by listing and discussing the assumptions of our model.

(a) The infinitely extensible plane is uniformly populated with customers with a density of one per unit of area.

(b) Each firm is faced with the same total cost function, $TC = K + cQ$, where K is fixed costs, c is the constant marginal cost of production, and Q is quantity produced and sold. This cost function is commonly used in location theory and we can take c as zero without loss of generality.

One way in which such a cost function could arise is through indivisibilities. To rationalize this precise function in this way we can assume that the only fixed costs are those associated with capital, and that there is an indivisibility in plant size such that the smallest possible plant is large enough to serve any of the markets for individual firms that we consider. We thus have $K = rI$ where r is the opportunity cost of capital and I is the investment associated with the minimum possible size of plant. Since indivisibilities are ubiquitous with any production involving machines,

---

* Associate professor of economics, University of British Columbia, and professor of economics, Queen's University, respectively. The present paper is a revised version of the Queen's Institute for Economic Research study paper no. 88, September 1972. We wish to acknowledge the helpful comments and suggestions of many colleagues, the valuable research assistance of Edward France, Allan Popoff, and Duncan Smeaton, and the generous support of the Queen's Institute for Economic Research.

[1] See Belá Bollobás and Nicholas Stern for a recent example of a full discussion of this proposition.

our cost assumption is not empirically uninteresting.[2]

(c) Transport costs per unit distance are constant. Consumers bear the cost of transport.

(d) Consumers buy from the firm whose delivered price is lowest.

(e) All firms charge the same mill price which is an exogenously imposed constant (the common mill price must exceed c and it is taken to be unity).

Assumptions (d) and (e) together imply that the market boundary between two adjacent firms is the perpendicular bisector of the line joining the two firms. Thus each firm's market is defined by a set of linear boundary segments whose positions depend solely on the locations of the firm and its neighbors. Assumption (e) allows us to concentrate on spatial rather than on price competition, but it is not necessary for the results that we obtain. The consequences of dropping it are considered in Section II.[3]

(f) All customers buy one unit of the product per period of time. This assumption greatly simplifies the analysis and exposition, but it is not necessary for the results that we obtain. The consequences of dropping it are also discussed in Section II.

(g) In selecting its location, each firm seeks to maximize its profits and takes the location of all other firms as given, i.e., it has a zero conjectural variation (ZCV). With respect to location ZCV is an appropriate assumption in at least two important cases: 1) where equilibrium is approached very rapidly so that firms do not have time to learn their opponents' reactions; and 2) when relocation occurs (if at all) only after a very long time lag, as in many locational problems.[4] (Since our firms are engaged in noncooperative games, any equilibria that we discover will be Nash equilibria.)

The assumptions made above affect the measurement of our profit variables. *Gross profit R* is total revenue minus total variable cost: $R = PQ - cQ$. Since we have assumed $c=0$ and $P=1$ and, since each unit of market area contains one customer who buys one unit of the product per period of time, we have $R = Q = Market\ Area$. *Pure profits Z* (also called net profits) are gross profits minus total fixed costs: $Z = R - K$. Thus in the model of this section, maximizing profits is the same thing as maximizing market area.

---

[2] As Nicholas Kaldor puts it, "Yet on an empirical level, nobody doubts that in any economic activity which involves processing or transforming basic materials—in other words, in industry—increasing returns dominate the picture for the very reasons given by Adam Smith in the first chapter of *The Wealth of Nations*: reasons that are fundamental to the nature of technological processes and not to any particular technology" (p. 1242). See also Paul Samuelson. Indeed if there were no indivisibilities and genuine constant returns to scale everywhere in a spatial economy in which transport costs were positive, then there would be no firms at all since all production would take place at the point of consumption so as to reduce transport costs to zero.

[3] It is important to note that our model with a parametric price that is common to all firms will have comparative static properties that are qualitatively similar to those of other models of price competition in which there is a single equilibrium price common to all firms. Consider, for example, the comparative static properties that are implied by the price-conjectural variation that is implicit in Edwin Mills and Michael Lav, and explicit in Martin Beckmann (1971). These authors assume that when setting its price, the firm assumes that each of its competitors will adopt the same price. With this assumption, as with our parametric price, the firm's anticipated market area is independent of the firm's own price. In the Mills-Lav and Beckmann case the existing firms charge the common profit-maximizing price and the general level of profits is raised or lowered by exit or entry. In our model the firms charge a common arbitrary price and the general level of profits is raised or lowered by exit or entry. Indeed anything that we prove for any arbitrary price must be true for one particular price, the monopoly price. Qualitatively these models behave in a similar fashion with respect to spatial competition.

[4] This does not mean that relocation never occurs, but only that the firm's locational decision is taken on the assumption that *over the relevant planning horizon* other firms will not relocate in response. Of course other conjectural variations can be studied, but in each new case the conditions of equilibrium will have to be suitably amended.

These assumptions outline the simplest model that will do our job. We wish to consider the conjectures: (i) that the Löschian hexagonal pattern is the unique equilibrium configuration on the infinitely extensible plane, and (ii) that if other configurations are arbitrarily imposed, the process of entry of new firms will convert these into hexagonal configurations. Our model provides a counterexample which is sufficient to refute both of these conjectures. It also shows some other configurations that can sometimes produce equilibria and it allows us to examine the relative stability of each of these under conditions of entry. In Section II we relax some of the assumptions of this model in order to deal with the possible objection that our assumptions are so restrictive that our counterexamples are of no real interest other than as pathological cases.

B. *The Technique of Analysis*

We analyze the behavior of our model using numerical simulation techniques. We do this because most of the questions we wish to ask are extraordinarily difficult, if not impossible, to answer using conventional analytical methods.

Where they are feasible, analytical techniques are usually preferable to numerical simulation techniques. Numerical methods can prove, for example, that a given configuration *is not* an equilibrium configuration by demonstrating the existence of a profitable move. They cannot, however, prove that a particular configuration *is* an equilibrium configuration. They are only strongly suggestive. The inevitable rounding errors of simulation routines limit the fineness of the grid of potential locations, and in any case it is impossible to evaluate potential profits at an infinite number of points. We have used numerical techniques solely because the problem seemed intractable with conventional analytical techniques, while numerical techniques do seem to allow us to proceed further than other investigators who have confined themselves to analytical methods.

The core of our technique is an algorithm (described in detail in our 1972a paper), which answers the following question: given the location of $n-1$ firms in some region of the infinitely extensible plane, what market can the nth firm expect to control if it locates at an arbitrary point in the region?[5] Using this algorithm it is an easy matter to produce a map which describes the profits that the nth firm could expect to have if it located at any one of a large number of alternative points, given the locations of all of its neighbors. We refer to such maps as market maps.

Figure 1 reproduces a part of one of these maps. The origin is shown by the dot within the circle, and the dots are spaced four units apart vertically and horizontally. The neighbors of the nth firm are shown by circled crosses. The numbers without parentheses indicate the nth firm's market area and hence by the assumptions in Section I, its gross profits in each of the positions indicated by the dots. Thus, for example, if the firm locates at the origin, its market area, and hence its profits, are 692 while if it locates at the point (8, 4) they are 698. (The numbers in parentheses show the profits in each loca-

---

[5] The algorithm was developed to analyze locational problems in a bounded market (see the authors, 1975a), but is easily adapted to the study of some types of behavior in infinitely extensible Löschian space. The basic analytical difference between unbounded and bounded space is that in the former a firm's market boundary must be composed entirely of boundary segments with other firms, whereas in bounded space a firm's market boundary can coincide over some of its range with the boundary of the market. Consider the problem of determining a firm's market area at some particular point in infinite space. The firm will, at least in all the cases in which we are interested, have a boundary with a small number of neighboring firms. The market area algorithm for the bounded space is adapted to the problem of a firm locating at a particular point in unbounded space simply by including all of the neighboring firms in the bounded space.

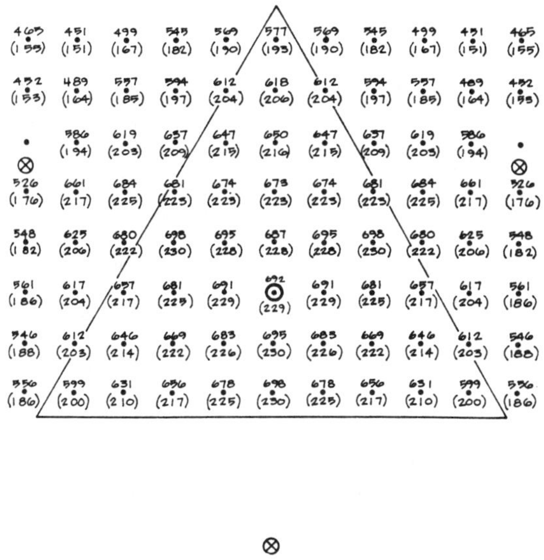

FIGURE 1. THE ABSENCE OF EQUILIBRIUM IN A NETWORK OF EQUILATERAL TRIANGLES

The numbers show the profits the *n*th firm would make by locating alternatively at each of the dots and with neighbors in the fixed positions shown by the circled crosses. Numbers in parentheses refer to the model of Section II, numbers not in parentheses refer to the model of Section I. Location of the *n*th firm at the origin, the point inside the circle, completes the symmetrical lattice of firms and gives the *n*th firm the market boundaries indicated by the dashed lines. Rows and columns are separated by 4 units in Figure 1 and by 6 units in all other figures.

tion that arise from the model in Section II.)

In our actual program, profits were calculated for many more points than are shown in our figures. Only 1/16 of the points are shown in Figure 1, and 1/36 of the points in all other figures. Furthermore, if we were uncertain about the precise location of a particular equilibrium, we could magnify any particular part of the market by placing our observation points as close together as we wished.

C. *Equilibrium in the Absence of Entry and Exit*

We now pass to a consideration of the behavior of our model. We consider, first, a situation in which firms are allowed neither to enter nor to leave the market. In the absence of entry and exit there is a single condition that is necessary and sufficient for all firms in the market to be in equilibrium:

Equilibrium Condition (i): *No firm can find a new location that offers it a larger anticipated profit (assuming ZCV) than that obtained in its present location.*

We first ask which of the three configurations of regular, space-filling polygons (triangles, squares, and hexagons) satisfy equilibrium condition (i). It is interesting that no answer to this question appears to exist in the literature. The reason probably lies with the extreme diffi-

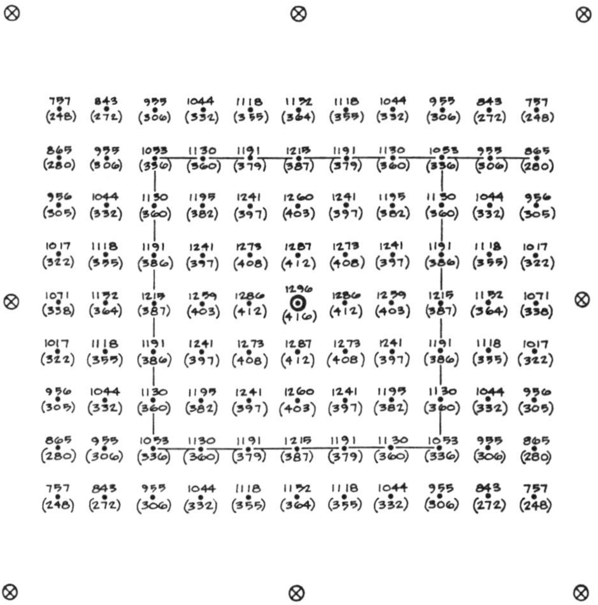

⊗   ⊗   ⊗

757	843	955	1044	1118	1152	1118	1044	955	843	757
(248)	(272)	(306)	(332)	(355)	(364)	(355)	(332)	(306)	(272)	(248)
865	955	1053	1130	1191	1215	1191	1130	1053	955	865
(280)	(306)	(336)	(360)	(379)	(387)	(379)	(360)	(336)	(306)	(280)
956	1044	1130	1195	1241	1260	1241	1195	1130	1044	956
(305)	(332)	(360)	(382)	(397)	(403)	(397)	(382)	(360)	(332)	(305)
1017	1118	1191	1241	1273	1287	1273	1241	1191	1118	1017
(322)	(355)	(380)	(397)	(408)	(412)	(408)	(397)	(380)	(355)	(322)
1071	1172	1215	1259	1286	1296	1286	1259	1215	1152	1071
(338)	(364)	(387)	(403)	(412)	(416)	(412)	(403)	(387)	(364)	(338)

⊗ (at left) ... ⊗ (at right) flanking center row

1017	1118	1191	1241	1273	1287	1273	1241	1191	1118	1017
(322)	(355)	(380)	(397)	(408)	(412)	(408)	(397)	(380)	(355)	(322)
956	1044	1130	1195	1241	1260	1241	1195	1130	1044	956
(305)	(332)	(360)	(382)	(397)	(403)	(397)	(382)	(360)	(332)	(305)
865	955	1053	1130	1191	1215	1191	1130	1053	955	865
(280)	(306)	(336)	(360)	(379)	(387)	(379)	(360)	(336)	(306)	(280)
757	843	955	1044	1118	1152	1118	1044	955	843	757
(248)	(272)	(306)	(332)	(355)	(364)	(355)	(332)	(306)	(272)	(248)

⊗   ⊗   ⊗

FIGURE 2. EQUILIBRIUM IN A NETWORK OF SQUARES
For the description, see Figure 1.

culty of using conventional analytical methods to deal with such problems.

To answer this question using our technique, we let all the firms be first arranged so that the network of market boundaries is composed of equilateral triangles. We select one firm and make its location the origin. We allow that firm to consider a large number of alternative locations and calculate the market area and hence the profits that it would obtain in each location. The triangular configuration is an equilibrium configuration if and only if the best location for the firm is at the origin. Next, repeat the experiment with the firms arranged so that there is a square network of market boundaries and, finally, so that there is a regular hexagonal network of market boundaries.

Figures 1, 2, and 3 show the results.

Intuition suggests and calculation confirms that the firm is always better off remaining within the area defined by its present neighbors rather than moving outside of that area to relocate in an already complete portion of the lattice of firms. Our maps are thus confined to this area. The broken lines indicate the firm's market boundaries when it locates at the origin, thus completing the regular lattice of firms.

Figure 1 shows that the triangular configuration does not satisfy condition (i): the firm at the origin, and hence *any* existing firm, wishes to relocate. The firm would prefer to locate at any of the three locations $(-8, 4)$, $(8, 4)$, or $(0, -8)$ where profits are 698 rather than at the origin where profits are only 692. Thus, given a chance, any firm will move from its posi-

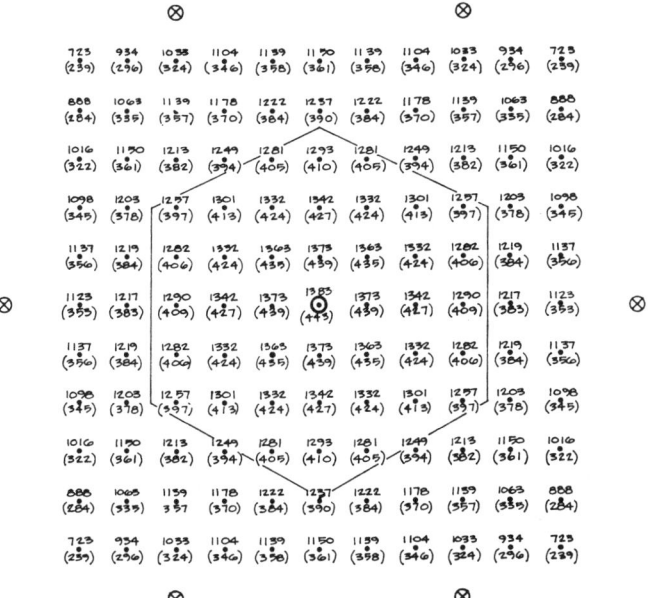

FIGURE 3. EQUILIBRIUM IN A NETWORK OF REGULAR HEXAGONS
For the description, see Figure 1.

tion in a regular triangular lattice. Figures 2 and 3 show that both the square and hexagonal configurations appear to satisfy condition (i): the firm at the origin, and hence any existing firm, does not wish to relocate since the market area and profits at the origin are higher than those at any other location. Thus two of the possible configurations of regular, space-filling polygons satisfy condition (i).

So far we have followed established practice in considering only those configurations of firms that give rise to identical, regular, space-filling polygons. We easily found counterexamples, however, to the conjecture that the only equilibrium configurations were regular, space-filling polygons. We found, for example, that some configurations of identical rectangles would fulfill equilibrium condition (i).

Specifically, we discovered by numerical experimentation that condition (i) is fulfilled by any rectangular lattice of market boundaries in which the ratio of the long to the short side of the rectangle is 26:10 or less. Figure 4 provides an example in which the ratio of the sides is 2:1. The figure shows that a firm that is surrounded by a rectangular lattice of other firms maximizes its market area and its profits (at a value of 968 in the present example) by locating at the origin, thus completing the rectangular lattice.

A network of firms and market boundaries composed of irregular hexagons also fulfills condition (i). In Figure 5 the firm that is free to move chooses to locate at the origin, earning gross profits of 1224 and completing the lattice of irregular hexagons. When it does this, each firm is

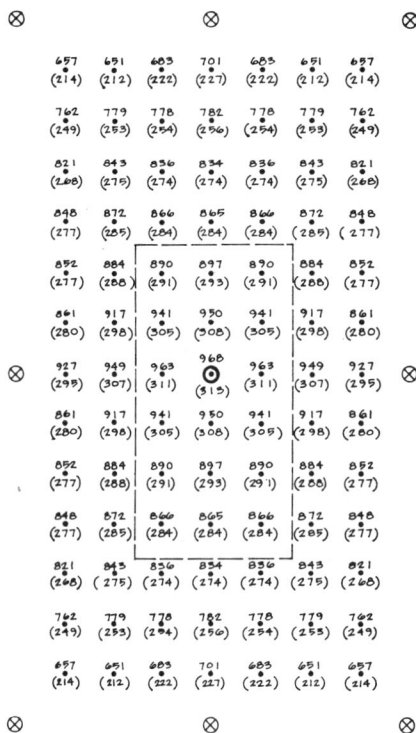

FIGURE 4. EQUILIBRIUM IN A NETWORK OF RECTANGLES WHOSE SIDES STAND IN THE RATIO 2:1

For the description, see Figure 1.

separated from two of its neighbors by 35 and from the remaining four neighbors by 39. This result shows that equilibrium condition (i) can be fulfilled by some configurations that give the firms identical, but nonregular, hexagonal market boundaries.

Our results suggest the further questions: "Can condition (i) be fulfilled: (a) if firms have markets that are not identical in shape but which are equal in area, and (b) if firms do not even have equal market areas?" Although we have not been able to show that identical market shapes or even equal market areas are required by our assumptions, neither have we yet succeeded in finding a configuration of nonidentical markets that satisfies condition (i). *In everything that follows, the argument is confined to situations in which the equilibrium configuration gives all firms markets that are identical in size and shape.*

D. *Equilibrium Configurations Under Freedom of Entry and Exit*

We now consider the case in which firms are permitted to enter and to leave the market. Condition (i) remains an equilibrium condition, but there are now two further conditions.

Condition (ii): *All possible locations for a new entrant within the network of existing firms offer anticipated gross profits, R^e, of less than K.*

Condition (iii): *No existing firm earns actual gross profits, R^a, of less than K.*

Taken together, (i), (ii), and (iii) are necessary and sufficient conditions for equilibrium in our free-entry model: (i) ensures that no existing firm wishes to relocate elsewhere in the market; (ii) ensures that no new firm wishes to enter; and (iii) ensures that no existing firm wishes to exit.

We now ask: Which of the configurations that satisfy condition (i) will also satisfy conditions (ii) and (iii)? Our measure of density of packing h is the reciprocal of the distance from a firm to its nearest neighbor. Within any configuration which gives all firms identical markets this definition of density of packing involves no ambiguity.[6]

---

[6] This definition of density of packing is sufficient for our purposes. In configurations composed of any one of the three regular space-filling polygons the distances to all neighbors are the same. In the irregular configurations that we consider, networks of irregular hexagon and the rectangles, there is no ambiguity in the measure since we hold constant the relative distances from a

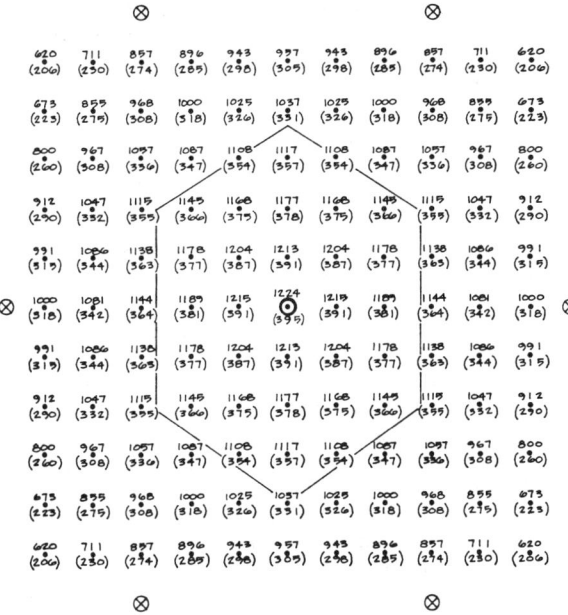

FIGURE 5. EQUILIBRIUM IN A NETWORK OF IRREGULAR HEXAGONS
For the description, see Figure 1.

We consider a particular configuration that gives all firms identical markets, which means that the ratios of the distances from a firm to each of its neighbors is held constant. We then vary the density of packing thus changing the absolute distances from each firm to each of its neighbors. The market area, and hence the gross profit of each existing firm, is a monotonically decreasing function of h: $R^a = R^a(h)$, with the properties

$$\frac{dR^a}{dh} < 0, \quad \lim_{h \to 0} R^a = \infty$$

and $\lim_{h \to \infty} R^a = 0$

---

firm to each of its neighbors. We hold the relative distances constant because we are only interested in whether or not a configuration can be made to satisfy the conditions for entry equilibrium by changing the density of packing. For a general, rigorous treatment of density of firms per unit of market area see Bollobás and Stern.

Now let R^e be the anticipated gross profits of a potential new entrant in its best possible location. Since the profits that a new firm can expect to earn (on a ZCV assumption) can be expressed as a function of the profits earned by existing firms which are in turn a function of h, we express R^e also as a function of h: $R^e = R^e(h)$.

Condition (ii) is fulfilled whenever $R^e(h) < K$. Condition (iii) is fulfilled whenever $R^a(h) \geq K$. Any new entrant must fit into an already completed lattice of firms and must expect to earn profits that are substantially lower than those earned by existing firms before entry occurs. Thus for any given value of h, h_0, $R^e(h_0) < R^a(h_0)$. To illustrate, numerical calculations show the ratios for R^e/R^a to be approximately 0.51 for a regular hexagonal configuration of firms, 0.56 for a square configuration, and 0.50 for a configuration of rectangles where the ratio of the lengths of the market boundaries is 2.0. (Although R^e and R^a are both functions of h their ratio is independent of h in each of the configurations that we consider.) It follows immediately that for any configuration of firms that satisfies condition (i), we can find a *range* of values for h that will allow conditions (ii) and (iii) to be fulfilled simultaneously.[7]

Thus the answer to the question with which we began this section is simply that any of the configurations that give identical market areas and that satisfy condition (i) can be made to satisfy (ii) and (iii) by packing the firms closely enough together so that the expected gross profit of any new entrant is less than K and far enough apart so that the actual gross profit of any existing firm is K or more.

It follows that equilibrium in our free-entry model is consistent with a multiplicity of configurations of firms (squares, rectangles, irregular and regular hexagons), and with a *range* of density of packing of firms (and hence of profits for each firm) in *each* of these configurations. The second of these conclusions has already been stated by Beckmann for hexagons (1968, p. 44). The first conclusion does not seem to have been stated in the literature before. We wish to emphasize that the multiplicity of equilibrium configurations would continue to exist even if zero profits were made a condition of equilibrium. For any of our configurations that satisfy condition (i) there is always a density of packing that will make profits exactly zero, thus satisfying conditions (ii) and (iii) at zero profits.

E. *The Effect of the Process of Entry on the Configuration of Firms*

We may wonder if the dynamic process of free entry is more likely to produce one of the equilibrium configurations, particularly regular hexagons, rather than any other. To consider this, we focus on two specific questions. Does the process of free entry into a square or rectangular configuration tend to transform it into the regular hexagonal configuration? Does the process of free entry into a regular hexagonal configuration tend to reproduce a regular hexagonal configuration?

Many entry dynamics are possible. The one that we use is based on a dynamic suggested for one-dimensional markets by H. Stephen Grace. We discover the set of points of entry offering the highest possible anticipated profits, on the assumption that there is only one new entrant. We then assume that there is simultaneous entry of one firm at each of these points.

Since we know from the previous section that any configuration in which condition (i) is satisfied for all firms can also be made to satisfy conditions (ii) and (iii) by suitable choice of h, we concentrate only on condition (i) in the entry process. This allows us to avoid a lengthy discussion of special cases which obscures the main points of interest.[8]

We first consider entry into a network of rectangular markets (in which lengths of the long and short sides of the market boundaries are X and Y). A new entrant's most profitable location is at the midpoint of the short side of an existing firm's mar-

---

[7] To show that $R^a(h_0) < R^a(h_0)$ when condition (i) is satisfied for all existing firms, we use a proof by contradiction. Assume that condition (i) is satisfied for all existing firms (each of whom is making profits of R^{a*}) before a new firm enters the market). We denote the profits that a potential new entrant expects as R^{e*}. If $R^{a*} < R^{e*}$, the assumption is obviously contradicted, since the entry position was available to any existing firm. If $R^{a*} = R^{e*}$, the assumption is also contradicted. Let (x_e, y_e) be the new entrants' best location, and (x_i, y_i) be the location of its ith neighbor. If the ith neighbor had chosen the point (x_e, y_e) before the new firm entered, it would have had profits greater than R^{e*} because it would not have had a neighbor at (x_i, y_i). Thus if R^{e*} were equal to R^{a*}, then the ith neighbor could have had profits greater than R^{a*} if it had located at (x_e, y_e); this contradicts the assumption that condition (i) is satisfied for the ith neighbor at the point (x_i, y_i).

[8] See our (1972b) paper for a full discussion of these lengthy obscurities.

ket boundary.⁹ When firms enter at each such point, the number of firms is doubled, and a new configuration of rectangular market areas (with sides of lengths $X/2$ and Y) is established. Thus the ratio of the long to the short side is changed by entry, but a new configuration of identical rectangular market areas is established.[10] If the configuration satisfied condition (i) before entry, it must satisfy it after entry.[11] Thus rectangles beget rectangles after each round of entry.

We next consider entry into a square network. To obtain the results shown in Figure 6, firms were placed in a square lattice and a single new entrant was allowed to calculate its market area, and hence its profits, at a large number of alternative entry points. The figure shows that the most profitable location for a new entrant is at the midpoint of each of the existing market boundary segments (where profits are 729). Letting a firm enter at each of these points produces the configuration shown by the circled crosses (original firms) and the dots (new entrants) in Figure 7. Condition (i) is no longer satisfied for the original firms. (The diamond in the top left-hand corner of Figure 7 shows one of the best possible points for relocation of the original firms; and such points recur throughout the market in similar locations.) *If* profits after entry were high enough to encourage a second round of entry and *if* this entry occurred before any relocation of firms already in the market, the square network would then be reestablished. The locations of the firms that would come into the market on the second round of entry are shown by the triangles in Figure 7. Condition (i) is now satisfied for all firms. Thus, squares beget squares but only after two rounds of entry and a fourfold increase in the number of firms.

Finally, we consider entry into a hexagonal network. Because the hexagon does not easily reproduce itself, the entry results are complex and their description becomes tedious. We nonetheless thought it worth briefly describing the process because of the enormous amount of attention that has been paid in the literature to the hexagonal configuration.

Beckmann (1968, p. 44) conjectured that a new entrant would wish to locate at the centroid of the equilateral triangle defined by three contiguous firms. If we let a firm enter at each such point, the number of firms is tripled and all firms again have identical, regular, hexagonal market areas. When we applied our simulation model to the entry problem in a hexagonal network, we discovered that Beckmann's conjecture does not apply in our model.[12] Figure 8 shows the market areas for a new

---

⁹ We have not reproduced the map for the rectangular case since it is so similar to the square case shown in Figure 6. In the square the best entry points bisect all the sides of the existing firms' market boundaries.

[10] The original ratio of the long to the short side of the market is $X:Y$. There are several cases: (a) $Y<X<2Y$. After entry, Y becomes the long side and the new ratio becomes $2Y:X$. After a second round of entry the ratio becomes $2X:2Y$ which is, of course, the original ratio. In the special case in which $X:Y=\sqrt{2}$ the ratio is unchanged after each round of entry since if $X/Y=\sqrt{2}$, then $2Y/X=\sqrt{2}$; (b) $X=2Y$. One round of entry creates a square configuration and after this the analysis of entry into square markets is appropriate. This is the special case in which rectangles do not beget rectangles; (c) $2Y<X$. In this case the short side remains the short side after entry, and the ratio of the long to the short side becomes $X:2Y$. Entry proceeds through r rounds until $X<2^rY$ and after this the analysis of case (a) applies.

[11] a) If $X<2Y$, the ratio of the long to the short sides alternates between two values $X:Y$ and $2Y:X$ which must both lie between the bounds of 1 and 2. b) If $X>2Y$, the ratio declines through successive rounds of entry until it reaches a value of less than 2 after which it alternates as in a) above. Thus, if the ratio of the sides is small enough so that condition (i) is satisfied in the initial configuration, entry can never cause it to increase to the point at which condition (i) is not satisfied.

[12] Beckmann's analysis appears to refer to any downward-sloping linear demand curve. Section II below shows that our results generalize at least to some downward-sloping demand curves and that Beckmann's conjecture cannot therefore be correct in general.

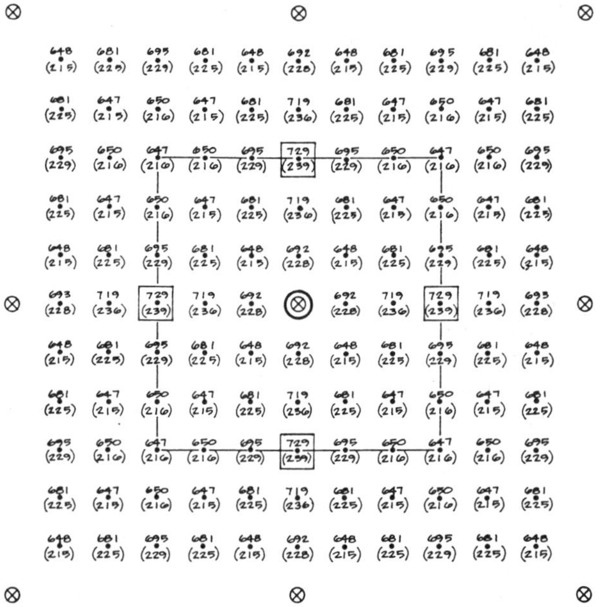

FIGURE 6. ENTRY INTO SQUARE NETWORK

The nth firm is located at the origin. Its location is shown by the double circled cross and its market boundaries by the broken lines; its neighbors are shown by single circled crosses. The numbers (in parentheses for the model of Section II and not in parentheses for the model of Section I) show the gross profits available to a single new entrant if it were to locate alternatively at each of the positions indicated by the dots. The best entry points are indicated by squares around both the dot that indicates the exact best point and the numbers that indicate gross profits at that point.

entrant in a number of alternative locations when existing firms are located in a hexagonal configuration at the circled crosses. Beckmann's conjectured entry points are shown by the six points marked with triangles. The market-maximizing entry points turn out to be much closer to the existing firms than Beckmann conjectured. The best entry points close to the firm located at the origin are marked by squares, and there are six such points around each of the existing firms. (The gross profits at these best entry points are approximately 708 while they are 692 at Beckmann's conjectured entry points. Note that because we are only reporting 1/36 of our actual observations our reported observations are close to but not actually at the best points.) If we let a new firm enter at each of the best entry points, we obtain the configuration shown by the circled crosses (original firms) and the dots (new firms) in Figure 9. This is not an equilibrium configuration since condition (i) is no longer satisfied for the original firms. These firms now find themselves surrounded by six very near neighbors and they could substantially increase their market areas by relocating. (The best places to relocate are shown by the triangles in Figure 9.)

In order to carry the analysis a stage

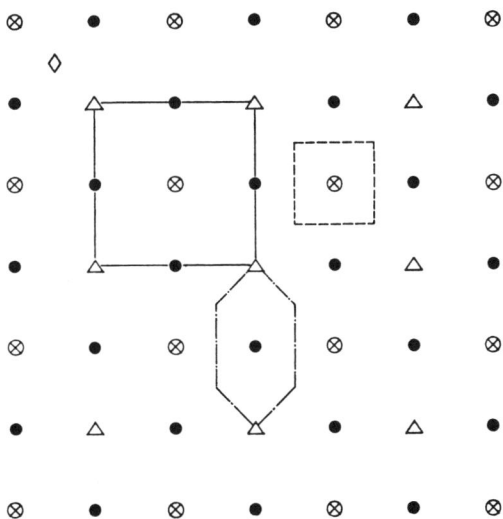

FIGURE 7. ENTRY INTO A SQUARE NETWORK

1) The original firms are shown by circled crosses. The market boundary of one such firm is shown by the solid lines. 2) The locations of new entrants after one round of entry are shown by dots. The market boundary of one such firm is shown by the dot-dashed line. 3) The locations of the new entrants after the second round of entry are shown by the triangles. The market boundary for one such firm is shown by the dashed lines (all firms, old and new, have identical market boundaries after the second round of entry).

further, we consider the effects of further rounds of entry that occur *before* existing firms are allowed to relocate. The second and third rounds of entry are shown in Figure 9 by the triangles and the squares, respectively. The second round still leaves a very irregular network of firms but a third round, if it occurs, reestablishes a hexagonal network. The three rounds, however require a twelvefold increase in the number of firms and, furthermore, the new configuration is not one of regular hexagons. There are no less than four types of market areas. The original firms have regular hexagonal markets, the firms that entered in the three rounds of entry all have irregular hexagonal markets. Condition (i) is not satisfied for the firms that entered in the first and second rounds of entry.

Finally, consider allowing those existing firms for which condition (i) is not fulfilled to relocate. We allow all of the firms that entered in the first round to relocate to their market-maximizing position. The first-round-entry firms are shown with a dot and the desired relocation is shown for six of them by the arrows in Figure 9. Calculation of the market-maximizing locations for these firms shows that this one set of movements establishes a regular hexagonal network of firms and no further movement is desired by any of the firms in the market.

The most important of our entry results may now be summarized. Entry into a square or a rectangular lattice does not tend to turn it into a hexagonal lattice. One round of entry into a hexagonal (or a square) lattice produces disequilibrium

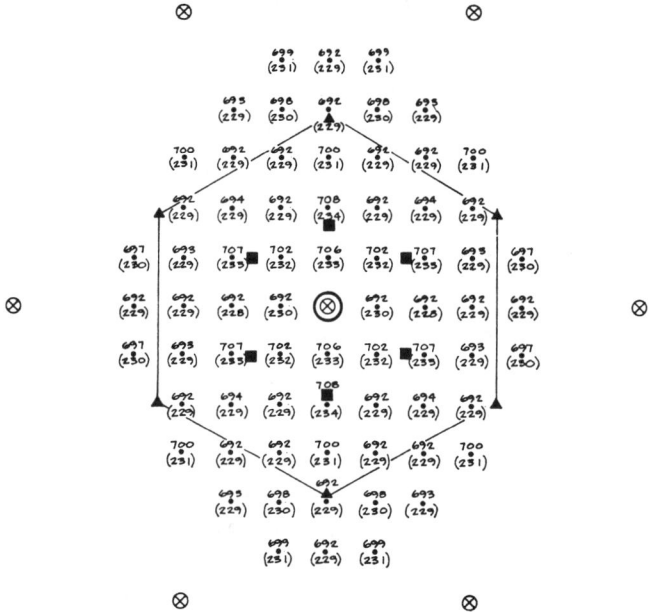

FIGURE 8. ENTRY INTO A REGULAR HEXAGONAL NETWORK

The *n*th firm is located at the origin. Its location is shown by the double circled cross and its market boundaries by the broken lines; its neighbors are shown by single circled crosses. The numbers (in parentheses for the model of Section II and not in parentheses for the model of Section I) show the gross profits available to a new entrant who locates alternatively at each of the positions indicated by the dots. Simultaneous entry at the points indicated by triangles would recreate a hexagonal configuration. The best entry points, however, are those indicated by the squares.

which tends to destroy the lattice. Of the three, therefore, the rectangular lattice seems to be the most robust and the hexagon the least robust in the face of the type of entry that we have considered.

II. Elasticity of Demand and Price Competition

In this section we relax two of the most restrictive assumptions of our model. In order to focus on the nature of equilibrium configurations in space, we have so far used a model in which the individual consumer's demand is perfectly inelastic (assumption (f)), and we have abstracted from price competition (assumption (e)). These restrictive assumptions considerably simplify the analysis and the exposition of the model but it is important to ask if they are necessary for the results that we obtain. In this section we simultaneously relax both assumptions and demonstrate that our results are not dependent on them.

We now assume that all individuals have the same downward-sloping demand function of a particular form and that firms maximize with respect to price as well as location. The demonstration that our results hold for a particular demand function and a particular type of price competition

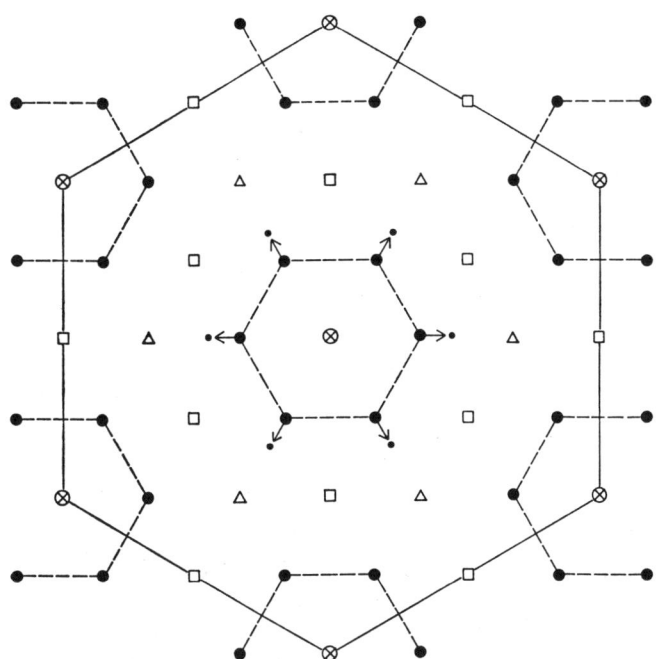

FIGURE 9. ENTRY INTO A HEXAGONAL NETWORK

Original firms are shown by circled crosses. Firms that enter on the first, second, and third rounds of entry are shown by the dots, triangles, and squares, respectively. Market areas are not shown. The lines are solely for visual aid: the original firms surrounding the one at the origin are linked by a solid line; each set of six first-round-entry firms that cluster around each original firm is indicated by a dashed line.

is a counterexample which disproves the conjecture (made by many readers of earlier versions of this paper) that our results are dependent upon our assumptions (e) and (f).

We assume that all customers have identical demand functions of the form

$$q = \exp[-P_d]$$

where q is quantity demanded and P_d is delivered price. For simplicity, we let transport costs be 1 per unit of distance. Delivered price at any point (X, Y) is then

$$P_d = P + [(X - X_0)^2 + (Y - Y_0)^2]^{1/2}$$

where (X_0, Y_0) is the location of the firm and P the firm's mill price.

We adopt the conjectural variations with respect to price which is implicit in Mills and Lav and explicit in Beckmann (1971). Any firm X in choosing its price assumes that all neighboring firms will charge the same price that X chooses. The firm maximizes expected profits with respect to price at any given location.

This price-conjectural variation implies that, just as in the model of Section I, the firm's anticipated market boundary will be composed of linear segments which are the perpendicular bisectors of the lines through the firm's own location and the locations of its neighboring firms. The firm's anticipated market area is independent of its price.

The firm's aggregated demand function will be

$$Q = \iint_{MA} \exp\left[-(P + ((X - X_0)^2 + (Y - Y_0)^2)^{1/2}\right]dxdy$$

$$= \exp[-P] \iint_{MA} \exp\left[-((X - X_0)^2 + (Y - Y_0)^2)^{1/2}\right]dxdy$$

The integration is over all points (X, Y) within the firm's anticipated market area, MA. This aggregated demand function will have the form

$$Q = M \exp[-P]$$

where M is dependent upon the firm's market area. With zero marginal costs of production, profit maximization at any location requires that the firm find the point of unit elasticity on its aggregated demand function. The point of unit elasticity occurs at a price of 1, and the firm's expectations with respect to its neighbor's price will be correct given that all firms pursue the same profit-maximizing behavior with the same price-conjectural variation.

All other assumptions of Section I are maintained. We analyze the firm's profit-maximizing behavior in this modified model using numerical techniques which are analogous to those described in Section I. At each point, we numerically evaluate the aggregated demand function. We ask the same questions of the revised model as were asked of the model in Section I. The numbers in parentheses in Figures 1–5 show data for this new model analogous to the data already referred to for the model in Section I. Since in this model Market Area $\neq Q \neq TR =$ Gross Profit, we must choose which of these variables to plot. The relevant variable is total revenue,

which is the same as gross profits (since Marginal Cost=0). In Figure 1, for example, the firm at the origin earns gross profits of 229 in our present model and of 692 in the model of Section I. In both cases, the firm does not wish to locate at the origin (it can earn 230 in the present model and 698 in the model of Section I at the points of maximum profits). In Figures 2 through 5, location at the origin does maximize profits. Since location of the nth firm at the origin completes the configuration in each case, we conclude that, just as with the model in Section I, equilateral triangles are not an equilibrium configuration, while configurations of squares and rectangles appear to be equilibrium configurations, as do configurations of regular and irregular hexagons.

Next, we consider entry (on the assumption that profits are large enough to induce it). Using the entry dynamic described in Section I, we discover that rectangles beget rectangles in one round of entry. In both the square and regular hexagonal networks (see Figures 6 and 8) one round of entry does not reproduce the configuration and there is therefore a tendency for these configurations to break up. These results are the same as those for the first round of entry in the model of Section I.[13]

III. Conclusions

(1) There is a wide range of configurations of firms—including squares, rectangles, regular and irregular hexagons, but not equilateral triangles—that satisfy the equilibrium condition of our models

---

[13] In subsequent work we have discovered that the best entry point varies with the elasticity of demand. Our results apply as long as elasticity is less than some critical value which varies with the parameters of the model. Above one critical value, rectangles do not reproduce themselves, while above another (very large) critical value, hexagons do reproduce themselves. These relationships are the subject of further research and the results will be published in study papers from the University of British Columbia and Queen's University under the title "Entry Experiments in Löschian Space."

with respect to the location of firms already in the market.

(2) Any of the configurations that satisfy the equilibrium condition for the location of firms already in the market can be made to satisfy the equilibrium conditions for free entry by packing the existing firms densely enough so that the expected profits of a new entrant are negative and loosely enough so that the profits of existing firms are nonnegative.

(3) Zero profits is not a condition of entry equilibrium in our model and thus there is a wide range of density of packing of firms in each of the configurations mentioned in conclusion (1) above that is consistent with entry equilibrium.

(4) On the dynamic assumption about entry that we have investigated, there is no tendency for entry to convert a nonhexagonal configuration into a hexagonal one; indeed a rectangular configuration is more likely to persist through rounds of entry of new firms than is a hexagonal configuration.

(5) The model used to establish conclusions (1), (2), (3), and (4) assumes zero elasticity of demand and an exogenously imposed parametric price. In Section II we demonstrated that none of these conclusions is critically dependent upon these two assumptions. In that section each customer has a downward-sloping demand curve and firms maximize with respect to both price and location. Conclusions (1) through (4) continue to hold.

Given that our results differ from those in the existing literature, we must ask why these differences arise. The basic reasons seem to be methodological.[14] Lösch and many of the location theorists who followed him did not make explicit conjectural-variation assumptions concerning either or both location and price (see, for example, Lösch, pp. 94–97). It is impossible, however, to know what profits a firm expects to earn in alternative locations unless we know what reaction it expects its neighbors to make to changes in its location and price. Therefore, in the absence of conjectural-variation assumptions, equilibrium is undefined and equilibrium conditions cannot be derived.

Not having well-defined equilibrium conditions, many location theorists beginning with Lösch (see pp. 94–97) have imposed what to them seemed to be reasonable equilibrium conditions. We may consider by way of illustration two of the commonly assumed conditions of zero profits and densest packing.[15]

The zero-profits condition is imposed on the argument that as long as the profits of existing firms are positive, it will pay new firms to enter. But this argument assumes that the expected profits of a new entrant, R^e, are the same as the actual profits of a typical existing firm, R^a (any existing firm will do as long as they have identical market areas). But Beckmann has shown (1968, p. 44) that there is a class of models for which $R^e(h_0) < R^a(h_0)$ so that for $R^e(h_0) = 0$ it is not necessary that $R^a(h_0) = 0$ (where h_0 is any specific density of packing).[16]

The assumed equilibrium condition of densest packing gives rise to the assumption that a regular hexagonal lattice is the

---

[14] See our (1972b) paper for a much more detailed discussion of this problem than is given here.

[15] For examples two recent articles, Kenneth Denike and John Parr, and John Hartwick, impose both zero profits and densest packing as conditions of equilibrium without deriving them from behavioral assumptions.

[16] Another commonly used argument is that if existing firms are making positive pure profits, a new firm could enter right alongside the old firm, slightly undercut its price, and drive the old firm out of business getting *all* of its profits. If firms make a ZCV assumption with respect to existing firms' prices and each new entrant undercuts the existing firm by a small but finite amount, price will eventually be driven down to the point at which profits are zero. Consideration of this frequently employed argument, which employs a price-conjectural variation different from the one used in Section II, is beyond the scope of this paper but our refutation of it can be found in our (1975b) paper.

unique equilibrium configuration. The argument would appear to run as follows: if firms are arranged in another configuration (say, rectangles), and just packed densely enough, i.e., a value of h chosen, so that $R^a(h) = 0$, they could all increase their profits by rearranging themselves into a hexagonal lattice. It is clear that if a rectangular configuration prevailed, all firms could increase their profits by agreeing collectively to rearrange themselves into a hexagonal configuration. It is equally clear from our models, however, that when each firm makes atomistic decisions based on conjectural variations with respect to other firms' locations and/or prices, there is no behavioral mechanism that will *necessarily* convert other configurations into hexagons (indeed we find it difficult to conceive of any behavioral mechanism suitable for atomistic decision taking that would be *sufficient* to do the job). Densest packing is not therefore an equilibrium condition of our models.

It seems to us, therefore, that many of the classic propositions of Löschian and post-Löschian location theory are suitable for analyzing optimal rules for collective decisions of a central-planning type, but are quite unsuitable for analyzing the outcome of decentralized decision making that is based on explicit conjectural-variation assumptions and that acts through the market mechanism.

REFERENCES

M. Beckmann, *Location Theory*, New York 1968.

———, "Equilibrium Versus Optimum: Spacing of Firms and Patterns of Market Areas," *Northeast Reg. Sci. Rev.*, 1971, *1*, 1–20.

B. Bollabás and N. Stern, "The Optimal Structure of Market Areas," *J. Econ. Theory*, Apr. 1972, *4*, 174–79.

K. G. Denike and J. B. Parr, "Production in Space, Spatial Competition, and Restricted Entry," *J. Reg. Sci.*, Apr. 1970, *10*, 49–63.

B. C. Eaton, "Free Entry in One-Dimensional Market Models: Pure Profits and Multiple Equilibria," *J. Reg. Sci.*, forthcoming.

——— and R. G. Lipsey, (1972a) "The Principle of Minimum Differentiation Reconsidered," disc. pap. no. 87, Queen's Univ., 1972.

——— and ———, (1972b) "Unsuspected Perversities in the Theory of Location," disc. pap. no. 88, Queen's Univ., 1972.

——— and ———, (1975a) "The Principle of Minimum Differentiation Reconsidered: Some New Developments in the Theory of Spatial Competition," *Rev. Econ. Stud.*, Jan. 1975, *42*, 27–49.

——— and ———, (1975b) "Freedom of Entry and the Rate of Profit," study pap. no. 190, Queen's Univ.; study pap. no. 210, Univ. British Columbia 1975.

H. S. Grace, "Professor Samuelson on Free Enterprise and Economic Efficiency: A Comment," *Quart. J. Econ.*, May 1970, *84*, 337–40.

J. Hartwick, "Lösch's Theorem on Hexagonal Market Areas," *J. Reg. Sci.*, Aug. 1973, *13*, 213–21.

N. Kaldor, "The Irrelevance of Equilibrium Economics," *Econ. J.*, Dec. 1972, *28*, 1237–55.

A. Lösch, *The Economics of Location*, New Haven 1954.

E. Mills and M. Lav, "A Model of Market Areas with Free Entry," *J. Polit. Econ.*, June 1964, *72*, 278–88.

P. A. Samuelson, "The Monopolistic Competition Revolution," in R. E. Keunne, ed., *Monopolistic Competition Theory: Studies in Impact*, New York 1967.

Reprinted from

THE AMERICAN ECONOMIC REVIEW

The American Economic Association

[3]

The introduction of space into the neoclassical model of value theory[1]

B. Curtis Eaton and Richard G. Lipsey

The themes of this paper are quite simple. First, economic activity is essentially a spatial phenomenon in the sense that it invariably involves the costly transportation of inputs and/or outputs through space. Second, economic activity is not a continuously variable phenomenon; instead it is characterized by lumpiness or indivisibilities both physically and temporally. Together these two characteristics of economic life imply some interesting and surprising things which are not encompassed by traditional, neo-classical economics. We wish to give these characteristics the same central place in theory that we believe they already hold in real economic activity. We believe that doing this will simultaneously greatly improve the explanatory power of the theory while actually simplifying it in some important respects.

Indivisibilities are universally associated with capital and they have two dimensions. Capital is physically indivisible in the sense that it is impossible to go on reducing indefinitely the amount of capital embodied in a given type of machine or productive process, reducing both the cost of making the capital and its output capacity per unit of time in direct proportion to each other. Capital is indivisible temporally because the durability of a piece of capital cannot be reduced indefinitely with proportionate reductions in the cost of producing it.

In some important cases physical indivisibilities are swept away by the general assumption of universal constant returns to scale. In a spatial context, physical indivisibilities do not need to be assumed away; indeed they are the *sine qua non* of the existence of firms, and even of exchange.

Temporal indivisibilities have been extensively treated in neo-classical theory. Labour services, for example, perish in the instant they are provided, but a labourer and a piece of capital necessarily have a duration in time. In spaceless neo-classical economics this temporal indivisibility of capital gives rise to the distinction between short-run and long-run equilibria. The senses in which capital is durable and the concept of exit of firms from an industry occurring when capital wears out has received considerable attention from theorists. Once space is introduced, the nature of the temporal indivisibility of capital equipment becomes very important, and a rich set of theoretical possibilities opens up when various assumptions, each of which seems to catch some aspect of reality, are introduced.

This paper is an interim report on some of the research we have been doing over the last several years. We did not begin with the claims laid out above as general hypotheses and then seek to substantiate them. Rather we originally set out to investigate some very specific and, we hope, practical problems in spatial economics. Only as our studies progressed did we begin to see that they had rather general implications for economic theory as a whole. In this report we reverse the order of our own work and begin by discussing some general implications of introducing space into value theory, and then pass on to detailed illustrations drawn from our own work. This means that we begin where our research frontier now is, and thus where we must be most conjectural, and only later progress to illustrations that draw on work already completed and on which we can thus pronounce with more authority and confidence.

I. Two equilibria and two versions of the 'neo-classical' model

A. Fixed numbers and free-entry equilibria

We distinguish two types of equilibria. A *fixed numbers equilibrium* is one in which the market is inhabited by an arbitrary number of firms, and it occurs when no firm can make a change in any variable under its control that will increase its expected profits. A *free-entry equilibrium* is one in which a fixed-numbers equilibrium holds for all existing firms and, in addition, no new firm wishes to enter the market and no existing firm wishes to leave. This distinction cuts across the Marshallian distinction between long and short-run. A fixed-numbers equilibrium can occur in the short run when existing firms are unable to change the size or location of their capital and in the long run when such adjustments are possible. Free-entry equilibrium is long run in the sense that new entry requires new capital. It may, however, be considered either over the life time of the capital of existing firms or after all capital has 'worn out' and been replaced and, if desired, relocated. This last distinction is unimportant in spaceless models with constant technology because, once entry occurs, the products of new firms are indistinguishable from those of old firms. In spatial models, however, each firm is differentiated from every other firm by its location. Where physical capital is immobile, new entrants will have different locations from existing firms and free-entry equilibria will normally be different before and after existing firms have had a chance to relocate. Furthermore, the circumstances under which they can or will relocate depend very much on the precise sense in which their physically-immobile capital is temporally indivisible.

B. Two versions of the neo-classical model

The Arrow-Debreu version of the neo-classical model is based on the concept of a fixed numbers equilibrium and is concerned with the existence of general equilibrium. The model is given a spatial as well as a temporal extension, since the *same* physical commodity at *different places* and/or at *different times* is treated as a *different commodity*. (See in particular Arrow and Debreu (1954) and Debreu (1959).)

The second version of the neo-classical model is one made familiar by Hicks in *Value and Capital* (1939). The Hicksian model is, at the same time, broader in scope and less-precisely formulated than the Arrow-Debreu model. It allows us to deal with firms, industries and whole economies in short-run and long-run contexts and with fixed and changing technologies. The Arrow-Debreu model may be thought of as a more highly formalized version of one aspect of the more general Hicksian model.

One apparent difference between the Hicksian and the Arrow-Debreu models is that the latter mentions space while the Hicksian model makes no explicit mention of it whatsoever. One view of the Hicksian model is that it is a spaceless or a point economy – i.e., all economic activity takes places at one point in space. Alternatively, by letting all costs of transportation be zero, one can, for all intents and purposes, collapse the spatial economy to a spaceless economy, and the Hicksian economy can thus be regarded as a spatially extended economy in which time and resource costs of transport are zero. In either case the economy is essentially spaceless.

C. Perfect competition

The basic concept of the neo-classical model in all its forms is that of perfect competition. The key distinguishing feature of perfect competition as a market form is the characteristic that firms are price takers. Economists sometimes speak as if this proposition is a logical deduction from the technical data that there is a very large number of firms in an industry. This, of course, is not correct. Even in a spaceless economy, as long as the ratio of any firm's output to industry output is positive – no matter how small it may be – that firm has some monopoly power over the market. Thus, as long as there is a finite number of firms in the industry – no matter how large the number – each firm actually faces a downward-sloping demand curve for its product.[2] In order to derive the perfectly elastic demand curve for that perfectly competitive firm's product it is thus necessary to make a behavioural assumption. This assumption is that *the firm incorrectly perceives its demand curve and thinks it is perfectly elastic*. The empirical applicability of models based on this assumption requires one of two things. First, real-world firms may correctly perceive their demand curve, but the differences between the *predicted behaviour* in the model where the firm assumes it can have *no* influence on price and the *real-world behaviour* where the firm can have a *slight* influence on price are trivial. Second real-world firms may characteristically make the same mistake as do the firms in the model, in which case the results of the model apply exactly.

In a spaceless economy the assumption of perfect competition is appealing if there is a large number of firms in each industry since the monopoly power possessed by any firm is inconsequential. As we shall soon see, however, the assumption of perfect competition in a spatial world removes what is for us one of the essential characteristics of a spatial economy – that all firms have substantial monopoly power. This is one important respect in which our conception of a spatial economy diverges from the Arrow-Debreu conception. The Arrow-Debreu model maintains perfect competition through the assumption that all firms believe that they face perfectly-elastic demand curves for all the commodities that they sell. Thus each firm incorrectly believes that it is in perfect competition with all other firms selling the same product irrespective of the location of firms and of the location of customers; in other words each firm believes that there is a perfectly elastic demand for its product at each point in space.

D. Perfect competition and the theory of the firm

Problems arise when we wish to determine, or at least restrict, the size of plants and firms. Once the firm acts as if it faces a perfectly elastic demand curve, there is nothing to restrict size from the demand side. *Size must be restricted from the cost side*. Hence, the extreme importance of eventually diminishing returns to scale in any competitive model that seeks to limit the size of plants and firms.

One version of the neo-classical model assumes strict constant returns to scale in all industries, fixed supplies of homogeneous factors of production and perfectly competitive markets for all commodities and factors. This is the version that is most familiar to modern students in the form of the Cambridge (Mass.) neo-neo-classical model that is used extensively, for example, in the real theory of international trade.[3] The model is one of *industrial* activity in spaceless economies. The model makes predictions about relative prices of commodities and factors as well as the quantities of inputs used and of outputs produced by each industry.

The model in this form does not explain the concentration of output in units called plants and the organization of plants by units called firms. The assumption of constant returns to scale means that all plants have horizontal long-run average cost curves. Since each plant, and hence each firm, is assumed to be a price taker at the existing market price p, it follows that each 'firm' will be indifferent as to its quantity produced when p = LRMC = LRATC.

If we want the model to have a theory of the size of plants and of firms, one method is to assume a U-shaped LRATC curve for that plant and for the firm. There is ample empirical evidence to support U-shaped *plant* LRATC curves (usually with a horizontal middle portion). The explanation for the falling part, which, as we shall see, is the critical part for our purposes, is usually found in indivisibilities of fixed factors (particularly plant and equipment) and scale economies in circulating capital (occasioned by such factors as the square-root rule for inventories). The rising portion is often attributed to the limitations of efficient management of a single integrated plant as its size increases. The U-shaped cost curve for *the firm* is less easily accounted for and seems to be based on less convincing evidence. The downward-sloping portion occurs for the same reason as for the plant when the firm is so small that it is a one-plant firm. But since the firm has the option open to it of replicating its plants and having them independently managed (so as to avoid the scale diseconomies of plant management), there seems no compelling reason why the firm should ever put up with any thing worse than constant returns to scale, at least for levels of output that are integer multiples of the output for which a single plant achieves its lowest LRATC.

If these arguments are accepted, the neo-classical model contains a theory of the size (or range of sizes) of the plant and of the size of the industry, but it is not so obvious that it contains a theory of the size of the firm. The usual way out taken in the literature is merely to *assume arbitrarily* that the firm faces a U-shaped LRATC curve.

E. General equilibrium in the neo-classical model

The Arrow-Debreu model is a model of fixed numbers equilibrium (the number of firms is fixed arbitrarily), and is concerned with the existence of general equilib-

On the Foundations of Monopolistic Competition and Economic Geography 45

rium under perfect competition. General equilibrium theorists are able to prove the existence of a perfectly competitive equilibrium when the production technology is convex (constant or decreasing returns to scale). The fixed numbers equilibrium is characterized by zero profits with constant returns to scale, and by positive profits with decreasing returns to scale.

With decreasing returns to scale LRMC exceeds LRATC. Each firm operates where price equals LRMC and since there are fixed numbers each firm will produce a positive output – thus the positive-profit result. It seems obvious that if there were free entry in this case, the size of firms would shrink to zero. That is, there would be no economic unit recognizable as a firm.

With constant returns to scale the free-entry equilibrium (if it exists) of the Arrow-Debreu model would also produce the result that the size of firms goes to zero. Since the model incorporates space, if transport costs are non-zero, all production would take place at the point of consumption and the costly activity of transportation would thereby be avoided. We elaborate on this point below. It thus appears to be necessary to introduce non-convexities into the spatial model to account for the existence of firms in free-entry equilibrium.

A U-shaped LRATC curve is necessary to give a determinant size of the firm in free-entry equilibrium. In this case, however, the non-convexities in the firm's production function makes impossible the proof of the existence of competitive equilibrium using present techniques even in a spaceless economy.[4] The best that can be done in G.E. models is to 'convexify' the economy by assuming that constant returns apply over the non-convex portion (i.e., the range of increasing returns to scale) of the production function, and then to prove the existence of an 'approximate equilibrium'. The degree of approximation improves as the number of firms in the industry increases.[5]

F. Some problems in the neo-classical model of perfect competition

It seems useful to summarize our discussion of the problems and inconsistencies in the model of perfect competition. Our basic view is, of course, that because space imparts monopoly power, the assumption of perfect competition is inappropriate. It is nevertheless useful to outline some problems in the spaceless model of perfect competition. Therefore, the comments below apply to a spaceless model of perfect competition except where explicit mention of space is made. We hope to show later that, when the assumption of perfect competition is abandoned, as it must be in a model which incorporates space along with non-convexities in production, many of these problems do not arise.

1. Increasing returns to scale throughout the entire range of output implies that firms will grow in size until some firm notices that it has market power, at which point the perfectly competitive model ceases to apply. The non-convexity in the production function makes it impossible to prove the existence of competitive equilibrium even in the fixed-numbers case.
2. Constant returns to scale throughout leaves size of units completely undetermined. The existence of a competitive equilibrium can be proven in this case if the number of firms is fixed arbitrarily. In a spatial context with free entry,

however, the size of firms shrinks to zero, since all production will take place at point of consumption.
3. Decreasing returns to scale throughout implies that in free-entry equilibrium the relevant units would shrink towards zero size even in a spaceless economy, since average costs can always be reduced by reducing the scale of operations. This is the easiest case[6] (strict convexity) for which to prove the existence of a fixed-numbers competitive equilibrium.
4. An upper limit to size requires that the relevant LRATC curves eventually turn upwards. This poses no problem for existence proofs providing the LRATC does not anywhere slope downwards.
5. A determinate size of the plant and firm requires that the relevant LRATC curves be U-shaped. In this case the best that can be done as far as an existence proof is concerned is to prove 'approximate equilibrium' by the 'convexifying technique' alluded to above.

II. A simplifying-complication

All theories are abstractions and when we introduce a particular abstraction from something that is accepted as empirically true we usually hope that, first, it will make our theory simpler while, second, that it will not have a critical effect on the result in which we are interested. Abstracting from space in the neo-classical model is usually thought of as fulfilling these general conditions. As a result, spatial economics has been relegated to a set of special topics such as urban economics, location theory and spatial models of oligopolistic competition. It is our view that the removal of space from the neo-classical model does not meet either of the conditions for a useful abstraction, at least for many purposes for which the neo-classical model is used.

First, it makes some problems more difficult than they are in a spatially extended world. In particular the concept of perfect competition with all of its difficulties can be dispensed with since the essence of spatial models, as we conceive of them, is that firms are always either monopolists or oligopolists in localized regions of space.[7] Out of the window, along with the concept of perfect competition, then goes a host of other related problems such as how to reconcile the Keynesian macro model with the micro theory of the behaviour of the perfectly-competitive firm. Second, although the spaceless model may successfully predict certain broad industry trends in response to such disturbances as changes in costs and demands, it is evident from our models that many predictions are often substantially altered by introducing space. This poses some urgent questions that are the subjects of some of our further researches. First, under what conditions will otherwise-similar models, that allow for and do not allow for space, give similar predictions? Second, where the predictions diverge substantially, which set are more nearly correct empirically (using 'more realistic' assumptions does not, of course, always guarantee 'more realistic' results). Third, it seems to us that the spaceless model fails to suggest many non-equilibrium conceptual possibilities that do arise from our spatial models, possibilities that may explain a range of real world phenomena we might otherwise fail to understand altogether, or else seriously misinterpret.

Let us see then what happens if we put space into the neo-classical model. We use the simplest case of one-dimensional space, and state a number of assumptions that outline a basic model. Assumptions indicated by an asterisk are subsequently relaxed at various places in this paper.

1. The economy is spread over the one-dimensional continuum of the real line.*
2. Households and hence labour supplies are distributed uniformly over that line, as are all other factor supplies.*
3. Demand for a commodity at each point in space is a decreasing function of the price at which that commodity can be delivered to that point in space. Demand over any interval of space is given by the point demand function weighted by the number of customers in that interval.
4. The transportation of goods is costly, at t per unit of distance per unit of commodity.*
5. Factors can be freely and instantly transported throughout the economy.* (This assumption renders the economy spaceless from the input side and its sole purpose is to allow us to concentrate for purposes of illustration on the spatial aspects of the output side of the economy.)
6. Each firm owns only one plant* and management is a perfectly homogeneous input. No two firms can occupy the same point in space.
7. There is freedom of entry into and exit from the industry.
8. Firms charge a mill price, p, and their delivered price at a point in space y units of distance from the firm is given by $P = p + ty$. Customers buy from the firm with the lowest delivered price.

Next, we come to the assumption about the production technology. Some discussion is necessary before this assumption is introduced. If we insisted on assuming constant returns to scale in our spatial model, we would get the unfortunate result that all production would take place at the point of consumption since there would be no reason to incur the transport costs that are necessary when commodities are produced at one place and consumed at another. Furthermore, diminishing returns to a factor implies that labour (assuming it wishes to maximize its real income) will spread itself evenly over all of the land in the economy. Hence, constant returns to scale plus completely homogenous factors[8] (with no more than one factor being physically immobile) implies a smooth undifferentiated distribution of production and consumption over the whole economy with *no geographical specialization, no firms* and *no exchange*. This is an economy that is the quintessence of self-sufficiency.

Fortunately, there is ample evidence that non-convexities are ubiquitous in any production using capital since no capital equipment is physically infinitely divisible. As Nicholas Kaldor puts it[9]

> Yet on an empirical level, nobody doubts that in any economic activity which involves processing or transforming basic materials – in other words, in industry – increasing returns dominate the picture for the very reasons given by Adam Smith in the first chapter of *The Wealth of Nations*: reasons that are fundamental to the nature of technological processes and not to any particular technology.

Instead of causing the difficulties already referred to in the spaceless model of perfect competition, non-convexities provide the crucial explanation for the geographical concentration of production into units called plants. We shall see later that non-convexity does not cause any other problems analogous to those it causes in the spaceless model. For these reasons we assume that any 'industry' we consider produces a single homogeneous product under conditions of declining plant, long-run average total costs, at least over some initial range of outputs. It does not matter whether the LRATC curve is U-shaped or declines throughout its whole range; the model works just as well in either case.

9. For concreteness we assume

$$LRATC = K/Q + c$$

so that LRATC asymptotically approaches c, which is of course short-run and long-run MC. The fixed cost, K, is associated with the indivisible amount of capital needed to set up a plant. The capital once established is geographically immobile, has a fixed finite life (i.e. capital is temporaly indivisible) and has no use other than that for which it is designed.*

10. Finally we introduce our behavioural assumption about how the firm perceives its demand curve: the firm correctly perceives that its demand curve is downward sloping. This assumption requires some further discussion.

In a spatial market all firms have some substantial monopoly power. Transport is costly so that firms will be able to charge a higher mill price than their distant competitors without losing all of their customers. Since, except at the firm's market boundaries, every point in space is severed by only one firm and since there is only a finite quantity demanded in any interval of space, it is natural to assume that each firm knows that it does not face a perfectly elastic demand for its product at each point in space. In the spaceless model with a large number of firms the error that the firm makes in incorrectly assuming that it faces a perfectly elastic demand curve is inconsequential and it is natural enough to assume that the firm may never discover its error. In the spatial model the error that the firm would make if it did assume it faced a perfectly elastic demand curve is anything but inconsequential and it seems clear that the firm would quickly discover this error if it made it. We therefore argue that it is natural to assume that the firm correctly perceives that it faces a downward-sloping demand curve. It is here that we differ significantly from the Arrow-Debreu model.

We may now consider some of the many implications of the introduction of space into the neo-classical model in which we are forced to assume some non-convexities in order to account for the localization of production in plants and for the exchange of commodities. We have also assumed freedom of entry and that each plant is owned by a separate firm. These assumptions are designed to make the model as competitive as is possible, although once space is introduced it is no longer appropriate to assume that firms believe that they are price takers.

III. Some implications of the introduction of space and production non-convexities into the neo-classical model

A. Geographical concentration

Increasing returns to scale due to indivisibilities makes it profitable to concentrate production in units called plants so as to gain the lower costs implied by higher outputs at any point in space. This production must then be transported by costly methods to its points of consumption. In general it will pay to produce another unit of output in an existing plant only as long as the marginal cost of production plus the cost of transporting the output to its point of consumption is less than the cost of producing the output at its point of consumption. This implies that production may not be carried to the point at which all scale economies are fully exhausted.

B. Transportation

Since more of the commodity is being produced at some point in the market (or over some segments of the market) than is being consumed, a further implication is that the commodity must be transported: the society will devote some resources to transportation. We may draw the same implication from the input side of the market if we momentarily relax assumption 5 and assume that transport of factors is costly. If there is a concentration of production at some points, then inputs into that production must be transported to the site of production. The geographical concentration of production occasioned by the indivisibility of capital thus implies the costly transportation of inputs over space. A further implication is that mobile factors, such as labour, will tend to concentrate near production centres so as to reduce transport costs. This immediately gives us a theory of one-plant towns. If we then developed a theory of the local clustering of plants in space we would have an elementary theory of cities.

C. Geographical dispersion

Although it pays to concentrate production geographically to gain the benefits of scale economies, the spatial extension of the market, and the resulting costs of transporting output to consumers, means that it will not generally pay to concentrate all production in one place (unless scale effects are very large). If we momentarily relax the one-plant firm assumption (assumption 6) and impose a quantity constraint on LRATC ($Q \leq Q^*$), we can see that production may be geographically dispersed. If a firm's market segment is large enough to dictate the construction of a second plant, the firm would never locate its second plant at the same point in space as its first plant because by choosing another location it could reduce the transport costs which consumers bear and thus increase quantity demanded from its two plants for any set of mill prices. A monopolist or a central planner would construct the number of plants and distribute them throughout the market, so as to minimize total costs of producing the good and delivering it to its point of consumption. Atomistic competition does not always yield this socially optimal result. It usually does, however, produce at least some geographical dispersion of plants.

D. Market power

We have already mentioned that in a spatial model each firm has some significant monopoly power. This arises because each firm is differentiated from every other firm by virtue of its unique location. The nature and implications of this monopoly power now require some careful study.

(i) Conjectural variations are necessary If we wish to study the behaviour of firms in space, it is necessary to know what each firm assumes about its neighbours' reactions to any change in price, location or other relevant decision variable. Until we know (or assume) this, we cannot say when a firm is in equilibrium, nor can we say what its behaviour will be if it is out of equilibrium. We use the term conjectural variation (CV) in a somewhat broader context than it is often used, to refer to any assumption a firm makes about the reactions of its neighbours to any change made by the firm. Without conjectural variations, equilibrium conditions cannot even be specified, and, hence, equilibrium is undefined.

(ii) Downward-sloping demand curves We can illustrate what we require by making the simple, and for our purposes the *most* troublesome, assumption of a zero price conjectural variation (ZVC): firm J assumes that all other firms will maintain their current price regardless of firm J's price. It is also convenient to assume for the moment that all customers buy one unit of the product per period of time independent of delivered price.

We now wish to derive one firm's demand curve. Assume that the firm in question, firm J, is located at the origin and that all other firms are dispersed at intervals of $\pm$ a (as shown in Figure 1a), and that all other firms charge the same mill price p*. Firm J's demand curve based on the ZVC is illustrated in Figure 1b. If J's mill price were above p* + ta, it would sell nothing since the delivered price of firms I and K at point J would be less than J's mill price. As J's mill price decreases from p* + ta quantity demanded increases smoothly until J's price is p* – ta. At this price J's delivered price at I and K equals the mill price p*, of firms I and K, and quantity demanded from J could be anything in the range 2a to 3a. Once J's mill price goes below p* – ta firms I and K are driven from the market and quantity demanded from J again increases smoothly as price decreases until, at price p* – 2ta, J's delivered price at H and L is equal to the mill price, p*, of firms H and L. Thus J's demand curve has the shape depicted in Figure 1b.

This awkward shape for firm J's demand curve does not look very promising. Fortunately, however, we are able to restrict J's behaviour so that the relevant part of J's demand curve is only the part that lies above the first kink. We are able to do this because we can establish that J's profit-maximizing price will never be such that it can undercut I or K's mill price at I or K's mill door. This argument runs as follows. (For simplicity we concentrate on firm K's reaction to J's price.) Firm J may be uncertain about what K's precise reaction will be to many mill prices charged by J. It can, however, be certain of one thing: as long as p_j + ta is greater than c, the common marginal cost of production, firm K will choose a price in the range

$$c \leq p_k \leq p_j + ta,$$

where p_k and p_j are K's and J's mill price and ta is, of course, the cost of transporting a unit of the commodity between J's plant and K's plant. Profit-maximizing behaviour of K implies that K will stay in the market as long as it can sell anything at a price greater than or equal to c. Thus J will anticipate that K will set its price in the range set out above. This implies that the first discontinuity in J's demand curve cannot occur until J's delivered price at K's mill door is equal to marginal cost, c. But for this to happen J's 'delivered price' at its own mill door must be less than c. Since J faces a downward-sloping demand curve, it will want to set MC = MR and thus have $p_j > c$. Thus the discontinuity is irrelevant and firm J faces a demand curve that is continuously downward sloping over the relevant range.[10] We call this the *no-mill-price-undercutting* restriction.

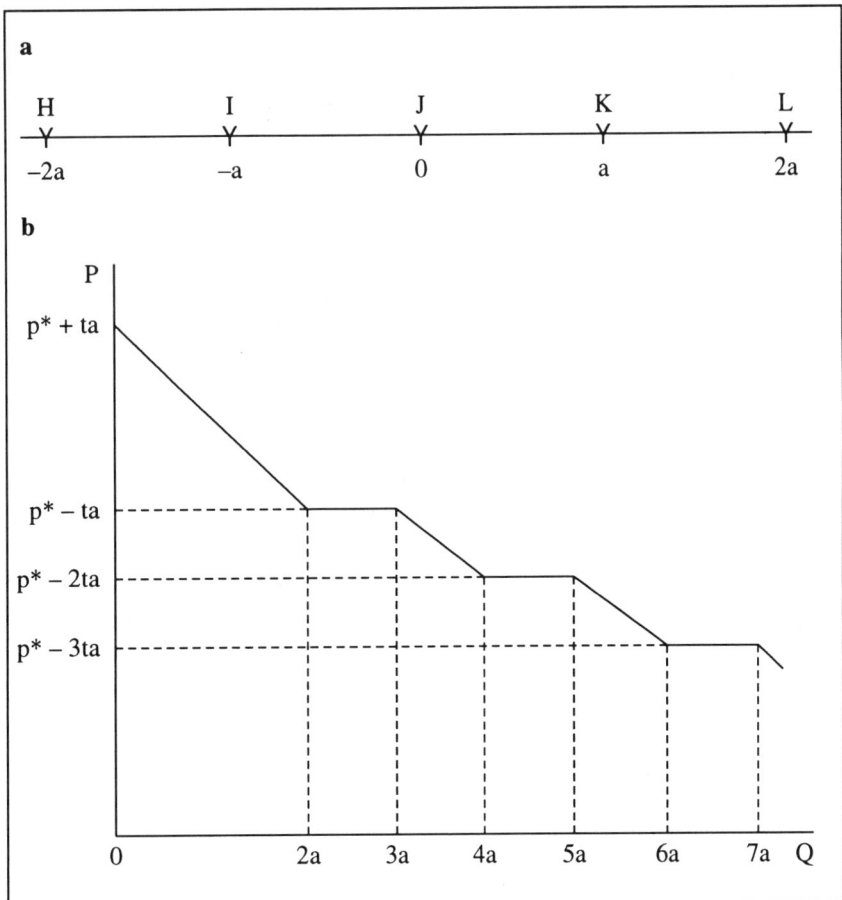

Figure 1. The derivation of firm J's demand curve

(iii) The existence of equilibrium It is now possible to prove the existence of an equilibrium in such a market in spite of the non-convexities.[11] We do this in our paper *Freedom of Entry and the Rate of Profit* (Eaton and Lipsey, 1976b) where we allow each customer to have a downward sloping demand curve rather than assuming, as we did above for expository simplicity, that each customer bought one unit per period independent of delivered price. The properties of this equilibrium are that all firms are equally spaced throughout the market and all are charging the same mill price. Since each firm's market demand curve expressed as a function of its mill price is downward sloping, equilibrium is compatible with rising, constant or falling marginal cost.

(iv) The size of firm is demand constrained The locational model provides a natural way of bounding the plant's demand at each price, thus making the size of the plant demand constrained. In the one-firm, one-plant model this allows the firm to reach equilibrium at a finite size in spite of unexploited economies of scale and perfect freedom of entry of new firms into the market. Indeed fixed-numbers equilibrium is consistent with rising, constant or falling short-run and long-run marginal costs (as long, of course, as MC is not falling faster than MR in which case output would expand until MC cuts MR from below). This follows obviously from elementary economic theory once it is established that each firm faces a downward-sloping demand curve. Free-entry equilibrium is considered below.

(v) Pure profits can exist in entry equilibrium One of the most important properties of the spatial model of value theory is that pure profits can exist even in free-entry equilibrium.[12] Consider entry into the market of Figure 2. A new firm must fit into a slot between two firms. The argument given above for the absence of mill price undercutting is also critical in the case of entry. An existing firm has sunk costs, a new firm considering entry has only avoidable costs. The new firm knows an existing firm would not allow itself to be driven out of the market at any price greater than its marginal cost, c. Thus the new firm knows it cannot hope to drive an existing firm out of the market at a price that would allow the new firm to cover its LRATC. Thus the new firm must expect to fit into a slot between two existing firms and have a market much smaller than that enjoyed by existing firms before entry. If the new firm charges the same price as the existing firm, it will have a market half

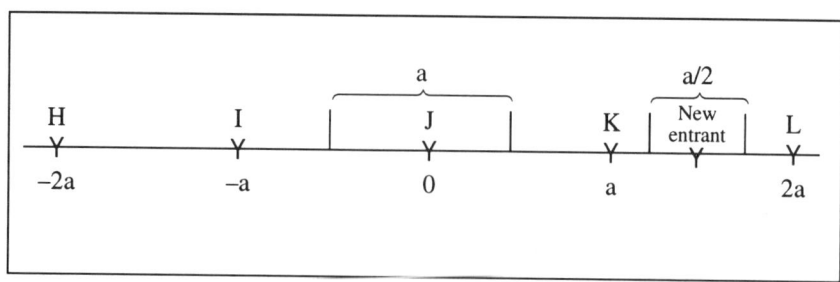

Figure 2. Entry of a new firm into a market occupied by equally spaced firms

as long as that enjoyed by existing firms before its entry. It may sell more to its customers by virtue of being closer to them than was their previous supplier but its total sales must always be less than the sales of its two neighbours before entry. Furthermore, as this effect, the elasticity effect, becomes negligible the expected sales of a new entrant expecting to charge the same price as an original firm go to half the sales of the original firm.[13]

Since LRATC is declining over some range, and since the demand curve of a new entrant is substantially to the left of existing firms' demand curves, it follows that the market can be in free-entry equilibrium with very large profits of existing firms and yet expected losses for new entrants. If the industry we are analysing is the only economic activity in the economy then it has zero opportunity cost of capital and our statement must be amended to read that the rate of return on capital of existing firms can be much higher than the rate of return expected by new firms. Some substantial conceptual problems would then have to be met. At this stage of our investigations we prefer to assume that there are non-spatial uses for capital – non-spatial industries, e.g., those that sell to a single point in space (such as an export node) and those that must locate at one point because of a resource concentration (an input node) – which yield a common rate of return i. We can then say that the rate of return in our spatial industry can be substantially higher than i (pure profits).[14] In Eaton and Lipsey (1976b) we prove that this rate can be as high as 2i!

(vi) Discontinuities in resource allocation Now consider entry into the market of Figure 2 as density of customers increases. Start with existing firms a distance apart and all earning zero profits (i.e., a rate of return on capital of i). Density increases and each firm sells more and its profits increase. There is no new entry, however, until potential new entrants expect at least a normal return of i on their capital. When this occurs, a new firm enters each slot and the number of firms doubles each being separated by a/2. As demand increases further, each firm sells more and earns increasing pure profits until another round of entry occurs with the number of firms again doubling and the distance between firms again halving.

(vii) A natural monopoly in every market segment The key characteristic of our spatial model of value theory is that $D^E(p) < D^X(p)$ for all relevant p, where $D^E(p)$ is the demand curve a new entrant expects to face and $D^X(p)$ is the demand curve actually faced by an existing firm before entry occurs. The difference between these two curves is substantial since the number of customers served by a new entrant that expects to charge the same price as that currently charged by existing firms is one half the number served by existing firms before entry. Firms enter until $D^E(p)$ lies below LRATC everywhere. Except for a tangency of $D^X(p)$ and LRATC there will be pure profits for existing firms. As market demand increases $D^X(p)$ increases, and with it outputs and profits increase, but although $D^E(p)$ also increases no new capital enters the industry until $D^E(p)$ is tangent to LRATC.

The natural monopoly characteristic of our model follows from the assumptions that purchasers visit only one firm to make their purchases. In other of our more elaborate models, purchasers engage in comparison shopping and thus visit two or more firms before making their purchases, and/or purchasers are indifferent between firms whose delivered price to the customer differs by less than some amount δ. In these cases firms are oligopolists rather than monopolists over the segment of the market from which they draw customers. Firms are, however, always in small-group competition over some segment of the market.

E. Non uniqueness

There is a wide range of density of packing of firms for any given set of demand and cost conditions that are consistent with entry equilibrium. Any density of firms that lies between the low density, where $D^X(p)$ is tangent to LRATC, and the high density, where $D^E(p)$ is almost tangent to LRATC, is consistent with free-entry equilibrium.

F. Comparative statics

Our model has comparative static results similar to those of spaceless economies and it has these whether MC is rising, constant or falling in the neighbourhood of equilibrium (as long as it intersects marginal revenue from below somewhere). For example, an iso-elastic increase in demand will be met by a rise in production of existing firms while a rise in costs will be met by a fall in production. The difference is that changes in the number of plants are not continuous: even in the limit as N gets very large, the number of plants tends to double or halve on each round of entry or exit as discussed in section D (vi).

G. Existence and stability of equilibrium

We have considered a wide variety of models that play interesting variations on the assumptions listed earlier in this paper. These researches lead us to the conclusion that there is no general presumption either that equilibrium always exists, or that where it exists it is unique, globally stable, or locally stable in most, let alone all, interesting spatial models.

We have already referred to Eaton and Lipsey (1976b) in which we show that equilibrium does exist in the infinitely extensible one-dimensional space considered above even when firms engage in price competition and employ a broad class of conjectural variations. In Eaton and Lipsey (1975) we show that equilibrium also exists for bounded one-dimensional spaces when firms sell at a parametric price.[15] We have also shown, in Eaton and Lipsey (1976a), that equilibrium exists for unbounded two-dimensional space: the infinitely extensible plane. In each case the equilibrium is non-unique. Furthermore, we have cases for the bounded line in which the equilibria are not globally stable. In one of our computer models (Eaton and Lipsey, 1976h) the density function of households is endogenous and high density areas grow up around firms (which sell at a parametric price). Originally we conjectured that our models would be more likely to be stable under the assumption of endogenous density functions since each firm would create its own peak in the density function whenever it was located and, so we thought, this would make relocation of firms less attractive than when the density function was exogenous. We found, however, that our models were not globally stable in that, although multiple equilibria existed, they were often never converged on when N firms entered in their profit-maximizing location and each firm was then allowed to relocate in turn.

More surprisingly, we have behaviour in a computer model (Eaton and Lipsey, 1975) that strongly suggests that there may be no equilibrium configuration in the bounded two-dimensional space of a disc.[16] The model referred to in this paragraph is a rather special one in which firms sell at a parametric price and make a zero CV assumption with respect to competitors' locations and customers buy one unit of the product per period of time irrespective of delivered price. Certainly neither a configuration of hexagons nor of any other regular space-filling pattern that we tried provided an equilibrium configuration. If an equilibrium does exist in this model it implies some unsuspected pattern of firms. We are inclined to believe that no such equilibrium does exist and we hold this view because of the nature of the movements that firms always make: peripheral firms always seek to pair with their neighbours and this always leaves their neighbours wishing to move. In all cases in this section we are referring to the equilibria that occur under atomistic decision-taking and to both fixed-numbers and free-entry equilibria.

H. History matters

It follows from the above that history is important in our models. We cannot understand the behaviour of our models just by knowing some timeless equilibrium toward which firms may or may not be gravitating. Even where the equilibria exist they are usually not unique and often are not globally stable, and in a very key case (the disc) we have reason to suspect that an equilibrium does not exist at all.

This does not mean we need to despair. It only means that to understand the system and to predict its behaviour we need to know some of its past history and its laws of motion but often do not need to know its equilibrium properties, even if it has any. Firms continue to change their behaviour indefinitely but each change follows the rules of rational behaviour, given the CV assumptions made by the firms. Thus if we know the configuration of locations and prices at any moment in time, we can predict what configuration will exist at some future point in time but we cannot do this through static equilibrium analysis.

This is a theme – the irrelevance of equilibrium theory – that many authors have stressed. Too often, however, critics of equilibrium theory feel it necessary to argue that such theory is totally useless.[17] Since some predictions of equilibrium theory are manifestly not false and are useful in real policy situations, little progress is going to be made as long as economists find it necessary to divide into two camps: the equilibrium-theory-can-do-nothing camp, and the equilibrium-theory-can-do-everything camp. It seems clear to us that equilibrium theory can do much, and equally clear that it cannot do everything. What we hope to be able to do is to isolate the circumstances in which equilibrium theory is useful and not useful.

For example, the traditional perfectly competitive markets of foreign exchange[18] and agriculture[19] are areas in which equilibrium theory appears useful. In many spatial situations, however, such as the theory of cities, it is not so clear that equilibrium exists. It may be that there is just perpetual change and predictions based on history and laws of motion is all we can hope for in the study of cities.[20] It clearly affects the predictions we can make if a real market is or is not in an equilibrium configuration and whether it is or is not gravitating towards a stable equilibrium configuration. We hope that one of the things that will come out of the spatial approach is some clues as to what to expect in which markets.

Another reason why history matters lies in sunk capital costs. In the perfectly competitive spaceless model with constant technology, the product of a new firm, once it enters the market, is indistinguishable from that of an old firm. In spatial models, this is not the case since every firm has a unique location. The locations of new firms will depend on the locations of existing firms. Since equilibrium is often not unique, many patterns of new firms can exist. To know the pattern of entry we need to know the pattern of existing firms. Different markets that are today identical in customer distributions and demands will have different equilibrium patterns of firms depending on their past histories.

I. Monopsony and secondary concentration effects

For this section we drop the assumption that factors of production can be costlessly transported and outline a few of the results obtained in Eaton and Lipsey (1976i).

Just as the firm has some monopoly power due to costs of transporting goods, it now also has some monopsony power due to costs of transporting factors. The firm can lower the price it is willing to pay for any factor without losing all of its nearby suppliers to more distant competitors. Every firm, or group of firms if there is more than one firm in a given location, is to some extent a monopsonist due to spatial extension of factor supplies plus costly transport. All firms thus face rising rather than perfectly elastic supply curves.

We have seen that the indivisibility in the production function results in a concentration of economic activity at points in space. More is produced at some points than is consumed there with the consequence that both output and inputs must be transported over space. But transportation is costly so that the suppliers of inputs and the demanders of the product have an incentive to move toward the producing firm. The consequence is a non-uniform distribution of input suppliers (to the extent that they can move), and of input demanders, with a local maximum around each producer. The tendency to increasing densities is balanced by decreasing returns to land in the various activities (housing for example).

An immediate consequence of this secondary concentration is to increase the monopoly and monopsony power of the producer. At every price the producer can now sell more of his good, and at every input price the producer can now attract more inputs. This of course implies increased profits at least in the short run. It also implies a type of 'cumulative causation' or 'poles of attraction' that has been discussed by such writers as Myrdal – firms attract customers and suppliers who in turn attract more firms.

We saw in previous sections that the monopoly power, which is an inevitable result in our spatial model, provides a demand constraint on the size of the individual firm. The monopsony power, which is also inherent in spatial markets, provides another constraint on firm size. As a firm in any given location increases the quantity of an input, say labour, that it uses the per unit cost of that input increases. Thus, even if real economies of scale are not exhausted, it is possible for LRATC to be increasing because of pecuniary diseconomies. Clearly, if there are constant real returns to scale for $Q > \bar{Q}$, LRATC will be increasing for $Q > \bar{Q}$, and possibly for some range of $Q < \bar{Q}$. Thus the monopoly power in space provides a demand constraint, while monopsony power provides a cost constraint on the size of the firm.

IV. Applications

We now give a few illustrations of situations in which the spatially-augmented neoclassical model is able to make sense of phenomena that seem hard to understand in the non-spatial version.

A. Rent creation and rent appropriation

We have discussed the existence of pure profits in free entry equilibrium in our spatial models. A person trained in Classical rent theory might wonder why the landlord does not appropriate the pure profits that can exist in free entry spatial equilibrium. The reason why this does not occur is discussed at length in Eaton and Lipsey (1976e). Only a brief mention of the argument can be given here. The key assumption in the classical theory of rent is that the profitability of production of some product, say corn on a given farm, is perceived by the producer to be unaffected by the transfer of any other single farm, including the neighbouring one, either into or out of corn production. This assumption does not hold in the model used in this paper. The value of a piece of land as a site depends critically on how many nearby sites are already used as inputs in the industry. Assume that between firms A and C, located on the real line at $-L$ and L, there is room for one additional firm to enter and make non-negative profits while, if two firms were to enter, their markets would be so small that both would make losses. In this example the most profitable location will be at the origin. In a particular example the firms might be shopping centres. In order to obtain the exclusive right to build the one potentially profitable shopping centre between A and C, an entrepreneur would pay an amount up to the discounted present value of the stream of pure profits he anticipated earning. But he would not have to pay anything like that amount to purchase the use of the best piece of land on which to build a supermarket since ownership per se of any piece of land, even the best site, does not provide exclusive rights to build anything, and many other pieces of land will do almost as well for the single shopping centre. Between $-L$ and L there are many potentially profitable sites for the shopping centre but room for only one. If there are many owners of land in the interval, the best price any one of them can hope to get from the one potential buyer is something slightly higher than the value of the land in alternative uses.

Who then does get the pure profits where they do exist? There is no obvious economic mechanism to determine which of the many possible new entrants will actually get its plant into the valuable gap in the market. This may be determined by political, historical, sociological or some other factors such as just plain superior foresight. But it will not be determined by ownership of one particular piece of land. Thus, whoever does appropriate the profits, it will not be the landowner (at least not *qua* landowner). If the ownership of the new centre is decided say by historical accident, then the profits will go to the original shopping centre owner, and he will earn a rent of historical accident. Thus the profits of the firms in the situations we have analysed in this paper are in the nature of economic rents. They accrue to the person who is first able to appropriate a right to operate a firm in a profitable location such as the one between –L and L. If the state sold a franchise, the profit would accrue to the state. If the shopping centre is 'up for grabs', and not subject to any right that is sold in a market, then the person who succeeds in making the grab appropriates the rent.

Of course if a firm locates immobile capital and leases land on a term less than the life of the capital, the landlord will be able to usurp the pure profits by raising rents once the lease comes up for renewal. (This same thing occurs in a neoclassical spaceless model if immobile capital is located on a fixed piece of land: the landlord can usurp the quasi rents if the rental agreement comes up for renewal before the capital wears out.) Even if this occurs, it does not upset our results. As long as the firm gains access to its land at a price that is fixed for some period into the future below its value to that firm, it can earn pure profits for some period of time and hence the present value of its stream of profits over its entire life time is positive.

This explains an empirical phenomenon that seems very puzzling when considered within the confines of the spaceless model: firms commonly sell for large 'going-concern' or 'goodwill' values. If there is freedom of entry in a spaceless model there is no reason why a single shop – say a clothing goods store – should sell for any significant goodwill value since the purchaser has the option of opening up a new store. But in the spatial model the reason is obvious. If, by historical accident or whatever reason, a firm occupies a finite slot between two competing firms that is big enough to offer pure profits to one firm but not two, the existing firm can earn a pure profit. The enterprise can be sold for the capitalized, 'goodwill' value of those profits. Our model leads to the expectation that positive goodwill values will be the rule rather than being the unexplained exception.

Another interesting implication relates to the phenomenon of land-rent creation and appropriation. Consider the building of a shopping centre in two different locations. In the first location, the centre is to be built towards the edge of a growing city but in an area where most of the land is already developed for housing (possibly with rather large lots attached to each house since land is cheap). If the shopping centre goes there it will raise the value of surrounding residential land and create a new peak in the population density function. It will not be easy for shopping centre developers to capture the land rents that they create since this would require buying up land from the hundreds of existing owners at a price that did not reflect the new values to be created by the shopping centre itself. Given transactions costs and the difficulty of keeping the reason for the large number of purchases secret, the shopping centre developers will probably not be able to do this and thus will end up giving a gift of the rents they create to the existing home owners. Second, assume that the shopping center owners go to the first plot of undeveloped land on the fringe of the city and buy up the land from a single farmer, perhaps paying him something more than the opportunity cost of the land in its agricultural use. They might, for example, pay the value of the land in urban, low-density development in the absence of the shopping centre. They can then develop both the shopping centre and a relatively high density residential subdivision around the shopping centre. In this way they are able to capture a significant portion of the rents they create for those residential plots of land that are now near to a new shopping centre.[21]

This explains at least two observed phenomena:

1. Why new developers on the edges of cities so often simultaneously develop a shopping centre and a residential subdivision.
2. Why 'holes' of low density emerge on the already subdivided fringes of cities, these 'holes' being bypassed in order to develop higher density residential areas on what was previously agricultural land.

This same insight has obvious applications to the isolated 'company town'. By locating a plant, perhaps a mining or smelting facility, in an isolated region the firm creates rents on surrounding land. It can and frequently does capture these rents by buying up land suitable for community development and establishing its 'company' town.

B. Multi-plant monopoly in space

In this section we drop the assumption that each firm may own only one plant. Consider a single firm, A, located in the centre of a bounded linear market as shown by point a_1 in Figure 3. Assume that the density of customers is high enough so that the firm is making profits but not so high that two new entrants on either side of A could cover costs. Now assume that at some future time T_2 the density of customers is expected to increase to such a point that two new entrants would make profits (but further new entrants would anticipate losses). If there are many potential new entrants, competition among them would push entry back in time to the point T_1 at which the present discounted value of losses from T_1 to T_2 exactly equalled the present discounted value of the profits to be earned from T_2 onwards. Two firms entering the market at T_1 would locate plants at the points that seemed best to them, at b_1 and b_2 in Figure 3.

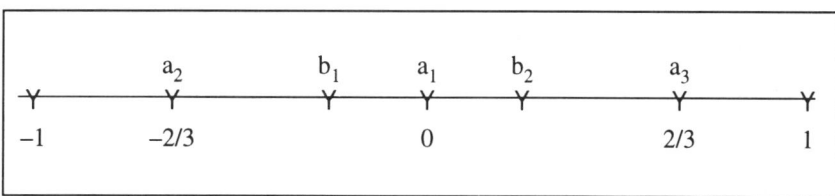

Figure 3. Spatial pre-emption by multi-plant firms

Now consider firm A's strategy. It can pre-empt entry by building two branch plants on either side of the market at any time before T_2. To see that it will be profitable for A to do so we reason as follows.

Assume initially that A locates its plants at b_1 and b_2, at time T_2 and that all three plants charge the same price as they would have charged if B had owned the plants at b_1 and b_2. Under these conditions, the plants would be exactly as profitable to firm A as to firm B. If there were no possibility of entry, the sales and profits that firm A's new plants take away from the old plant at a_1 could not be regarded as net additions to firm A's sales and profits. But when entry of new firms will occur at T_2, firm A's expected stream of profits and sales from its plant at a_1 fall abruptly at T_2. Thus all of the sales and profits of A's new plants represent net additions to the stream of sales and profits that A could expect if it did not build these plants. Since under the assumed conditions the plants add the same amount to A's profits as they would to those of a new entrant, the plants have the same value to A as to a new entrant.

The above analysis assumes that A adopts the same price and the same location for its new plants as would a newly entering firm. A can, however, be expected to do better than this with respect to both price and location. Consider price first. If firm A controls the entire market, it is clearly free to charge the profit-maximizing set of prices, p_m, given the locations of the two new plants. If A does not build the two new plants then with more than one firm in the market, we would anticipate at least some price competition. Even if the price competition is only transitory in nature, the stream of profits will be temporarily reduced while this price competition occurs. Thus, if the entry of a new firm with plants at b_1 and b_2 can be expected to lead to a set of prices that is depressed whether permanently or temporarily below the profit maximizing price, the value of the new plants in their given locations is higher to firm A than to a newly-entering firm.

Now consider location. If firm A establishes both of the new plants, it can choose the best location for them in conjunction with its plant at a_1. It can be shown that the best place for firm A to establish its new plants is a $-2/3$ and $2/3$, and that all three plants will charge a common price. These best locations are shown in Figure 3 by the points a_2 and a_3. When A adopts this locational configuration, all three plants are in the middle of identical markets running from -1 to $-1/3$, from $-1/3$ to $1/3$ and from $1/3$ to 1.

The new entrant, however, cannot in general be expected to locate its plant at these points. Instead it will tend to locate closer to a_1 than $-2/3$ and $2/3$ since the new entrant regards sales that it takes from A's plant at a_1 as net additions to its sales. One such locational configuration is illustrated in Figure 3 by the plants at b_1 and b_2. Thus, total profits generated from the entire market will, in general, be larger when firm A owns and chooses the sites for, and the prices charged by, the new plants than when some new firm B locates them and chooses the price that they will charge. Thus it will always pay the existing firm A to pre-empt an expanding market at a time (before T_2) at which potential new entrants must expect losses. Although many more details are worked out in our paper (Eaton and Lipsey, 1976c) it should be clear that we have suggested a theory of the growth of multi-plant firms in spatial markets. This model seems to us to make sense out of the widely observed empirical phenomenon of one firm establishing many retail plants in the same market.

C. Predatory pricing
So far we have considered cases in which a new firm will not follow the strategy of mill price undercutting. This is likely to be the case when each plant is owned by a separate firm. The multi-plant monopoly profits that arise from the market pre-

emption strategy considered in the previous section, however, raise the possibility that mill price undercutting may be a profitable strategy when a potential multi-branch firm considers entering a market currently occupied by N independent, single-plant firms.

This strategy is known as predatory pricing in the literature and the present state of play appears to be as follows. Proponents of predatory pricing argue on empirical grounds that there are documented cases that look like predatory pricing. Opponents argue, using a spaceless model, that predatory pricing does not make sense in theory. They say that if firm B enters the market and drives A out by predatory pricing it cannot then raise prices to earn monopoly profits because it would then lay itself open to a predatory price attack from a new potential entrant, C. Here the debate now stands; one side the strategy does not make sense theoretically; the other side says 'but it does seem to happen'.

A possible resolution of this impasse seems to arise from the spatially extended model and depends on the key insight that pure profits are consistent with free-entry equilibrium. Assume a market containing a large number of plants each owned by an independent firm. In general these plants will not be at the joint-profit-maximizing locations and, if there is any price-competition among them, they will not be charging the joint profit maximizing price.

A new firm could now enter, establishing branches throughout the market in what would be the joint-profit-maximizing locations in the absence of the independents. It can then predatory price (adopt the mill-price undercutting strategy) and drive out the independents. Once they are eliminated the multi-plant monopoly can charge the price that yields it maximum profits consistent with a new entrant just expecting losses. This new firm will earn profits in excess of the joint profits of the independents because its plants will be in superior locations and it can charge the joint-profit-maximizing price. The firm is protected from the entry of a second multi-branch firm that tries to eliminate the first by predatory pricing because the second firm can at best expect profits equal to the first firm's profits after the first firm exits – and making the first firm exit will bring transitory losses. Thus the market is more valuable to the first multi-branch firm than to the independents, and the multi-branch firm can afford to predatory price. It can also afford to buy out the independents (on the threat of predatory pricing) at a price that goes as high (if the predatory price threat were not taken seriously) as the present value of the independent firms and still earn pure profits. Once the market is pre-empted by a multi-branch monopoly, the predatory-price strategy does not appear profitable to a second multi-branch firm considering entry.

One strand of the anti-predatory price literature argues that since the new entrant can buy out the existing firms at their present market value, the threat of predatory pricing should be enough and it should never be observed actually to occur. Assume, however, that the independent firms are not in the joint-profit-maximizing locations so that the new firm would wish to build new plants, and if it owned the old plants, merely discard them or sell them off for other uses. (The strategy of building plants in the joint-profit-maximizing locations is also attractive because, in general, these locations also minimize the market available to a new entrant). It now has two options. First it can buy up the independents at the capitalized value of their present profits. Second, it can build its new plants and predatory price, thus reducing the profits of the independents to negative values. It may then be able to buy out the independents at a saving in costs that more than compensates it for the short period over which its new plants suffer losses because of its predatory-price policy.

Thus the spatial model appears capable of reconciling theory and evidence in a way that the spaceless model cannot.[22]

D. Keynesian underemployment equilibrium and micro behaviour

A problem that greatly concerns theorists today is how to reconcile a Keynesian underemployment equilibrium with perfectly competitive behaviour in product markets when prices are inflexible downwards. Even if market demand diminishes, there is no reason why any one perfectly competitive firm should produce less if market price is inflexible downwards (in the sense that at the present price market demand is less than desired market supply). If firms face perfectly elastic demand curves they should never come to rest in a situation in which marginal cost does not equal price. The downward-sloping demand curves for each firm in the spatial model provide a simple resolution of this theoretical puzzle. Assume that our linear market is inhibited by a number of producers of some raw material, say iron ore or lumber. Because of the spatial dispersion of producers and consumers, each firm has some monopoly power and each firm faces a downward-sloping demand curve. If market demand now falls off, each firm can now sell less at a fixed price and each will voluntarily reduce its output to meet the finite demand that it faces over its own market segment (given downward inflexibility of prices).

Once again, we see that ridding ourselves of the spaceless, perfectly competitive model provides a simple resolution of problems that otherwise seem difficult, or even intractable.

E. Comparison shopping and the attraction of homogeneous firms

In these final two sections we briefly mention two problems that are already agreed to be spatial problems but on which we believe our models cast fresh light. The clustering together of firms selling similar products is a frequently observed empirical phenomenon. The explanation that is almost universally accepted by economists is the one that comes from Hotelling's famous 1929 article. Firms seek to minimally differentiate themselves from their competitors, and the resulting clustering is socially wasteful because it raises transport costs. In Eaton and Lipsey (1975) we proved that the clustering of firms is necessary in Hotelling's model only at the market peripheries – the two extreme firms, at either end of the market will be located side by side. Other firms in the market may or may not be clustered into local groups. Indeed if individual customer demand is responsive to price, interior firms will be equally spaced (see Eaton and Lipsey, 1976b).

There is now a problem: if Hotelling's model does not explain the clustering of similar firms that we observe in the world, what does? One explanation that seems to apply to much of what we see in the world arises from comparison shopping. If households visit say, three shops before making a purchase then in equilibrium firms will cluster together in clusters of at least three firms.[23] In this example the socially optimal configuration of firms would have groups of three firms equally spaced along the market. Although the socially-optimal configuration of firms does not, in this model, arise from atomistic decision taking among independent firms, much of the local clustering that does occur is a transport-cost-reducing response to the needs of comparison shoppers, rather than being a universally wasteful phenomenon as it is in Hotelling's model.

We are also able with our model to account for a frequently-observed phenomenon that has no rationale whatsoever in Hotelling's model. It is commonly observed that department stores who contribute capital to the formation of shopping centres actively encourage the location of competing firms within the shopping centre. Although a firm may not be able to prevent the nearby location of a competing firm in the Hotelling model, there are no circumstances in which it would encourage such a phenomenon. Our model provides a reason why one store would do so and so provides a possible explanation, absent from the Hotelling model, of this phenomenon. The reason is provided by the proof in our article of the proposition that when customers visit 2 stores (to use a simple example) before making their purchases, the sales of a group of two stores at a particular location will be more than double the sales of an isolated store at that location. In these circumstances it clearly pays an isolated store to persuade a second store competing with it to locate next door to it.[24]

This model also makes sense out of what we refer to as the automobile plaza. In many growing cities land values have increased to the point where it is not profitable to maintain an automobile retaining firm in the core of the city. What we have observed in several cities is that when automobile firms relocate on cheaper land they jointly buy up a large plot of land and establish an automobile plaza in which several firms retail different automobiles. Again this phenomenon is inconsistent with the Hotelling model but is easily understood in the comparison shopping model.

F. The theory of shopping centres, the attraction of heterogeneous firms, and the suburbanization of cities

Up to this point we have concentrated on the implications of indivisibilities in the production process in the context of a spatial model. There are, however, two other types of indivisibilities which are central to an understanding of spatial patterns of retail firms. The indivisibilities are central to the activity of shopping – traveling from domicile to retail stores, purchasing products and transporting them from retail stores to domicile. The first indivisibility of concern is the indivisibility of the automobile. This indivisibility implies that there is frequently excess capacity for the transportation of goods from retail stores to domicile. The second indivisibility is the indivisibility of the shopper. This indivisibility implies that the shopper can economize on his or her time input to the activity of shopping by purchasing several commodities on one trip. Together the two indivisibilities imply the phenomenon of multi-purpose retail trips.

In this section we consider the implications of these indivisibilities for the spatial attraction of firms selling heterogeneous products which are purchased by shoppers with different frequencies. Consider a simple example in which four goods are bought with the following frequencies: good 1 every period, good 2 every second period, good 3 every fourth period and good 4 every 8th period. Table 1 illustrates, showing which goods are bought in each period.

Assume initially that all firms are located in a central business district, that the population of the city grows and the number of firms in the CBD grows as well. Sooner or later some new firm may consider locating in the suburbs rather than becoming yet another firm in the CBD. Clearly if the decision is atomistic it will be a firm selling product 1 that will suburbanize first; if a firm selling any other product went to the suburbs on its own, it would get little or no custom since it is always bought in conjunction with other products that are sold only in the CBD.

Table 1. Commodities purchased in each period

Time period	Commodities purchased (The pattern repeats itself every 8 periods).
1	1, 2, 3, 4
2	1
3	1, 2
4	1
5	1, 2, 3
6	1
7	1, 2
8	1
9	1, 2, 3, 4

The product that is most frequently bought on its own will be the first to be suburbanized. Once a firm selling good 1 locates in the suburbs and if demand continues to grow it will eventually pay a firm selling good 2 to locate in the suburbs along side of the already existing firm selling good 1 because, when nearby customers wish to buy goods 1 and 2 alone, they will go to the suburban stores. The firm selling 1 confers an externality on the firm selling 2 because if the firm selling 1 were not there it would never pay the firm selling 2 to suburbanize on its own. What may not be so obvious is that the firm selling 2 confers an externality on the firm selling 1. When the firm selling 1 is in the suburbs on its own it is only visited when customers want to buy good 1 on its own. When the firm selling 2 is there as well, the firm selling 1 is visited every time customers want to buy 1 on its own or 1 and 2 in combination (but not in combination with 3 and 4). *The externalities are reciprocal.* Clearly, when the firm selling 1 wishes to suburbanize it will pay it to bribe the firm selling 2 to come along with it even if the sales of the firm selling good 2 in the suburbs would not quite cover its own costs. In Eaton and Lipsey (1976f) we prove that cooperative suburbanization of firms selling different products in a city whose size is growing will occur sooner and will lead to firms being located further out towards the edge of the city than when each type of store makes it suburbanization decision atomistically. This then is the essence of the theory of suburbanization of firms through the institution of shopping centres.

V. Conclusion

Our general conclusions then are that space matters; that space matters a great deal; that many phenomena that appear inexplicable when inserted into a spaceless model are explicable in a spatial model; that space deserves a central rather than a peripheral position (the metaphor is conscious) in neo-classical value theory; that many theoretical problems concerning the difficulties of perfect competition are finessed in a spatial model because, in our models at least, perfect competition never exists; and that an informed view on the basic methodological question of the extent to which comparative static equilibrium theory is a useful tool for understanding economic reality may be radically changed when we move over from spaceless to spatially extended models.

Notes

1. An earlier version of this paper was read at the meetings of the Canadian Economic Association in Quebec (May 31, 1976). The paper is a general survey of the work we have done, largely in 1974–75, under the support of the Killam Foundation for Professor Lipsey and the Canada Council for Professor Eaton. We are greatly indebted to Lloyd Paquin and Clive Southey for detailed comments and criticism and to the University of Colorado at Boulder for providing us with facilities for our work.
2. The standard reference for this result is R. J. Aumann (1964). Earlier recognitions can, however, be documented although none of the earlier writers went on to do what Aumann did: to prove that for an exchange economy, with a continuum of traders, the core coincides with the set of equilibrium allocations.
3. In the international version of the model, 'countries' – each of which is a spaceless, point economy – are separated by factor immobility assumption rather than by the assumption of positive transport costs. (The latter is sometimes added but only as a very minor 'frill'.)
4. The main theorem for proving the existence of competitive equilibrium states the following.

    Def: Consider a set S and correspondence ψ from S to S.
    A fixed point of the correspondence ψ is an $x' \in S$ such that $x' \in \psi(x')$.

    Theorem: (Kakatani): If S is a non-empty, compact, convex subset of R^m, and if ψ is an upper semi continuous correspondence from S to S such that for all $x \in S$ the set $\psi(x)$ is non-empty and convex, then ψ has a fixed point.

    A non-convexity in the production function implies that $\psi(x)$ is not convex and consequently the conditions of the theorem are not met.
5. See R. Starr (1969).
6. Easiest in the sense that it only requires the Brower fixed point theorem and not the Kakatani theorem.
7. Our view is very close to that expounded by Kaldor in his brilliant 1935 article on Imperfect Competition.
8. Homogeneous land requires that all natural resource be available in the same proportions in all land in the economy.
9. N. Kaldor (1972, p. 1242). Of particular importance in a spatial model are economies of scale in transportation. Economies of scale in transportation imply that any production which requires the transportation of inputs (from resource nodes, for example) and/or outputs will be characterized by decreasing costs at least up to the level of output at which the economies of scale in transportation are exhausted. We do not, however, study scale economies in transportation in this paper.
10. If for an existence proof we need to have a demand function defined for all $p_j \in (0, \infty)$, we can arbitrarily assume $q = q(p^*)$ for all $p_j \leq p^* - ta$. This will pose no problems since we know that the equilibrium value of p_j must satisfy $p_j > p^* - ta$.
11. As seen in Figure 1b, J's entire demand curve for a strict zero CV assumption (i.e., mill price undercutting *is* permitted) is semi upper continuous. Thus is might be possible to prove the existence of an equilibrium even if mill price undercutting is permitted. Since, however, no-mill-price-undercutting is such an obvious implication of the assumption that firms are profit maximizers, it seems to us uninteresting to follow the route of allowing mill price undercutting to occur.

12. Arrow and Hahn (1971, pp. 151–69) have proven the existence of equilibrium for a fixed-numbers equilibrium in a spatially extended economy with production non-convexities and downward-sloping demand curve. Not surprisingly since numbers are fixed, equilibrium is consistent with positive profits.
13. This elasticity effects goes to zero either as the elasticity of the demand at each point goes to zero – so that proximity to customers does not influence sales, or as the density of packing of firms in the market goes to infinity – so that the difference between the firm's mill price and its delivered price at its market boundary goes to zero for *any* downward-sloping demand curve.
14. Archibald and Rosenbluth (1975) demonstrate that pure profits are consistent with equilibrium in a model in which goods are distinguished by different locations in characteristics space as opposed to the physical space in our model.
15. An example of the former space is a line of finite length, a bounded linear market; an example of the latter is the circumference of a circle: there are no boundaries but the market is of a finite length.
16. A. Shaked (1975) has proven that equilibrium does not exist in this model for the case of N = 3. No such non-existence proof has been demonstrated for larger N but our computer model strongly suggests that it does not exist.
17. See, e.g., Kaldor (1972). Although we are critical of Kaldor's view that equilibrium theory is totally irrelevant, it should be apparent from the substance of this paper that we are in substantial agreement with many of the points Kaldor makes. We think it is both factually wrong and a tactical mistake, however, to assert to economists who use it every day with some success, that equilibrium economics is totally irrelevant.
18. When Canada was on a fixed exchange rate in the period the late 1960s the government attempted to keep the growth of the Canadian money supply at a low level in an attempt to keep the Canadian inflation rate below the U.S. rate. This policy induced exactly the crisis predicted by the static Mundell model that makes the money supply endogenous when the exchange rate is fixed.
19. The understanding of the agricultural problem that existed throughout most of the twentieth century as arising from a set of markets with slowly shifting demand curves due to low income elasticities, rapidly shifting supply curves due to productivity growth combined with short-term erratic fluctuations in supply, and low price elasticities was a major triumph of early empirical work combined with the crude but, in this case effective, tools of comparative-static equilibrium analysis.
20. Even if cities are in a perpetual state of long-term disequilibrium, movement is slow because of the long life of fixed capital. Thus short-term equilibrium analysis is able successfully to predict, for example, the disastrous effects of rent controls in spite of the possible absence of long-term full equilibrium.
21. In an important paper C. Southey (1974) considers some of the problems that arise when producers create rents in surrounding land and seek to maximize the sum of the profits from normal production plus the rents that they create and appropriate. In our paper discussing this rent application (1976e) we make detailed comparisons between our results and Southey's.
22. This section is a brief summary of the argument that is detailed in Eaton and Lipsey (1976a).
23. In Eaton and Lipsey (1976d) we prove that if customers visit R firms before making a purchase, firms will always be grouped in clusters containing at least R firms. Like so many propositions in economics that are intuitively appealing, this one turns out to be difficult to prove.
24. This section gives a brief summary of the argument in Eaton and Lipsey (1976d).

Bibliography

Archibald, G. C. and Rosenbluth, G. (1975). The 'New' Theory of Consumer Demand and Monopolistic Competition. *Quarterly Journal of Economics, LXXXIX* (4), 569–90.

Arrow, K.J. and Debreu, G.L. (1954). Existence of Equilibrium for a Competitive Economy. *Econometrica*, **27**, 265–90.

Arrow, K.J. and Hahn, F.H. (1971). *General Competitive Analysis*. Edinburgh: Oliver and Boyd.

Aumann, R.J. (1964). Markets With a Continuum of Traders. *Econometrica*, **32**, 39–50.

Debreu, G. (1959). *Theory of Value*. New York: Willey.

Eaton, B. Curtis and Lipsey, Richard G. (1975). The Principal of Minimum Differentiation Reconsidered: Some New Developments in the Theory of Spatial Competition. *Review of Economic Studies*, **XLII** (1), 27–50.

Eaton, B. Curtis and Lipsey, Richard G. (1976a). The Non-Uniqueness of Equilibrium in the Loschian Model. *American Economic Review*, **66** (1), 77–93.

Eaton, B. Curtis and Lipsey, Richard G. (1976b). Freedom of Entry and the Rate of Profit. *Institute for Economic Research*. Queen's University Discussion Paper No. 207.

Eaton, B. Curtis and Lipsey, Richard G. (1976c). The Theory of Spatial Pre-Emption: Location as a Barrier to Entry. *Institute for Economic Research*. Queen's University Discussion Paper No. 208.

Eaton, B. Curtis and Lipsey, Richard G. (1976d). Comparison Shopping and Clusters of Homogeneous Firms. *Institute for Economic Research*. Queen's University Discussion Paper No. 226.

Eaton, B. Curtis and Lipsey, Richard G. (1976e). The Theory of Rent in A Spatial Economy with Production at Discrete Points. *Institute for Economic Research*. Queen's University Discussion Paper. Forthcoming, Summer 1976.

Eaton, B. Curtis and Lipsey, Richard G. (1976f). Shopping Centres, Suburbanization and the Attraction of Heterogeneous Firms. *Institute for Economic Research*. Queen's University Discussion Paper. Forthcoming, Summer 1976.

Eaton, B. Curtis and Lipsey, Richard G. (1976g). A Theory of Rational Predatory Pricing: Predatory Monopolistic Practices in a Spatial Context. *Institute for Economic Research*. Queen's University Discussion Paper. Forthcoming, Autumn 1976.

Eaton, B. Curtis and Lipsey, Richard G. (1976h). A Model of Oligopolistic Spatial Competition when Customer Density is Determined Endogeneously: A Theory of Shopping Centres. *Institute for Economic Research*. Forthcoming, Summer 1976.

Eaton, B. Curtis and Lipsey, Richard G (1976i). Some Effects on the Spatial Distribution of Firms on Factor Markets. *Institute for Economic Research*. Queen's University Discussion Paper. Forthcoming, Autumn 1976.

Hicks, J. R. (1939). *Value and Capital*. London: Oxford University Press.

Hotelling, H. (1929), 'Stability in Competition', *Economic Journal*, **39** (March), 41–57.

Kaldor, N. (1935). Market Imperfection and Excess Capacity. *Economics* N.S.2, 33–50.

Kaldor, N. (1972). The Irrelevance of Equilibrium Economics. *Economic Journal*, **82**, 1237–55.

Shaked, A.L. (1975). Non-Existence of Equilibrium for the 2-dimensional 3-firms Location Problem. *Review of Economic Studies*, **XLII** (1), 51–6.

Southey, C. (1974). Spatial Rents, Spatial Competition and Efficiency. *Canadian Journal of Economics*, **VII** (2), 260–72.

Starr, R. (1969). Quasi-Equilibria in Markets with Non-Convex Preferences. *Econometrica*, **37**, 25–38.

[4]

Spatial monopoly, natural monopoly, pure profits, and land rents

B. Curtis Eaton and Richard G. Lipsey

In our paper 'Freedom of Entry and the Existence of Pure Profit' (Eaton and Lipsey, 1976a) we demonstrated the existence of an equilibrium in a spatial model in which all firms in the market enjoyed positive and significant pure profits while potential new entrants could not expect to cover their costs of production. We concluded that in models such as ours zero-profit is not a condition of free-entry equilibrium. Although this conclusion is still a subject of controversy, several other investigators have reached similar conclusions, e.g., Salop (1976) and Schmalensee (1977).

The key characteristics of these models are (i) that long run average total costs of production (LRATC) fall over some initial range of output starting at zero due to indivisibilities in capital, and (ii) that costs of transactions are significant and positively related to distance of the customer from the firm with whom he transacts. As a result of the second characteristic, firms are spread out over the market. This geographical dispersion of firms effectively segments the market and confers on each firm an element of monopoly power over segments of the market that are closer to that firm than to any other firm. The dispersion of firms also means that any new entrant must fit into a space between existing firms and as a result will sell significantly less at any price than would an existing firm have sold at the same price before entry occurred. This result, in combination with characteristic (i), decreasing LRATC over some range, implies that it is quite possible for potential new entrants to anticipate negative profits while firms already in the market enjoy positive pure profits.

The profits in this model are, in a sense, rents of location and this observation gives rise to the first question that we ask in this paper: Is it conceivable that landowners could appropriate these profits as land rents? This question turns out to be relatively easy to answer and it is handled in Section II.B.

The model in the zero-profits paper, and the models in the other papers cited above, are based on inelastic expectations with respect to future profits (all firms anticipate that their current flow of profits will persist into the indefinite future). The second question addressed in this paper is: Will the pure-profit result survive when firms explicitly recognize any potential that exists for intertemporal variation in the profits that they earn? This question turns out to be much more difficult to answer than the first question and we examine it in the context of a timeless equilibrium in Section II.C and in the context of changing market conditions in Section III.

These are the two main questions dealt with in this paper. Along the way, however, we make comparisons between our results and those that obtain in the Classical theory of spaceless natural monopoly. (The comparison of results is interesting because the equilibrium of the firm of our spatial model looks very much like that of a firm in a Classical natural monopoly situation – in both cases the demand curve intersects one firm's LRATC so that pure profits exist but would be below the LRATC if there were two firms in that segment of the market, and, as a result, pure profits persist.)

In the final section we compare and contrast the behaviour of land rents and profits in a neo-classical model and in our spatial model. Since we believe that each model applies to a significant portion of the economy we believe these comparisons and contrasts are necessary if we are to build up anything like a complete tool kit for analysing all of the major sectors of the economy. (Industries which have the characteristics of our spatial model are most retailing, much of primary production – e.g., forest products and cement – and many geographically dispersed light manufacturing industries.)

I. The model

In this section we outline the model used in this paper. It captures the significant features of the model used in Eaton and Lipsey (1976a), but is more general in certain respects.

1. The economy has a non-spatial, perfectly competitive sector in which the going rate of return on capital is i and in which the opportunity cost of using land is A per year. There is a single spatially decentralized industry, Z, which is the subject of our detailed analysis.
2. The market for Z consists of a one-dimensional line of infinite length over which customers are evenly spread at a constant density of C per unit of distance.[1]
3. All firms are faced with the same long-run cost function which displays declining average costs at the outset due to capital indivisibilities.
4. Fixed capital once installed is geographically immobile and has no opportunity cost. We consider a number of alternative assumptions concerning the nature and durability of capital.
5. Each plant is owned by a separate firm.[2]
6. Transport costs are significant and positively related to distance travelled. Customers bear the cost of transport.
7. Customers buy from the firm whose delivered price (mill price plus transport cost) is lowest.
8. Each customer has a downward-sloping demand curve in terms of delivered price.
9. Since fixed capital is immobile and has no opportunity cost by assumption 4, each firm assumes that all other firms will maintain their locations as long as they remain in the market. Thus we do not consider the possibility of firms changing their locations in response to any actions of competing firms. This follows logically from our assumption that capital is immobile and, once

installed, has no opportunity cost, for in this situation if a firm wishes to 'relocate' it must abandon its present plant and re-enter the market at another location. Thus in this model it is appropriate to consider firms exiting from the market and entering into the market, *but their locations are fixed while they are in the market.*

10. Assumptions are required concerning the firm's expectations. As we mentioned above, Eaton and Lipsey (1976a) incorporated inelastic expectations with respect to the flow of future profits (as do the other models cited above). Here we substitute the following assumptions concerning firms' expectations.

10a. Firms are identically motivated.

10b. Given the locational configuration of firms in the market and the density of customers, all firms – existing firms as well as new entrants – can accurately calculate the flows of costs and revenues. This allows us to avoid the specification of an explicit conjectural variation with respect to price. It has the advantage that the characteristics of equilibrium that we discover are not dependent on firms entering the market with given expectations, only to have these expectations disappointed.

10c. All firms are able to foresee correctly the potential for entry and exit from the industry.

II. The long-run persistence of pure profits

A. *Initial conditions*

Two salient characteristics of long-run equilibrium in unbounded linear spatial models[3] that are established in Eaton and Lipsey (1976a) are that all firms charge the same price, p*, and all are equally spaced over the whole market and thus located in the centre of identical individual market segments.

The locational pattern is illustrated in Figure 1. The firms, U, V, W, and X occupy a segment of the market from –4L to 4L and, like all other firms in the market, are spaced out a distance 2L apart. Firm V, for example, is in the middle of its own individual market that stretches from –2L to zero.

The intuition of the positive pure profit result is easily explained, by reference to Figure 1. Consider a new firm considering entry into the market segment between firms V and W. If the entrant expects to charge the common price p* it must expect to have a market segment of half the distance of that controlled by existing firms before entry i.e., its market will only be L in length. Indeed if the firm and its two neighbours end up charging *any* common price, whatever its value, the new entrant will serve a market of only L in length. It follows from this that the entrant's expected demand curve must lie substantially to the left of the demand curves facing V and W before entry. Since all firms' LRATCs are decreasing over some initial interval, a free-entry equilibrium is possible in which the demand curves of existing firms in the market lie above their LRATCs while the expected demand curve for a new entrant into any slot between two existing firms lies below its prospective LRATC. Entry occurs until the expected demand curves facing new entrants are to the left of their expected LRATCs, but except by coincidence this

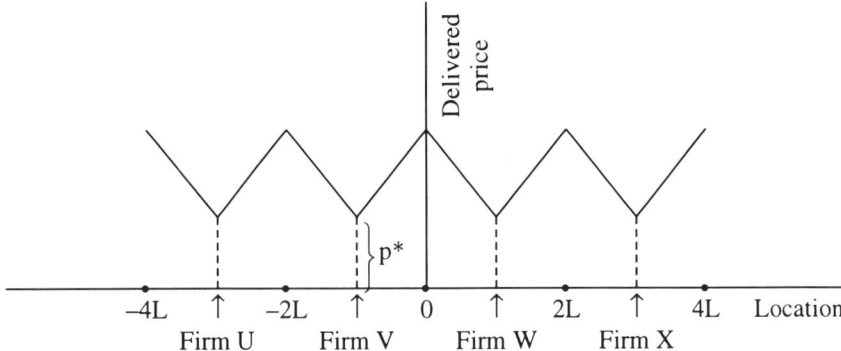

Figure 1. The equilibrium locations of four firms along a segment of the linear market

will occur when the demand curves of existing firms lie to the right of their LRATCs and, hence, existing firms earn pure profits. In this free-entry equilibrium existing firms can earn pure profits while potential new entrants expect losses. This is the sense in which the equilibrium of any one firm in this spatial model is analogous to a situation of natural monopoly.

We begin our analysis by placing the existing firms in a position of free-entry equilibrium with positive pure profits. To do this we arbitrarily space all firms out a distance 2L apart as shown in Figure 1 and then select an appropriate value for the density of customers along the line. There will be a certain density C_0, which will just allow existing firms to earn zero profits. (In this case their demand curves will be tangent to their LRATCs.) There will be a second, significant higher density, C_1, at which potential new entrants will expect zero profits. (Their expected demand curves will be tangent to their expected LRATCs.) We choose the actual density of customers, C, such that $C_0 < C < C_1$. Customer density and all other relevant characteristics are expected to remain unchanged indefinitely. Now the market is in free-entry equilibrium with positive pure profits for existing firms and negative expected profits for potential new entrants.

B. Will landlords convert the pure profits into land rent?

Will the pure profits that are consistent with free-entry equilibrium persist or will they be removed by some form of behaviour not analysed in any of the models mentioned above? One possibility, that landlords will appropriate these profits as land rents, is studied in this section.

In order to make the 'land market' as competitive as possible, assume that land is divided up into parcels of size, s, where L/s is a large number, and where each parcel is owned by a separate individual. We also assume that initially firms lease their land from landlords for a rent that is fixed over the period of the lease. Various cases arise according to the period of the lease.

We first consider the possibilities open to landlords who can do nothing other than choose the price at which they offer their land. Because all firms in the market are in an identical position we need to consider only one of them. We thus ask if firm W's pure profits will be appropriated by some landlord or landlords who hold land in the interval between –L and 3L. We begin with some definitions. *Gross profits* are the firm's total revenues minus current avoidable costs (variable costs). *Fixed costs* are a sum equal to the competitive rate of return on all sunk capital (valued at its historical cost rather than current opportunity cost). *Pure profits* are gross profits minus fixed costs. Our initial conditions are such that all existing firms earn pure profits. Hence gross profits must be greater than fixed costs as defined above.

To begin our study of the question posed in the heading we consider firm W's pure profits as a function of its alternative possible locations within its present slot between firm V and X. These are depicted in Figure 2 by the function π^W, which is drawn on the assumption that the price of land is A (see assumption 1). Firm W's profits are a maximum at its existing location L. This is because quantity demanded at any price is a maximum at L and decreases monotonically and symmetrically as the firm's location departs from L.[4] Intuitively, quantity demanded (and hence profits) is a maximum at L for any price because in locations other than L, average transport costs over the firm's market area are higher and quantity demanded correspondingly lower. L is not, however, the only location that promises pure profits. Indeed any location between a and b in Figure 2 promises non-negative profits.

Assume that the firm's land lease comes up for renewal when it still has fixed capital in existence.

By how much can the landlord now raise the firm's rent? The landlord can usurp all of the firm's 'fixed costs'. As defined these represent a return on sunk costs sufficient to make the firm sink them again if it had to do so. But in its present location the sunk costs are sunk while if the firm moved it would have to discard its present capital and spend to build a new plant. Thus the landlord can extract all of the firm's fixed costs (quasi rents in Marshall's sense of the term) without it being worthwhile for the firm to relocate. The landlord can also extract an amount equal to the difference in pure profit that can be earned in the firm's present location L and the next best location, call it L_1. But the landlord can extract no more. If he

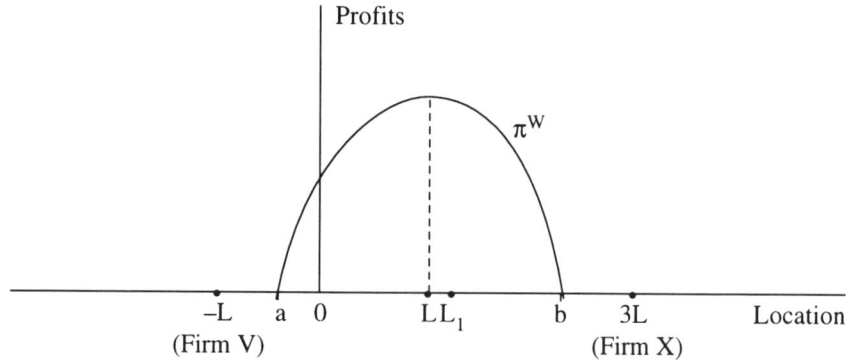

Figure 2. The profit function for firm W in the slot between firms V and W (π^W is drawn for a price of land of A)

raises rent sufficiently to appropriate any further of the firm's pure profits, the firm can abandon its present plant and build a new one at L_1 and increase its profits. A glance at Figure 2 should convince the reader, that as the amount of land needed by the firm goes to zero, so the difference between the profits that can be earned at L, the best site, and at L_1, the next best site, goes to zero. As this happens the amount that the landlord can extract from the firm in these circumstances approaches the firm's fixed costs, and the amount that cannot be extracted approaches the firm's pure profits. For simplicity we use this limiting result, but when we speak of the landlord appropriating the firm's fixed costs we shall mean fixed costs plus the difference between $\pi(L)$ and $\pi(L_1)$.

We conclude that even if the firm is silly enough not to get control of its land over the period of life of its fixed capital, all that the landlord can appropriate for himself is the firm's quasi rents – its return on sunk costs. We may also note in passing that this result is exactly the same as in the spaceless neo-classical model of monopoly. If the monopolist builds an immobile plant on land and the lease comes up for renewal before the plant has reached the end of its life the landlord can appropriate the monopolists quasi rents but not its pure profits.[5] Of course the existence of this possibility dictates that profit maximizing firms who own their own fixed capital will also either own their land or lease it over a period equal to the life time of their capital. (Of course if they rent both land *and* fixed capital then they have no sunk costs – other than those connected with moving – that can be appropriated by the landlord.)

It is probably worth noting that there is one strategy open to the landlord that will allow him to usurp the pure profits providing W's rental contract comes up for renewal during the life time of its plant. The strategy is as follows: The landlord, or an entrepreneur who is cooperating with him, buys up a nearby piece of land at the going price A and builds a plant identical to W's plant. When W's rental contract comes up for renewal the landlord raises the rent so high that W cannot even cover his variable costs and thus forces W out of business. The 'landlord' is now the owner of a firm near to W's present location. This strategy is open to W's landlord and no one else because only he is in a position to costlessly drive W out of business. If landlords do engage in this strategy then firms will always own their own land or lease it for the life time of their capital.

It is once again worth noting that this possibility also occurs in the standard spaceless neo-classical model of monopoly. If the firm is silly enough not to have the requisite control over its land, the landlord can build a new plant and then drive out the old firm by raising its rent sufficiently. The profits that accrue, however, are still properly regarded as profits to the firm and not a return to land. To see this note that the landlord-entrepreneur can buy up a new piece of land at a price A, build a plant on it, then abandon the old plant, and the profits will follow the plant while the value of the abandoned piece of land will revert to A.

C. *Will new firms enter hoping to drive out old firms?*

We now come to the second major possibility. The positive profit result in previous models is based on the assumption of inelastic profit expectations. If a new firm enters a slot between two firms it must expect negative profits while its neighbours continue in existence. We now consider the possibility that a new firm may enter each slot in the market *hoping to drive out at least one of the old firms* and that this behaviour will force profits to zero. For this analysis everything turns on the nature of the firm's capital and on what we mean by 'the long run'. We consider 3 types of capital.

Type I capital has infinite life, and no expenditure is required to maintain the capital. In this case existing firms' profits will not be reduced or usurped by new entrants. There appear to be at least three ways to argue this result. It is worthwhile examining each argument since analogous arguments apply to types II and III capital.

Argument 1: The first argument relies on assumptions 10a and 10c, that all firms, existing firms as well as potential entrants, are identically motivated and able to foresee correctly the potential for entry. Let us *assume* that a new entrant, Firm E, is able to drive an existing firm, Firm X, out of the market. (We argue below that this will *not* be possible in this model.) By assumption 10c Firm E must recognize that if it were successful in driving X out of the market, it would then be in exactly the same position as the firm it had just driven out of the market. Hence Firm E would anticipate that some other new entrant, E_1, would then enter the market to drive E out. Thus even if Firm E could drive some existing firm out of the market it would not be profitable for it to do so since it would then be open to the same move from E_1.

Argument 2: But firm E will not be able to drive X out of the market and expect to earn profits even if it does not worry about the entry of E_1. Notice first that firm X will stay in the market as long as it can make any sales on which it can cover its avoidable costs of production. This implies that if E is to drive X out of the market, E must charge a price so low that its delivered price at X's mill is less than X's avoidable costs. (We call this strategy *mill price undercutting*.) On a flow basis this strategy will look decidedly unprofitable to firm E, all of whose costs are avoidable *until it actually does enter the market*. Notice next that E cannot anticipate driving X out of the market by sustaining losses over some period of time which are to be more than recouped by profits earned after X's departure. Firm X will recognize that when E is charging the price calculated to drive X out of the market (i.e., a price such that E's delivered price at X's mill is *less than* X's avoidable costs), E is not covering its avoidable costs (much less its total costs), and will therefore anticipate that E must raise its price in the future. In anticipation of this price increase, X will simply remain ready to serve the market when E's price is increased. Thus firm E must anticipate that at any point in time and at any price at which it can cover its costs, firm X will also be in the market. Since the market segment is not large enough to allow two firms to cover their total costs, entry must look unprofitable to E. With Type I capital *inelastic expectations with respect to the flow of future profits are the correct expectations*.

We use the second argument throughout this paper. The argument implies that no firm will entertain the strategy of mill price undercutting as a viable strategy to drive another firm out of the market, because the firm must realize (as long as the other firm's capital is in place) that as soon as the other firm can cover its costs of production it will recommence production. This argument is elaborated at length in Eaton and Lipsey (1976a), Section II.

Argument 3: Firm E must recognize that if it does enter the market, firms E and X will be indistinguishable (except in their locations) since capital is infinitely lived. Thus firm E must anticipate that if a price war ensues and one firm is eventually driven from the market, firm E has at best[6] a probability of 1/2 of being the survivor. If the war between E and X is settled instantly and costlessly on E's entry, firm E stands to gain the present value of X's pure profits, π, if it wins, and to sacrifice the present value of its sunk costs, S if it loses. Thus E's expected profits are $0.5\pi - 0.5S$. For this value to be positive we require $\pi > S$ which means a gross profit, $\pi + S$, of twice the competitive rate of return on capital. Thus equilibria in which existing firms earn up to twice the competitive rate of return on capital are possible without new firms being tempted to enter in the hope of driving existing firms out of business.[7] *The possibility of predatory entry – entry that will be profitable only if an existing firm can be driven from the market – does not restrict the possibilities in this model for free entry equilibrium to be consistent with large positive pure profits for existing firms.*

We find each of these arguments convincing. We rely mainly on the second argument in the remainder of this paper.

Type II capital has a fixed, finite life which cannot be changed by varying maintenance costs. Plants built at time t wear out all at once – like the Deacon's one horse shay – at time $t + d$. Now a new entrant does have a strategy available to it that will allow it to drive an existing firm out of the market.

Consider first the case in which there is only one potential new entrant, E, and firm X does not worry about the threat posed by E. Firm E waits until firm X's plant is just about to wear out and then builds a plant as close to X as is possible. When firm X comes to replace its capital it is in the position of a potential new entrant: there is not room in this slot in the market for X and E to operate with normal profitability; E is in the market with sunk costs and all of X's costs are variable; X has no incentive to build a new plant in order to stay in the market. The new entrant has usurped the market segment and will earn pure profits from then on.

Now assume that there are many potential new entrants who would like to accomplish what E accomplished in the above case. (In fact everyone with capital to invest would like to replace X who is earning pure profits.) Let X have built its present plant at time T_0. Its life is d periods. If a firm E builds a new plant at $T_0 + d - f$ it will earn pure flow profits after a time period of f has passed. There is, however, room for only one firm to replace X and whoever gets in first will become that firm. At this point we invoke the *no-mill-price-undercutting caveat*. Since firm X will serve the market until time $T_0 + d$ as long as it can cover avoidable costs, it follows that the best that E can do is to share the market with X until $T_0 + d$. Thus the sooner does E's entry occur the longer is the period over which X and E coexist and the longer the period over which E will fail to cover its total costs. *Competition among potential new entrants will push entry backward in time to the point at which the discounted present value of E's flow of profits is zero.* (We call this point in time T_1.) Say that E enters at T_1; until $T_0 + d$ both firms are in the market and there is no price at which both can cover their total costs. Firm E's flow profits are depicted by the solid line in Figure 3. Figure 3 is drawn on the assumption that E has the foresight to realize that a new firm E^1 can do to E at $2T_1 - T_0$ what E did to X some d periods earlier.

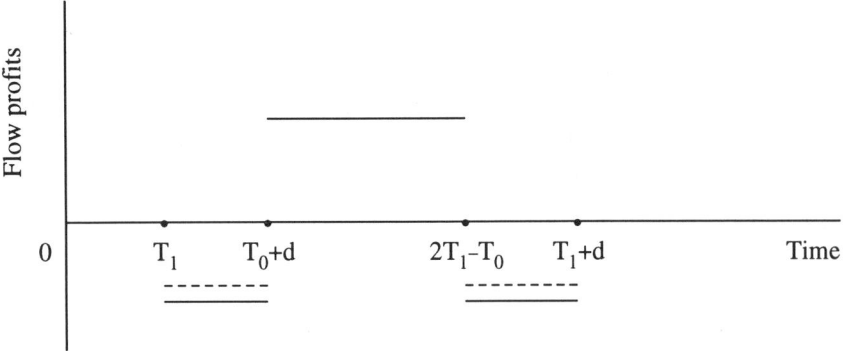

Figure 3. A time series for profits of firm E entering at T_1 in a slot between two firms who are earning pure profits and whose capital wears out at $T_0 + d$

In this case each firm expects a stream of pure profits with a present discounted value of zero evaluated at its time of entry. Capital in the industry alternates between too much (it is earning a current rate less than the competitive rate of return i) and too little (it is earning a current rate of more than i). Current flow profits alternate between positive and negative amounts.[8] This situation is obviously exactly the same as the one facing a Classical spaceless natural monopolist whose plant has a fixed life time. Any new firm that builds a plant just before the original firm's plant wears out will be in possession of the market and it will not pay the original firm to replace its plant. Competition among potential new entrants will push the date of building a new plant backward in time until the discounted value of the flow of profits (negative, then positive, then negative) is zero.

Type III capital has a life time of d years when installed if no maintenance expenditures are incurred, and a maintenance expenditure of M dollars per year will extend the life of the capital by one year. Thus any firm which has spent M dollars per year on maintenance since its capital was installed enters the year with capital which will last d more years.

In this case firm X in the initial pure profits equilibrium will be maintaining its capital and at any moment of time it will have capital that will last d further periods if it ceases to spend further on maintenance.

If a new firm E enters the market along side of X the two firms will be in identical situations in relation to their capital: both firm's capital will last forever if they spend M dollars per year on maintenance and both will last d years if they cease maintenance expenditure. In the previous case of one-horse-shay capital E was able to drive X out of the industry by presenting X with a situation in which E had sunk costs and X did not (when X's capital wore out and E had only recently entered). In the present case E cannot do this to X. If E does enter it is similar in all respects to X (except for its location) and therefore has no more than a 0.5 probability of winning any battle for survival that it joins with X. Firm E will then not find it profitable to attempt to drive X out of the market. This is analogous to argument 3 with Type I capital above.

A variant of argument 1 for Type I capital also has force in this case. Assume that E believes that it *can* drive X from the market. After having driven X out of the market, E must recognize that it is now in the same position as was X before E's entry. Since all firms are identically motivated (assumption 10a) and are able to foresee the potential for entry (assumption 10c), E must recognize that some other new entrant will enter the market attempting to drive E from the market. E will then not perceive the strategy of driving X from the market to be profitable, even if he believes that he will succeed.

In this section we have reached two major conclusions. First, landlords will not be able to appropriate the pure profits which arise in spatial models by converting these profits into land rents. Second, competition between existing firms and new entrants will not always reduce profits to zero. Indeed, only in the case of one-horse-shay capital will entry of new firms reduce profits to zero.[9]

III. The origin of the profits

The analysis of Section III was conducted from an initial situation in which the density of firms and customers was such that existing firms earned pure profits and new entrants expected losses if old firms remained in the market. We now extend the behaviour backwards in time to allow for the circumstances that originally produced the pure profits. To do this we start the model off with existing firms earning zero profits. We then introduce a change in customer density that offers existing firms positive profits. To do this we return to the situation illustrated in Figure 1 and impose the density of customers C_0 which just allow existing firms to earn zero profits. We now let the density of customers increase. The behaviour of the model depends critically on whether or not this change is anticipated.

The situation analysed in Section II arises immediately if there is an *unanticipated* discrete change in density such that $\Delta C < C_1 - C_0$. (Recall that C_1 is the density that just promises zero flow profits to a new firm entering each slot in the market.) If the change is unanticipated the existing firms earn pure profits once it occurs. These profits will persist indefinitely with Type I and Type III capital but will eventually be competed away, in the manner earlier analysed with Type II (one-horse-shay) capital.[10]

It is worth noting that even in the case of Type II capital the pure profits last far longer than they do in the neo-classical spaceless model. In the neo-classical model pure profits due to a rise in demand persist only as long as it takes to establish new capital in the industry – *the length of the long run depends only on the gestation period for new capital*. In the spatial model the time during which the pure profits persist depends on the length of life of existing capital. If this is fifty years, for example, it may be say forty years after the rise in demand before it will pay new firms to enter the industry in expectation of usurping the market when the old capital expires – *the length of the long run is a function of the life time of existing capital*. Since this capital can be very long lived, the short term result of the persistence of pure profits may be of more practical importance than the (very) long run result of the driving of profits to zero due to the entry of new firms some time before old capital has worn out.

If the change ($\Delta C < C_1 - C_0$) were *anticipated* then what happens depends again on the nature of capital. If it is Type I or Type III then there is no way a new firm can drive out an old firm. Entry will not occur and when the change in customer density occurs existing firms will begin to earn pure profits. With Type II capital (one-horse-shay) new firms will enter before the old firm's capital wears out so as to be in possession of the market when the old firm's capital does wear out and thus to usurp the pure profits. Whether this happens before or after the time at which ΔC occurs depends on the length of the remaining life of the existing firm's capital at that point in time.[11]

We now pass to the more difficult cases in which $\Delta C > C_1 - C_0$ so that a round of net new entry will be profitable once the change has occurred. We remind the reader of the restriction that each firm owns only one plant. In what follows we do not specifically analyse the manner in which pure profits are driven to zero with Type II capital. It should, however, be obvious that with the one firm-one plant restriction pure profits in this case will always eventually be driven to zero. Table 1 gives the four cases that we need to analyse.

Table 1. The equilibrium level of pure profits when a round of entry is profitable

Change in Customer Density	Anticipated	Unanticipated
Discrete Change ($\Delta C > C_1 - C_0$)	1. Zero profits due to 'early' entry of new firms.	3. Either the result is indeterminant (the core is empty) or there are pure profits which are a return to superior knowledge.
Continuous Change	2. Zero profits due to 'early' entry of new firms.	4. There are pure profits which are a return to luck.

Case 1: We assume that at T_2 there is a discrete change in density $\Delta C > C_1 - C_0$. To keep the exposition as simple as possible we assume that ΔC is small enough so that only one new firm will enter in each segment of the market. With a full expected discrete change occurring at time T_2 there will be no pure profits. There is room for only one firm in each slot between two existing firms and there will be many potential new entrants (since this use of capital at time T_2 offers a higher return than the competitive return in all other industries in the economy). Competition among new entrants will drive entry back in time to T_1 when the flow of pure profits, negative until T_2 and positive thereafter, has a discounted present value of zero. Again we have alternating periods of too much capital and too little as we had with Type II capital in previous sections.

Case 2: Density is increasing at a constant rate through time. At T_2, T_4, T_6 ... a round of entry would yield a *current* flow of zero pure profits to the new entrants.

Because the growth of the market is anticipated and because the number of possible entrants on each round is small relative to the number of potential entrants, competition among potential entrants will push each round of entry back in time to T_1, T_3, T_5 ... at which the present value of the flows of pure profits of each entering firm is zero.

The general conclusion is that fully *anticipated* changes that would make a round of entry profitable when they occur will not generate pure profits because entry will occur before the change that justifies them. The potential for either overinvestment and negative profits due to overestimation of future changes or underinvestment and positive profits due to underestimation of future changes is as obvious as it may be important in practical applications.

We now pass to the interesting case of unanticipated changes. It is convenient to consider case 4 before case 3 which is more complex.

Case 4: The market is growing at a constant rate that is *unanticipated*. This means that the Hicksian elasticity of expectations is zero: everyone expects that the current level of demand will persist forever. A round of firms now enter the market at time T_2, T_4, T_6 ... On entry they will earn zero profits but they will then earn a rising level of pure profits until a new round of entry occurs. The time series of pure profits of a firm that enters at T_2 will look as in Figure 4.

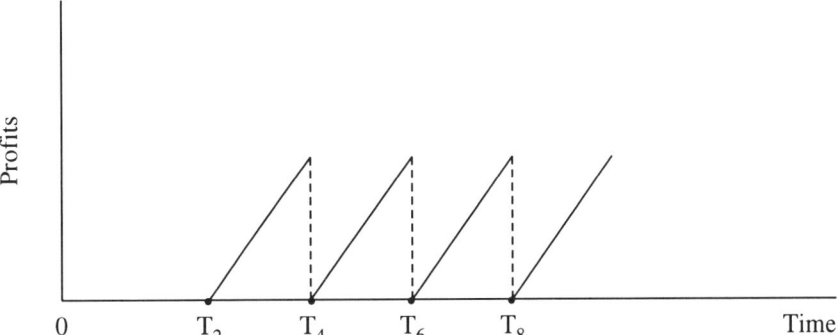

Figure 4. A time series of profits of a firm in a market where customer density is growing at a constant rate while the elasticity of expectations with respect to this density is zero

When firms enter on each round they expect zero profits and are thus indifferent between investing in the Z industry and any other industry in the economy. Subsequently pure profits emerge and these profits are a return to pure luck, to having had the luck to have chosen to invest in this industry rather than the many other apparently equally profitable investment opportunities in the economy.

Case 3: At time T_2 there occurs an *unanticipated*, discrete change in customer density, $\Delta C > C_1 - C_0$, but ΔC is again small enough so that there is room for only one new entrant in each market segment. This is the most complex of the cases and we must analyse it with care.

The initial conditions are that everyone wakes up one morning to find that the step change in density has occurred. Entry promises pure profits but there is room for only one firm in each market slot. To analyse this situation we give the economy a Walrasian auctioneer who will close the bidding when he has a contract that cannot be upset by any other coalition of potential buyers and sellers who are excluded from the proposed bargain.

Consider first the situation as it would look to a single potential new entrant, E_1, who possesses a franchise giving him the exclusive right to enter the now-profitable slot in the market between firms X and Y who are located at $-L$ and L in Figure 5. The pure profit function for E_1 is illustrated in the Figure, and is drawn on the assumption that the price of land is zero so that true pure profits are given by $\pi^{E_1} - A$. The mid-point location is the best, but any other location between a and b offers some pure profits (since $C > C_1$). Once E_1 chooses any location, say zero, all other locations then offer losses since the increase in density is large enough to support only one new firm in each segment. Firm E_1 having located at zero, the profit function for a second potential new entrant would look as does π^{E_2} in Figure 6, and the land in the interval $-L$ and L would be only worth its value in alternative uses, A.

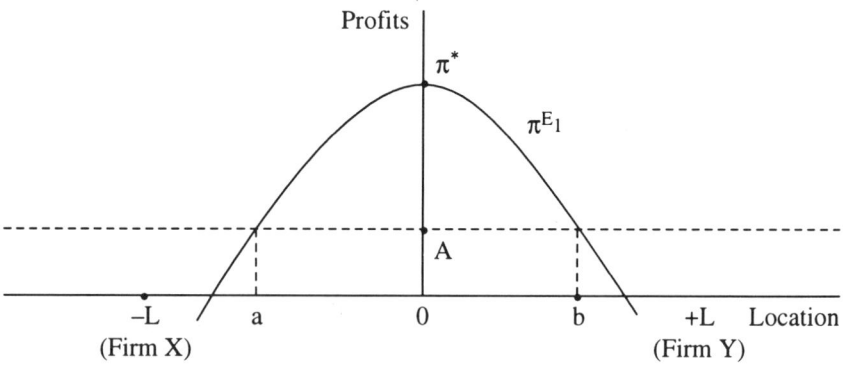

Figure 5. *The expected profit function for a new entrant E_1 considering entry in a slot between firms X and Y when customer density exceeds C_1 (π^{E_1} is drawn for a zero price of land)*

Since there is only one potential buyer (by virtue of his holding the exclusive franchise) and many potential sellers, competition among suppliers of land to be the one successful seller will force the price E_1 pays down to A, and E_1 will locate at 0.

Now consider the opposite extreme in which there is no franchise for entry, and thus there are many potential new entrants who compete against each other to be the new entrant, but where all of the land between a and b is owned by *one* landlord. Now competition among potential new entrants will force the price of any piece of land in location l up $\pi^{E_1}(l)$ (see Figure 5). The landowner can offer any one piece of land at point l and be sure that competition will force the price up to $\pi^{E_1}(l)$. *Since once one piece of land is sold, all the rest will revert in value to A* (there is not room in the slot for 2 firms), self interest dictates that the landlord will offer the most profitable piece of land (that at zero). In this case all of the pure profits will accrue to the one landowner.

On the Foundations of Monopolistic Competition and Economic Geography 81

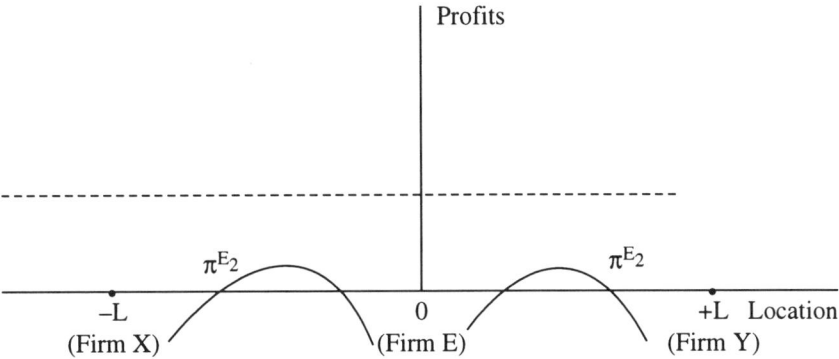

Figure 6. The expected profit function for a new entrant E_2 considering entry into the slot between firms X and Y after E_1 has already entered at the midpoint of this slot (π^{E_2} is drawn for a zero price of land)

Now consider our actual case in which there are many potential new entrants and many landowners in the range between a and b. Any bargain that the auctioneer can suggest between one buyer and one seller of land can be upset by a coalition of at least one other potential new entrant and one other landlord. The core of the economy that displays this bargaining problem is empty.

To establish this we argue as follows. Consider any suggested bargain between *one* landowner and *one* potential new entrant at any mutually acceptable price P in the range $A \leq P \leq \pi^*$, where π^* is the value of pure profits obtainable at 0 [i.e., $\pi^* = \pi^{E_1}(0)$]. Notice, first, that for any P > A, the remaining landlords will be willing to offer their land for less than P and the remaining potential new entrants will be willing to accept those offers of land in the range from a to b that promise pure profits at a price less than P. Notice, second, that for any $P < \pi^*$, unsuccessful new entrants will be willing to offer a higher price for any parcel of land that offers pure profits at a price of P. Unsuccessful landowners will be willing to accept such offers. Next we must consider the two end points of the range of P. Notice, first that at a suggested offer of P = A any unsuccessful new entrant will be willing to offer a bit more than A and any unsuccessful landlord will be willing to accept this price rather than be left out of the bargain and have his land revert to A in value. Notice, second, that at the price $P = \pi^*$ there are no unsuccessful new entrants who are willing to put in a higher bid. All unsuccessful landlords will, however, be willing to offer their land at prices less than π^* but in excess of A. Any unsuccessful new entrant will be willing to accept any of these offers that promises some pure profits at the offered price.

The above argument establishes that the auctioneer can never close the bidding. There is no single trade that he can suggest that cannot be upset by many pairwise coalitions between one unsuccessful, would-be new entrant and one unsuccessful landowner.

If we wish to proceed further we must change our assumptions. We can make either of two changes which have the same effect. First we can assume that some foresight is possible and that before the event different people begin to form expectations about it at different times. In this case the first potential new entrant to form expectations that lead him to enter the market, possibly only shortly before density increases, gains the pure profits which become a return on superior foresight. Second, we can stick to our assumption of zero foresight and then assume that knowledge about the event after it has happened does not diffuse instantaneously. In this case the first potential new entrant who gains sufficient knowledge to cause him to enter the market obtains pure profits as a return on superior knowledge. We would expect one of these results to occur in the real world. Thus, although the indeterminate case can arise in the pure model, we would expect any real world case in which a change was more or less unanticipated to give rise to persistent pure profits.

It is worth noticing that in all of these cases the profits accrue to the firm and not to the land. To establish this we argue as follows. Assume that the landowner at the origin is the first person to learn of the change. To gain the pure profits he would have to become an entrepreneur himself and build the plant. If instead he merely imparted his knowledge to another entrepreneur and then asked of him a rent of π^*, the entrepreneur could obtain other land at a price of A and locate his plant there earning pure profits greater than zero although less than $\pi^* - A$. Furthermore, once the firm is established in its slot in the market it can move to another site (i.e. build a new plant on the new site and then destroy its old plant) and take its profits with it. The land at the old site is then worth only A.

We conclude, therefore, that when the rise in density is not foreseen, existing firms and new entrants earn profits and these profits are not translated into land rents by competitive bidding of new entrants. The analysis of the first part of the paper is then needed to establish whether or not the profits will eventually be competed away by new entrants who seek to displace the firms already in the market.

IV. Comparison with Classical rent theory

Consider first the neo-classical theory of the allocation of different units of a factor among firms in an industry when different units of the 'same' factor contain different numbers of efficiency units. Let different units of labour for example, be of different efficiencies – each contains a different number of efficiency units. There will be a common price for an efficiency unit but different prices for different labourers. Now any one firm will be indifferent as to whether it hires an efficient or an inefficient labourer. This standard theory provides an explanation of how different labourers get priced but it provides no explanation of the allocation of a particular unit of labour to a particular firm.

Notice that if our results for cases 3 and 4 had been that the landlords usurped the pure profits, we could have no theory of the location of the plants in the spatially dispersed industry, Z. If, for example, the new entrant in Figure 5 faced a rent-of-land function that followed the profit function he would be indifferent as to where he placed his plant. *A theory of plant location in our spatial model requires that the firm appropriates at least a proportion of the pure profits, the proportion appropriated being a strictly monotonically increasing function of the full pure profits evaluated when all land is priced at A.*

In our model there is room for only one new firm to enter the slot between firms X and Y. If the new entrant faced prices of land that exactly reflected the differential profitability of each piece of land to that firm there would be no explanation of which piece was allocated to Z production and which pieces to all other uses (at cost A).

The difference between the neo-classical theory of the pricing of different units of non-homogeneous labour and our theory of the pricing of land to industry is as follows. In the neo-classical theory there are many units of labour and many purchasers of these units. The value of a unit of labour to one purchaser is independent of whether or not another unit is purchased by another potential purchaser. In our theory there is room for only one new firm in the slot between a and b. Although each unit of land in this range is different each offers pure profits. Once, however, one unit is purchased and used to establish a plant, all other units offer losses to a second plant producing Z and thus all other units are worth only A. *The value of one unit of land is not independent of the use to which other units are put.*

Now consider the Classical theory of the allocation of land to an industry such as wheat. This theory is originally due to von Thunen. Let all industries in the economy except the wheat industry be indifferent as to their spatial location and have a reserve price of land of A. Let all wheat be sold in a central market place located at the origin in Figure 5 and transported there at a cost of t per unit distance. The reservation price of land for wheat producers will be the tent-like function shown in Figure 5 and all land between a and b will be allocated to wheat production.

In this case landlords do obtain all of the extra profitability of wheat land close to the origin; the actual rent function will follow the tent-like function in Figure 5 and land between a and b will be devoted to wheat production. This theory does explain the allocation of land to the wheat industry but it does not explain the allocation of one piece of land to one wheat farmer. All wheat farmers are indifferent between all pieces of wheat land between a and b.

The difference between this model and our spatial model is in the absence of a central market place. As a result there is room for only one firm between a and b and, once that firm is established, all other land is only worth A. In our model the landlord cannot usurp the rent of location of a single firm locating between a and b in Figure 5 and, if he could, the firm would be indifferent between alternative locations between a and b, as is a single wheat farmer in the Classical model.

V. Conclusions

We do not believe that our model describes the whole economy. We do believe, however, that it describes a significant part of it. Industries such as agriculture require models such as the Classical von Thunen model for their analysis. Spatially concentrated industries such as automobiles and steel can be analysed with the Classical spaceless model. Spatially decentralized industries such as retailing, many resource-based industries, and much light manufacturing require a model such as the one we have presented here. Not only is the theory of location different for each type of industry so also is the theory of value and distribution. Industries of this type can display pure profits in free-entry equilibrium. Their capital will expand or contract in large discrete jumps, and, where they do earn pure profits, these profits will not be converted into land rents. Indeed the analysis of natural monopoly seems more relevant to this type of model than does the neo-classical model of perfect competition since the locations of firms effectively segment the market and entry occurs until each firm's demand curve intersects its LRATC, while potential new entrants find that their potential demand curves lies everywhere inside their potential LRATCs.

Notes

1. The assumption of infinite length is made merely to avoid problems of locating firms at the market boundary. These problems can be handled but at a substantial increase in complexity and no change in the characteristics in which we are here interested. See Eaton and Lipsey (1975).
2. This is designed to keep the economy as competitive as possible. Some of the consequences of dropping this assumption are analysed in Eaton and Lipsey (1976b), and are considered at various points in this paper.
3. Our linear market is unbounded because it is infinitely long. The other commonly-used method of constructing an unbounded one-dimensional model is to let the market be an unbounded line, e.g., the circumference a circle. See Eaton and Lipsey (1975), Eaton (1976), Schmalensee (1977), and Salop (1976) for examples of this type of unbounded one-dimensional model. Analytically the difference between the two types of models are trivial.
4. This result is derived in Eaton and Lipsey (1976a).
5. Of course, if the land between a and b was owned by a single landowner he could extract all of the firm's pure profits by virtue of his monopoly position in the land market. Again this is exactly analogous to the case of a natural monopoly. Any agent which has monopoly control over any necessary productive input will be able to extract all the natural monopolist's pure profits.
6. Firm X occupies a slot in the market between firms W and Y. Firm X is optimally located in the mid-point of the slot firm E hopes to enter and drive X out. Since X is already in the optimal location firm E must accept a second-best location. Thus E is at some competitive disadvantage to X as far as location is concerned. In the text we ignore this added complication.
7. In the Appendix to Lipsey and Eaton (1976a) we prove that if profits of existing firms exceed twice the normal rate of return then it will appear profitable for new firms to enter expecting the old firms to remain in the market. Thus a free entry equilibrium in this model will *never* leave a rate of profit for existing firms high enough to tempt a new entrant to come in hoping to displace an existing firm in a war that it has a probability of less than unity of winning.
8. In the text we have restricted each firm to one plant. If we drop this restriction there is a method by which X can and will protect its position in the market. Firm X could maintain control of the market segment by establishing a second plant just before T_1. If X pursues this strategy in anticipation of entry of another firm at T_1 it can effectively forestall entry of the competing firm. It will be profitable for X to do so because it could, by owning both plants itself, avoid costly price and/or non-price competition over the time interval T_1 to $T_0 + d$, and the flow of profits over this interval would be greater than if a competitive firm owned the new plant – see e.g., the dotted line in Figure 3. This implies that the opportunity to establish a new plant at time T_1 is more valuable to X than to any other firm. In this manner X could maintain control of its market segment, but the pure profits it could earn would be substantially reduced. This argument is elaborated in Eaton and Lipsey (1976b).
9. Even in this case, if existing firms have enough foresight to see the threat of entry, they will be led to forestall entry and maintain control of their market segment, by building a second plant at a point in time at which its discounted present value to a new entrant would be zero. The pure profits they will enjoy in this case will be substantially reduced but will still be positive. But this result requires that we drop the assumption of one-plant firms.
10. Provided existing firms do not forestall entry of new firms in the manner outlined in notes 8 and 9.
11. In this case existing firms again have the incentive to maintain control of the market by establishing new plants before new entrants find it profitable to do so if we allow firms to have more than one plant.

References

EATON, B. Curtis, (1976), 'Free Entry in One-Dimensional Models: Pure Profits and Multiple Equilibria', *Journal of Regional Science*, **16** (1).

EATON, B. Curtis and LIPSEY, Richard G. (1975), 'The Principle of Minimum Differentiation Reconsidered: Some New Developments in the Theory of Spatial Competition', *Review of Economic Studies*, **LXII** (1), January.
EATON, B. Curtis and Lipsey, Richard G. (1976a), 'Freedom of Entry and the Existence of Pure Profit', Queen's University Discussion Paper No. 207.
EATON, B. Curtis and Lipsey, Richard G. (1976b), 'The Theory of Spatial Pre-Emption: Location as a Barrier to Entry', Queen's University Discussion Paper No. 208.
SALOP, S., (1976), 'Monopolistic Competition Reconstructed or Circular Fashions in Economic Thought', mimeographed.
SCHMALENSEE, Richard, (1977), 'Brand Proliferation and Entry Deterrence: The Ready to Eat Cereals Case', mimeographed, Department of Economics, University of California, San Diego.

[5]

A comment on location and industrial efficiency with free entry*

B. Curtis Eaton and Richard G. Lipsey

In the November 1976 issue of the *Quarterly Journal of Economics* J.M.A. Gee uses a computer simulation model to investigate some problems in industrial location and industrial efficiency in a bounded two-dimensional space. His purpose is to set up a model of firm behaviour and to compare the resulting locational patterns with the optimal locational pattern. The results are interesting and suggestive in several important aspects. They are also at variance with the results obtained in our investigation of the same basic problem (Eaton and Lipsey, 1975).

In this note we study Gee's model in one-dimensional space where analytical results can be obtained. We then compare and contrast Gee's results with those obtained by other investigators. This allows us to shed light on the causes that lie behind Gee's results and on the reasons for the divergence of his results from those obtained in other studies.

Gee's two main substantive conclusions are as follows:

1. The introduction of transport costs in a spatially extended model does not appear to cause a general tendency toward 'instability'; instead the firms tend to settle down in a stable locational pattern.
2. The stable locational patterns of firms that results from free entry diverge to a considerable degree from the optimal pattern in two major ways:
    i. there are not enough firms in the market in the sense that substantial pure profits (as much as 3 times the competitive rate of return) persist when entry ceases;
    ii. the firms that are in the market are not in the optimal, transport-cost minimizing, locational configuration.

Gee also argues that these results do not seem to be crucially dependent upon two of his major assumptions: the assumption with respect to pricing behaviour of firms and the assumption that the market is bounded.

In this note we argue the following propositions:

a. Gee's conclusion 1 depends critically on his assumptions. Given other assumptions commonly used in the literature, the Eaton-Lipsey results of instability in

---

* A shortened version of this paper was published in the *Quarterly Journal of Economics*, August 1979

locational patterns in general, and the breakdown of the hexagonal configuration in bounded markets in particular, apply.
b. Gee's conclusion 2(i) is a general result that does not depend on his particular assumptions. Indeed it is a property of most spatial models in which a zero profit condition is not imposed by assumption.
c. His result 2(ii) depends in his own model on the omission of a key long-run equilibrium condition, and when this condition is added the firms that are in the market will be optimally located in long-run equilibrium.
d. This result, that firms in Gee's model will be optimally located when all relevant long-run equilibrium conditions are satisfied depends, in turn, on Gee's pricing assumptions that firms price discriminate among different points in the market. With the more usual assumption of mill-price-plus-transport-cost pricing (called hereafter *mp + t pricing*) the firms in the market will not be optimally distributed even in long-run equilibrium. Since we can think of some real world cases in which Gee's assumption of price discrimination[1] seems applicable and of others in which the more common assumption of mp + t pricing seems applicable, it appears important to establish analytically where and why differences in behaviour occur when one of these pricing assumptions is substituted for the other.
e. On the basis of our analysis we reassert the view, challenged by Gee, that the behaviour of locational models such as Gee's *does* depend critically both on the pricing behaviour of firms and on whether or not the market is bounded.[2]

I. The model

Gee's model is as follows. Single-plant firms sell a homogeneous product to customers located at discrete points which are spread at regular intervals over a bounded, two-dimensional market. Customers buy one unit of the product per period irrespective of price. Firms can locate only at the points at which the customers are located, and there can be no more than one firm at any point. All firms have variable costs that for simplicity are assumed to consist only of the transport costs of delivering their product from mill door to customer's location. Firms have fixed costs that require *net revenues* (the excess of revenues over variable costs) of K per year in order to induce the firm to incur them. Firms are profit maximizers and hence will never sell their product at a delivered price less than its transport cost. Contrary to the assumption commonly made in the literature, firms price discriminate between different geographical points. They do this by selling their product at each point that they do serve at a price that just prevents the next most advantageously sited competitor from capturing that point in the market. These assumptions imply (i) that a firm's market area will be the set of points closer to it than to any other firm and (ii) that the firm's price at any point in its market area is equal to the transport cost between that point and the next closest firm.

Gee's model uses two long-run equilibrium conditions: (i) no firm in the market can be earning net revenues of less than K (no desired exit), and (ii) at all possible locations the expected net revenues of potential new entrants must be less than K (no desired entry).

The dynamics of the model consist of setting the first firm down in the middle of the market and then letting firms enter one at a time at the most profitable point. Once it has entered a firm may not relocate in the market. Entry proceeds until no potential new entrant expects net revenues of K or more. Any existing firm whose net revenues are less than K is then allowed to exit and potential entrants again survey the market for profitable points of entry. Entry and exit cease when both equilibrium conditions are simultaneously fulfilled.

In order to investigate Gee's model analytically we assume that: (1) the market is a one-dimensional line segment; (2) customers are spread continuously and uniformly over the market; and (3) firms can locate anywhere in the market. This gives us the one-dimensional continuous analogue to Gee's two-dimensional market where customers and firms can locate only at discrete points

II. Location of firms

We first consider the best point for the location of a new firm entering the market. We assume for convenience that the length of the market, transport costs, and the density of customers are all unity.[3] Two cases need to be studied: a peripheral and an interior firm. Figure 1 illustrates the case of a peripheral firm. The market stretches from 0 to 1. Firm A wishes to locate at some point a in the peripheral market segment between firm N, located at $\bar{n}$, and the market boundary at 1. The firm's costs of serving a consumer at any point x are $a - x$ to the left of a and $x - a$ to the right. Its price is $x - \bar{n}$ and its market stretches from $(\bar{n} + a)/2$ to 1. Profits are given by

$$\pi = \int_{\frac{\bar{n}+a}{2}}^{a}[(x-\bar{n})-(a-x)]dx + \int_{a}^{1}[(x-\bar{n})-(x-a)]dx - K,$$

$$= -(3a^2)/4 + \bar{n}^2/4 + a\bar{n}/2 + a - \bar{n} - K.$$

Profit maximization requires that

$$\frac{\partial \pi}{\partial a} = \frac{-(3a)}{2} + \frac{\bar{n}}{2} + 1 = 0,$$

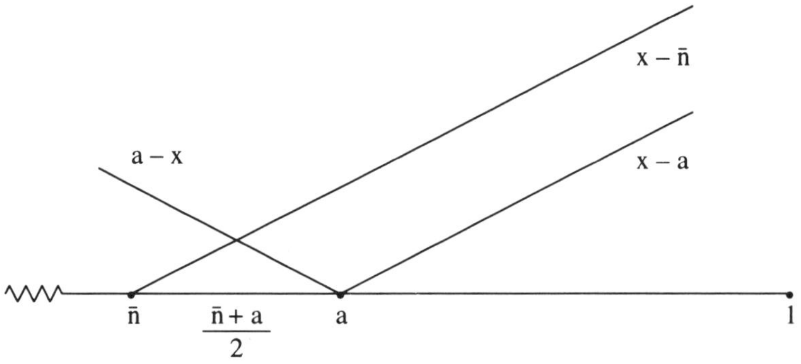

Figure 1

or

$$a^* = (\bar{n}+2)/3,$$

where the star denotes the optimal value. Thus the optimal location of the firm is in the middle of its market segment, one third of the way in from the market boundary towards $\bar{n}$.

Figure 2 illustrates the situation when firm A is choosing a location on an interior market segment between firms M and N located at $\bar{m}$ and $\bar{n}$. Firm A's profit function must be derived separately for $a \leq (\bar{m}+\bar{n})/2$ and for $a \geq (\bar{m}+\bar{n})/2$. The figure shows firm A to the left of this point. For any such location the profit function is

$$\pi = \int_{\frac{a+\bar{m}}{2}}^{a}[(x-\bar{m})-(a-x)]dx + \int_{a}^{\frac{\bar{m}+\bar{n}}{2}}[(x-\bar{m})-(x-a)]dx$$

$$+ \int_{\frac{\bar{m}+\bar{n}}{2}}^{\frac{a+\bar{n}}{2}}[(\bar{n}-x)-(x-a)]dx - K,$$

$$= -a^2/2 + a\bar{n}/2 + a\bar{m}/2 - \frac{\bar{n}\bar{m}}{2} - K.$$

Differentiation with respect to a yields

$$\frac{\partial \pi}{\partial a} = -a + \frac{\bar{m}+\bar{n}}{2} > 0, \quad \text{for } a < \frac{\bar{m}+\bar{n}}{2}.$$

Thus when a is less than $(\bar{m}+\bar{n})/2$ profits increase with a.
The analogous procedure when a is to the right of $(\bar{m}+\bar{n})/2$ yields

$$\frac{\partial \pi}{\partial a} = -a + \frac{\bar{m}+\bar{n}}{2} < 0, \quad \text{for } a > \frac{\bar{m}+\bar{n}}{2}.$$

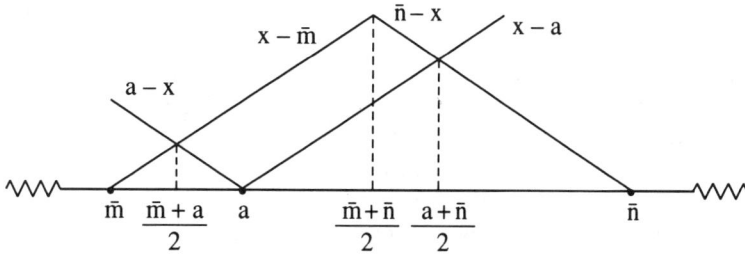

Figure 2

Thus when a exceeds $(\overline{m}+\overline{n})/2$ profits decrease with a.

These results establish that A maximizes its profits by locating at $a^* = (\overline{m}+\overline{n})/2$; that is, A will locate in the middle of its market.

We may now use these results to consider the importance of market boundaries in Gee's model. For comparison we first consider a market that is the entire real line. We space firms equally along the line but in a loose enough packing that each firm is earning pure profits.[4] Entry now proceeds in a series of rounds with one new firm entering at the mid-point between each pair of existing firms on each round. Entry stops when another round promises negative profits for new entrants. The locational pattern of firms will be the transport cost minimizing pattern at all times, since transport cost minimization requires only that firms be in the middle of their market segments (see Eaton and Lipsey, 1975).

We now add boundaries by letting the market be a line segment running from 0 to 1. We follow Gee's procedure by beginning with only one firm located in the centre of the market. The first round of entry will locate two new firms at 1/6 and 5/6. The second round will locate four new firms at 1/18, 1/3, 2/3, and 17/18 as shown in Figure 3. This leaves the firms at 1/3 and 2/3 no longer in the middle of their market areas.

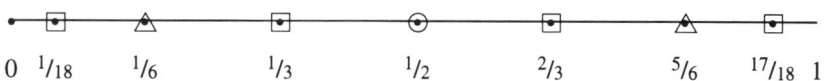

⊙ denotes original firm
△ denotes first round entrant
▣ denotes second round entrant

Figure 3

The general result is as follows: let L and R be the left and right hand peripheral firms after r rounds of entry. Any new round of entry that locates a new firm in the peripheral and/or interior segment of L's market will leave L no longer in the middle of its market. Similarly for R. Transport costs are obviously not minimized and the location pattern is not optimal. This is Gee's result.

Notice, however that any firm that is not in the centre of its market area would wish to move to the center of its market if it had the chance to do so – as it would, for example, if its fixed capital had to be replaced. A long-run equilibrium such as Gee's which allows firms to abandon the market because their profits are less than K should also allow the firm to move to an alternative site if that site provided larger profits. We therefore add a third equilibrium condition to the model: (iii) no existing firm should be able to increase its profits by relocating.[5] In Eaton and Lipsey (1975, model 2) we show in a one-dimensional model that, whether the market is bounded or unbounded, if firms always choose to locate in the middle of their markets, transport costs are minimized in long-run equilibrium. In Gee's model firms do choose to locate in the middle of their markets. Hence the locational pattern of firms in long-run equilibrium when condition (iii) is added to Gee's two conditions on entry and exit is optimal in both a bounded and an unbounded linear market.

Finally let us change the pricing assumption from Gee's price discrimination to the more commonly assumed mp + t pricing. All other assumptions are as stated previously and the third long run equilibrium condition is also employed. Eaton and Lipsey (1975) have established for this model the following results that are relevant to the present study. (1) The optimal locational configuration is one of many possible equilibrium configurations when the market is the real line. (2) The optimal configuration is *not* an equilibrium when the market is a line segment (because the two peripheral firms must be paired with their neighbours). If we change one more of Gee's assumptions and allow for downward sloping rather than perfectly inelastic demand curves we get the result established by Smithies (1941), and further studied by Eaton (1972), that each peripheral firm will want to be closer to its neighbour than the location that would put is at the mid-point of its market, although it may not want to come as close as possible.

We have now established the following results. The non-optimal distribution of firms in equilibrium in Gee's model depends critically on his omission of the equilibrium condition with respect to relocation of existing firms. When this condition is added, the distribution of firms is optimal in Gee's model whether the space is the real line or a line segment. The optimal distribution of firms in Gee's model amended by the addition of the equilibrium condition for relocation depends critically on Gee's pricing assumption which is what makes firms wish to seek out the middle of their market segments. With the more commonly used assumption of mp + t pricing the optimal distribution of firms is possible in an unbounded market but impossible in a bounded market because peripheral firms wish to locate too close to their neighbours – for the reasons originally studied by Hotelling (1929) and further analysed in detail by Eaton and Lipsey (1975).

III. The number of firms in the market

Gee also finds that too few firms enter his market in the sense that entry stops while existing firms are earning substantial pure profits. This result does not depend on any of the specific assumptions made by Gee but rather on the discrete nature of entry into any spatial model. Kaldor (1935), in his debate with Chamberlin, and Beckman (1968), in the context of a specific spatial model, have both noted that new entrants must fit in between existing firms and thus must typically expect markets discretely smaller than those enjoyed by existing firms before new entry occurs. This means (as was shown by Eaton and Lipsey, 1976a) that if firms charge a parametric price, a free-entry equilibrium is possible in which new entrants expect to earn negative profits while existing firms are earning substantial pure profits. Eaton and Lipsey (1976b) establish that these profits can persist even if existing firms engage in some types of price competition (indeed the rate of return on capital can be as much as *twice* the competitive rate of return). Gee's model provides an important extension of this result by showing that it holds for another interesting type of price-selling behaviour.

IV. Stability of locational structure

Gee's model does produce a stable 'equilibrium' of locations in a bounded space. The configuration is stable in the sense that his equilibrium conditions for entry and exit are satisfied. We have already noted, however, that Gee does not use an equilibrium condition for relocation. Thus his experiments throw no light on whether or not his model would provide a stable pattern of firms if the third equilibrium condition were added to it.

More importantly, however, there is already a significant body of literature showing that his result does not generalize to the mp + t pricing assumption. Lerner and Singer (1941) demonstrated the absence of equilibrium in Hotelling's (1929) model when three firms serve a bounded one-dimensional market. Eaton (1972) produces a similar demonstration when individual demand curves are downward sloping and linear. Eaton and Lipsey (1975) transfer Hotelling's model to a bounded two dimensional space (a disc) and cast doubt on the existence of a locational equilibrium for any number of firms greater than two. In particular they demonstrate that the familiar hexagonal pattern of market areas is not an equilibrium configuration in a bounded two dimensional space given mp + t pricing. A. Shaked (1975) has proved the non-existence of equilibrium for three firms in the Eaton-Lipsey model.

V. Conclusion

Price discrimination of the type analysed by Gee leads firms to wish to locate in the centres of their markets. This means that once equilibrium conditions with respect to entry, exit *and* relocation are satisfied the firms in the market will be optimally distributed whether the market is bounded or unbounded. Mp + t pricing gives the same result in unbounded markets. It does not do so, however, in bounded markets because of the incentive for peripheral firms to crowd in too close to their neighbours. This means that any equilibrium configuration of firms that does exist will be non-optimal.

When equilibrium conditions with respect to entry, exit, and relocation are satisfied there will generally be too few firms in a spatial market in the sense that existing firms can be earning significantly more than (up to twice as much as) the competitive rate of return on capital. This result occurs in many spatial models in which zero profits is not imposed by assumption. It has been proved to hold even when existing firms engage in price competition by Eaton and Lipsey (1976b).

Stable distributions of firms in which no firms wish to enter, exit or relocate exist in some models but not in others. In particular there is strong doubt (see Eaton and Lipsey, 1975) that they exist in two-dimensional bounded markets when firms follow mp + t pricing.

Clearly the results derived from many spatial models do vary significantly depending on the pricing behaviour of firms and whether or not the market is bounded.

Notes

1. Gee's model of pricing behaviour is really a multiple basing point pricing system where the location of every firm is a basing point. See Stigler (1949) for some analysis of basing point price systems.
2. There are three basic types of spatial markets (i) unbounded and infinitely extensible, (ii) un-

bounded but of finite size and (iii) bounded. In one and two dimensions these are illustrated by (i) the real line and a Euclidean plane, (ii) the circumference of a circle and the surface of a sphere and (iii) a line segment and a bounded plane. In Eaton and Lipsey (1975) we show that the behaviour of several models depends critically on whether or not the market has boundaries so that behaviour is much the same in spaces (i) and (ii) above, but different in (iii).
3. Gee introduces variables for size of the market, number of customers at each point in space and transport costs per unit of distance but for our purposes all of these can be set to unity.
4. If we set firms down haphazardly and let them readjust their locations until no firm wanted to change location the process would converge to equal spacing since on each move each firm would move to the middle of its market segment.
5. If the firm abandons the market because profits are less than K, this implies that capital is no longer fixed and consideration is being given to replacing it. At such a point in time the alternative possibility of moving to another site if it offers larger profits must also be open to the firm. Gee makes some attempt to deal with this possibility in the experiment that he describes on page 567, but his numerical procedure is clearly not equivalent to the equilibrium condition described in the above text.

Bibliography

Beckman, M. (1968), *Location Theory* (New York: Random House).
Eaton, B. (1972), 'Spatial Competition Revisited', *Canadian Journal of Economics*, 5 (May), 268–77.
Eaton, B.C., and Lipsey, R.G. (1975), 'The Principal of Minimum Differentiation Reconsidered: Some New Developments in the Theory of Spatial Competition', *Review of Economic Studies*, **42** (January), 27–49.
Eaton, B.C. and Lipsey, R.G. (1976a), 'The Non-Uniqueness of Equilibrium in the Loschian Location Model', *American Economic Review*, **66** (March), 77–93.
Eaton, B.C. and Lipsey, R.G. (1976b), 'Freedom of Entry and the Existence of Pure Profit', U.B.C. Department of Economics, Discussion Paper 76–18. (May), and Queen's University Institute for Economic Research, Discussion Paper No. 207 (February).
Gee, J.M.A. (1976), 'A Model of Location and Industrial Efficiency with Free Entry', *Quarterly Journal of Economics* **90** (November) 557–74.
Hotelling, H. (1929), 'Stability in Competition', *Economic Journal* **39** (March), 41–57.
Kaldor, N. (1935), 'Market Imperfection and Excess Capacity', *Economica*, **2**, 33–50.
Lerner, A. and Singer, H. (1941), 'Some Notes on Duopoly and Spatial Competition', *Journal of Political Economy*, **45** (February), 423–39.
Shaked, A. (1975), 'Non Existence of Equilibrium for the 2-Dimensional 3-Firm Location Problem', *The Review of Economic Studies*, (January), **XLII** (129), 51–6.
Smithies, A. (1941), 'Optimum Location in Spatial Competition', *Journal of Political Economy*, **49** (June), 423–39.
Stigler, G. (1949), 'A Theory of Delivered Price Systems', *American Economic Review*, **39** (December).

[6]

The Economic Journal, **88** (*September* 1978), 455–469
Printed in Great Britain

FREEDOM OF ENTRY AND THE EXISTENCE OF PURE PROFIT[1]

The neoclassical model of perfect competition is spaceless, and assumes constant returns to scale. Since real economies are spatially extended and most production technologies display an initial region of increasing returns due to capital indivisibilities,[2] the applicability of the neoclassical model requires that abstracting from space and scale effects does not seriously affect its properties.

It is well known that *either* space[3] *or* "minor" scale effects[4] can be added to the neo-classical model without serious consequences. It is our contention, however, that the *simultaneous* introduction of space and any range of increasing returns significantly alters the properties of the model. Zero profit is no longer a property of free-entry equilibrium. Furthermore, even as the number of firms in the market is increased without limit, the behaviour of the model remains stubbornly oligopolistic.

A survey of the literature shows that zero-profit is imposed as a condition of free-entry equilibrium in the vast majority of spatially extended models.[5] Thus our contention in this paper is in direct opposition to the assumption usually made, either explicitly or implicitly, that the neoclassical zero-profit result survives the introduction of space and some scale effects.

Kaldor (1935, pp. 42–3) gives a classic statement of the non-zero profit result:
Let us now introduce indivisibilities and economies of scale. The movement of new firms into the field will then not continue until the elasticities of demand for the individual producers become infinite; it will be stopped long before that by the increase in costs as the output of producers is reduced. *But there is no reason to assume that it will stop precisely at the point where the demand*

---

[1] The present paper is a revision of Queen's Study Paper No. 207, Eaton and Lipsey (1976b). The work was done while the authors held visiting appointments at the University of Colorado at Boulder during the session 1974–5. We are grateful to the Killam Foundation and the Canada Council for support for Professors Lipsey and Eaton respectively.

[2] See Kaldor (1972, p. 1242) for a theoretical discussion and Johnston (1960) for some empirical evidence.

[3] If space is added to the constant-returns, neo-classical model, its main features are unaffected. The minimisation of transport costs will require, however, that production is spread smoothly over space so that there will be no economic unit recognisable as a firm. For an excellent discussion see Koopmans (1957).

[4] If production non-convexities are introduced into the spaceless neoclassical model, no insuperable difficulties are caused as long as the scale effects are "small" (see, for example, Starr, 1969).

[5] Reactions to other papers of ours that have presumed the non-zero profit characteristic of the model presented in this paper (see, for example, Eaton and Lipsey, 1976a) have convinced us that we are not dealing with a straw man. Examples in which the zero-profits condition is imposed in spatial models include Beckman (1971, 1974), Böventer (1969), Chamberlin (1933), Denike and Parr (1970), M. Greenhut (1952), M. L. Greenhut (1975), Greenhut and Ohta (1975), Losche (1954), Mills and Lav (1964), Ohta (1976), Southey (1974), and Telser (1969). Examples of models in which a zero profit condition is specifically ruled out are Eaton (1976), Tullock (1965), Kaldor (1935), and Zeuthen (1933). Beckman (1968) makes one of the basic points that market areas of new entrants are significantly smaller than those of existing firms, but he does not there go on to consider the consequences for profits while elsewhere he has imposed a zero profit condition. Eaton and Lipsey (1976a) derived the non-zero profit result but assumed a parametric price.

and cost curves are tangential. For, on account of the very reason of economies of scale, the potential producer cannot hope to enter the field profitably with less than a certain magnitude of output; and that additional output may reduce demand, both to his nearest neighbours and to him, to such an extent that the demand curves will lie *below* the cost curves and all will be involved in losses. The interpolation of a third producer in between any two producers may thus transform profits into losses. *The same reason therefore which prevents competition from becoming perfect – i.e. indivisibility – will also prevent the complete elimination of "profits".* It will secure a "monopolistic advantage" to anybody who is first in the field and merely by virtue of priority. The ultimate reason for this is that it is not the original resources themselves, but the various uses to which they are put that are indivisible – you can divide "free capital" but you cannot invest *less* than a certain amount of it in a machine – and consequently the investment of resources cannot be so finely distributed as to equalise the level of marginal productivities.

There are at least three problems with Kaldor's intuitively appealing argument. First, as our survey of the literature reveals, the great majority of writers either reject it, or are unaware of it. Second, the argument is not based on an explicitly formulated model and thus there is no way of dealing with such counter assertions as "once price competition is allowed for pure profit will be driven to zero". Third, Kaldor provides no way to study the potential quantitative significance of his qualitative result. Our work provides an analytical underpinning for Kaldor's argument. It rigorously demonstrates that pure profit will not necessarily be driven to zero by price competition and/or free entry of new firms,[1] it allows the conditions that contribute to the non-zero profit result to be explored; it allows further consequences of these conditions to be deduced; and it permits quantitative estimates of the magnitude of positive profits in equilibrium when specific cases are studied.

I. THE MODEL

We now outline our basic model and in section VII we consider the consequences of relaxing its more restrictive assumptions.

(*a*) The market is a one-dimensional line of infinite length over which customers are spread at a constant density.

(*b*) Average total cost is $ATC = K/Q + c$, where Q is quantity produced, c is a constant marginal cost, and K is the fixed cost associated with a minimum indivisible unit of capital. This cost function is the most convenient way to capture the empirical phenomenon that ATC declines over some initial range. We do not impose a capacity constraint because, as we argue in section VII, it is only the declining portion that is relevant to our argument.

(*c*) Fixed capital is geographically immobile and its value in any other use is less than its replacement cost, i.e. there are sunk costs.

(*d*) No firm owns two adjacent plants. This assumption is used to avoid the

---

[1] For a survey of all our work on the consequences of introducing space and scale effects into the neo-classical model see Eaton and Lipsey (1977).

possibility of monopolistic behaviour on the part of adjacent plants, and thus to ensure that firm behaviour is as competitive as possible. (See Eaton and Lipsey (1976c) for a discussion of the use by multi-plant firms of locational configurations as barriers to entry.)

(e) Transport costs are borne by customers and are t per unit of distance per unit of product.

(f) Each customer patronises the firm with lowest delivered price.

(g) Demand at each point is $q = f(p_d)$, where p_d is delivered price and $f' < 0$. The function f has no price intercept and its elasticity $\to -\infty$ as $p_d \to \infty$. f has either a quantity intercept or is asymptotic to the quantity axis (i.e. customers face a budget constraint).

(h) In selecting price and location all firms, existing firms as well as new entrants, seek to maximise profits subject to the same set of conjectural variations. They also have static expectations with respect to the flow of future profits. We refer to a firm's conjectural variations concerning other firms' price and location decisions as PCV and LCV respectively.

(i) In selecting its location, each firm takes the location of all other firms as given ($ZLCV$). We show in section VII that this assumption is not as restrictive as it might at first appear.

(j) The price any firm expects a neighbouring firm to charge, V, is dependent upon its own price, p, the price currently charged by the neighbouring firm, v, and the distance between the two firms, D:

$$V = g(p, v, D) \quad (0 \leqslant g_1 \leqslant 1,\; g_3 \geqslant 0,\; g_{33} \leqslant 0). \tag{1}$$

The restriction on g_1 assures that V is non-decreasing in p, and that firms do not expect their neighbours to "overreact" to their price changes. The restrictions on g_3 and g_{33} assure respectively that firms expect a neighbour's price not to decrease with distance between the firms, and that the rate of increase is non-increasing with distance. We qualify our PCV by ruling out *mill-price undercutting*: no firm, i, assumes that any other firm, j, will allow i to charge a mill price such that i's delivered price at j's mill door is less than j's mill price. Our reasons for imposing this qualification are explored in section II.

There is a problem with the PCV in (1) because, without further restriction, there is no guarantee that a firm's price expectations will be realised in equilibrium. One way out is to further restrict (1) to ensure that price expectations are fulfilled in equilibrium. We do not consider this problem further but simply note, first, that it arises out of a difficult problem of oligopolistic interdependence, and second, that many specific functions within the general class of (1), including the linear PCV, $V = ap + (1-a)v$ ($0 \leqslant a \leqslant 1$), do have the desired property. The linear case includes the two cases which have received the most attention in the literature: when $a = 1$ each firm assumes that competitors will match any price (denoted $UPCV$) and when $a = 0$ each firm assumes that its competitors will not alter their price (denoted $ZPCV$). If we can prove our non-zero-profit contention for even this linear PCV case we will have dealt with the majority of cases in the literature in which a zero-profit condition has been imposed.

Constant-numbers equilibrium refers to an equilibrium when the number of firms is fixed, and *free-entry equilibrium* refers to an equilibrium when there is freedom of entry and exit. We use the terms *pure profit* and *gross profit* to refer respectively to total revenue minus long run total cost and to total revenue minus variable cost.

There is one condition that is necessary and sufficient for constant-numbers equilibrium: (i) *no firm can find a combination of location and price that offers it a larger anticipated gross profit than that obtained with its present combination of location and price*. Free entry equilibrium requires, in addition to the above: (ii) *all possible combinations of location and price for a potential new entrant offer anticipated gross profit of less than K*; and (iii) *no existing firm earns actual gross profit of less than K*.

II. MILL-PRICE UNDERCUTTING

We now pass to a consideration of the basic question: Is zero profit a condition of equilibrium in this model? One frequently encountered argument for answering this question in the affirmative follows. Assume that any existing firm, A, is making positive pure profit. Any new firm, B, can enter right beside A, undercut A's price ever so slightly, and capture all of A's market. Hence B can expect to have profit virtually as large as A's. If any firm is earning positive pure profit entry will occur, and hence positive pure profit is not consistent with free-entry equilibrium.

Notice, first, that this argument is based on the unqualified *ZPCV*. To see the importance of this assume instead *UPCV*: B assumes that A will match any price that B charges. Now B cannot expect to capture all of A's market and profit. As long as ATC is falling over some range of output and as long as B does not expect to capture all of A's market, there will be a range of positive pure profit for A that will cause B to anticipate negative pure profit if it were to enter alongside A with a *UPCV* assumption.

Many *PCV*s are, of course, quite arbitrary. One firm is trying to foresee another's profit-maximising reactions. Arbitrary rules such as *ZPCV* and *UPCV* are used because these reactions are difficult to foresee. Where, however, the reactions can be foreseen we should allow for them, and we now consider one particular reaction that is easily foreseeable.

Firm B, considering locating anywhere in A's market – whether right next to A or elsewhere – may be uncertain what A's precise reactions will be, but B can be certain of one thing: A will not voluntarily leave the market as long as there exists any price greater than average variable cost (AVC) at which A can sell goods. Thus B can expect A to set its mill price, p^A, in relation to B's mill price, p^B, as follows: $AVC < p^A < p^B + tD$ (where D is the distance between the two firms).

Since B has not actually entered the market, all of its costs are avoidable; A, however, has some fixed costs. Thus $ATC > AVC$ and it follows that there is *no* price that B can choose such that, after A's reaction, both of the following are true: (i) $p^B + tD < p^A$, i.e. A allows itself to be driven from the market; and (ii) $ATC \leq p^B$, i.e. B does not make negative pure profit. *If B has even the most elementary foresight B will never assume that it can drive A out of the market, and also earn non-negative pure profit*. Indeed, if B tries to capture all of A's market by undercutting A's mill price, B can expect A to follow it all the way down to a price ($p = AVC$) at which B's entry looks decidedly unprofitable. This is our reason for ruling out mill price undercutting.

III. LOCATION AND PRICE DECISIONS

The next step in our analysis is to study the price and location decisions of a firm, B, locating between two other firms, A and C. Locate A at $-L$, C at L and let both charge a common price, v.

Let b_C denote B's anticipated market boundary with C – the point at which B expects the two firms to have the same delivered price. Then b_C must satisfy

$$p + t(b_C - x) = g(p, v, L - x) + t(L - b_C), \qquad (2)$$

where x is B's location, and from (1), $g(p, v, L-x)$ is the mill price B expects C to charge. Solving for b_C yields

$$b_C = \frac{1}{2t}[g(p, v, L-x) - p + t(L+x)]. \qquad (3)$$

The delivered price, P_C, that B anticipates at b_C is

$$P_C = \tfrac{1}{2}[p + g(p, v, L-x) + t(L-x)]. \qquad (4)$$

Aggregate expected quantity demanded from firm B from x to b_C is

$$\int_x^{b_C} f[p + t(z-x)]\, dz, \qquad (5)$$

where f is the individual demand function, z is distance measured from the origin, and hence $p + t(z-x)$ is delivered price. Letting $u = p + t(z-x)$, the above expression is easily reduced to

$$\frac{1}{t}\int_p^{P_C} f(u)\, du = \frac{1}{t}[F(P_C) - F(p)], \qquad (6)$$

where F is an indefinite integral of f.

Obtaining the expressions analogous to (3)–(6) for the market segment to the left x allows us to derive firm B's expected demand:

$$Q(x, p) = \frac{1}{t}[F(P_A) + F(P_C) - 2F(p)], \qquad (7)$$

where P_A is the delivered price at its anticipated market boundary with A and is equal to $[p + g(p, v, L+x) + t(L+x)]/2$.

Firm B must choose price and location so as to maximise profit. It can, however, make these decisions sequentially. For any price that B chooses, B will wish to maximise quantity demanded at that price: if it pays B to sell anything at all it will pay B to sell as much as possible since marginal cost is constant. To maximise sales at any price we require as a necessary condition that

$$\frac{\partial Q}{\partial x} = \frac{1}{2t}\{f(P_A)[t + g_3(p, v, L+x)] - f(P_C)[t + g_3(p, v, L-x)]\} = 0. \qquad (8)$$

Notice first that when $x = 0$, $P_A = P_C$ and condition (8) is satisfied.

Then consider

$$\frac{\partial^2 Q}{\partial x^2} = \frac{1}{2t}\{(\tfrac{1}{2})f'(P_A)[t+g_3(p,v,L+x)]^2 + f(P_A)g_{33}(p,v,L+x) \\ + (\tfrac{1}{2})f'(P_C)[t+g_3(p,v,L-x)]^2 + f(P_C)g_{33}(p,v,L-x)\}. \quad (9)$$

The first and third terms in the braces are negative since f' is negative, and the second and fourth are non-positive by the restriction on g_{33} in (1). Then Q is strictly concave with respect to x, and since equation (8) is satisfied when $x = 0$ the global maximum of quantity demanded occurs at $x = 0$, i.e. B will locate at the midpoint of the interval between the two firms.

Letting $x = 0$ in (4) yields the common anticipated delivered price at the two market boundaries, P:

$$P = \tfrac{1}{2}[p + g(p,v,L) + tL]. \quad (10)$$

From (7) B's expected demand curve when it locates at the origin is

$$Q(0,p) = \frac{2}{t}[F(P) - F(p)]. \quad (11)$$

The first-order condition for a maximum of B's gross and pure profits (which differ only by a constant, K) is derived by differentiating $(p-c)Q - K$ with respect to p. The first-order condition is easily reduced first to

$$F(P) - F(p) + (p-c)\left[f(P)\frac{\partial P}{\partial p} - f(p)\right] = 0 \quad (12)$$

and second, using $\partial P/\partial p = (g_1 + 1)/2$ from (10), to

$$\frac{p-c}{F(P) - F(p)}\left[\frac{f(P)(g_1 + 1)}{2} - f(p)\right] = -1. \quad (13)$$

Thus a firm locating between two other firms which charge a common price will maximise its anticipated profits by locating at the midpoint of the interval between the two firms and charging a price which satisfies (13).

IV. POSITIVE PURE PROFIT IN CONSTANT-NUMBERS EQUILIBRIUM

It is often argued that if positive pure profit is being earned, any existing firm will necessarily be tempted to cut its price in an effort to gain a larger share of the profitable market (particularly if it makes a ZPCV assumption). This would imply that positive pure profit is inconsistent with equilibrium.

In the Appendix we prove the existence of an equilibrium in which firms are evenly spaced throughout the market charging a common price, p^*, which is independent of fixed costs, K. Given a value of K, assume that by chance pure profit is zero at price p^*. Now reduce K. This produces positive pure profit but causes no competitive price cutting since it leaves p^* unchanged.

The importance of this demonstration is in showing that price competition between existing firms in the market will not necessarily drive pure profit to zero. Our general PCV includes the special case of ZPCV, which is very conducive to price cutting since any firm feels it can cut its price without *any* retaliation from other firms. Even in this case, an equilibrium p^* exists in which pure profit may be earned but in which each firm is not motivated to cut price.

V. PURE PROFIT IN FREE-ENTRY EQUILIBRIUM

Having shown that price competition among existing firms will not necessarily drive pure profit to zero, even when they adopt *ZPCV*, the remaining question is whether or not *entry* (in addition to the price competition that is an integral part of the model) will do so. To show that it will not we argue as follows.

Let the existing firms be in constant-numbers equilibrium, spaced L units apart charging the common equilibrium price, p^*. Equation (11) in conjunction with (10), yields the demand curve facing an existing firm in constant numbers equilibrium:

$$Q^E = \frac{2}{t}\left\{F\left[\frac{p}{2} + \frac{g(p,p^*,L)}{2} + \frac{tL}{2}\right] - F(p)\right\},$$
$$g(p,p^*,L) + tL > p > g(p,p^*,L) - tL. \quad (14)$$

The constraints on p are required because if p were above the upper limit, quantity demanded would be zero since the firm's neighbours would undersell the firm at every point in the market; while if p were below the lower limit the "no-mill-price undercutting" restriction would be violated.

Now consider entry of a new firm between any two of the existing firms. Since the existing firms are charging a common price, the new entrant would locate at the midpoint between the existing firms which leaves it only $L/2$ units from each of its neighbours. The new entrant's expected demand function, Q^{NE}, will then be

$$Q^{NE} = \frac{2}{t}\left\{F\left[\frac{p}{2} + \frac{g(p,p^*,L/2)}{2} + \frac{tL}{4}\right] - F(p)\right\},$$
$$g(p,p^*,L/2) + tL/2 > p < g(p,p^*,L/2) - tL/2. \quad (15)$$

Comparison of (14) and (15) shows that

$$Q^{NE} < Q^E \text{ since } \tfrac{1}{2}(p + g(p,p^*,L) + tL) > \tfrac{1}{2}(p + g(p,p^*,L/2) + tL/2).$$

It follows from this that if all firms have the same costs it is possible for the expected demand curve for new entrants to lie everywhere below ATC, which is the condition for no new entry, while the demand curves for existing firms lie above ATC at p^*, which is the condition for positive pure profit.[1]

---

[1] The argument in the last paragraph of the text appeals to geometric intuition. A formal proof proceeds by contradiction. (1) Assume a fixed-numbers equilibrium with gross profits of existing firms of $\Pi^E(p^*) > 0$. (2) Assume there exists some p^{**} for which $\Pi^{NE}(p^{**}) \geq \Pi^E(p^*)$. From the text we know that $Q^E(p^{**}) > Q^{NE}(p^{**})$. Given constant marginal costs this implies that $\Pi^E(p^{**}) > \Pi^{NE}(p^{**})$. But by (2) above $\Pi^{NE}(p^{**}) \geq \Pi^E(p^*)$ so that $\Pi^E(p^{**}) > \Pi^E(p^*)$, which contradicts (1) above. Thus we know that when (1) holds we also have $\Pi^{NE}(p^{**}) < \Pi^E(p^*)$ where p^{**} is the price that maximises Π^{NE}. Now choose K such that $\Pi^E(p^*) > K > \Pi^{NE}(p^{**})$ and positive pure profits exist in free-entry equilibrium.

VI. AN EXAMPLE

The qualitative result proved above would be unimportant if the quantitative divergence from the competitive rate of return on capital were insignificant. We can, however, show by example that the divergence from the competitive rate of return may be substantial.

Let the individual demand function be

$$q = e^{-p_d}. \tag{16}$$

Let all firms adopt a *UPCV*. If existing firms are L units apart, aggregate quantity demanded from any firm is, using equation (11),

$$Q = \frac{2}{t}(-e^{-(p+tL/2)} + e^{-p}) = \frac{2e^{-p}}{t}(1 - e^{-tL/2}). \tag{17}$$

Application of the profit-maximising condition in equation (13) yields the profit-maximising price, $p^* = 1 + c$, which is the constant-numbers equilibrium price. Gross profit for existing firms at price p^* is

$$\Pi^{*E} = \frac{2e^{-(1+c)}}{t}(1 - e^{-tL/2}). \tag{18}$$

A new entrant would have neighbours a distance of $L/2$ away and maximum gross profit for the new entrant would be

$$\Pi^{*NE} = \frac{2e^{-(1+c)}}{t}(1 - e^{-tL/4}), \tag{19}$$

since the profit maximising price for the new entrant is also $1+c$.

Entry will not occur if $\Pi^{*NE} < K$, or, substituting for Π^{*NE} (from (14)) in the inequality and rearranging terms, entry will not occur if

$$e^{-tL/4} > 1 - \frac{tKe^{1+c}}{2}. \tag{20}$$

Inspection of (18) reveals that if the market is to be served at all, K must be less than $2e^{-(1+c)}/t$, since with a market of infinite length gross profits are $2e^{-(1+c)}/t$. If this restriction is satisfied, the right side of (20) is positive, and, squaring both sides, entry will not occur if

$$e^{-tL/2} > 1 - tKe^{1+c} + \left(\frac{tKe^{1+c}}{2}\right)^2. \tag{21}$$

Maximum profit for existing firms will occur when the left side of (21) is just greater than the right. Thus the supremum of profit of existing firms will occur when (21) holds with equality. Then substituting the right side of (21) for $e^{-tL/2}$ in (18) we obtain the supremum of Π^{*E}, $\hat{\Pi}^E$.

$$\hat{\Pi}^E = 2\left(K - \frac{tK^2 e^{1+c}}{4}\right). \tag{22}$$

It is convenient to express K as a proportion of $2e^{-(1+c)}/t$, the maximum value of K at which the market will be served.

$$K = 2\delta e^{-(1+c)}/t \quad (0 < \delta \leqslant 1). \tag{23}$$

Combining (22) and (23) we obtain

$$\hat{\Pi}^E = \frac{2e^{-(1+c)}}{t}(2\delta - \delta^2). \tag{24}$$

If we assume for convenience that capital has an infinite life, fixed costs of K would arise from a capital expenditure of K/i, where i is the normal rate of return on capital. Then the rate of return on capital associated with $\hat{\Pi}^E$ is $i\hat{\Pi}^E/K$, which yields,

$$r = i(2-\delta). \tag{25}$$

As δ approaches 1, r approaches i and as δ approaches zero r approaches $2i$. *Thus the rate of return consistent with free entry equilibrium in this model can be as much as twice the normal rate of return on capital.*[1]

It is fairly easy to understand the reason for the limits on r. As $\delta \to 1$, one firm can just cover its costs in a market of infinite length and hence $r \to i$. The maximum value of r is approached as $\delta \to 0$. Letting $\delta \to 0$ means that the density of packing of firms per unit of market length, Δ, $\to \infty$. As $\Delta \to \infty$, the difference between mill price and price at the firm's market boundaries approaches zero. Thus the difference between sales at these two points also approaches zero. As this occurs, the advantage in sales that a new entrant gets from having the customers in its market segment closer to its plant than they were to the plant that served them before entry goes to zero. The only remaining influence on the relation between sales of a potential new entrant and the sales of an existing firm is the *number* of customers served (since virtually the same amount is sold to all customers). Since a new firm always gets one half the number of customers that were served by an existing firm before entry, sales and hence profits of the new firm go to half those earned by existing firms before entry as $\Delta \to \infty$. Thus $r \to 2i$.

VII. SOME RESTRICTIVE ASSUMPTIONS REMOVED

In this section we discuss how several of the restrictive assumptions of our basic model might be relaxed. We conjecture that for a more general class of models than we have considered so far *if a fixed numbers equilibrium exists, zero profit is not a condition of free-entry equilibrium.* We thus do not consider existence of equilibrium in this section, but merely note that the position we are assailing, that zero profit is a condition of equilibrium, has no meaning in any model in which equilibrium does not exist.[2]

Demand Conditions. In order to prove the existence of equilbrium we assume that the individual demand function has no price intercept and that its elasticity

---

[1] Eaton (1976) develops a model based on ZPCV in which the maximum rate of return is 1·7i.
[2] Indeed there is some reason to believe that equilibrium may not exist in some otherwise sensible-looking models of spatial competition in bounded two-dimensional space. See Eaton and Lipsey (1975) and Shaked (1975).

goes to infinity as price goes to infinity. Neither of these assumptions has any real bearing on the question of zero profit. As long as firms are in equilibrium and equally spaced along the linear market with all points in the market being served, the expected sales, and hence profit, of a potential new entrant must be substantially lower than those of existing firms, irrespective of the precise shape of the demand curve.[1]

Locational Conjectural Variation. It is often argued that the positive profit result depends on the *arbitrary assumption* that new entrants base their decisions on the expectation that existing firms will not move. Indeed we have used this assumption so far. In this section we examine conditions under which this expectation is the correct one. Our analysis takes us some way towards developing a theory of appropriate *LCV*'s and thus away from arbitrarily assuming some particular *LCV*. We first study the example of the previous section and then, in an intuitive fashion, explore the problem in a more general context.

The immobility of firms must arise either because there are location-specific fixed costs, or because there are costs of moving fixed capital. We capture both of these sources of immobility by postulating that a proportion, λ, of the firms' fixed costs are "location specific". We then ask when it is appropriate for a new entrant to regard the location of existing firms as fixed.

Let there be a constant-numbers equilibrium in the example of the previous section with all firms located L units apart. Suppose a new entrant thinks of entering at the midpoint of the interval between two firms. If neither of the two existing firms move, the excess of an existing firms' revenue over avoidable costs would be

$$\frac{e^{-(1+c)}}{t}[(1-e^{-tL/2})+(1-e^{-tL/4})] > \frac{3e^{-(1+c)}}{2t}(1-e^{-tL/2}) = G, \qquad (26)$$

since its profit maximising price would still be $1+c$ and its market would extend $L/2$ units in one direction and $L/4$ in the other. To simplify the arithmetic we will assume that the excess of revenues over avoidable costs is G. Without further assumptions we do not know what profits the existing firm would expect if it were to move. For the purpose of argument let us make the strongest assumption: if the existing firm moves, it believes that it will set off an instantaneous process of adjustment which will leave it with a market of the same size as its market before entry. This clearly biases the analysis towards the movement of the existing firm. On this assumption the excess of revenues over avoidable costs will be

$$H = \frac{2e^{-(1+c)}}{t}(1-e^{-tL/2}) - \lambda K. \qquad (27)$$

---

[1] Assuming that elasticity goes to infinity as price goes to infinity is sufficient to avoid such problems as the non-existence of equilibrium if demand is everywhere inelastic. The existence proof is actually easier if the individual demand curve has a price intercept. In this case the aggregated demand curve will also have a price intercept and it is obvious that as p goes to the price intercept, the left-hand side of equation (30) goes to $-\infty$. However, the positive-profit argument is quite tedious if the individual demand function has a price intercept. The difficulty arises because for very high prices (for existing firms and for the new entrant) the two demand curves in (14) and (15) are coincident because price is so high there are unserved gaps in the market.

The existing firm will not move if $G > H$. Using (26) and (27) and substituting for K from (23) the condition that $G > H$ is easily reduced to

$$e^{-tL/2} > 1 - 4\lambda\delta = \theta_1. \qquad (28)$$

It is then quite clear that if λ and/or δ are sufficiently large the existing firm will never move, even if it believes it could regain its whole market by moving. If $\lambda\delta > \frac{1}{4}$ the existing firm will never move regardless of how large L is. Accordingly it would be rational for the new entrant to regard the location of existing firms as fixed. This is sufficient to show that there are circumstances under which a new entrant, rationally calculating the location policies of existing firms, would regard their locations as fixed.

But we can say more. Combining (21) and (23) we can rewrite the conditions under which entry is not profitable if new entrants adopt a ZLCV:

$$e^{-tL/2} > 1 - 2\delta + \delta^2 = \theta_2. \qquad (29)$$

Imagine a market in which L is very large, large enough so that neither inequality (28) nor (29) holds and hence entry occurs reducing L. (For (28) not to hold $\lambda\delta < \frac{1}{4}$ is necessary.) If $\theta_1 < \theta_2$, then as we decrease L (28) will bind before (29) does, and L will eventually become small enough so that (28) holds while (29) does not – existing firms will not move but entry on a ZLCV will still be profitable. In this case the analysis of the previous section, based on ZLCV, tells us all there is to know about equilibrium in the model. When $\theta_1 > \theta_2$, L will eventually become small enough so that (29) holds while (28) does not – ZLCV is then not always appropriate, given that any existing firm believes that it can recapture its whole market by moving. In this case entry will continue until the rate of return in the market is just i, or until L is small enough so that (28) holds and existing firms will no longer move. The second possibility will occur if $\lambda > \frac{1}{4}$, and the supremum of Π^{*E} will occur when (28) holds with equality, which yields a maximum rate of return of $4\lambda i$. In this case ZLCV is not initially appropriate but entry proceeds until it becomes appropriate.

The range of possibilities is outlined in Fig. 1. For any combination of λ and δ above the line $\theta_1 = \theta_2$, ZLCV is always appropriate and the maximum rate of return is $i(2-\delta)$. In the triangular region bounded by the vertical axis, and the lines $\theta_1 = \theta_2$ and $\lambda = \frac{1}{4}$, ZLCV eventually becomes appropriate but the possibility of pure profit persists, $r = 4\lambda i$. For $\lambda < \frac{1}{4}$, ZLCV is inappropriate and $r = i$. Recall that this argument is based on inequality (26); it should be noted that the argument significantly understates the conditions under which ZLCV is appropriate. ZLCV is in fact always appropriate for combinations of λ and δ above the line, $\lambda = (1-\delta)/2$.

It is fairly easy to understand at least some of the forces contributing to these results. Let us ignore the elasticity of the individual demand function and assume that all firms charge the same price. Then, when faced with a new entrant in the middle of one of its market segments an existing firm will not move if

$$3\Pi(L)/4 > \Pi(L) - \lambda K,$$

or if $\Pi(L) < 4\lambda K$, where $\Pi(L)$ is gross profit which declines with L. There will be no entry on ZLCV if $\Pi(L)/2 < K$, or if $\Pi(L) < 2K$. As L decreases existing firms will not move while entry on a ZLCV is still profitable if $4\lambda K > 2K$, or if $\lambda > \frac{1}{2}$. Thus when we ignore elasticity of demand, ZLCV is always appropriate when $\lambda > \frac{1}{2}$ and questionable when $\lambda < \frac{1}{2}$. Even when $\lambda < \frac{1}{2}$, the possibility of pure profits in free entry equilibrium exists – zero profits will characterise equilibrium only if $\Pi(L) > 4\lambda K$ (existing firms are still willing to move) when L is small enough so that $\Pi(L) - K = 0$. This implies that ZLCV is inappropriate and that zero profits will characterise equilibrium only if $\lambda < \frac{1}{4}$.

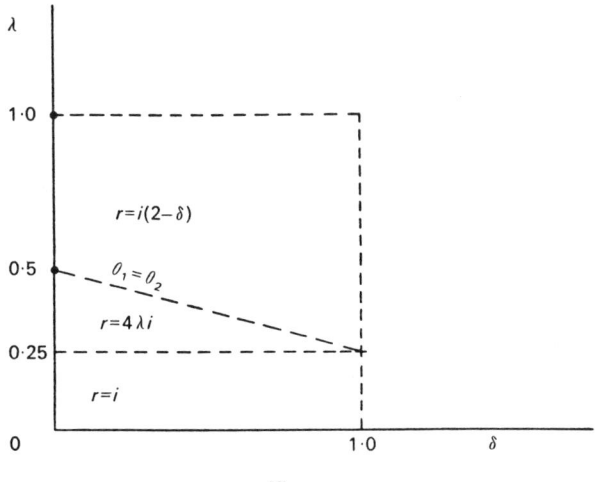

Fig. 1.

Cost Conditions. The key result in our model is that the expected demand curve of a new entrant lies strictly, and in most cases very far, to the left of the demand curve of an existing firm. This will bring entry to a halt before profits of existing firms are reduced to zero as long as average total costs are initially declining. To see why ATC only needs to decline initially we alter our cost assumption to make ATC constant or rising beyond an arbitrary positive output $\bar{Q}$. As long as the potential demand curve of a new entrant, Q^{NE}, lies somewhere above ATC, entry will continue. This is necessarily the case if Q^{NE} intersects ATC in the latter's flat or rising portion. As entry proceeds, however, Q^{NE} must finally be pushed everywhere to the left of ATC. At this point entry stops even though Q^E, the demand curve for an existing firm, lies above ATC (because Q^E lies substantially to the right of Q^{NE}). Entry thus proceeds until a situation akin to the classical natural monopoly is created in each segment of the market. In each segment one firm faces a demand curve that lies above ATC over part of its range, while a second firm considering entry into that market faces an expected demand curve that lies everywhere below its potential ATC curve. Thus it is obvious that the introduction of a capacity constraint into our cost function would change nothing.

VIII. SUMMARY AND CONCLUSIONS

We have demonstrated that zero pure profit is not a necessary condition of free-entry equilibrium in a model in which the market is spatially extended and long-run cost curves decline over some initial range. We have shown that neither price competition among existing firms nor the entry of new firms will necessarily drive profits to zero. This is true even when firms assume that they can cut their own price without reaction from their competitors, and when new entrants rationally calculate whether or not their entry will force existing firms to relocate. We have further shown, in a specific example, that rates of return on capital of up to *twice* the competitive rate are possible in free-entry equilibrium.

It is interesting to speculate on the proportion of the economy to which the positive-pure-profit result may apply. Some intuitive feel for the range of applicability may be developed by considering the conditions that are critical for the result: (i) the average total cost curve is declining over some initial range; (ii) customers are geographically spread out, and are intermingled with firms; (iii) transport is costly;[1] and (iv) once the firm enters the market it has location-specific sunk costs.

We believe that condition (i) captures a phenomenon that is nearly ubiquitous. Condition (ii) describes a large number of markets, but not those in which all producers are concentrated in a single geographical location, nor those in which geographically dispersed producers sell in a single centralised market. Conditions (iii) and (iv) would seem to be almost universally true.

The model of this paper is formulated in terms of geographical differentiation among firms. There would seem, however, to be significant applications to product differentiation, where firms sell products with different locations in characteristics space, and a new product fitting in between two established ones must expect a market significantly smaller than those obtained by "neighbouring" products before entry. For a discussion of some of the issues involved in handling monopolistic competition in characteristic space see Archibald and Rosenbluth (1975) and for a practical application that uses some of the properties developed in our model see Schmalensee (1977).

It would thus appear that the positive-profit result applies to a significant range of spatially dispersed activities in both the manufacturing and the retailing sectors of the economy, as well as to some cases of product differentiation. Evidently the neoclassical proposition that profits tend to zero under conditions of

---

[1] Demsetz (1971) argues that quantity demanded will not be a declining function of delivered prices because the rent gradient for residential sites will adjust so as to make all consumers have the same real income and, since there is only one good on which to spend this income, demand will be the same everywhere in the market, and will vary only with mill price. Demsetz's discussion assumes only one argument in household's utility functions; but if land enters the utility function as well the rent gradient will ensure equal real incomes and hence no income effects throughout the market. But there will be a substitution effect: households close to their nearest firm will face higher rents and a lower delivered price than will households more distant from their nearest firm. The substitution effect will then guarantee that firms face a downward-sloping demand curve in terms of delivered price. Even if Demsetz's argument were correct it would not upset our conclusion since if customer demand is insensitive to delivered price a new firm entering a segment of the market would not only expect to get exactly half the number of customers, it would also expect exactly half the sales enjoyed by existing firms before its entry.

free-entry requires serious amendment when account is taken of the geographical intermingling of producers and consumers and of capital indivisibilities.

University of British Columbia
Queen's University, Canada
Date of receipt of final typescript: November 1977

B. CURTIS EATON
RICHARD G. LIPSEY

APPENDIX

The existence of constant numbers equilibrium

Place firms A, B, and C at $-L$, 0, and L respectively. We must prove that there exists a common price, v^*, charged by A and C that leads B to charge the same price. Let $v = p$ in (10) to obtain $P = [p + g(p, p, L) + tL]/2$. With P so defined we show that (13) can always be satisfied for some positive finite value of p.

Since $0 \leqslant g_1 \leqslant 1$ the term in brackets in (13) is always negative and as $p \to 0$ the first term in (13) is also negative. Hence the left side of (13) goes to some positive limit as $p \to 0$.

To see what happens to the left side as $p \to \infty$ rewrite (13) as

$$(p-c)\left[\frac{f(P)-f(p)}{F(P)-F(p)}\right] + (p-c)\left[\frac{f(P)(g_1-1)/2}{F(P)-F(p)}\right] = -1. \qquad (30)$$

As $p \to \infty$ the second term on the left in (30) will either decrease without bound or will approach some non-positive limit. Using the Cauchy mean value theorem write the first term on the left in (30) as

$$(p-c)\left[\frac{f(P)-f(p)}{F(P)-F(p)}\right] = (p-c)\frac{f'(\hat{p})}{f(\hat{p})} \quad (p < \hat{p} < P). \qquad (31)$$

Then consider

$$\lim_{p \to \infty} \frac{(p-c)f'(\hat{p})/f(\hat{p})}{\hat{p}f'(\hat{p})/f(\hat{p})} = \lim_{p \to \infty} \left(\frac{p}{\hat{p}} - \frac{c}{\hat{p}}\right) = 1. \qquad (32)$$

So the limits on the top and bottom on the left in (32) are identical, but by assumption (g) the limit in the bottom is $-\infty$ since the bottom is the elasticity of the individual demand function. We have then established that as $p \to \infty$, the numerator in (32), the left side of (31) and the left side of (30) go to $-\infty$. Then since the left side of (13) is continuous, and since it approaches a positive limit as $p \to 0$, and $-\infty$ as $p \to \infty$ there exists at least one positive finite p which satisfies (13), call it p^*. Now let all firms be placed L units apart charging price p^*. No firm will wish to move and no firm will wish to change its price. Thus the constant-numbers equilibrium condition is satisfied.

REFERENCES

Archibald, G. C. and Rosenbluth, G. (1975). "The "New" Theory of Consumer Demand and Monopolistic Competition." *Quarterly Journal of Economics*, vol. 89, no. 4, pp. 569–90.

Beckmann, M. (1968). *Location Theory*. New York: Random House.

—— (1971). "Equilibrium Versus Optimum: Spacing of Firms and Patterns of Market Areas." *Northeast Regional Science Review*, vol. 1, no. 1, pp. 1–20.

—— (1974). "A Theorem on Perfect Competition in Spatial Markets." *Regional Science Association Papers and Proceedings*, vol. 33, pp. 3–12.
Böventer, E. von (1969). "Walter Christaller's Central Places and Peripheral Areas: The Central Place Theory in Retrospect." *The Journal of Regional Science*, vol. 9, no. 1, pp. 117–24.
Chamberlin, J. (1933). *The Theory of Monopolistic Competition*. Cambridge: Harvard University Press.
Denike, K. G. and Parr, J. B. (1970). "Production in Space, Spatial Competition, and Restricted Entry." *Journal of Regional Science*, vol. 10, no. 1, pp. 49–63.
Demsetz, H. (1971). "On the Regulation of Industry: A Reply." *Journal of Political Economy*, vol. 79, pp. 356–63.
Eaton, B. C. (1976). "Free Entry in One-Dimensional Models: Pure Profits and Multiple Equilibria." *Journal of Regional Science*, vol. 16, no. 1, pp. 21–33.
—— and Lipsey, R. G. (1975). "The Principle of Minimum Differentiation Reconsidered: Some New Developments in the Theory of Spatial Competition." *Review of Economic Studies*, vol. 42 (1), no. 129, pp. 27–49.
—— (1976a). "The Non-Uniqueness of Equilibrium in the Löschian Location Model." *American Economic Review*, vol. 56.
—— (1976b). "Freedom of Entry and the Existence of Pure Profits." Queen's University Discussion Paper, no. 207. Kingston, Ontario.
—— (1976c). "The Theory of Spatial Pre-Emption: Location as a Barrier to Entry." Queens' University Discussion Paper, no. 208. Kingston, Ontario.
—— (1977). "The Introduction of Space into the Neo-Classical Model of Value Theory." In *Studies in Modern Economics* (ed. M. J. Artis and A. R. Nobay), pp. 59–96. Oxford: Basic Blackwell. (Also printed as Queen's University Discussion Paper, no. 239. Kingston, Ontario.)
Greenhut, M. (1952). "The Size and Shape of the Market Area of a Firm." *Southern Economic Journal*, vol. 17, no. 4, pp. 526–38.
Greenhut, M. L. (1975). "A Theoretical Mapping from Perfect Competition to Imperfect Competition." *Southern Economic Journal*, vol. 42, no. 2, pp. 177–92.
—— and Ohta, H. (1975). *The Theory of Spatial Pricing and Market Areas*. North Carolina: Duke University Press.
Johnston, J. (1960). *Statistical Cost Analysis*. New York: McGraw-Hill.
Kaldor, N. (1935). "Market Imperfections and Excess Capacity." *Economica*, vol. 2, pp. 35–50.
—— (1972). "The Irrelevance of Equilibrium Economics." ECONOMIC JOURNAL, vol. 82, no. 328, pp. 1237–55.
Koopmans, T. C. (1957). *Three Essays on the State of Economic Science*. Essay No. 1. New York: McGraw-Hill.
Lösch, A. (1954). *The Economics of Location*. New Haven: Yale University Press.
Mills, E., and Lav, M. (1964). "A Model of Market Areas with Free Entry." *Journal of Political Economy*, vol. 72, no. 3, pp. 278–88.
Ohta, H. (1976). "On Efficiency of Production Under Conditions of Imperfect Competition." *Southern Economic Journal*, vol. 43, no. 2, pp. 1124–35.
Shaked, A. (1975). "Non Existence of Equilibrium for the 2-Dimensional 3-Firm Location Problem." *The Review of Economic Studies*, vol. 42, no. 129, pp. 51–6.
Schmalensee, R. (1977). "Entry Deterrence in the RTE Cereal Industry" Working Paper 961–77, Alfred P. Sloan, School of Management MIT, Cambridge, Mass.
Southey, C. (1974). "Spatial Rents, Spatial Competition and Efficiency." *Canadian Journal of Economics*, vol. 52, no. 2, pp. 260–72.
Starr, R. (1969). "Quasi-Equilibrium in Markets with Non-Convex Preferences." *Econometrica*, vol. 37, pp. 25–38.
Telser, L. (1969). "On the Regulation of Industry: A Note." *Journal of Political Economy*, vol. 77, pp. 937–52.
Tullock, G. (1965). "Optimality with Monopolistic Competition." *Western Economic Journal*, vol. 4, pp. 41–8.
Zeuthen, F. (1933). "Theoretical Remarks on Price Policy: Hotelling's Case with Variations." *Quarterly Journal of Economics*, vol. 49, pp. 231–53.

The Theory of Market Pre-emption: The Persistence of Excess Capacity and Monopoly in Growing Spatial Markets

By B. Curtis Eaton and Richard G. Lipsey

University of British Columbia and Queen's University

There is a substantial literature on the use of excess capacity as a means of preventing entry into monopolistic or oligopolistic markets. Some of the interest in this issue stems from the famous anti-trust judgment against the Aluminum Company of America (Alcoa) written by Judge Learned Hand:

> It was not inevitable that it [Alcoa] should always anticipate increases in demand for ingot and be prepared to supply them. Nothing compelled it to keep doubling and redoubling its capacity before others entered the field. It insists that it never excluded competitors, but we can think of no more effective exclusion than progressively to embrace each new opportunity as it opened, and to face each new comer with new capacity already geared into a giant organization....[1]

Much of the subsequent debate among economists on the issue of excess capacity as a possible barrier to entry was in a static framework, and virtually all of it has been in the standard spaceless context.[2]

In the present paper we consider a spatial market in which demand is increasing. We demonstrate that, if the growth of the market is foreseen, it will *always* pay existing firms to pre-empt the market by establishing new plants before the time when it would first pay new firms to enter. In such markets, monopolies or oligopolies will persist; plants will be built well before their outputs are required and even when current receipts and costs yield losses. Such markets will exhibit the excess capacity that many investigators have thought they discerned;[3] and this excess capacity will occur as a result of the early building of new capacity to which Judge Hand referred.

We also show that, if the existing monopoly firm will not pre-empt—or is prevented from pre-empting—the market by building capacity before it is needed, competition among potential new entrants will lead to the establishment of the unneeded capacity at virtually the same time that it would have been established by the profit-maximizing monopolist.

I. A Model of Market Pre-emption

We begin by specifying assumptions with respect to the nature of the market, the cost conditions of firms and the behaviour of firms and customers. Next we construct a set of *initial* conditions which guarantee that an *existing* firm with one plant is in a position of natural monopoly. We then allow the number of customers to increase at some future date, and demonstrate two propositions:

(a) if the existing monopolist does not establish new capacity to meet the increased demand, competition among potential new entrants will lead to the establishment of new capacity some time *before* the date at which demand increases; and

(b) the existing monopolist will always find it profitable to pre-empt the market by establishing new capacity at a time just earlier than the earliest date at which any potential new entrant would find it profitable to do so.

The first proposition, which we call *pre-emption by new entrants*, ensures that there will be temporal excess capacity in this market—capacity that is installed before it is needed. The second proposition, which we call *monopoly pre-emption*, ensures that, unless the monopoly firm either misjudges the situation or is in some way restrained, it will always maintain its monopoly even though the market grows large enough to sustain many plants. In this section we confine ourselves to cases in which there are only a few firms in the market. In Section II we investigate behaviour when the number of firms in the market is large.

(a) *Assumptions*

We consider a one-dimensional market, two units in length, with a uniform density of customers, D. Each customer has the same downward-sloping demand curve, $q = f(w)$, where w is delivered price, the firm's mill price plus transport costs. Transport costs per unit of product, $t(Z)$, are an increasing function of distance, Z, from firm to customer. Each customer buys from the plant with the lowest delivered price.

All firms have the same cost curves. Their production exhibits increasing returns to scale over a limited range of output at the plant level owing to capital indivisibilities; and, hence, average total costs of production (ATC) decline over some initial range of output. Once the firm's capital is installed it has no opportunity cost and is immobile. (All that we require is that firms have some sunk costs but it is convenient to assume that all capital costs are sunk.)

Firms maximize profits and we assume that *firms are capable of accurately calculating the flows of costs and revenues that will be associated with any plant*; that is, we adopt the assumption of perfect foresight with respect to the flow of profits. (In Section (e) below we examine in some detail the role that this assumption plays in our model.)

We assume that no firm entertains the strategy of *mill-price undercutting*. That is, no firm will charge a mill price low enough so that its delivered price at a competitor's mill door is lower than the competitor's mill price. Elsewhere we have outlined in detail our reasons for adopting this assumption.[4]

(b) *Initial conditions*

Initially let firm A serve the entire market with a plant located in the centre of the market at a_1 in Figure 1. The aggregated demand curve faced by the plant will be

$$Q = 2D \int_0^1 f\{p_A + t(Z)\} \, dZ$$

where p_A is A's mill price. Since the market is symmetrical about the plant and the density of customers is D, we integrate from 0 to 1 and multiply by $2D$. There will be some density, $D = D_0$, such that the aggregated demand curve is just tangent to the ATC curve in the declining portion of that curve.

Now consider the situation that would face a plant owned by another firm, B, and located at an arbitrary point b_1 in the market segment from -1 to a_1 in Figure 1. The *no-mill-price-undercutting* assumption implies that B's market would be

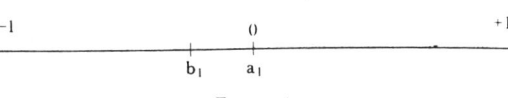

FIGURE 1

confined to some part of the interval from -1 to a_1. Thus the number of customers in B's market would be less than half the number of customers that would be in A's market in the absence of B's plant at b_1. From this it follows that the density of customers, D_2, that would allow the plant at b_1 just to cover its costs must be greater than D_0, the density that allows the single plant serving the whole market from its location at a_1 to cover its costs.

We adopt as an *initial condition* a density of customers, D_1, such that $D_0 < D_1 < D_2$, and we let firm A serve the market with a plant located at a_1. Firm A is thus earning pure profits, but given the initial density of customers, D_1, entry of other firms will not occur. We have thus specified our initial conditions so that firm A is in a position of profitable natural monopoly.

(c) *Market pre-emption*

We now consider entry when the market grows. We use comparative static analysis of a market that undergoes a single, once-for-all increase in density. It would of course be possible to consider a market that was growing continuously. While this would make it necessary to use more complicated analytical techniques than the ones we do employ, it seems to us that it would add very little to the results in which we are interested.

We assume that at some time in the future, T_2, density will increase discretely to $D_3 > D_2$. This increase in density is foreseen and, since $D_3 > D_2$, the increase is sufficient to ensure that a new firm (or firms), if given the opportunity at time T_2, would enter each of the intervals $(-1:0)$ and $(0:1)$ in Figure 1. For simplicity, we further assume that D_3 is not large enough to permit *two* new plants to be profitably operated in each of these intervals.

We ask, first: when will the two new plants be established *if firm A does nothing to pre-empt the market?* By hypothesis the new density, D_3, which occurs at T_2 is great enough so that one new plant in each interval could earn revenues in excess of costs after T_2, but neither plant could cover costs prior to T_2. Since the increase in density is foreseen, competition among potential new entrants will ensure that the opportunity to establish these plants at T_2 will not present itself. There exists some time $T_1 < T_2$ such that the present value of each of the two new plants will be zero. If at time T_1 the two new plants were established at their individual, profit-maximizing locations (say b_1 and b_2 in Figure 2), each plant would earn only a normal rate of return because the present value of profits earned after T_2 would be just offset by the losses incurred from T_1 to T_2. The existence of many would-be entrants will push the actual date of entry back in time to T_1.

This establishes the proposition concerning pre-emption by new entrants: if firm A does nothing to block entry, then some new entrant will pre-empt the

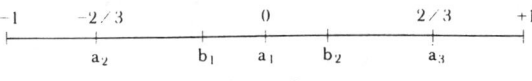

FIGURE 2

market by establishing plants at time T_1 in anticipation of the growth in density at T_2. Intertemporal excess capacity then arises in the sense that new capital is established in the market before the increase in density that justifies its existence.

The interval of time, $T_2 - T_1$, over which excess capacity exists is a function of the flow of profits that a new entrant into each half of the market could earn after T_2. This depends on customer density, which determines demand, and on costs. If ATC is declining or constant over the relevant range, then profits, and hence the size of $T_2 - T_1$, approach an upper limit as D_3 approaches D_4, where D_4 is the customer density that would allow two new plants in each of the intervals $(-1:0)$ and $(0:1)$ to cover costs.

It is useful for future arguments to define two terms:

(i) R_1 is the discounted present value at T_1 of A's plant at a_1 when new entrants establish two new plants at b_1 and b_2 at T_1.

(ii) R_2 is the discounted present value at T_1 of all three plants when A owns the plant at a_1 and new entrants establish two new plants at b_1 and b_2 at T_1.

We have of course chosen T_1 such that $R_2 = R_1$.

We ask, second: what will happen if firm A considers pre-empting the market for itself? It could, of course, effectively prevent the entry of any new firm by establishing a plant of its own in each of the intervals $(-1:0)$ and $(0:1)$ prior to time T_1. If A did this, there would be no entry of new firms at T_1. Is it in firm A's own interest to block entry in this manner, assuming that A foresees the potential for entry at T_1? Consider the consequences if A were to replicate the configuration of locations and prices that would be brought about by other firms entering the market. Just before T_1 let A establish plants at b_1 and b_2 and let A charge the prices that would emerge if new entrants owned the plants at b_1 and b_2. If there were no possibility of entry, the sales and profits that A's new plants at b_1 and b_2 take away from the old plant at a_1 could not be regarded as net additions to firm A's sales and profits. But if A does not pre-empt, new firms will enter at T_1, and firm A's stream of profits and sales from its plant at a_1 will fall abruptly at T_1. *Thus all of the sales and profits of A's new plants at* b_1 *and* b_2 *represent net additions to the stream of sales and profits that A could expect if it did not build these plants.* Since the plants add the same amount to A's profits as they would to those of a new entrant, the plants have the same value to A as to new entrants.

But A will not replicate the configuration of locations and prices that would be brought about by other firms entering the market. In the first place A will choose different locations for the new plants than would new entrants. Firm A will locate the new plants at $-2/3$ and $2/3$, points a_2 and a_3 in Figure 2, so that each plant will serve one-third of the market. This puts the three plants in their joint profit-maximizing locations. New entrants would not, however, adopt these locations; rather, they would locate plants nearer to a_1. The force that leads new entrants to locate nearer to a_1 than $-2/3$ and $2/3$ is the one analysed by Hotelling (1929) and Smithies (1941): the new entrants have no competitors to worry about on their outside flanks and they can gain customers by crowding in towards their competitor at a_1. In addition, firm A can charge the joint profit-maximizing price when it owns all three plants. Normally when there is more than one firm in the market we would expect price competition to result in prices for each plant that differed from the joint profit-maximizing prices.

We now need one further definition:

(iii) R_3 is the discounted present value at T_1 of the three plants when firm A chooses the joint profit-maximizing locations and prices.

Monopolistic pre-emption is now easily proven. The value to A of establishing two new plants in the market at T_1 is $R^A = R_3 - R_1$. The value to new entrants of the two plants (located at b_1 and b_2) is $R^B = R_2 - R_1 = 0$. Since $R_3 > R_2$ (for the two reasons stated above) it follows that $R^A > 0$. It will thus pay firm A to establish new plants just prior to T_1. This proves the monopoly pre-emption result. The value to A of monopoly pre-emption depends on the difference between the profitability of the market when three plants are owned by A and two of the plants are owned by new entrants.

(d) *Extensions of the argument*

The argument of the previous section is easily extended to interior segments of the linear market. Suppose that at T_0 firm A owns two adjacent plants and that at some time in the future, T_2, density will increase sufficiently to allow a new entrant to earn revenues in excess of costs in the market segment bounded by A's plants. There will exist a time $T_1 < T_2$ such that a new entrant would expect only a normal return on its investment and, if A does nothing, some new entrant will pre-empt the market at T_1. Monopoly pre-emption will, however, occur since the new plant will be worth more to A than to the new entrant. In this case A's advantage stems only from joint profit-maximizing prices. A enjoys no locational advantage since both A and a new entrant would locate their new plants at the midpoint of the interval between existing plants. The absence of a locational advantage for A is, however, an artefact of the one-dimensional market. In a two-dimensional spatial market an independent firm entering a hexagonal or a rectangular lattice of firms would not choose the joint profit-maximizing location (see Eaton and Lipsey, 1976b). If one firm owned all adjacent plants in the lattice it would, of course, choose the joint profit-maximizing location. Thus in two-dimensional space A again has both a locational and a price advantage over new competitors in interior market segments.

The analysis is also easily extended to a market that grows in length, holding the density of customers constant. Beginning with the initial conditions in Section (b) let the length of market increase at time T_2 sufficiently to allow a new entrant to earn revenues in excess of costs. If A does nothing, some new entrant will pre-empt the market at some time $T_1 < T_2$, but since A will choose the joint profit-maximizing prices and locations while new entrants will not do so (for reasons similar to those in Section (c)), A itself will establish the new plants just before T_1.

(e) *The role of expectations*

Expectations play a critical role in a model such as ours and there is, of course, some expectations assumption that will yield virtually any conceivable result. We wish to confine our expectations assumptions to the class that may be called *consistent expectations*: those expectations that are consistent with realizations. It seems to us that this is a desirable property to require of expectations in our model since it avoids outcomes that are caused by a mistaken view of market conditions and market processes.

In our model we have employed the strongest form of consistent expectations, *perfect* foresight. Our two basic results on competitive and monopoly pre-emption will hold, however, with weaker forms of consistent expectations. We consider below two cases of imperfect foresight.

First, firms may be uncertain of the outcome of the competitive process and hence of the equilibrium prices that will emerge should new firms enter the market. If the entrant's equilibrium price is a random variable with a distribution that is known to all firms, and if all firms are risk-neutral, then our argument goes through as before. We merely replace the perfectly foreseen values of revenues and profits with expected values. The gap between T_1 and T_2 will be unchanged whenever the expected value of the profits is identical to the perfectly foreseen value. When the existing monopoly firm A values the market at T_1 on the assumption that A pre-empts it, A has no uncertainty since A can set any prices it wishes. Hence A's valuation is unaffected by the uncertainty over the outcome of the competitive process. Thus neither the time at which pre-emption by new entrants would occur nor the incentive for monopoly pre-emption is affected by this uncertainty.

Second, assume that T_2, the time at which demand will increase, is a random variable with a known distribution. New entrants again perform the appropriate expected-value calculations, and again there will exist a $T_1 < \bar{T}_2$ such that the present value of expected profits is zero, where $\bar{T}_2$ is the mathematical expectation of the time of market growth.

The monopolist's problem is, however, slightly more complex than when T_2 was certain. As long as the realization of T_2 is later than T_1 then his pre-emptive strategy of building new capacity just before T_1 works as before. But if there is an "unlucky" realization that yields $T_2 < T_1$, then at T_2 there will be a scramble to establish capacity to meet the *existing* extra demand. The monopolist may then lose its monopoly position. To reduce the probability of this happening the monopolist may pre-empt the market by building new capacity discretely before T_1. This strategy will not, of course, eliminate the possibility that the market will actually grow before the monopolist pre-empts, and our pre-emption results must be cast in probabilistic terms when there exists uncertainty with respect to growth in the market.

The above examples show that, although perfect foresight is sufficient, it is not necessary for our results. All that we require is consistent expectations: that firms correctly apprehend the nature of any uncertainties that they face.

II. Comparisons with Spaceless Models

The pre-emption arguments developed above obviously apply, with modification, to spaceless natural monopoly, the situation in which the minimum efficient scale of production is large relative to market demand. When there is an anticipated increase in demand at some future time, (a) competition among potential entrants will ensure that if the monopolist does nothing entry will occur before the increase in demand occurs, while (b) if the monopoly firm anticipates entry, it will be led to pre-empt the market by establishing the new capacity at a time just earlier than the earliest time at which it would be profitable for a new entrant to do so. In the spaceless case the monopolist's incentive to pre-empt the market arises only from the ability to avoid price competition. One important difference between the two models then is that in a spatial model the monopolist has an added incentive to pre-empt the market since he can increase the total profit that can be extracted from the market; he does this by choosing joint profit-maximizing locations as well as prices.

The really important differences between the two models emerge when initially the number of customers is large enough so that there are many plants in the market. In spaceless models the potential for profits owing to a range of increasing returns to scale is quickly dissipated as the number of plants serving the market increases. That is, the problem of natural monopoly in spaceless models arises only where the ratio of minimum efficient scale to market demand is large. In spatial models the problem of natural monopoly is undiminished when the market is served by a large number of plants. Since the potential for profit remains in spatial models and vanishes in spaceless models as the market grows, the incentive for new entrants or existing firms to pre-empt the market via premature entry remains in spatial models and vanishes in spaceless models. It is after all the possibility of earning profits after an anticipated market growth occurs that leads firms to create capacity before the growth occurs. These arguments are elaborated below.

The propositions we wish to argue are the following. The interval $T_2 - T_1$ falls rapidly to zero as the number of plants initially serving the market is increased in the spaceless model, but does not fall at all as the number of plants initially serving the market is increased in a spatial model.

We first turn to the spaceless model and, for concreteness, consider a limit pricing strategy. Let the market demand arise from the aggregation of demands of identical individuals. As the number of individuals over which we aggregate increases, the absolute value of the slope of the market demand curve at any price decreases towards zero. As this occurs the limit price converges to the minimum cost of production, and the pure rate of return on capital goes to zero.

Now let the number of customers be large enough so that the divergence of the market price, the limit price, from the minimum cost of production is arbitrarily small. Take this as an initial condition and assume that, at some future point in time, T_2, the number of customers will grow enough so that one new entrant could earn pure profits while two would earn losses. The pure profits earned by a single new entrant will be arbitrarily small since the divergence of current price from costs of production is arbitrarily small. Since the profits anticipated subsequent to T_2 are arbitrarily small, the time T_1 comes arbitrarily close to T_2. It follows then that, as the number of customers in the spaceless model increases, T_1 goes to T_2 and excess capacity owing to pre-emption by new entrants disappears. It also follows that the monopolist's incentive to pre-empt vanishes as the market grows. The key to this asymptotic result is that the potential in static equilibrium for pure profit, which is due to barriers to entry arising solely from decreasing unit costs over an initial range of output, vanishes as the market grows through an increase in the number of customers.[5]

Now consider a spatial model. As we have shown elsewhere (Eaton and Lipsey, 1978), the potential for pure profit in free-entry equilibrium in a spatial market does not diminish as the number of customers, and hence the number of plants, is increased. We give here a very brief summary of this argument.

Consider a segment of a linear spatial market with a large number of plants spread out over the market equidistant from each other. If a firm enters a slot between any two existing plants, it will serve, at any common price, half the number of customers as are served by existing plants before its entry. If we assume for simplicity that profits are proportional to customers served, then each existing plant would need to be earning a rate of return on capital of at least $2i$ before a new firm would enter and expect a return of i (where i is the minimum rate of return on capital that will induce entry). Given a uniform increase in density over the whole market, if entry is profitable in one interval between two existing plants, it will be profitable in every interval. Thus plants per unit of space will tend to double on each successive 'round of entry' as density increases. After each round of entry, however, the disadvantage of any new entrant compared with existing firms remains the same: expected customers of the former are only half those of the latter before entry. Thus the rate of profits that can be earned by existing plants without inducing entry does not diminish as density increases.[6]

Now adopt a high initial customer density with a monopolist owning plants spread evenly throughout the market and all charging the joint profit-maximizing price, and let the monopolist have enough plants so that entry is unprofitable. Then let an increase in density at some future time, T_2, be foreseen, the increase being the maximum that would support one but not two new plants in each segment between two existing plants. Since the rate of profit that will be foreseen on a new unit of capacity at T_2 does not diminish as initial customer density is increased, it follows that $T_2 - T_1$, the interval over which competitive pre-emption would create excess capacity, will also not diminish as initial density is increased. It further follows that the incentive for an existing monopolist to pre-empt the market does not diminish as customer density is increased.

III. Summary and Conclusion

The underlying cause of the results in this paper is that large positive pure profits can persist in free-entry equilibrium in spatial models. This result, stated in Eaton and Lipsey (1978), arises because any potential new entrant can expect a demand of the order of only half that enjoyed by existing firms before entry. Thus if an anticipated future increase in demand makes it profitable to install new plants, those plants may earn (depending on the initial density of customers and plants and the amount of the increase in demand) up to twice the competitive rate of return. Competition among potential entrants for the opportunity to earn the pure profits occasioned by the increase in demand will push new entry backwards in time until the present value of the flow of all future profits is zero. In such markets the capacity will be installed well before it is needed. Because the monopolist can extract more profits from the market by locating in a joint profit-maximizing location and charging joint profit-maximizing prices, it will always pay the monopolist to pre-empt the market by installing new capacity just earlier than the earliest point in time that it would be profitable for a new entrant to do so.[7]

We have analysed only the case in which an existing monopolist pre-empts the market by building new plants and operating them at a price less than ATC until market demand increases. Other forms of spatial pre-emption are obviously possible. The firm might build the plant and leave it idle (this would make sense if marginal costs were greater than the current profit-maximizing price). The firm could announce its plans to build in the market and then find its plans subject to a series of "unexpected" delays. Provided that new entrants believed that the existing firm's plans were serious, new entry might be deterred at low cost. If only a few sites were available (a situation not allowed for in our present model) the monopolist could buy them up and put them to other uses and then use one for its new plant when the market did expand.

What public policies could prevent the excess capacity from emerging? The case is similar to a common property problem: premature entry occurs because there exists no property right to establish new capacity in the market, so that the only effective means for establishing such a right is premature entry. The State could, of course, establish property rights by auctioning off the rights to establish new capacity in various segments of a growing market. This would prevent premature entry and would allow the State to appropriate the pure profits available in the market. In order to prevent the monopolist from buying the right and then simply not exercising it, the right, if not acted upon by some specified date, would revert to the State.

Finally, we might wonder if we have proven too much. We have shown that it will always pay an existing firm to blockade entry by locating new plants in an expanding market at a time before it will pay a new firm to enter. We know, however, that new firms do sometimes enter expanding markets. How is this? Our proof employed the assumption of perfect foresight. There are many ways in which imperfect foresight can cause entry of new firms. If either the market grows unexpectedly, or the change comes to be expected only at a time at which new entry is already profitable, the market is "up for grabs" and a scramble may ensue between new entrants and existing firms. It is also possible that either existing or new firms may make mistakes. On the one hand, if the market is very large, local knowledge of one part of it may give a potential new entrant foresight that is superior to that of the distant head office(s) of the existing multi-plant firm(s). On the other hand, new firms may enter the market on false expectations. Once built, the plants will be operated by someone as long as variable costs can be covered. This leads to the general conclusion that, the more stable and easily predictable is market growth, the more will the expanding market be served by new branches of existing firms, while the more erratic and unpredictable is market growth, the greater the possibility of new firms entering to serve part of the expanding market.

Our model is not designed to explain what number of multi-plant firms inhabit a market. Should the market come to be served by more than one firm for whatever reasons, including those sketched above, these firms will, individually and jointly, have the incentive and the ability to block further entry into the market by building new branch plants at a time when it will not pay new entrants to do so.

ACKNOWLEDGMENTS

This paper is a revised version of Eaton and Lipsey (1976c). The research for it was done while the authors were Visiting Professors at the University of Colorado at Boulder during 1974–1975. We acknowledge the generous support of the Killam Foundation for Professor Lipsey and the Canada Council for Professor Eaton. For a general survey of our work in spatial economics see Eaton and Lipsey (1976a).

NOTES

[1] U.S. vs. Aluminum Company of America et al., 44F. Supp. 97(1941) 148F. 2d 416(1945), p. 431.

[2] See, e.g., Pashigian (1968), Needham (1971), and Wenders (1971).

[3] See, e.g., Esposito and Esposito (1974).

[4] The argument is detailed in Eaton and Lipsey (1978). It focuses on the fact that existing firms have sunk costs while all costs of potential new entrants are avoidable. Thus the lowest price that

will allow an existing firm to cover avoidable costs is lower than the lowest price that will allow a potential new entrant to cover avoidable costs. It then follows that a new entrant would be forced to charge a price lower than its avoidable cost if it wished to undercut the existing firm's mill price. This is clearly not profitable since all the new entrant's costs are avoidable.

[5] Another way of seeing this result is to note that, as the demand curve gets flatter, the fall in price needed to sell the output of one more indivisible unit of capital operated at its least-cost output gets smaller and smaller. Thus the excess of price over costs that can occur when N plants sell their optimal outputs without allowing an $N + 1$th plant to cover its costs diminishes to zero. Hence the rate of pure profit that can be earned by existing units of capacity in free-entry equilibrium also diminishes to zero in a spaceless model.

[6] The intuitive argument in the text is based on the simplifying assumption that the firm's revenues are proportional to the number of customers. Actually in this model a new entrant will expect to have the same number of customers but more than half the revenues as are enjoyed by an existing firm before entry given any common price. Although the new entrant has only half the customers, it is closer to them and thus will have a lower delivered price over its market than would the original firm for any common mill price. Thus for every common price the ratio of *sales of a new plant to sales of an existing plant before entry* is more than half. Interestingly enough, however, as density of customers and hence density of plants is increased this price effect diminishes, since the distance to a firm's market boundary diminishes. Thus the difference between a firm's mill price and the delivered price at its market boundary diminishes as well. For this reason, as density increases, the ratio defined above *diminishes* towards one-half. This means that the profits that can be earned by existing plants without inducing entry *increases*. Thus in a spatial model the maximum possible duration of the interval $T_2 - T_1$ *increases* as density increases—the opposite result to the one in a spaceless economy (see Eaton and Lipsey, 1978, expecially Section VI).

[7] See Schmalensee (1977) for an interesting case to which the analysis of our paper seems to apply.

REFERENCES

EATON, B. C., and LIPSEY, R. G. (1976a). The introduction of space into the neoclassical model of value theory. In *Studies in Modern Economics* (M. J. Artis and A. R. Nobay, eds.). Oxford: Basil Blackwell.

—— (1976b). The non-uniqueness of equilibrium in the Löschian location model. *American Economic Review*, **66**, 77–93.

—— (1976c). The theory of market pre-emption: location as a barrier to entry. Queen's University Discussion Paper No. 208.

—— (1978). Freedom of entry and the existence of pure profit. *Economic Journal*, **88**, 455–469.

ESPOSITO, FRANCES FERGUSON and ESPOSITO, LOUIS (1974). Excess capacity and market structure. *Review of Economics and Statistics*, **56**, 188–194.

HAND, LEARNED (1941). U.S. vs. Aluminum Company of America *et al.*, 44 F. Supp. 97(1941), 148 F. 2d 416(1945).

HOTELLING, H. (1929). Stability in competition. *Economic Journal*, **29**, 41–57.

KALDOR, N. (1935). Market imperfections and excess capacity. *Economica*, **2**, 35–50.

MODIGLIANI, F. (1958). New developments on the oligopoly front. *Journal of Political Economy*, **66**, 215–232.

NEEDHAM, D. (1971). *Economic Analysis and Industrial Structure*. New York: Holt, Rinehart & Winston.

PASHIGIAN, B. P. (1968). Limit price and the market share of the leading firm. *Journal of Industrial Economics*, **16**, 165–177.

SCHMALENSEE, RICHARD (1977). Entry deterrence in the RTE cereal industry. Working Paper 961–77, Alfred P. Sloan School of Management, M.I.T., Cambridge, Mass.

SMITHIES, A. (1941). Optimum location in spatial competition. *Journal of Political Economy*, **49**, 423–439.

WENDERS, JOHN T. (1971). Excess capacity as a barrier to entry. *Journal of Industrial Economics*, **20**, 14–19.

COMPARISON SHOPPING AND THE CLUSTERING OF HOMOGENEOUS FIRMS*

B. Curtis Eaton and Richard G. Lipsey†

In his famous 1929 article on duopoly in space, Hotelling [15] explained why two competing duopolists would locate together in the center of the market rather than adopting the socially optimal, transport minimizing locations. Local clustering of firms is a matter of common observation in many markets, and it is part of the conventional wisdom of economists to refer to Hotelling and to the socially wasteful nature of clustering whenever local clusters are encountered in the real world. Boulding has contributed to this conventional wisdom by laying sweeping claims for the applicability of Hotelling's model. After explaining the workings of the model he goes on to observe:

This is a principle of the utmost generality. It explains why all the dime stores are usually clustered together, often next door to each other; why certain towns attract large numbers of firms of one kind; why an industry, such as the garment industry, will concentrate in one quarter of a city. It is a principle which can be carried over into other "differences" than spatial differences. The general rule for any new manufacturer coming into an industry is "make your product as like the existing products as you can without destroying the differences." It explains why all automobiles are so much alike and why no manufacturer dares make a car in which a tall hat can be worn comfortably. It even explains why Methodists, Baptists, and even Quakers are so much alike, and tend to get even more alike. [4, p. 484.]

People who follow the conventional wisdom and accept statements such as those made by Boulding are assuming that Hotelling's model generalizes to a much wider set of market conditions than those covered explicitly by the model.

The theoretical work on this subject does not, in fact, support Boulding and the conventional wisdom. Smithies [22] showed that when demand is responsive to delivered price, the tendency for Hotelling's duopolists to gravitate to the market's center is weakened. Papers by Lerner and Singer [16] and by Eaton and Lipsey [6] demonstrate that if the number of firms serving Hotelling's one-dimensional market were increased, firms would never be grouped in clusters larger than two firms, and that clustering is a necessary condition of equilibrium only at the peripheries of the market. A subsequent paper by Eaton and Lipsey [10] demonstrates that when demand is responsive to delivered price, firms in the interior of a

---

*This paper is a revised version of Eaton and Lipsey [7]. The authors wish to acknowledge the generous support of the Killam Foundation, which supported Professor Lipsey, the Canada Council, which supported Professor Eaton, and the Department of Economics of the University of Colorado, which provided us with an exceedingly pleasant and stimulating atmosphere in which to work.

†Associate Professor of Economics, University of British Columbia and Professor of Economics, Queen's University, Kingston, Ontario, respectively.

Date received: November, 1977.

one-dimensional market will be equally spaced. Thus, a clustering of even two firms cannot occur except at the peripheries of the market when Hotelling's model is so amended.

It is now clear that there is a major gap between theory and observation. Hotelling's model is not able to explain local clustering of firms in markets with more than two firms. Indeed, once the assumptions are relaxed very slightly in the direction of realism, Hotelling's model predicts that no two firms should be clustered together, except on the peripheries of the market. This hiatus is important not only because we always want to be able to explain what we see, but also because the Hotelling explanation carries with it the welfare condemnation—local clusters are a universally wasteful phenomenon—while other explanations may not do so.

In contrast to general economists, the conventional wisdom among geographers, market researchers, and economists who concern themselves with space appears to be that clustering of firms occurs in response to consumers' desires to make comparisons between goods. Lösch [17] appears to be the first to suggest this intuitive argument. He clearly attributes the existence of special business districts to "the preference of consumers for ... comparing qualities of differentiated products." Other early statements of this position are attributable to Berry and Garrison [3] and to Nelson [18]. Indeed, all recent taxonomies of types of retail goods include shopping goods as one classification. (See Holton [13] and Porter [19] for examples.) In Holton's words: "Shopping goods ... are ... those goods for which the probable gain from making price comparisons among alternative sellers is thought to be large relative to the consumer's appraisal of searching costs." The implication is that the forces affecting location of retailers of shopping goods are different from the forces affecting other types of retail goods.

A body of evidence indicates that the conventional wisdom of geographers and market researchers is not without empirical support. There is considerable evidence to the effect that consumers do engage in comparison shopping (for example, Golledge, Rushton, and Clark [12] and Bucklin [5]), and that retailers of shopping goods do tend to cluster (for example, Berry [2], Horton [14], and Rogers [20]).

Although the proposition that clusters of firms are to be understood as a response to consumers' comparison shopping has been accepted as part of the conventional wisdom of geographers and market researchers, there does not exist a tightly formulated theory of the locational response of firms to the comparison shopping of consumers. In the absence of such a theory the proposition remains only an intuitively appealing hypothesis and, perhaps more importantly, it is impossible to ask whether, or to what extent, clustering of firms is socially wasteful.

In the present paper we consider the forces influencing the locations of independent, profit-maximizing firms that sell similar commodities when consumers engage in comparison shopping, i.e., more than one store is visited before a purchase is made. We find that the forces analyzed in this model make the existence of local clusters of firms throughout the entire market a necessary condition of equilibrium. We also find that, in contrast to the Hotelling model, local clustering of firms can serve a socially useful purpose by helping to minimize the costs of transport between firms and comparison shoppers.

Although the socially optimal configuration of firms does not, in this model, arise from atomistic decision-making among independent firms, much of the local clustering that does occur is a transport-cost-reducing response to the needs of comparison shoppers, rather than being a universally wasteful phenomenon as it is in Hotelling's model.

1. THE MODEL

We deal with the simplest model that will suffice to isolate the forces in question. The assumptions and definitions are presented (and numbered) and then discussed.

The Market

(1) The market is a bounded line one unit in length. The boundaries of the market are at 0 and 1 on the real line.

(2) Customers are spread continuously over the market at a uniform density.

Customer Behavior

(3) All customers purchase an identical quantity of the commodity once each period. Before making a purchase each customer visits two stores that sell the commodity to compare their offerings; we say he "samples" these stores. Customers bear the cost of transport to obtain information, and they seek to minimize this cost which is directly proportional to distance travelled.

It follows that each customer will choose the stores that he samples so as to minimize his cost of travel which is accomplished by minimizing the distance travelled. If a customer based at point x wishes to sample firms located at $\bar{a}$ and $\bar{b}$, the distance he travels is

$$|\bar{a} - x| + |\bar{b} - \bar{a}| + |x - \bar{b}|$$

Since prices are fixed by assumption (7) below, customers must be comparing nonprice factors such as quality, delivery dates, and servicing arrangements when they sample firms prior to making their purchases. The assumption that customers sample a fixed number of firms before making their purchases is, of course, arbitrary. An alternative would be to solve the customer's optimal search problem with the number of searches as an endogenous variable. This optimal search problem is, however, much more complex in a spatial model than in the spaceless models that have usually been studied in the search literature, and it is doubtful if analytical solutions can be developed. Indeed, those investigators who have studied this problem in models similar to ours have been forced to fall back on numerical simulation techniques. (See, for example, Bacon [1].) It is easier to display the problems involved in solving the optimal search problem after our model has been developed; we discuss them in Section 5. In the meantime, we offer the following justification for our procedure. Since our objective is to study the effects on the location of firms of the known fact that comparison shopping does occur, we merely assume this behavior and then go on to investigate its consequences.

What really matters in our model is that the number of stores visited before a purchase is made, R, should be greater than one. The results that we obtain for $R = 2$ extend in a direct and obvious way to cases in which $R > 2$.

(4) Having sampled two stores, the customer returns to his base and costlessly orders his purchase from the preferred store. The store then delivers the goods at no charge. This is a model of visits to obtain information, telephone orders, and costless delivery.[1]

(5) The probability that a customer who samples any store actually makes a purchase from that store is one half; thus, all stores expect the same ratio of visits by customers to sales to customers, namely 2:1.

All that we require is that for each store, sales are a monotonically increasing function of samplings (so that maximizing the number of samplings it receives also maximizes its sales). The assumption that the ratio is the same for all stores, however, does simplify the algebra and seems appropriate for cases in which the stores are selling products that are identical in price and broadly similar in characteristics.

We wish to satisfy ourselves, and if possible our readers, that we have not set up a theory which will be an empirically empty box. Possible real world analogues to our theory suggest that we have not done so. Consider, for example, two competing men's clothing stores. Each tries to cover the whole distribution of customers' tastes with respect to such characteristics as sizes, cut of clothing, color, brand name of manufacturer, etc. Since the number of possible combinations of characteristics is very large, each store cannot be sure of offering any given customer exactly what he requires at any given moment in time. Both stores hold inventories that are random samplings across the whole distribution of combinations of characteristics. On the average, the stores will share all the customers in the ratio that reflects the relative abilities of their average inventories to come closest to satisfying the desires of their potential customers, 0.5 in this case.

Firm Behavior

(6) All stores have the same cost function made up of a constant fixed cost, K, and a variable cost of v per unit of output

$$TC = K + vQ \qquad v < 1$$

(7) All stores charge the same exogenously imposed price, which we take to be unity. The units of quantity are chosen so that one unit of the commodity is bought each period over the entire market.

---

[1]Different, and much more complex, models occur in the cases in which the customer must return to the store of his choice to make his purchase personally (in which case the order in which the stores are visited matters) and/or the firms levy a delivery charge that is an increasing function of distance (in which case the firm's ratio of samplings to sales will vary with the ratio of the distance travelled by the household to the firm in question to the distance travelled by the household to the other firm it samples). The proof of the crucial characteristic (3) becomes more complex in the no-telephone-order model than in the present model.

This fixed-price assumption allows us to concentrate on the locational aspect of competition between firms. It is, in any case, the appropriate assumption whenever resale price maintenance is enforced.

Comparison shopping for price could, however, be easily accommodated in our model. Consider, for example, two automobile dealers selling very similar cars with similar costs of production and similar list prices (e.g., Broncos and Blazers). Each dealer bargains with each customer over the price of the trade-in and the discount from list price. Each dealer will generate a distribution of prices at which his final deals are struck. The distributions of the two dealers will be very similar and can be assumed for purposes of analysis to be identical. The probability that one customer, with a given bargaining ability, receives a lower offer from one firm rather than the other is 0.5. Comparison shopping will now occur and the two dealers will divide their total sales equally. In this case our model applies exactly when the parametric price is replaced by the mean of the common distribution of prices.

(8) Each firm owns only one store.

We impose this assumption to keep the model as competitive as possible. Firms are named by upper case letters from A to K while the location of each store is denoted by its corresponding lower case letter, which is unbarred when location is variable and barred when it is fixed. Firms are lettered in alphabetical order starting from the left of the market.

(9) No two stores can be closer together than a small, arbitrary distance δ.

It greatly simplifies the algebra to assume that δ is zero when we come to measure distances from a customer's base to paired firms while still allowing the customer to distinguish which of the paired firms is on the left and which on the right. We refer to groupings of two, three, and four firms with each firm separated from its neighbor(s) by the minimum distance δ as pairs, triplets and quartets.

(10) In choosing its location, each firm assumes that each other firm will leave its location unchanged.

This assumption of a zero conjectural variation with respect to location is suitable for many locational problems where relocation is extremely costly and occurs, if at all, only with a long time lag.

(11) Firms seek to maximize their expected profits subject to the conjectural variation outlined in (10).

Assumptions (6) and (7) imply that profit maximization is the same as sales maximization. Assumption (5) implies that sales are maximized by maximizing the number of customers who sample the firm, and assumption (2) implies that this is done by maximizing the length of the market segment over which households sample the firm in question. Thus profit-maximizing firms will seek to maximize the length of the segment over which customers sample the firm; we call this the firm's market segment.

2. EQUILIBRIUM IN THE LOCATIONS OF FIRMS WHEN THE NUMBER OF FIRMS IS GIVEN

In this section we consider equilibrium when the number of firms is fixed at any particular value, N. Equilibrium requires only that no firm be able, by

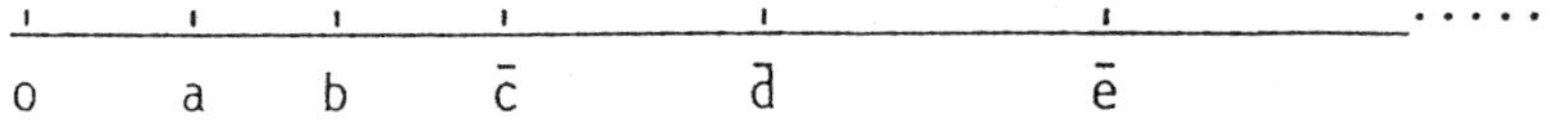

```
|      |   |   |   |   |   |          .  .  .  .  .
0      a   b   c̄   d̄       ē
```

FIGURE 1:   Peripheral Triplets.

relocating, to increase its profits. We first develop some general properties that must hold in any equilibrium configuration and then go on to consider what equilibrium configurations of firms are possible.

(1) Peripheral firms must be grouped in at least a triplet.

Consider firms A, B, and C when there is at least one further firm, D. Place the firms as shown in Figure 1 and let firm B move to its profit-maximizing location within the interval $\bar{a}, \bar{c}$. Firm B will wish to pair with C moving to $\bar{c} - \delta$. The intuitive reason for this is as follows: since all customers visit two firms, firm B loses none of its customers located between it and the market boundary at 0 by moving toward C, but B gains customers located on its right by reducing the distance that they must travel to visit B and C (rather than visiting D and C or perhaps D and E).[2] Now consider firm A's location. It is clear that everyone to the left of A can do no better than to sample firms A and B, while customers to the right of A have the additional alternative of sampling B and C. As A moves towards firm B it thus loses no customers on its left while it picks up customers on its right. A thus maximizes its market area by pairing with B.[3] A similar argument establishes that the three right-hand peripheral firms must be grouped in *at least* a triplet.

(2) No single grouping of firms can contain more than four firms.

In any larger grouping of firms all of the customers visiting the group from the left will visit the first two firms in the group and all of the customers visiting the group from the right will visit the last two firms in the group. Any firms between the first two and last two will receive no customers.[4]

(3) No firm can be unpaired.

This characteristic is the key to the behavior of the whole model. Because the proof is extremely tedious it is not presented here.[5] However, some intuitive feel for the result can be developed by considering the case of a firm locating between

---

[2] B's left-hand market boundary is fixed at zero while its right-hand boundary is at x^*, where the journey to B and C is the same distance as the journey to C and D:

$$|x^* - b| - |\bar{c} - b| + |\bar{c} - x^*| = |x^* - \bar{c}| + |\bar{d} - \bar{c}| + |\bar{d} - x^*|$$

and so $x^* = b + \bar{d} - \bar{c}$. When B is confined to the interval between 0 and $\bar{c}$, its market is maximized at the value $\bar{d}$ by making $b = \bar{c}$.

[3] When B and C are paired at $\bar{b}$, firm A's left-hand market boundary is fixed at 0 and its right-hand boundary is at a, since anyone to the right of a must travel to $\bar{b}$ and will sample B and C and so avoid an additional journey to a. Thus A's market is a, and this value is maximized within the segment $(0, \bar{b})$ by setting $a = \bar{b}$.

[4] The generalizations of results (1) and (2) are that peripheral groups must contain at least $R + 1$ firms and that no group can contain more than $2R$ firms, where R is the number of firms that each household samples before making its purchases.

[5] The proof of characteristic (3) is contained in Eaton and Lipsey [7] and is available on request. Although the proof is tedious, we think it is not without interest. The nature of the problem under investigation dictates that discontinuities and nondifferentiabilities abound; therefore, standard

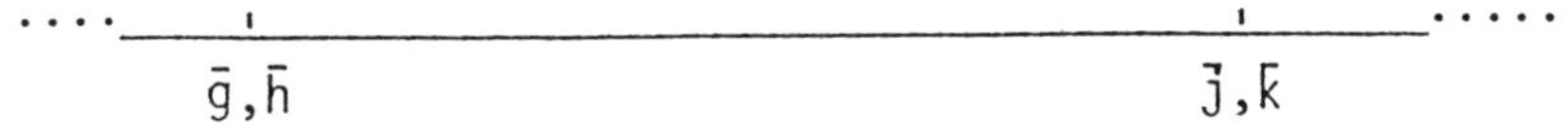

```
. . . ._____|_____|_____. . . . .
       ḡ,h̄                                        j̄,k̄
```

FIGURE 2: The Principle of Paring.

two clusters of firms. Consider Figure 2 in which four firms, G, H, J, and K are located in the interior of the market as two pairs, and firm I considers locating in the interval between them. If firm I locates at the midpoint of the interval it will have no customers, since everyone to then left of i will prefer to go directly to $\bar{h}$ and $\bar{g}(=\bar{h})$ rather than travel rightward to i and then leftward to $\bar{h}$; while everyone to the right of i will prefer to go directly to $\bar{j}$ and $\bar{k}(=\bar{j})$ rather than go left to i and then right to $\bar{j}$. As firm I departs for the midpoint location, customers between the midpoint and i will stop at I and then travel only to the first firm in the nearest pair. It follows from this that firm I maximizes its market segment at a value of half the length of the interval in which it is locating by joining either of the pairs of firms.

Characteristic (3) dictates that in equilibrium all firms will be in a grouping that contains at least two firms. Taken together, characteristics (1), (2), and (3) require that there be a grouping of three or four firms on each of the market peripheries and that the rest of the firms be distributed throughout the interior of the market in groupings of two, three, or four firms.

(4) The market area of each grouping (pairs, triplet, or quartet) extends half the distance to the neighboring group of firms on either side of the group in question.

When all firms are members of groups, households will minimize travel costs by travelling to one group only and making their desired comparisons in this one location. Travel costs will be minimized by going to the nearest group, and thus the boundary between the market areas of two adjacent groups will be at the midpoint between them.

(5) No firm's whole market segment can be less than any other firm's half market segment (where a firm's half market segment is defined as the distance from the firm to one of the boundaries of its market segment).

This follows obviously from the fact that any firm (I) can obtain another firm (J's) half market segment as its whole market segment by pairing with J on the side of the desired half market segment. It is a simple corollary of this proposition that all firms whose markets are concentrated wholly to one side of them (all firms in any quartet and the two outside firms in any triplet) must have markets that are identical in size. From this follows another simple corollary that the middle firm in a triplet that shares customers with both the outside firms must have a market exactly twice as large as the markets of the two outside firms of the triplet.

It follows from the first of these corollaries that if $\bar{a}$ is the distance of the first group of firms from the left-hand market boundary then the second group of firms

---

techniques of analysis are not applicable. Our proof of characteristic (3) illustrates one approach to problems which inevitably involve discontinuity and nondifferentiability. For an application of these techniques to another spatial economic problem see Eaton and Lipsey [9]. For a survey of our work in the area of spatial economics see Eaton and Lipsey [8].

```
_____|_____|_____ . . . . . . . . . . _____|_____|____
0          ā          ·3ā                        1-3ā          1-ā    1
```

FIGURE 3: Equilibrium Configurations at the Peripheries of the Market.

must be exactly $3\bar{a}$ from the market boundary and the last and the second last groupings must be $1 - \bar{a}$ and $1 - 3\bar{a}$ from the right-hand boundary respectively. The reason is that the first and last firms in the two peripheral groups must have all of their market segments concentrated on one side of them, and so all of them must have market segments of $\bar{a}$ in length. The first firm in the left-hand grouping, firm A, has $\bar{a}$ by definition. For the last firm in this group to have $\bar{a}$ the next group must be located at $3\bar{a}$. This configuration is illustrated in Figure 3.

(6) The locations of triplets and quartets are uniquely determined at the midpoints of the market that they serve.

This is the only way in which characteristic (5) can hold for triplets or quartets. If (6) did not hold, the outside firm in the grouping facing the shorter market segment would move over and pair with the outside firm facing the longer market segment and capture all of its market.

(7) The location of any pair of firms that is neither the second nor the penultimate group of firms is not unique within its interval.

Consider the pair H and I located at h in an interval between the pair F and G on the left and the pair J and K on the right. The joint market for the pair of firms H and I stretches from its left-hand boundary at $(\bar{f} + h)/2$ to its right-hand boundary at $(\bar{k} + h)/2$. The market segment is thus $(\bar{k} + h)/2 - (\bar{f} + h)/2$, and is independent of h. Thus, an interior pair of firms is indifferent as to where it locates within its interval. Of course, for the market to be in equilibrium, characteristic (5) must be satisfied, and this places some limits on the locations of interior pairs.

These characteristics allow us to study the configurations of firms that are possible when the model is in equilibrium. We first consider the special cases where N is small and the equilibrium configuration is unique. When $N = 1$, there can be no comparison shopping, and when $N = 2$ the two firms get all of the customers no matter where they locate. When $N = 3$, characteristic (1) dictates that the three firms should be located in a triplet and characteristic (6) dictates that the triplet should be located at the midpoint of the market. When there are four firms in the market, the only way to satisfy characteristic (1) is for A, B, and C to be in one triplet and for B, C, and D to be in another triplet, which, taken together, requires that all four firms be in a quartet. Characteristic (6) then requires that the quartet be located at the center of the market. There is no equilibrium for $N = 5$. Characteristic (1) requires that ABC and CDE be the two triplets at each end of the market, but since C is common to both triplets this can only occur if the firms are grouped in a single quintet. This, however, violates characteristic (2). (This is analogous to the non-existence of equilibrium for $N = 3$ in Hotelling's model.)

When $N = 6$, characteristic (1) requires that there be two triplets consisting of ABC and DEF. Characteristic (5) then requires that these be located at the first and third quartiles. This gives firms A, C, D, and F market segments of $1/4$, and firms B and E market segments of $1/2$.

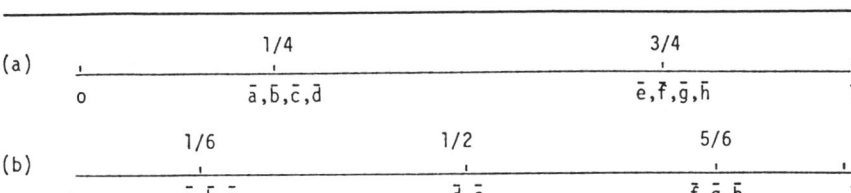

FIGURE 4: Equilibrium Configurations With 8 Firms.

When $N = 7$, characteristic (1) requires that ABC and EFG be the two triplets at the extremes of the market. Characteristic (3) requires that firm D be located so as to make one of the two peripheral groups into a quartet. Characteristic (5) requires that the two groups be located at the first and third quartiles. In this configuration the middle firm in the one triplet (B or F) has a market segment of $1/2$ while the other 6 firms have market segments of $1/4$.

For $N \geq 8$ the equilibrium configuration ceases to be unique. Figure 4 illustrates the two possible configurations for $N = 8$. In the first configuration there are two quartets located at the first and the third quartiles respectively. In the second configuration there are two triplets located at $1/6$ and $5/6$, while a pair of firms is located at the midpoint of the market. This is the only location for the interior pair that will satisfy the necessary symmetries at the edges of the market that are illustrated in Figure 3.

There is no point in going much further because as N is increased, the number of combinations that will provide triplets or quartets at the two extremes of the market and pairs, triplets, or quartets elsewhere increases, thus increasing the number of equilibrium configurations. To mention just one other example, there are four possible configurations for $N = 10$. Three of these contain only three clusters of firms, and thus have unique locations of the clusters at $1/6$, $1/2$, and $5/6$. These configurations are quartet, pair, quartet; quartet, trio, trio; and trio, quartet, trio. The fourth configuration contains four clusters (trio, pair, pair, trio) and the locations of the four clusters are not unique.[6]

3. FREE-ENTRY EQUILIBRIUM

A free-entry equilibrium requires that no firm can increase its profits by relocating, that no existing firm earn negative profits, and that there exists no location offering positive profits to a new entrant.[7]

A necessary and sufficient condition for free-entry equilibrium is that a market segment of $\bar{a}$ should just yield zero profits. (Otherwise, new firms would wish to join, or old firms would wish to leave the first two clusters counting from

---

[6] Let A, B, C be located at $\bar{a}$; D,E at $3\bar{a}$; F, G at $1 - 3\bar{a}$; H,I,J, at $1 - \bar{a}$. Markets for D, E, and F, G are $1/2 - 2\bar{a}$. We require that $1/2 - 2\bar{a} \geq \bar{a}$ or $\bar{a} \leq 1/6$. In addition, firm A (or C, or H, or I) can have a market as small as half of firm D's (or E's, or F's, or G's) market without violating any equilibrium conditions. Thus we require $1/4 - \bar{a} < \bar{a}$, or $\bar{a} \geq 1/8$. Therefore, in equilibrium $1/8 \leq \bar{a} \leq 1/6$.

[7] There is a problem here with respect to our working assumption to treat δ as being zero. If we say that δ is really zero and a firm will enter if its expected profits, Π^e, are non-negative, i.e., $\Pi^e \geq 0$, then if firm I is making zero profits in the location i with all of its market concentrated on one side, say its left, firms will continue to enter indefinitely, each seeking to pair on the left with the last firm to locate at i. Since δ is zero, each new firm will not be significantly to the left of the firm with whom it is

the left and the right-hand ends of the market.) If either of the peripheral groupings is a triplet, the middle firm must have a market segment of $2\underline{a}$, and, given the cost curve of assumption (6), must have significant positive profits. If either of the second and/or the penultimate groups is a pair, the firms in these pairs will have market segments of $\underline{a}$ on their side that extends to the market boundary, and of up to $\underline{a}$ on their other side.

For any triplet and/or quartet anywhere in the market, the size of each firm's market is unique: $\underline{a}$ for all firms except the middle firm in the triplet whose market is $2\underline{a}$. The market segment of pairs can be anything from $\underline{a}$ to $2\underline{a}$ for each firm in the pair (although both firms in any one pair have identical market segments).

Thus equilibrium under freedom of entry and exit requires a unique market segment, and, hence, profits for all firms in all groups except pairs. In the case of pairs, the market can vary between $\underline{a}$ and $2\underline{a}$, while in the case of the middle firm in a triplet the market must be $2\underline{a}$. Evidently entry equilibrium is consistent with wide variations among the profits of individual firms in the industry.

4. SIGNIFICANCE

Optimality

We use a simple working definition of the socially optimal distribution of N firms, i.e., the distribution that minimizes the total cost of travel between customers and firms. Note that we do not consider the optimal number of firms, but simply the optimal distribution of firms when N is given. In the Hotelling model the optimal distribution occurs when N firms are spread along the line with each firm in the center of a market $1/N$th of the length of the whole market.

There is a strong intuitive appeal to the argument that, since customers always visit two firms, the optimality properties of our model can be found by grouping firms into pairs and then applying the results that apply to single firms in Hotelling's model to each of our pairs of firms. Thus in the present model the optimal distribution of firms occurs when the firms are paired and placed in the center of identical markets. The proof of this proposition can be found in Eaton and Lipsey [7]. (If N is odd, the location of the Nth firm is of no importance, since it has no effect on total distance travelled.)

Thus although the pairing of firms may represent a nonoptimal configuration arising in response to the forces analyzed by Hotelling [15] it may also represent an optimal configuration arising in response to the forces of comparison shopping analyzed in this paper. To someone applying the Hotelling model to the world, any clustering together of shops represents a departure from optimality. Two of the most important insights following from the present model are, first, that there are reasons for the clustering of firms that are basically different from those analyzed

---

pairing, and its market will be the same as that of the previous entrant. To avoid this ridiculous result we must recognize that treating δ as zero is only a convenient simplification for the fixed members case; δ must in fact be a finite magnitude—although it can be as small as we like. When a new firm comes in to pair with firm I, it thus expects a market smaller than firm I's market by $\delta/2$. Instead of changing assumptions at this stage to allow for a nonzero δ, we can achieve the same result by using a strong instead of a weak inequality in the entry condition: a new firm will enter if and only if $\Pi^e > 0$.

in the Hotelling model, and, second, that when comparison shopping exists, a movement towards clustering of similar firms may represent a movement towards, rather than away from, optimality. It remains to be seen how close to, or far away from, the optimal configuration the actual competitive equilibrium can come in the present model. The optimal configuration is not an equilibrium configuration in our model. This is because of the necessity for the two groups of firms on the periphery to be at least triplets—characteristic (1). The closest one can come to the optimal distribution in equilibrium is to have a triplet on each end and $(N - 6)/2$ pairs (N even) distributed evenly throughout the rest of the market. This gives one fewer group of firms than in the optimal grouping and a higher total distance travelled. The difference between the distance travelled when the firms are optimally distributed and when they are distributed in the equilibrium configuration that comes closest to optimality clearly goes to zero as N goes to infinity.

Finally we ask what configurations will give the maximum possible departure from optimality. The general conclusion is that the transport-cost-maximizing configuration is the one that minimizes the number of groups of firms serving the market, given that the groups must be either pairs, triplets, or quartets. In these situations for large N, the equilibrium transport costs are roughly twice the value of transport costs in the optimum configuration.

Shopping Centers

In the atomistic development of a city, a firm cannot prevent the nearby location of a competing firm. In Hotelling's model, such a phenomenon is universally harmful to the initial firm which therefore would do nothing to encourage it. Hotelling's model cannot therefore explain the common observation that does seem very odd at first sight: when a department store takes part in the development of a shopping center it positively encourages the location in that shopping center of firms in direct competition with the department store. Foster [11] has investigated this phenomenon. He writes:

Developers not only concede in rent to sign the anchor department store but they often relinquish their freedom to select other tenants in the center. The department store often demands that a certain space be occupied by apparel and shoe retailers in the center. (The rationale... is to assure the merchandise offering of the department store is balanced by a competitive offering for purposes of comparison shopping.) (p. 322.)

The model of comparison shopping provides a theoretical explanation of this behavior by predicting that it will always pay an isolated firm selling goods that are subject to comparison shopping to encourage a competitor to locate nearby. More precisely we can show that if a single store is joined by a second competing store selling the same commodity, the sales of the pair will be more than twice that of the single store. The proof is as follows. In our discussion of characteristic (3) above, we showed that a single firm locating between two pairs of firms who are separated by a distance L will obtain a market, M, such that $0 \le M < L/2$. A market of zero is obtained if the firm locates at the mid point of the interval, while the market approaches $L/2$ as the firm approaches (but does not join) one of the two pairs. Characteristic (4) shows that if the unpaired firm is joined by a second firm the pair will enjoy a market of $L/2$.

The fact that the sales of a pair of firms located at any point will be more than twice the sales of a single firm located at the same point is a reflection of the fact that the two firms confer a positive demand externality on each other. In our model, where customers visit only two firms, these demand externalities are exhausted when the number of firms in a group is two. The entry of a third or fourth firm at this location serves only to dissipate the economic rents available at the location; no customers are better off, but existing firms are worse off since their profits are reduced by entry of further firms.

This result implies that any shopping center would include exactly two retail outlets for our comparison shopping good. Shopping centers exist to collect the rents of location, and clearly the rents from the comparison shopping good at any location are maximized when the number of retail outlets is two.

In our model of independent retailers, groups of three or four retailers are possible. Such groups are evidence of excess capacity and inefficiency. The shopping center, which internalizes the demand externality, will avoid this inefficiency.

The recent growth of automobile plazas, where competing firms selling different makes of automobiles group together as a conscious joint decision, can be understood as an attempt on the part of independent retailers to internalize the demand externalities.

Range of Applicability

It seems obvious that the comparison shopping model applies to some, but not all, situations of spatial competition. The model strictly requires that households visit more than one store each time a purchase is contemplated. Under what circumstances would we expect repeated comparison shopping to occur? First, the need arises when information gathered in the past is of little or no use in guiding today's behavior—i.e., when product characteristics and/or prices are changing rapidly relative to frequency of purchase. More complex models occur if the customer needs to make comparisons less frequently than he needs to make purchases, but we see no reason why the tendency of firms to cluster would not generalize to such models. Second, the time and money costs of making comparisons must not be too high relative to the expected value of the gain to be made from making the comparison. This requires that the commodity in question not be too inexpensive. The typical commodity to which our model applies is then a consumer durable, bought infrequently by consumers who thus feel the need to engage in comparisons each time they do make a purchase. (Porter [19] provides a good discussion of shopping goods which emphasizes these same points.)

5. AN ACHILLES HEEL?

Our model uses the arbitrary search rule that consumers visit R stores before selecting the good they wish to purchase. There has, of course, been a great deal of work on the consumers' search problem when information is imperfect. (See Rothchild [21] for a survey of much of this literature.) It would seem reasonable to ask how we justify our arbitrary search assumption in the face of this impressive body of literature.

Virtually all of this rational search literature assumes that the marginal cost of search is either a constant or an increasing function of the number of searches. Where the models go beyond the analysis of the optimum search behavior of a single individual to analyze market implications, they usually assume that all searchers have the same cost-of-search function. These assumptions are appropriate for many models that are either spaceless or are spatially extended but have a continuum of buyers and sellers with nonzero density at each point.

In our model there is a continuum of buyers, but not of sellers. Consider the consequences for the search problem facing any one of our households. Figure 5 illustrates this problem for a household located at the origin ($r_1, r_2 \ldots$ and $l_1, l_2 \ldots$ give the locations of firms to the right and to the left of the origin, respectively). The total costs of making one, two and three searches are:

$$TC_1 = \text{Min}\,(r_1, |l_1|)$$
$$TC_2 = \text{Min}\,(r_2, r_1 + |l_1|, |l_2|)$$
$$TC_3 = \text{Min}\,(r_3, r_2 + |l_1|, r_1 + |l_2|, |l_3|)$$

(where transport costs are one per unit of distance). The marginal cost of the nth search is $MC_n = TC_n - TC_{n-1}$. The following characteristics are obvious from this enumeration of up to three searches: (a) in general we can have $MC_N \leq MC_{N-1}$; (b) households in different locations have different search-cost functions; (c) a change in the location of one firm can radically alter any household's search-cost function.

The solution of a single consumer's optimal search problem for a given set of firm locations would seem to be much more complex in our spatial model than it is in standard search models. Indeed, we see no way to generate an analytical solution when the number of searches is an endogenous variable. (Bacon [1], for example, has analyzed a similar problem in a spatial context and was forced to adopt numerical simulation techniques.)

If the solution of the single household's search problem is difficult, the solution of the firms' locational problem is much more so. For any possible location, the firm would have to solve the choice problem of *each* household in the market and calculate the number of customers who would sample a firm in that location. It would then choose from all possible locations the one that maximized the number of customers sampling the firm. We suspect that an analytical solution to the firm's locational problem could not be developed, and we are sure that, if it could be developed, it would require an extended and very complex analysis. We have thus adopted an alternative: we know that comparison shopping does occur

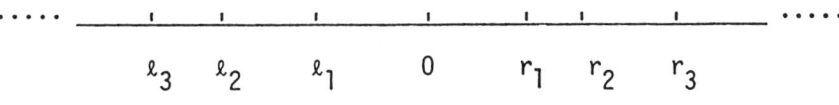

FIGURE 5: The Consumers' Search Problem.

and we wish to analyze the implications of this type of shopping on the clustering of firms. To do this we impose arbitrary search behavior on the household and then see what follows in respect to the locations of firms.

6. EXTENSIONS

We have used the simplest model of comparison shopping that allowed us to establish some general theoretical points. First, we have shown that comparison shopping provides a theoretically valid explanation of the clustering of firms throughout the market while Hotelling's model does not. Second, we have shown that the clustering of firms can be socially valuable in reducing transport costs rather than being a universally wasteful phenomenon as it is in Hotelling's model.

Our model is also capable of extension to explain actual patterns of clustering that have been noted in the applied literature. To do this, certain of our arbitrary assumptions would have to be relaxed, and the resulting more complex models might require numerical methods for their analysis. In conclusion, two of the directions for relaxation of assumptions may be mentioned and some of their general effects noted.

First, we could introduce a terminal cost of shopping at a single store or at a cluster of stores. This would introduce a powerful additional force towards clustering. A single store located between two clusters of stores would then get no custom regardless of its location since stopping there would cause the customer to incur an unnecessary additional terminal cost.

Second, we could assume that the location of firms within a single cluster had no effect on the firms' sales. Two situations would bring this about. Either any customer who stopped at a cluster of M firms could sample all firms in that cluster, or he could sample a subset of the M firms chosen randomly. In either case, all firms in a cluster would expect the same number of samplers. We would then lose the characteristic of our model that firms cared where they were located within any cluster; this would introduce some range of indeterminacy in the relative distances separating clusters of firms. This alternative assumption may be empirically more appealing than our assumption (9) which allows customers to distinguish between the locations of firms in any one cluster. We have not adopted the alternative in the body of the paper since it makes all of the analysis, and in particular the proof of the principal of pairing, more complex than it already is.

REFERENCES

[1] Bacon, R. W. "An Approach to the Theory of Consumer Shopping Behavior," *Urban Studies*, 8 (1971), 55–65.
[2] Berry, B. J. L. *Commercial Structure and Commercial Blight: Retail Patterns and Processes in the City of Chicago*, University of Chicago, Department of Geography Research Paper No. 85, 1963.
[3] Berry, B. J. L. and L. Garrison. "Recent Developments in Central Place Theory," *Papers, Regional Science Association*, 4 (1958), 107–120.
[4] Boulding, K. *Economic Analysis*, Volume 1: *Microeconomics*, 4th Edition. New York: Harpers, 1966.
[5] Bucklin, P. "Retail Gravity Models and Consumer Choice: A Theoretical and Empirical Critique," *Economic Geography*, 47 (1971), 489–497.
[6] Eaton, B. C. and R. G. Lipsey. "The Principle of Minimum Differentiation Reconsidered: Some

New Developments in the Theory of Spatial Competition," *Review of Economic Studies*, 42 (1975), 27–49.

[7] ——. "Comparison Shopping and the Clustering of Homogeneous Firms," Queen's University Discussion Paper No. 226, 1976.

[8] ——. "The Introduction of Space into the Neo-Classical Model of Value Theory" in M. J. Artis and A. R. Nobay (eds.), *Studies in Modern Economics*, Oxford: Basil Blackwell, 1977, pp. 59–96.

[9] ——. "Microeconomic Foundations of Central Place Theory," Queen's University Discussion Paper, No. 327, 1978.

[10] ——. "Freedom of Entry and the Existence of Pure Profit," *Economic Journal*, forthcoming.

[11] Foster, J. R. "Real Estate Financing and the Opportunity Cost for Shopping Center Occupancy," *Land Economics*, 44 (1968), 319–329.

[12] Golledge, R. G., G. Rushton, and W. A. V. Clark. "Some Spatial Characteristics of Iowa's Dispersed Farm Population and Their Implications for the Grouping of Central Place Functions," *Economic Geography*, 42 (1966), 261–272.

[13] Holton, R. M. "The Distinction Between Convenience Goods, Shopping Goods, and Specialty Goods," *Journal of Marketing*, 23 (1958), 53–56.

[14] Horton, F. E. "Location Factors as Determinants of Consumer Attraction to Retail Firms," *Annals of the Association of American Geographers*, 48 (1968), 787–801.

[15] Hotelling, H. "Stability in Competition," *Economic Journal*, 39 (1929), 41–57.

[16] Lerner, A., and H. Singer. "Some Notes on Duopoly and Spatial Competition," *Journal of Political Economy*, 45 (1937), 145–186.

[17] Lösch, A. *The Economics of Location*. (W. H. Woglom and W. F. Stolper, trans.) New Haven: Yale University Press, 1954.

[18] Nelson, R. L. *The Selection of Retail Locations*. New York: F. W. Dodge Corporation, 1958.

[19] Porter, M. E. "Consumer Behavior, Retailer Power and Market Performance in Consumer Goods Industries," *Review of Economics and Statistics*, 56 (1974), 419–436.

[20] Rogers, A. "A Stochastic Analysis of the Spatial Clustering of Retail Establishments," *American Statistical Association Journal*, 60 (1965), 1094–1103.

[21] Rothchild, M. "Models of Market Organization with Imperfect Information: A Survey," *Journal of Political Economy*, 81 (1973), 1283–1308.

[22] Smithies, A. "Optimal Location in Spatial Competition," *Journal of Political Economy*, 49 (1941), 423–439.

[9]
The Block Metric and the Law of Markets

B. Curtis Eaton[1]

Department of Economics, University of British Columbia, Vancouver, British Columbia V6T 1W5, Canada

AND

Richard G. Lipsey

Department of Economics, Queen's University, Kingston, Ontario, K7L 3N6, Canada

Received November 29, 1977; revised March 2, 1978

> The "Law of Markets" as originally stated by Fetter and amended by Hyson and Hyson is based on the assumption that the transportation of goods is along a line segment from firm to customer. In many situations the assumption that transportation is along a block-like network of roads is a better approximation of reality. In this paper we establish the "law of markets" appropriate to the block metric. We discover that with such a metric there exist significant discontinuities in a firm's demand functions and we argue that these discontinuities have important implications for the types of competitive strategies open to firms.

In 1924 Fetter stated his "Law of Markets" [3, p. 525]:

> The boundary line between the territories tributary to two geographically competing markets for like goods is a hyperbolic curve. At each point on this line the difference between freights from the two markets is just equal to the difference between the market prices, whereas on either side of this line the freight difference and the price difference are unequal. The relation of prices in the two markets determine the location of the boundary line; the lower the relative price the larger the tributary area.

Fetter's law clearly deals with the delivery of goods from plant to customers directly along a straight line; distance between two points is measured by the Euclidean metric. The Euclidean metric is appropriate for situations in which a few producers are spread over the whole nation and the vicissitudes of the highway or rail network can be ignored so that, to a good approximation, transportation from point to point is along a straight line.

However, in many rural areas and most cities transportation is along a network of roads which is closely approximated by a block-like grid and the Euclidean metric is not appropriate. In these circumstances the correct

---

[1]Author to whom correspondence should be addressed.

metric is what Nash and Beckmann [7] refer to as the "Manhattan" metric, or more simply the *block metric*: the distance between two points, with roads oriented north–south and east–west, is the sum of the north–south and the east–west distances separating the points.

Our purpose in this paper is to establish the "law of markets" appropriate to the block metric. The law turns out to be substantially different from the law applicable to the Euclidean metric. In the concluding section we suggest some potentially important applications which arise out of the differences.

Fetter assumed that transport costs were the same from each firm. Hyson and Hyson [5] have generalized Fetter's analysis to cover the case in which transport costs from different firms are different because, for example, the modes of transport differ. In the Appendix we examine the analogous problem with the block metric.

I. THE BLOCK METRIC AND THE LAW OF MARKETS

We assume that customers are distributed over a bounded two-dimensional space and that they purchase a homogeneous commodity from either of two firms. Firm A is located at point a with Cartesian coordinates (X_a, Y_a) and B is located at b with coordinates (X_b, Y_b).

Define K as $(P_b - P_a)/t$, where P_b and P_a are mill prices of A and B and t is unit transport cost, the cost of transporting a unit of product a unit of distance. We refer to K as "A's net margin of advantage."

With the block metric the distance between firms A and B is

$$D = |X_a - X_b| + |Y_a - Y_b|. \tag{1}$$

The distance from any point (X, Y) to firm A is then

$$D_a = |X_a - X| + |Y_a - Y|, \tag{2}$$

and the distance from (X, Y) to B is

$$D_b = |X_b - X| + |Y_b - Y|. \tag{3}$$

Then the market boundary between A and B is the locus of points such that $D_a - D_b = K$, or

$$|X_a - X| + |Y_a - Y| - |X_b - X| - |Y_b - Y| = K, \quad -D < K < D. \tag{4}$$

To begin the case-by-case analysis of market boundaries we will assume that $X_a < X_b$, $Y_a < Y_b$, and $X_b - X_a > Y_b - Y_a$. These assumptions are incorporated in Fig. 1. The points (X_a, Y_a), (X_b, Y_b), (X_a, Y_b) and (X_b, Y_a)

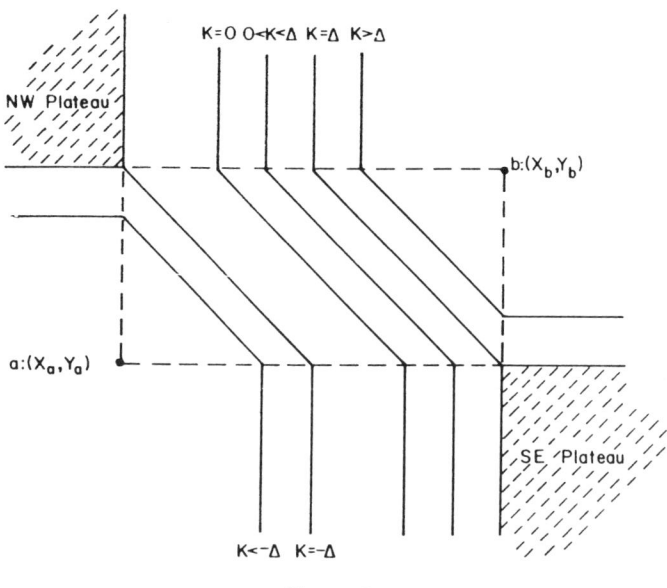

FIGURE 1

define the rectangle shown by broken lines in the figure. We refer to the market boundary within this rectangle as the *interior boundary*. A market boundary outside the rectangle is referred to as an *exterior boundary*.

To determine the interior boundary we can, given the restrictions that $X_a < X_b$ and $Y_a < Y_b$, rewrite Eq. (4) as

$$(X - X_a) + (Y - Y_a) - (X_b - X) - (Y_b - Y) = K,$$

which yields the interior boundary,

$$X = (K + X_a + X_b + Y_a + Y_b)/2 - Y. \tag{5}$$

We now wish to show that the exterior boundaries emanate from the points where the interior boundary intersects the rectangle and that the exterior boundaries are perpendicular to the sides of the rectangle at the points of intersection. We begin by considering the intersection of the interior boundary with the side of the rectangle $Y = Y_a$. Evaluating Eq. (5) at $Y = Y_a$ we obtain

$$X_1 = (K + X_a + X_b - Y_a + Y_b)/2. \tag{6}$$

Note that

$$X_1 \gtreqless X_b \text{ as } K \gtreqless X_b - X_a + Y_a - Y_b = \Delta > 0.$$

$\Delta > 0$ since, by assumption, $X_b - X_a > Y_b - Y_a$. This result implies that the interior boundary will intersect the rectangle in Fig. 1 along the side $Y = Y_a$ if $K < \Delta$. In this case the exterior boundary for the area such that $Y < Y_a$ will be the vertical line $X = X_1$, defined in Eq. (6). To see that this is so, note that all points such that $X < X_a$ and $Y < Y_a$ are clearly in A's market area as long as $K > -D$, and all points such that $X > X_b$ are clearly in B's market area as long as $K < \Delta$. Thus the X coordinate of the exterior market boundary is bounded below by X_a and above by X_b. Then when $Y < Y_a$ and $X_a < X < X_b$ Eq. (4) can be rewritten as

$$(X - X_a) + (Y_a - Y) - (X_b - X) - (Y_b - Y) = K.$$

Solving for X yields $X = X_1$.

If $K > \Delta$ the interior boundary will intersect the rectangle along the side $X = X_b$. Letting $X = X_b$ in Eq. (5) and solving for Y we discover that the intersection occurs at

$$Y_1 = (K + X_a - X_b + Y_a + Y_b)/2. \qquad (7)$$

In this case the exterior boundary for the area $X > X_b$ is the horizontal line $Y = Y_1$. Firm B clearly dominates the area where $X > X_b$ and $Y > Y_b$ if $K < D$, and A dominates the area $Y < Y_a$ if $K > \Delta$ so that the Y coordinate of the exterior market boundary must satisfy $Y_b > Y > Y_a$. With $X > X_b$ and $Y_b > Y > Y_a$ Eq. (4) can be rewritten to eliminate the absolute value signs, and then solving for Y yields $Y = Y_1$.

Next observe that when $K = \Delta$ all customers in the area such that $X > X_b$ and $Y < Y_a$, labeled the SE plateau in Fig. 1, are indifferent between patronizing A or B. For all points in this region $D_a - D_b$ is a constant, Δ, and hence if A's net margin of advantage is Δ, customers will be indifferent between firms A and B. We refer to areas over which $D_a - D_b$ is constant as *plateau areas*. If K assumes a value such that customers in a plateau area are indifferent between A and B, we refer to the plateau as a *zone of indifference*.

A procedure parallel to the above establishes that if

$$K > X_a - X_b + Y_b - Y_a = -\Delta < 0,$$

the interior boundary intersects the rectangle along the side $Y = Y_b$ and the exterior boundary for the area $Y > Y_b$ is the vertical line

$$X_2 = (K + X_a + X_b + Y_a - Y_b)/2. \qquad (8)$$

If $K < -\Delta$ the interior boundary intersects the rectangle along the side $X = X_a$, and the exterior boundary for the area $X < X_a$ is the horizontal line

$$Y_2 = (K - X_a + X_b + Y_a + Y_b)/2. \qquad (9)$$

If $K = -\Delta$ all customers in the NW plateau in Fig. 1 ($Y > Y_b$ and $X < X_a$) will be indifferent between A and B; the plateau is a zone of indifference.

Now consider the continuity properties of the market boundary. In contrast to the model with Cartesian distance, the market of either firm expressed as a function of K exhibits significant discontinuities. Starting with $K = 0$, a glance at Fig. 1 reveals that as K increases (because, for example, firm A decreases its price) A's market increases continuously until K reaches Δ. At this value of K, A's market increases discretely since all customers in the SE plateau who formerly patronized B are now indifferent between patronizing A or B. As K is increased further A captures the entire SE plateau. Thus as K increases A's market area is discretely increased as K passes through Δ so that A captures both of the plateau areas. Analogous changes in B's market area occur as K is decreased; for a while B's market area increases continuously as K decreases but as K passes through $-\Delta$, B's market area increases discretely as B adds the NW plateau to its own market area.

Some special cases must now be considered. First assume that $X_b - X_a = Y_b - Y_a$; i.e., the rectangle in Fig. 1 is reduced to a square. In this case $\Delta = 0$ since all points in the two plateaus are equidistant from firms A and B. Thus when $K = 0$ both plateaus are zones of indifference. A marginal increase in K would then allow A to capture both plateaus and a decrease in K would allow B to capture them.

A second special case arises when either $X_a = X_b$ or $Y_a = Y_b$. In this case there are no plateaus and the market boundary is a line perpendicular to the line joining points a and b, moving toward point b as K increases and toward a as K decreases.

A large number of other cases would seem to arise if we drop the restrictions ($X_a < X_b$, $Y_a < Y_b$, $X_b - X_a > Y_b - Y_a$) that underlie the analysis pictured in Fig. 1. However, except for the two special cases discussed above, the locations of the two firms will always define a rectangle. If, as in Fig. 1, one firm is above and to the right of the other the interior boundary will have a slope of -1, and if one firm is above and to the left of the other the interior boundary will have a slope of $+1$. In all the rectangular cases the exterior boundaries emanate from the points where the interior boundary intersects the rectangle, and the exterior boundaries are perpendicular to the sides of the rectangle at the points of intersection. The discontinuities in market areas as a function of K characterize all the rectangular (and square) configurations.

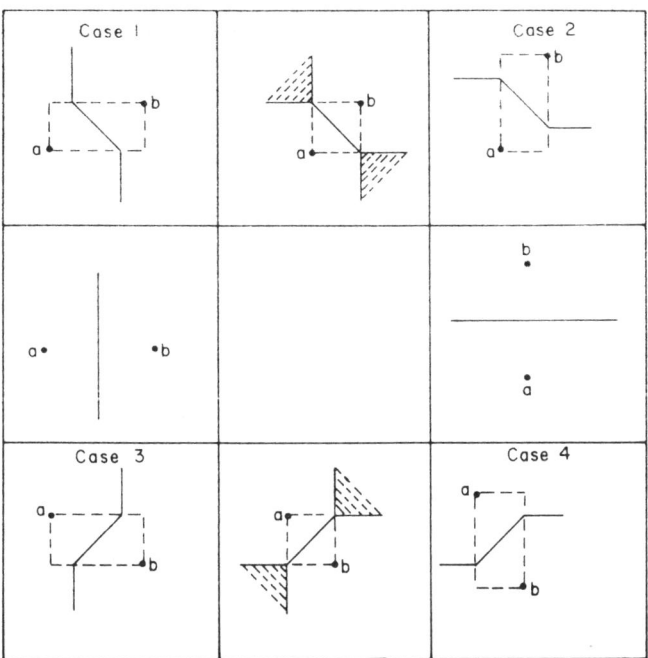

FIGURE 2

To this point we have held the locations of firms fixed and allowed K to vary. Now let us hold K constant at a value of zero and let one firm's location vary. In Fig. 2 we have drawn the market boundaries with $K = 0$ for all possible cases and have labeled the four cases in the corners of the diagram as cases 1, 2, 3, and 4.

We arbitrarily pick case 1 as the initial configuration and allow A's location to vary. First let the Y coordinate of A's location vary, holding X_a constant. Denote the variable Y coordinate of A's location at Y'_a. As Y'_a increases the market boundary will remain in case 1 and A's market area will change continuously until Y'_a approaches Y_b. As Y'_a passes through Y_b, A's market boundary will pass through the special case in column 1 of Fig. 1 into case 3, and A's market area will change continuously. Now hold Y_a constant (at its initial value) and let the X coordinate, X'_a, of A's location vary. As long as X'_a is less than $X_b - Y_b + Y_a$ the market boundary remains in the case 1 and A's market changes continuously but as X'_a passes through the point $X_b - Y_b + Y_a$, A's market boundary passes through the special case of the square configuration in row 1 of Fig. 1 to case 2. At this point there is an obvious discontinuity in A's market area. When $X'_a < X_b - Y_b + Y_a$, A captures the NW plateau and B captures the

SE plateau. When $X'_a = X_b - Y_b + Y_a$ the plateaus are shared (the special case of the square configuration), and when $X'_a > X_b - Y_b + Y_a$, A captures the SE plateau and B the NW. More generally as long as $Y'_a < Y_b$ and $X < X_b - Y_b + Y'_a$, the market boundary remains in case 1; and as Y'_a passes through Y_b the market boundary passes through the special case of column 1 of Fig. 2 into case 3; as A's location passes through line $X'_a = X_b - Y_b + Y_a$ the market boundary passes through the special case of row 1 of Fig. 2 to case 2, and there is an obvious discontinuity in A's market area.

II. SIGNIFICANCE

In this section we suggest some ways in which the results in Section I may help in understanding actual competitive behavior. Some of the statements made follow fairly obviously from what has gone before; some are more conjectural.

1. The plateaus give a discontinuity to any firm's market area expressed as a function of K. Any change in either firm's price that shifts K beyond one of the two critical values $(\Delta, -\Delta)$ allows one firm to capture the other's plateau. This provides a strong incentive for firms to engage in price competition whenever K is close to Δ or $-\Delta$. The closer the configuration of the two firms is to a square, the closer Δ is to zero and the stronger the incentive. Indeed if the firms are in a square configuration with a common price both plateaus will be zones of indifference and there will be a very large payoff to the slightest bit of successful price cutting.

When price competition is seen to be undesirable or even unavailable (e.g., because of retail price maintenance legislation) there are many alternative forms of "K-competition" open to the firms. One method is to try to reduce their customers' time costs of purchasing from them. This can be done, for example, by building large parking lots to reduce parking congestion and hence overall travel time and by having sufficient floor space and sufficiently large displays (and hence large inventories) to eliminate shopping congestion even at peak periods. These techniques lead to "excess capacity": more capacity than is necessary to meet the average load of demand. Firms can pressure local governments to change traffic patterns by road building, traffic light installation, etc.

Advertising is another obvious weapon for K-competition. If a plateau is almost, or only just, in one firm's market area it is an obvious target respectively for offensive and defensive advertising campaigns. Selective advertising within any plateau, such as can be done by mail, the direct distribution of circulars, and door-to-door canvassing, is a technique that tends to minimize costs by localizing the appeal where it is needed while promising a large profit if a whole plateau area (or a significant part of it) can be swung from one firm to the other.

All of the above and other, similar forms of behavior are obvious ways of shifting the boundary dividing the market areas of two stores whether the appropriate metric is block or Euclidean. *The analysis of the present paper demonstrates that, when the block metric is appropriate, there may be large and quite disproportionate returns to a small amount of successful K-competition.*

The illustrations of nonprice competition used above are not well defined in our model and some caution is therefore necessary. An assumption that is sufficient to give definition to nonprice competition in our model is the assumption of identical tastes. However, it is clear that this assumption is not tenable in many situations.

2. Consider cases in which the plateau areas are zones of indifference. This can arise because either (a) the firms are in a square configuration with the boundary defined by the $K = 0$ contour, or (b) the firms are in a rectangular configuration with the boundary defined by a value of K at either Δ, or $-\Delta$. In case (a) both of the plateaus are zones of indifference; in case (b) only one of the plateaus can be a zone of indifference. Any theory that allows for these possibilities must have a way of dividing the indifferent customers between the two firms. If, as seems likely, there is a stochastic element in this division then, since the plateau areas can be very large, the firms may be subject to larger intertemporal fluctuations in demand. This will inevitably lead to a higher total capacity between firms A and B than would exist if each firm had one plateau firmly within its own market area. Such extra capacity would seem to serve no socially useful purpose since customers are indifferent as to which firm they patronize.

Devletoglou [1] has analyzed a duopoly model in space, with the Euclidean metric, in which consumers are indifferent between the products of the two firms as long as the difference in delivered prices from the two firms is less than some "minimum sensible." The minimum sensible, of course, implies a "zone of indifference," and Devletoglou demonstrates that the zone of indifference implies excessive inventory costs. The introduction of a minimum sensible in our model would, of course, increase the likelihood that one or both plateaus are zones of indifference.

3. The existence of equilibrium seems more questionable with the block metric. If we hold constant all locations and all but one firm's price, then the market area and hence the quantity demanded from the one firm whose prices are varied is (i) a continuously decreasing function of the firm's price with the Euclidean metric (as long as one firm does not come to dominate another) but (ii) is a discontinuous function with the block metric—with a discontinuity occurring at each price such that customers in a plateau are indifferent between the two firms.

4. If we depart from the duopoly model considered so far, then as the space becomes more densely packed with firms a new range of issues is raised by the block metric. What is the optimal packing of firms? What configurations are equilibrium configurations? Losch [6, pp. 133 − 134] and Fox and Kumar [4] have considered packing configurations which leave firms with square market areas, and a recent paper by Donaldson and Eaton [2] demonstrates that this configuration is the optimal configuration under the block metric.

5. There are many interesting nonfirm applications. Assume, for example, that A and B are two stops on a bus or subway commuter line, located at a and b. If passengers travel to the closer station, the boundary of their two catchment areas is found by setting $K = 0$ in Eq. (8). Now assume the existence of congestion (that is not caused by the travelers going to the station) that adds an amount of time, δ, to the journey of every traveler going to a. This congestion shifts the boundary from the contour $K = 0$ to the contour $K = d$, where d is the distance that can be traveled toward b in time interval δ. If the two stations were nearly in a square configuration even a small δ could throw all of A's plateau to B. A very large shift in custom would have accompanied a small, congestion-induced change in K. These large responses to small changes in incentives are changes that may be uninfluenced by, and are sometimes even unpredictable by, planners and can be very upsetting to normal planning.

These examples are merely those that seem to us to be fairly obvious illustrations of the potential importance of the block as opposed to the Euclidean metric. Any one of them could be the subject of a full paper. We hope that these examples are sufficient to demonstrate the potential for applied application of the theory worked out in the earlier part of this paper.

APPENDIX: UNEQUAL TRANSPORT COSTS AND THE LAW OF MARKETS

In the text we have followed Fetter in assuming that transport costs to both firms are the same. When transport is along the same road grid this might seem the most natural assumption. We can, however, imagine situations in which it is appropriate to assume differential transport costs, such as the case analyzed by Hyson and Hyson [5] with the Euclidean metric. For example, one firm might obtain a rebate from the firm delivering its goods while the other did not, or one firm might refund transportation costs incurred by its customers while the other did not (sometimes downtown retailers refund their customers' bus fares while suburban retailers do not). In this appendix we briefly examine the case in which transport costs differ.

Let t_a and t_b be the unit transport costs of firms A and B. The market boundary between A and B will satisfy

$$t_a D_a - t_b D_b = P_b - P_a.$$

Ignoring the special cases (where $X_a = X_b$, $Y_a = Y_b$, or $(X_a - X_b) = (Y_a - Y_b)$) the points a and b will define a rectangle. The market boundary will be a polygon which contains the firm with the higher transport costs. Depending on the magnitude of the price differential the polygon will have eight, six, or four sides. These three possibilities are illustrated in Fig. 3, which is drawn on the assumption that $t_b = 3t_a$. If P_b is low enough relative to P_a the market boundary will be the nonconvex octagon in the figure. If we hold P_a constant and let P_b increase the market boundary will become first a nonconvex hexagon and eventually a

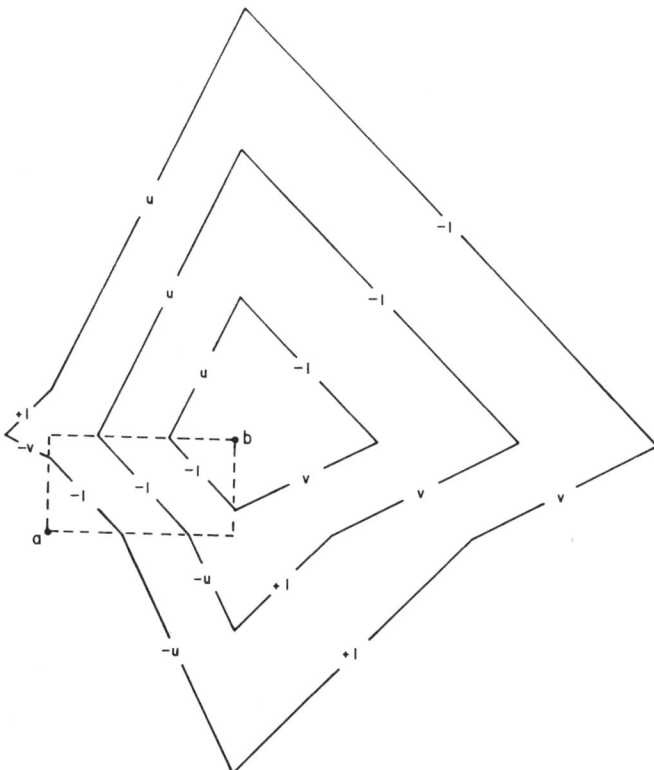

FIG. 3. The symbols at the midpoint of each line segment are the slopes of the segments. The symbols u and v are defined as follows: $u = (t_a - t_b)/(t_a + t_b)$; $v = (t_a + t_b)/(t_a - t_b)$.

trapezoid. Note that when $t_a \neq t_b$ the plateaus disappear, as do the discontinuities in the firms' demand functions. The slopes of the various segments of the market boundary are provided in the figure.

REFERENCES

1. N. Devletoglou, A dissenting view of duopoly and spatial competition, *Economica* **32**, 140–160 (1965).
2. D. Donaldson and B. C. Eaton, "Transporation Networks and Optimal Packing Patterns," mimeographed (1978).
3. F. A. Fetter, The economic law of market areas, *Quart. J. Econ.* **39**, 520–529 (1924).
4. K. Fox and T. K. Kumar, The functional economic area delineation and implications for economic analysis and policy, *Pap. Reg. Sci. Assoc.* **22**, 57–85 (1965).
5. C. D. Hyson and W. P. Hyson The economic law of market areas, *Quart. J. Econ.* **64**, 319–324 (1950).
6. A. Losch, "The Economics of Location," Yale Univ. Press, New Haven, Conn. (1954).
7. D. H. Nash and M. J. Beckmann, On exponential densities and urban form, *J. Urban Econ.* **3**, 304–307 (1976).

Exit barriers are entry barriers: the durability of capital as a barrier to entry

B. Curtis Eaton*

and

Richard G. Lipsey**

We argue that the effectiveness of capital as an entry barrier depends critically on its durability and that this aspect of capital has been largely ignored. We examine strategic decisions with respect to capital durability in two models. In a broad range of cases an active policy with respect to durability and replacement of capital is necessary to maintain a position of market power. Such policies will result in capital that is "too durable" or "too soon replaced" or "too well maintained" relative to the cost minimizing solution (for a given time path of output).

1. Introduction

■ In his seminal essay on bargaining, Thomas Schelling (1956) distinguishes threats and commitments. Both are designed to influence a competitor by impressing him with the consequences of his actions. Both take the same form: "If you take action X, I shall take action Y, which will make you regret X." The distinguishing characteristic of a threat is that the actor has no incentive to carry out action Y either before or after action X. The distinguishing characteristic of a commitment is that, X having occurred, it is in the actor's self-interest to take action Y. A fanatic may carry out a threat, and may thus make "credible threats." A maximizer would not carry out his threats and thus cannot make his threats credible. There would seem, therefore, to be little place for threats in maximizing models.

In this paper we examine the use of product-specific capital goods as vehicles for entry-deterring *commitments*. It may seem surprising that there is anything left to say on this subject in view of such works as Caves and Porter (1977), Dixit (1979, 1980), Eaton and Lipsey (1978, 1979), Schmalensee (1978), and Spence (1977, 1979). These papers deal, however, with what may be called the atemporal aspect of capital as a barrier to entry: a monopolist strategically commits a quantity of capital which is sufficient to produce a negative *flow* of profits to a new entrant. This may be called a *type-A artificial monopoly* (A

---
* University of British Columbia and Yale University.
** Queen's University and Yale University.

This is a shortened version of Eaton and Lipsey (1980), in which proofs may be found of results asserted in the present article. We are indebted to G. C. Archibald, Y. Kanemoto, and J. Roemer for comments and suggestions.

for "atemporal"). *Type-A natural monopoly* occurs when nonstrategic profit-maximizing behavior commits enough capital to produce a negative flow of profits to an entrant. Capital indivisibilities and decreasing costs are at the heart of this analysis. One firm can profitably serve such a market but two cannot.

The point of this paper is that it is not indivisibilities and decreasing costs *per se* which create barriers to entry. Rather, it is the intertemporal commitment of specific capital to a market, in combination with decreasing costs which creates an entry barrier. We thus focus on the durability of capital in the creation of entry barriers. We define a *type-T natural monopoly* (T for "temporal") to be one in which *cost minimizing* decisions with respect to durability, replacement, and maintenance of capital imply that there is no point in time at which entry is profitable, and a *type-T artificial monopoly* to be one in which *strategic decisions* with respect to capital prevent there being any point in time at which entry is profitable.

To see the potential importance of durability as an entry barrier, first consider two extreme cases under static demand and cost conditions. At one extreme is a type-*A* natural monopolist who has no sunk costs. (This would arise, for example, if capital were not product-specific and could be bought, sold, and rented on perfect markets.) Although only one firm can serve this market profitably, there exists no vehicle for commitment to the market. With no sunk costs the market is "up for grabs" at each instant. The absence of capital fixity and associated fixed costs thus seems to imply chaos. At the other extreme, the durability of capital (plant) is exogenous and infinite. Now a type-*A* natural monopolist has a permanent commitment to the market: as long as he can cover his avoidable costs he will remain in the market. As a result, he need never consider the possibility of the entry of new firms.

Second, consider the intermediate case in which a type-*A* natural monopolist's plant has an exogenous and finite durability, $0 < H < \infty$. When unconcerned about entry, the monopolist replaces his plant every H years. But a potential new entrant could establish plant just as the monopolist was about to renew his plant. The market would then belong to the new entrant. But foreseeing that strategy, the existing monopolist would renew his plant a little sooner. But foreseeing this, a potential new entrant would establish his plant sooner yet, and so on. In this case it is clear that the type-*A* natural monopolist must concern himself with the threat of entry; he is not a type-*T* natural monopolist.

In this article we study the strategic use of capital to create a type-*T* artificial monopoly. It is useful in analytical studies to separate strategic decisions with respect to the creation of the two types of monopoly. To isolate the creation of type-*A* artificial monopoly, it is convenient to assume type-*T* *natural* monopoly by letting the durability of capital be infinite (Spence, 1979; Dixit, 1980). Similarly, to isolate the creation of type-*T* artificial monopoly, it is convenient in this article to assume a type-*A* *natural* monopoly. (Our results extend in a fairly obvious way to a firm that has erected entry barriers to create a type-*A* artificial monopoly as well as to oligopolists who wish to maintain their place in the market.)

Our analysis shows that the textbook, type-*A* natural monopoly is not necessarily a type-*T* natural monopoly and that it is impossible for the monopolist to separate cost-minimizing decisions from profit-maximizing ones.

2. Model 1: one-hoss shay capital

■ The basic assumptions of model 1 are as follows. There is an indivisible, product-specific capital good, called plant, which is large enough that a monopolist would require only one unit of it. There are constant returns to the variable factor up to plant capacity.

If there were two firms in the market, each with one unit of plant, their common capacity and common short-run marginal costs would imply a symmetric resolution of the duopoly problem. The symmetric resolution might be Cournot-Nash, or it might be based on some conjectural-variation formulation. Indeed any symmetric resolution will allow us to define what we require: R_1 is the rate of flow of revenues over variable costs when one firm serves the market; R_2 is the rate of flow of revenues over variable costs for either firm when two firms serve the market. We assume that R_1 and R_2 are time invariant, that firms know them with certainty, and that $R_1 > 2R_2 > 0$. These inequalities imply that the resolution of the duopoly pricing problem is not joint profit maximizing and that duopolists cover variable costs.

In model 1 plant of durability H costs $C(H)$ and requires no maintenance. We assume that

$$\lim_{H \to 0} C(H) > 0, \quad C'(H) > 0, \quad \text{and} \quad C''(H) \geq 0 \text{ for } H > \hat{H}. \quad (1)$$

These restrictions guarantee that H will always be chosen to be positive and finite. The deterioration of this "one-hoss shay" capital depends on its age and is independent of intensity of use. Since R_2 is positive, a firm which has plant is committed (in Schelling's sense of the word) to stay in the market until its plant expires.

If a monopolist replaced plant of durability H every $H - \Delta$ periods, its minimum commitment to the market would be Δ. The discounted present value of this policy to a monopolist would be

$$V(\Delta, H) = \frac{R_1}{r} - \frac{C(H)}{1 - \exp[-r(H - \Delta)]}. \quad (2)$$

It is, of course, Δ that is the deterrent to entry and, given Δ, H will be chosen to maximize profits. Define

$$\tilde{V}(\Delta) = \frac{R_1}{r} - \frac{C(h(\Delta))}{1 - \exp[-r(h(\Delta) - \Delta)]}, \quad (3)$$

where $h(\Delta)$ is the profit-maximizing (or cost-minimizing) value of H, given Δ. It can be shown that $h'(\Delta) > 0$. Let $\check{H} = h(0)$. Type-A natural monopoly requires that

$$\tilde{V}(0) = \frac{R_1}{r} - \frac{C(\check{H})}{1 - \exp[-r\check{H}]} > 0 > \frac{R_1}{2r} - \frac{C(\check{H})}{1 - \exp[-r\check{H}]}. \quad (4)$$

The first inequality implies that one firm could more than cover costs and the second implies that two could not.

We assume that entry will occur if and only if the discounted present value of an entrant's profits is greater than zero, and thus we adopt the following definitions. An entry-preventing policy (EPP) is a policy such that the discounted present value of an entrant's profits is always less than or equal to zero. An optimal, entry-preventing policy (OEPP) is an EPP that maximizes the monopolist's present value evaluated at any point in time when he is replacing his plant.

To provide an intuitive explanation of the problem we *assume* that an OEPP exists, denoted by Δ^*, and that potential entrants consider only this policy. Subsequently we show directly the existence of an OEPP with $0 < \Delta^* < h(\Delta^*)/2$. The present value of an entrant's pursuing policy Δ^* is

$$E(\delta,\Delta^*) = -C(h(\Delta^*)) + R_2 \int_0^\delta \exp[-rt]dt$$

$$+ R_1 \int_\delta^{h(\Delta^*)-\Delta^*} \exp[-rt]dt + V(\Delta^*) \exp[-r(h(\Delta^*) - \Delta^*)],$$

where δ is the length of time until the sitting monopolist's plant expires. To interpret this expression let the origin in time be the time of entry. The entrant's initial plant would cost $C(h(\Delta^*))$ and he would earn R_2 from time 0 to δ. Since Δ^* is, by assumption, an EPP, the sitting monopolist would not renew plant and entry would be deterred at all future times. Thus the entrant would earn R_1 from δ to $h(\Delta^*) - \Delta^*$ at which time he would renew his plant and his present value would be $V(\Delta^*)$. $E(\delta,\Delta^*)$ can be rewritten as

$$E(\delta,\Delta^*) = \tilde{V}(\Delta^*) - (R_1 - R_2) \int_0^\delta \exp[-rt]dt. \tag{5}$$

The second term is the new entrant's "price of admission": the difference between profits when the market is served by two firms rather than one firm for the length of time until the sitting monopolist exits. This is also, of course, the measure of the barrier to entry at any point in time. Let Δ be the sitting monopolist's policy. Then

$$E(\Delta,\Delta^*) = \max_\delta E(\delta,\Delta^*) = \tilde{V}(\Delta^*) - (R_1 - R_2) \int_0^\Delta \exp[-rt]dt, \tag{6}$$

which is the maximum present value of an entrant.

Thus the monopolist's problem is

$$\left.\begin{array}{c} \max_\Delta \tilde{V}(\Delta) \\ \text{subject to} \\ E(\Delta,\Delta^*) \leq 0. \end{array}\right\} \tag{7}$$

Both $\tilde{V}(\Delta)$ and $E(\Delta,\Delta^*)$ are decreasing in Δ, and thus the maximization problem posed in (7) is solved by finding $\bar{\Delta}$ such that $E(\bar{\Delta},\Delta^*) = 0$. But Δ^* is an OEPP by assumption and thus $\bar{\Delta} = \Delta^*$. So, if it exists, Δ^* must satisfy $E(\Delta^*,\Delta^*) = 0$. $E(0,0) = \tilde{V}(0)$, which is positive by the first inequality in (4). $E(\Delta,\Delta)$ is decreasing in Δ and goes to $-\infty$ as Δ goes to ∞. Thus, there exists a unique $\Delta^* > 0$ such that $E(\Delta^*,\Delta^*) = 0$. It can be shown that the second inequality in (4) implies that $\Delta^* < h(\Delta^*)/2$. Intuitively, if Δ^* were greater than $h(\Delta^*)/2$, costs of plant would exceed the costs of having two units of plant in the market at all times, which could not be profitable, given our definition of natural monopoly.

At the outset we assumed existence of Δ^*, and thus the argument above is only an intuitive argument. We can however use the result that Δ^* is the unique value of Δ such that $E(\Delta,\Delta)$ is equal to zero to show directly that Δ^* is the unique OEPP. Note first that $E(\Delta_m,\Delta_e)$ is the maximum present value of an entrant with policy Δ_e, if Δ_e is an EPP, when the sitting monopolist's policy is Δ_m. Note that the first derivatives of E with respect to Δ_m and Δ_e are negative. We use a proof by contradiction to demonstrate that Δ^* is the unique OEPP.

Proof: (i) Assume $\Delta_1 < \Delta^*$ is an EPP and that the sitting monopolist's policy is Δ_1. Then, since Δ_1 is an EPP, $E(\Delta_1,\Delta_1) \leq 0$, otherwise an entrant adopting policy Δ_1 would not be deterred. But we have shown that for $\Delta_1 < \Delta^*, E(\Delta_1,\Delta_1) > 0$, which contradicts our assumption that Δ_1 is an EPP. Thus $\Delta_1 < \Delta^*$ is not an EPP. (ii) Now assume that Δ^* is not an EPP and that the sitting monopolist's policy is Δ^*. Since Δ^* is not an EPP, there exists an EPP, Δ_2, such that $E(\Delta^*,\Delta_2) > 0$. But since $E(\Delta^*,\Delta^*) = 0$ and E is decreasing in its second argument, $\Delta_2 < \Delta^*$. But, by the argument in (i), $\Delta_2 < \Delta^*$ cannot be an EPP, a contradiction. Thus Δ^* is an EPP.[1] (iii) The argument in (ii) implies that any policy, $\Delta > \Delta^*$, is an EPP. But since $\bar{V}(\Delta)$ is decreasing in Δ, Δ^* is the unique OEPP. *Q.E.D.*

For completeness we must show that the monopolist prefers the OEPP to the policy of "graceful exit": allowing entry to occur and then exiting when his plant expires. In the absence of entry prevention, entry would occur $\Delta^* - \epsilon$ periods before the sitting monopolist's plant expired, where ϵ is arbitrarily small. As ϵ goes to zero, the present value of graceful exit approaches

$$G(\Delta^*) = R_2 \int_0^{\Delta^*} \exp[-rt]dt > 0. \qquad (8)$$

Note that

$$\bar{V}(\Delta^*) - E(\Delta^*,\Delta^*) = (R_1 - R_2) \int_0^{\Delta^*} \exp[-rt]dt.$$

But since $E(\Delta^*,\Delta^*) = 0$, we have

$$\bar{V}(\Delta^*) = (R_1 - R_2) \int_0^{\Delta^*} \exp[-rt]dt, \qquad (9)$$

and since $R_1 > 2R_2$, we have $V(\Delta^*) > G(\Delta^*) > 0$.

We have shown in model 1 that an active policy of entry prevention is necessary—that type-A natural monopoly does not imply type-T natural monopoly—and that this strategy is profitable. Protecting this monopoly position involves the dissipation of monopoly rents and is wasteful of scarce resources, since the monopolist replaces plant before it is economically obsolete. The dissipation of monopoly rents through early replacement of capital and the resulting resource waste will be smaller the stronger is duopoly price competition, and the smaller are the monopoly profits (*ceteris paribus* the smaller is

---

[1] This argument assumes that the entrant considers only entry-preventing policies. We show in Eaton and Lipsey (1980), footnote 2, that nonentry-preventing strategies are never profitable.

R_2 or R_1). Regulation that reduces monopoly profits may thus reduce the social waste analyzed in this paper.

Since $\Delta^* > 0$ and $h'(\Delta) > 0$, it follows that $h(\Delta^*) > \bar{H}$. In other words, the strategy of entry deterrence leads the monopolist to choose plant which is more durable than the cost-minimizing durability. This result does not reflect an additional burden since, given Δ^*, durability is chosen to minimize costs.

3. Model 2: maintaining plant

■ In model 2 we assume that plant costs K, $K > 0$, and that maintenance costs, m, are a convex function of age of plant, a:

$$m = g(a), \quad g'(a) > 0, \quad g''(a) \geq 0. \tag{10}$$

Notice that we have three categories of costs in this model: sunk costs of plant; costs of maintaining plant which are avoidable only by not producing and which are invariant with respect to output; and the constant marginal costs of production. Define $C(S)$ to be the discounted present cost of a new plant over a service life of S periods. Then

$$C(S) = K + \int_0^S g(a) \exp[-ra] da. \tag{11}$$

The restrictions on $g(a)$ imply that $C'(S) > 0$ and $C''(S) > 0$.

$C(S)$ satisfies the restrictions on the cost function in model 1, and it follows immediately that the monopolist could create a minimum commitment to the market, Δ, by replacing plant, *with a prepaid maintenance contract of S periods*, every $S - \Delta$ periods. By analogy with model 1 there exists a Δ^* which maximizes profits, subject to entry's being unprofitable. Further, it is easily demonstrated that the optimal service life associated with Δ^* is less than the cost-minimizing service life, so that plant is replaced before its economic life is over.

Our purpose in model 2 is to explore another entry-preventing strategy when plant is maintainable. Accordingly, define S to be the policy of replacing plant every S periods. The present value to a monopolist of this policy is

$$V(S) = \frac{R_1}{r} - \frac{C(S)}{1 - \exp[-rS]}. \tag{12}$$

$V(S)$ is pseudoconcave in S, decreases without bound as S goes to zero and as S goes to infinity, and therefore has a unique maximum.[2] Let $\tilde{S}$ be the value of S which maximizes $V(S)$.

We wish to argue that, in the event of entry, the sitting monopolist would stay in the market until his maintenance costs rose to R_2. We argue as follows: if $g(a)$ were less than R_2, and if the monopolist paid $g(a)$, then he and the entrant would face identical avoidable costs, the resolution of the duopoly problem would be symmetric, and the monopolist would enjoy the flow R_2; therefore, the monopolist will incur the maintenance costs if and only if $g(a) \leq R_2$. Alternatively, in the event of entry the monopolist could sign a binding maintenance contract with a third party, and his avoidable costs would then be just

---

[2] Pseudoconcavity of $V(S)$ requires that when $V'(S) = 0$, $V''(S) < 0$, which is easily verified. See Diewert, Avriel, and Zang (1977) for a useful taxonomy of concavity.

the marginal costs of production. An optimal maintenance contract would run until $g(a) = R_2$.

Let A be the age of plant such that $g(A) = R_2$. Then if the monopolist chooses a policy $S \leq A$, his minimum commitment to the market is $A - S$. If he chooses $S > A$, his minimum commitment to the market is zero.

Then we seek the existence of a policy S^* which solves

$$\max_{S} V(S)$$

subject to

$$E(S,S^*) \leq 0, \quad (13)$$

where

$$E(S,S^*) = \begin{cases} V(S^*) - (R_1 - R_2) \int_0^{A-S} \exp[-rt]dt, & \text{if } S \leq A, \\ V(S^*), & \text{if } S > A. \end{cases} \quad (14)$$

$E(S,S^*)$ is interpreted as the present value of an entrant's pursuing policy S^* when the monopolist's policy is S.

Several cases require attention. First, suppose the monopolist adopts policy $\tilde{S}$. It is clear from (14) that if A is large enough relative to $\tilde{S}$, the monopolist need not pursue an active policy of entry prevention. Let $\bar{A}$ be the value of A in (14) such that $E(\tilde{S},\tilde{S}) = 0$. Then, if $A \geq \bar{A}$, $S^* = \tilde{S}$, and entry prevention is costless. This is a case of type-T natural monopoly.

Denote by S_1 and S_2 the minimum and maximum values of S such that $V(S) = 0$. Pseudoconcavity of $V(S)$ then implies that $V(S) > 0$ in the open interval (S_1,S_2) and $V(S) < 0$ for $S < S_1$ and for $S > S_2$. When $A \leq S_1$, the constraint in (13) cannot be satisfied in the profitable range of production. Thus $S^* = S_1$ and $S^* = S_2$ are the only solutions to the problem posed in (13) and $V(S^*) = 0$. In this case it is clear that the use of a prepaid maintenance contract to deter entry is the preferred strategy.

Finally, consider the case when $S_1 < A < \bar{A}$. $E(S_1,S_1) < 0$, since $S_1 < A$, and $E(\tilde{S},\tilde{S}) > 0$, since $A < \bar{A}$. Both $V(S)$ and $E(S,S^*)$ are increasing in S when $S_1 < S < \tilde{S}$, and thus S^* must satisfy $E(S^*,S^*) = 0$. Since $E(S,S)$ is increasing in S in this interval, there exists a unique S^*, $S_1 < S^* < \tilde{S}$ such that $E(S^*,S^*) = 0$. An argument parallel to that in model 1 shows that S^* is the unique OEPP. Since $S^* < \tilde{S}$, plant is replaced before its economically useful life is over.

We have shown that when plant is maintainable, there exist circumstances where entry deterrence is costless, the case of type-T natural monopoly. When an active policy of entry deterrence is necessary, the monopolist has two options, both of which require the replacement of plant before its economically useful life is over. Since a potential entrant has the same options, the monopolist must choose the more profitable option.

4. Conclusions

■ Our analysis suggests a need for revision of the concept of natural monopoly. A fully insulated natural monopoly must have both type-A and type-T natural monopoly. If it has only the former, it may be able to use specific capital to create a type-T artificial monopoly.

Profit maximization does not imply cost minimization in our models. Thus, when one is considering the creation of artificial barriers to entry, taking minimized costs as a primitive can be misleading. Product-specific capital is a natural vehicle for commitment, and firms who so use it will violate cost minimization.

It may be useful to consider the argument that a successful entry-preventing strategy must be based on commitment, not threat, in the context of the creation of a type-T monopoly. To make an entry-deterring threat in model 1, the sitting monopolist must threaten that in the event of entry, he will stay in the market *long enough* that the entrant's present value at time of entry will be nonpositive. "Long enough" is Δ^* periods. If the sitting monopolist's plant has at least Δ^* periods of remaining economic life, then the threat is a commitment, because the sitting monopolist's plant can more than cover its variable costs. If his plant has less than Δ^* periods of remaining economic life, the threat is not a commitment: fulfilling it would require building new plant at a time when it promises a negative present value. Δ^* can be interpreted as the monopolist's minimum commitment to the market or as the minimum *barrier to his exit*. It is in this sense that barriers to exit are barriers to entry.

The intuitive appeal of our results suggests to us that they will survive generalization of our assumptions with respect to capital. Two obvious possibilities are capital that decays exponentially or capital that decays only with use. Specific capital is a natural vehicle for commitment to the market, and commitment is valuable to the firm, since it inhibits entry. Accordingly a profit-maximizing firm will choose the specifications of specific capital (its durability and/or time of replacement and/or level of maintenance, etc.), so that marginal cost is equal to a positive marginal value in inhibiting entry. This choice will often result in specific capital that is "too durable" or "too soon replaced" or "too well maintained" relative to the unconstrained cost-minimizing solution.

The entry-deterring strategies that we have analyzed would be relatively easy to detect in a world of static demand and technology. They would, however, be much harder to detect in the real world of changing demand and technology. The entry-preventing firm may then appear as the "alert" firm, establishing capacity to meet growing demand, and as the "progressive" firm, investing early in new technologies.

Application to policy is clearly premature. The purpose of this article is to reveal a gap in our present theories of natural and artificial monopoly. To do this we use stark concepts of capital. At a minimum, analysis of more "realistic" assumptions with respect to capital and corroborating empirical work are necessary before the social waste that occurs in our models can be held to be likely and/or significant. In this context it is important to note that although waste of capital always occurs in model 1, it may be unnecessary in model 2.[3]

References

CAVES, R.E. AND PORTER, M.E. "Barriers to Exit" in R.T. Masson and P.D. Qualls, eds., *Essays on Industrial Organization in Honor of Joe S. Bain*, Cambridge: Ballinger, 1976.

——— AND ———. "From Entry Barriers to Mobility Barriers: Conjectural Decisions and Contrived Deterrence to New Competition." *Quarterly Journal of Economics* (May 1977), pp. 241–261.

---

[3] Since writing this paper, our attention has been drawn to Caves and Porter (1976), in which the issues discussed in this paper are foreshadowed. See especially their pages 44–45.

DIEWERT, W.E., AVRIEL, M., AND ZANG, I. "Nine Kinds of Quasi Concavity and Concavity." Discussion Paper 77-31, University of British Columbia, 1977.
DIXIT, A. "A Model of Duopoly Suggesting a Theory of Entry Barriers." *Bell Journal of Economics* (Spring 1979), pp. 20–32.
———. "The Role of Investment in Entry Deterrence." *Economic Journal* (March 1980), pp. 95–106.
EATON, B.C. AND LIPSEY, R.G. "The Theory of Market Preemption: The Persistence of Excess Capacity and Monopoly in Growing Spatial Markets." *Economica* (May 1977).
——— AND ———. "Freedom of Entry and the Existence of Pure Profit." *Economic Journal* (September 1978), pp. 455–469.
——— AND ———. "Exit Barriers Are Entry Barriers." University of British Columbia Discussion Paper No. 80-3, February 1980.
SCHELLING, T.C. "An Essay on Bargaining." *American Economic Review* (June 1956), pp. 281–306.
SCHMALENSEE, R. "Entry Deterrence in the Ready-to-Eat Breakfast Cereal Industry." *Bell Journal of Economics* (Autumn 1978), pp. 305–327.
SPENCE, A.M. "Entry, Capacity, Investment, and Oligopolistic Pricing." *Bell Journal of Economics* (Autumn 1977), pp. 534–544.
———. "Investment Strategy and Growth in a New Market." *Bell Journal of Economics* (Spring 1979), pp. 1–19.

Capital, commitment, and entry equilibrium

B. Curtis Eaton*

and

Richard G. Lipsey**

A primary concern of recent oligopoly literature has been the use of product-specific capital to impose asymmetric market solutions, including the deterrence of entry. This article explores the surprisingly neglected topic of the correspondence between the nature of product-specific capital (PSC) and the properties of entry equilibrium. The nature of PSC determines the type of entry with which firms must be concerned (predatory entry, where the entrant replaces an existing firm, or augmenting entry, where the entrant does not), the instruments available to effect asymmetry, the ability to impose asymmetric solutions, and their profitability.

1. Introduction

■ A recent focus of research on entry barriers has been on sunk capital as a vehicle by which existing firms can make entry-barring commitments (Caves and Porter, 1976, 1977; Dixit, 1979, 1980; Eaton and Lipsey, 1979, 1980; Spence, 1977, 1979). In this article we briefly review two of the models from this literature and add another. Our purpose is to explore the relationship between the nature of capital and entry equilibrium.

The value of entry is the discounted present value of the flow of profits expected by an entrant. Since entry will occur when this value is positive, an established firm that seeks to deter entry must pursue a course of action that makes the value of entry nonpositive. As the problem is usually formulated, the course of action is to promise to produce a postentry stream of output large enough to have the desired effect on the value of entry.

The equilibrium concepts in Dixit (1980) and in Eaton and Lipsey (1980) rely on Schelling's (1956) distinction between threats and commitments. Both take the same form: "If you take action X, I shall take action Y, which will make you regret X." The distinguishing characteristic of a threat is that the actor has no incentive to carry out action Y, while the distinguishing characteristic of a commitment is that, X having occurred, it is in the actor's self-interest to take action Y. We rely on commitment in our equilibrium concept. Entry

---

* University of Toronto.
** Queen's University.
The work on this article was done while the authors held visiting appointments at Yale University. We acknowledge the helpful comments of Drew Fudenberg and Andrew Mueller on an earlier draft.

deterrence then requires that the established firm unambiguously *commit* itself to a course of action which will deter entry.

The essence of commitment in our model is the ability to create irreversibilities, to "tie one's own hands" in Schelling's words. If capital is to be used as a vehicle for commitment, it is then clear that the capital must be *product-specific* in some degree; otherwise, past expenditures on capital are recoverable, and incurring such expenditures does not "tie one's own hands." We use PSC to denote "product-specific capital." In this article we focus on product-specific plant, equipment, and entry capital. We define the degree of product specificity by the index $1 - R$, where R is the ratio of *value of existing capital in its best alternative use to replacement cost of existing capital*. In the formal analysis we assume for convenience that R is zero. The range of items included in PSC could be expanded to include informational advertising, brand image advertising, firm-specific human capital, and any other items that represent nonrecoverable costs to existing firms, but avoidable costs to new entrants. Our definition of an index of specificity would, however, require amendment in some of these cases (e.g., brand-image advertising).

Given the sunk capital of the existing firm or firms, it is apparent that a model of duopoly, or oligopoly, is required to determine the value of entry. This basic insight, which turns Bain's fundamental insight around, can be found in Dixit (1980) and in Eaton and Lipsey (1979). Bain observed that *we cannot meaningfully analyze oligopoly problems without explicit attention to the possibility of entry*. Dixit (1980) and Eaton and Lipsey (1979) observe that as long as we insist on commitment and not threat, *we cannot analyze entry deterrence without an underlying model of oligopoly*. Thus, there is a correspondence between models of oligopoly and entry equilibrium.

Although the existing literature emphasizes PSC as the vehicle by which a flow of capital services, and hence of output, can be committed to the market by existing firms, surprisingly little attention has been paid to the nature of the PSC that does the job. Two important aspects of PSC are its durability and its divisibility. The title of this article, "Capital, Commitment, and Entry Equilibrium," reflects our basic purpose, which is to explore the correspondence between the nature of capital and entry equilibrium when the equilibrium concept is based on commitment. We demonstrate that the properties of entry equilibrium vary dramatically as the durability and divisibility of PSC change, and that definition cannot be given to the concept of entry equilibrium in the absence of knowledge of the nature of PSC.[1]

2. Variations on a theme

■ **Assumptions of convenience.** For simplicity, we assume that the market is not large enough to support three firms, and that demand and cost conditions are time-invariant and known with certainty. We then examine the behavior

---

[1] Our first attempt to deal with the correspondence between the nature of capital and entry equilibrium can be found in Eaton and Lipsey (1977), where we consider the problem in a model of spatial competition. In a recent paper, Schmalensee (1980) argues that capital cannot be a significant barrier to entry where the ratio of minimum efficient scale to market demand is small. In models of spatial competition and in some models of product differentiation, the location of firms serves to segment the market. Each firm is then in localized competition with a small number of other firms, and capital acts as a significant barrier to entry even when there is a large number of firms in the whole market.

of an established firm, referred to as ONE, to determine the circumstances in which it is possible and profitable to deter entry of a second firm, referred to as TWO.

We capture decreasing unit costs by assuming that there is a fixed cost of entry associated with *entry capital*, which is product-specific. Production involves the services of a completely product-specific capital good, *production capital*, and a composite input. We assume a fixed-proportions technology involving the services of production capital and the composite input. We choose the unit of production capital so that one unit is required to produce a unit of output. With these assumptions, average total costs of production for any output $x \leq k$ can be written as

$$C = f + wx + rk, \qquad (1)$$

where k is quantity of production capital or the firm's capacity, r is the cost of the flow of services of a unit of production capital, w is the cost of the variable input per unit of output, and f is the flow of fixed costs associated with entry capital.

Entry barriers may arise in the natural course of events or they may be the result of conscious strategies. To clarify this distinction, we define *nonstrategic behavior* to be behavior unconstrained by the threat of entry, and *strategic behavior* to be behavior with entry deterrence as its objective. Correspondingly, we define a *natural monopoly* to be one in which the monopolist makes nonstrategic decisions and the value of entry is nonpositive and an *artificial monopoly* to be one in which the monopolist makes strategic decisions so as to make the value of entry nonpositive at all points in time (and where it would be positive, given nonstrategic decisions). We turn now to an examination of entry equilibrium in circumstances which are distinguished by assumptions with respect to the divisibility and durability of capital.

☐ **Immortal capital.** Assume that production capital is infinitely durable and perfectly divisible. Assume that entry capital is infinitely durable and completely indivisible. By completely indivisible, we mean that the services of a second unit of this capital are never required for any of the outputs considered by any of the firms in our model. Assume that the underlying duopoly model is the Cournot model and that firms foresee the Cournot quantity-setting equilibrium. By making strategic decisions with respect to production capital, ONE can alter its reaction function and hence the duopoly solution. This yields a simplified version of Dixit's (1980) model. In Figure 1 the line $M'M$ is ONE's "full-cost reaction function"—the reaction function when *avoidable* incremental unit costs are $w + r$. The line $N'N$ is ONE's "variable-cost reaction function"—the reaction function when *avoidable* incremental unit costs are w.

ONE's actual reaction function is dependent on k_1, ONE's capacity. First suppose that $k_1 \leq M$. ONE's reaction function is $N'N$ for $x_1 < k_1$, $M'M$ for $M \geq x_1 > k_1$, the horizontal axis for $x_1 > M$, and the vertical line from $M'M$ to $N'N$ for $x_1 = k_1$. Second, suppose $k_1 > M$. ONE's reaction function is $N'N$ for $x_1 < k_1$, the horizontal axis for $x_1 > k_1$, and the vertical line from $N'N$ to the horizontal axis for $x_1 = k_1$. The line RR' in Figure 1 is TWO's full-cost reaction function. This is the only reaction function we need to consider for TWO, since all its costs are avoidable.

FIGURE 1

ENTRY DETERRENCE WITH IMMORTAL CAPITAL

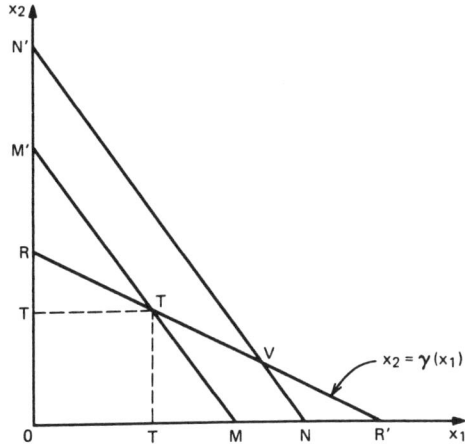

Suppose TWO incurs the fixed cost of entry. The resolution of the duopoly problem then depends on ONE's capacity, k_1. Denote equilibrium values by a hat, TWO's reaction function by $\gamma(x_1)$, the coordinates of point V in Figure 1 by (V_1, V_2), and the coordinates of point T by (T, T) (since the point T is on the line $x_2 = x_1$). Then

$$\hat{x}_1 = \min(k_1, V_1), \qquad (2a)$$

$$\hat{x}_2 = \gamma(\hat{x}_1). \qquad (2b)$$

Now define $\pi(x_i, x_j)$ ($i = 1, 2; j = 2, 1$) to be the ith firm's flow of revenue net of variable costs. Assume that $\pi(x_i, x_j)$ is concave. Define $\bar{\pi}(x_i, x_j)$ ($i = 1, 2; j = 2, 1$) to be

$$\bar{\pi}(x_i, x_j) = \pi(x_i, x_j) - rx_i. \qquad (3)$$

Concavity of $\pi(x_i, x_j)$ implies that $\bar{\pi}(x_i, x_j)$ is also concave.

Let $B = (B_1, B_2)$ be the point on RR' such that $\bar{\pi}(B_2, B_1) - f = 0$. B_1 is thus ONE's "limit quantity." Define S to be the value of x_1 which maximizes $\bar{\pi}(x_1, \gamma(x_1))$. S is then ONE's output at the von Stackelberg solution. Define $\tilde{S} = \min(S, V_1)$. We can now examine ONE's profit-maximizing behavior.

Case (i): $B_1 > V_1$. ONE cannot create an artificial monopoly. Suppose $k_1 = B_1$. TWO will realize that, should he enter, the duopoly solution would be at V, which promises him positive profits. Thus, $k_1 > V_1$ does not create a commitment to produce $x_1 > V_1$ after entry. Given that he cannot deter entry, ONE will choose $k_1^* = \tilde{S}$ and TWO will enter, producing $x_2^* = \gamma(\tilde{S})$.

Case (ii): $M < B_1 \leq V_1$. ONE can create an artificial monopoly by setting $k_1 = B_1$. TWO will realize that the duopoly solution would be at B, which promises TWO nonpositive profits. Entry deterrence may not be preferred, however, since ONE's net worth as an artificial monopolist may be less than his net worth in the best duopoly solution $(x_1 = \tilde{S}, x_2 = \gamma(\tilde{S}))$. If ONE does choose to deter entry by setting $k_1^* = B_1$, ONE's output will also be B_1, and ONE will not hold excess capacity.

Case (iii): $B_1 \leq M$. The limit output is less than the monopoly output, and ONE has a natural monopoly.

The influence of the discount rate on the ability to prevent entry is of interest. As the discount rate falls, the limit output, B_1, increases since the opportunity cost of entry and production capital is diminished. The diminished cost of production capital also shifts TWO's full-cost reaction function, RR', upward. As a result, V, decreases. For interest rates below the level such that $B_1 = V_1$, entry deterrence is impossible.

□ **Radioactive capital.** In this subsection, we amend the model by assuming that production capital decays with time at some continuous rate, z, which is subject to choice. The model of the preceding subsection is then the special case of the radioactive model when $z = 0$. Let $\alpha(z)$ be the cost of producing one unit of capital with rate of decay z. We assume that $\alpha(z)$ is twice continuously differentiable and that

$$\alpha'(z) < 0, \qquad \alpha''(z) \geq 0, \qquad \lim_{z \to 0} \alpha(z) = \infty, \qquad \lim_{z \to \infty} \alpha(z) > 0. \qquad (4)$$

Let $\beta(z, i)$ be the present discounted cost to the firm of *maintaining* one unit of capital forever, where i is the appropriate discount rate. Then

$$\beta(z, i) = \alpha(z) + \frac{z\alpha(z)}{i}. \qquad (5)$$

The second term on the right is the present discounted cost of the stream of replacement expenditures. The restrictions in (4) on the limits of $\alpha(z)$ ensure that z will always be chosen to be positive and finite. The cost-minimizing value of z, $\hat{z}$, will then satisfy $\beta_1(\hat{z}, i) = 0$ and $\beta_{11}(\hat{z}, i) \geq 0$. For convenience, we assume that $\beta_{11}(z, i) > 0$ for all $z > 0$. Then $\hat{z}$ is unique. Define r to be the cost of the flow of services of a unit of capital,

$$r = i\beta(z, i). \qquad (6)$$

The minimum value of r, $\hat{r}$, is $i\beta(\hat{z}, i)$. Average total costs are given by equation (1) above, where r is now defined by (6).

ONE's optimal entry-deterring problem is to choose a time path of committed production-capital services to maximize net worth, subject to the constraint that TWO's value of entry be nonpositive at all points in time. Since revenues and costs are time invariant, the problem reduces to choosing a capital stock, k_1, and a rate of decay, z_1, that will be maintained forever. ONE's monopoly net worth can be written as

$$\phi(k_1, z_1) = \int_0^\infty \pi(x_1^*, 0)e^{-it}dt - k_1\beta(z_1, i) - F,$$

where $x_1^* = \min(k_1, N)$ is the profit-maximizing value of x_1, given k_1, and F is the cost of the entry capital. Evaluating the integral,

$$\phi(k_1, z_1) = \frac{\pi(x_1^*, 0)}{i} - k_1\beta(z_1, i) - F. \qquad (7)$$

In Figure 2 QQ' is the locus of values of k_1 which maximize ϕ, given z_1. On this locus the iso-net-worth contours are horizontal. The slope of QQ' is

FIGURE 2

ENTRY DETERRENCE WITH RADIOACTIVE CAPITAL

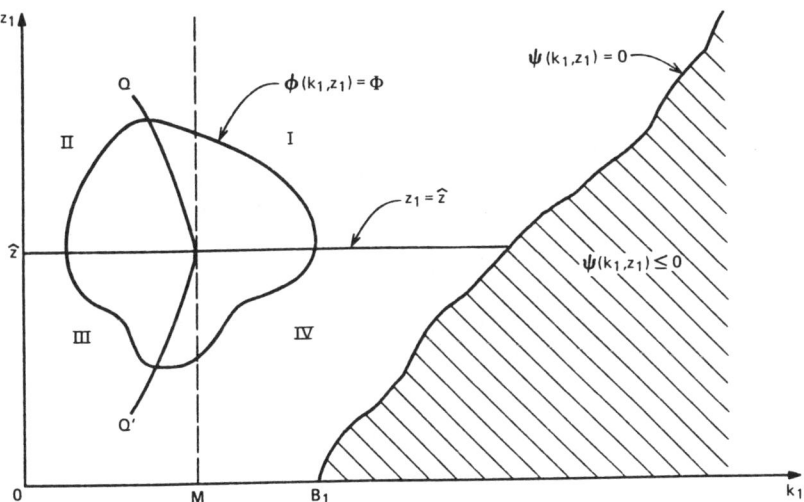

positive for $z_1 < \hat{z}$ and negative for $z_1 > \hat{z}$, since r increases with $|z_1 - \hat{z}|$. The locus of values of z_1 which maximize ϕ, given k_1, is the horizontal line $z_1 = \hat{z}$, and on this locus the iso-net-worth contours are vertical. The two lines intersect at the unconstrained maximum of ϕ: at $z_1 = \hat{z}$ and $k_1 = M$. Differentiating ϕ, we have

$$\left. \frac{dz_1}{dk_1} \right|_{\phi(k_1, z_1) = \bar{\phi}} = \frac{\partial x_1^* / \partial k_1 \pi_1(x_1^*, 0)/i - \beta(z_1, i)}{k_1 \beta_1(z_1, i)}. \qquad (8)$$

At points to the right (left) of QQ', the numerator in (8) is negative (positive). At points below (above) the line $z_1 = \hat{z}$, the denominator in (8) is negative (positive). Thus, in quadrants II and IV of Figure 2, the iso-net-worth contours are positively sloped, and in I and III they are negatively sloped. ϕ is concave when $z_1 > \hat{z}$, but when $z_1 < \hat{z}$, it is not necessarily so. Thus the iso-net-worth contours in quadrants III and IV are not necessarily convex.

To evaluate TWO's value of entry and hence write the constraint for the entry-deterring problem, we must determine the resolution of the duopoly problem through time. If TWO considers entering at some point in time, $t = 0$ for convenience, when ONE's stock of production capital is k_1, ONE's *minimum* commitment of capital services at time $t > 0$ is $k_1 e^{-z_1 t}$, and TWO must foresee this minimum commitment. ONE might commit more—particularly if he engaged in strategic investment decisions after TWO entered—but he cannot commit less. We assume that after TWO enters, both ONE's and TWO's short-run output and long-run investment decisions are determined in Cournot fashion and are foreseen—i.e., we rule out postentry strategic behavior. Then we have

$$x_1^t = \min [V_1, \max (k_1 e^{-z_1 t}, T)], \qquad (9a)$$

$$x_2^t = \gamma(x_1^t), \qquad (9b)$$

where γ is TWO's *minimized* full-cost reaction function. This process of adjustment will follow some portion of line segment VT in Figure 1. If $k_1 > V_1$, it will trace out the entire segment, and the duopoly will remain at V for a positive period of time.

This is not the only possible assumption either about behavior after entry or about the final equilibrium, but this one has a number of desirable features. First, it is the assumption that is most conducive to TWO's entry, since any rational strategic behavior on ONE's part after TWO's entry must reduce the value of entry to TWO. Second, it follows from the first point that any strategy that is entry barring on these assumptions about postentry behavior is *a fortiori* entry barring under alternative assumptions. Third, since the only barrier to entry in this model is the capital ONE has committed to the market before TWO's entry, this is the case that isolates exactly what we wish to study: the effect of precommitted capital as a barrier to entry. If we were to allow postentry strategic behavior, the long-run duopoly solution which is least conducive to entry allows ONE to achieve the von Stackelberg solution. In this case the adjustment process would trace out the segment of TWO's reaction function from V to the von Stackelberg point (provided, of course, that this lies to the left of V).

Now define
$$\hat{\pi}(x_i, x_j) = \pi(x_i, x_j) - \hat{r}x_i. \tag{10}$$

Then the value of entry is
$$\psi(k_1, z_1) = \int_0^{t_1} \hat{\pi}(x_2^t, x_1^t)e^{-it}dt + \frac{\hat{\pi}(T, T)}{i} e^{-it_1} - F, \tag{11}$$

where t_1 satisfies
$$k_1 e^{-z_1 t_1} = T. \tag{12}$$

When $k_1 > T$, $\psi_1(k_1, z_1) < 0$ and $\psi_2(k_1, z_1) > 0$. Redefine B_1 to be the value of x_1 such that
$$\hat{\pi}(\gamma(B_1), B_1) - \hat{f} = 0. \tag{13}$$

When $B_1 < V_1$, the entry constraint, $\psi(k_1, z_1) = 0$, is positively sloped and intersects the k_1-axis at $k_1 = B_1$. In addition, the value of k_1 on the constraint goes to infinity as z_1 goes to infinity, since for any given value of k_1, sunk capital services at any point in time go to zero as z_1 approaches infinity. In Figure 2, we illustrate the constraint for the case when $M < B_1 < V_1$. For future reference, denote by $\bar{k}_1$ and $\bar{z}_1$ the values (if any) which solve the optimal entry-deterring problem: maximize $\phi(k_1, z_1)$ subject to $\psi(k_1, z_1) \leq 0$.

In the event that TWO does enter, ONE will allow its capital to decay to the amount T and will then begin replacing it. ONE's net worth is then

$$\theta(k_1, z_1) = \int_0^{t_1} \pi(x_1^t, x_2^t)e^{-it}dt - k_1\alpha(z_1)$$
$$+ \frac{\pi(T, T)}{i} e^{-it_1} - \alpha(\hat{z})\int_{t_1}^{\infty} [z_1 k_1^t + \hat{z}(T - k_1^t)]e^{-it}dt. \tag{14}$$

The last term, which represents the present discounted cost of capital replacement after the duopoly has converged to T, requires explanation. ONE will then choose the cost-minimizing rate of decay, $\hat{z}$, and the unit cost of replacement capital will be $\alpha(\hat{z})$. At any instant the firm will hold k_1^i units of its original capital stock which decays at rate z_1, and it will hold $(T - k_1^i)$ units of capital which decays at rate $\hat{z}$. Denote by $\bar{k}_1$ and $\check{z}_1$ the values which maximize $\theta(k_1, z_1)$. It can be shown that $\bar{k}_1 > \tilde{S}$ and $\check{z}_1 < \hat{z}$.

We now outline the possible solutions to ONE's profit-maximizing problem. We use k_1^* and z_1^* to denote ONE's profit-maximizing choices.

Case (i): $B_1 > V_1$. Entry deterrence is impossible since TWO could earn positive profit at V, and $k_1^* = \bar{k}_1$, $z_1^* = \check{z}_1$. The long-run duopoly solution is the symmetric Cournot solution at T, but the duopoly does not immediately go to T. Rather ONE pursues what might be thought of as a dynamic von Stackelberg strategy. Recall that $\bar{k}_1 > \tilde{S}$ and $\check{z}_1 < \hat{z}$. Thus on TWO's entry the instantaneous duopoly solution is asymmetric, but as ONE's capital decays, the duopoly converges to the symmetric solution.

Case (ii): $M < B_1 < V_1$. In this case, illustrated in Figure 3, there are three notable features of the optimal entry deterring strategy. First, $\bar{k}_1 > B_1$, so that the optimal entry-deterring capacity always exceeds what would be the optimal entry-deterring capacity if capital were immortal. Second, $\bar{k}_1$ may exceed N, in which case ONE would hold excess capacity as a barrier to entry. Third, $\check{z}_1 < \hat{z}$ and ONE's capital is more durable than the cost-minimizing durability. ONE may or may not choose to deter entry in case (ii), since $\phi(\bar{k}_1, \check{z}_1)$ may or may not exceed $\theta(\bar{k}_1, \check{z}_1)$.

Case (iii): $T < B_1 \leq M$. Two possibilities require attention. First, if $\hat{z}$ is sufficiently small, the point $(M, \hat{z})$ will lie below $\psi(k_1, z_1) = 0$, and we have a case of natural monopoly: $k_1^* = M$, $z_1^* = \hat{z}$. When production capital is immortal we necessarily have natural monopoly when $B_1 \leq M$. Second, if $\hat{z}$ is large enough, strategic behavior is required to deter entry. Again $\check{z}_1 < \hat{z}$ and $\bar{k}_1$ may exceed N, so that excess capacity is a possibility. (Curiously, we have not been able to show that $\bar{k}_1$ is necessarily larger than M.) Again ONE may or may not find strategic entry deterrence preferable to the dynamic von Stackelberg duopoly strategy.

Case (iv): $B_1 \leq T$. This is another case of natural monopoly: $k_1^* = M$, $z_1^* = \hat{z}$.

When strategic entry deterrence is the preferred strategy, the artificial monopolist will *always* choose capital that is more durable than the cost-minimizing durability, and he may or may not hold excess capacity as a barrier to entry. When the dynamic von Stackelberg strategy is preferred, the first firm in the market will choose to make its initial capital stock more durable than the cost-minimizing durability, but all capital subsequently devoted to the market by either firm will have the cost-minimizing durability.

In model 2 the interest rate influences the ability to prevent entry. A decline in the interest rate moves B_1 right and V left, just as in model 1, but it also raises the present value of the distant profits proportionately more than it raises the present value of the early losses. This also makes entry more attractive and diminishes the scope for entry prevention.

☐ **One-hoss-shay capital.** Assume that there are no product-specific production inputs and hence that there is no production capital. Assume also that the indivisible entry capital now has a finite life of H years. (Alternatively, we

FIGURE 3

EXCESSIVE DURABILITY AND ENTRY DETERRENCE

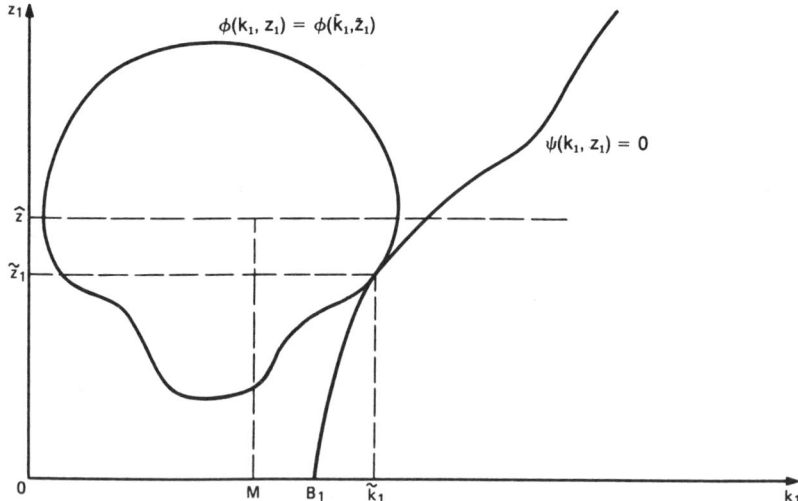

could assume that there is no entry capital and that production capital is completely indivisible with a finite lifetime of H years.) We then have a special case of Eaton and Lipsey (1980) which we summarize briefly below.

In this model ONE cannot (by the definition of an indivisible unit of capital) increase the flow of output it is committed to produce after TWO's entry by precommitting itself to a second unit of indivisible capital. Thus, if a duopoly is profitable, there is no strategic investment decision ONE can make to bar TWO's entry.

This kind of entry, which has been our sole concern up to this point, may be called *augmenting entry*—entry by TWO in the expectation of creating a duopoly. Now consider ONE's situation if the market is not large enough to support a profitable duopoly. With one-hoss-shay capital, ONE must now worry about what may be called *predatory entry*—entry by TWO in the expectation of replacing ONE as the sitting monopolist. This possibility arises because as the age of ONE's capital approaches H, the time over which ONE has capital committed to the market (*ONE's temporal commitment to the market*) approaches zero. If ONE behaves nonstrategically, planning to replace its capital after H periods, TWO could enter the market just before ONE's capital reached age H. ONE would then find himself in the position of a potential new entrant, and replacement of his capital would no longer be profitable.

ONE can affect the value of TWO's entry by replacing his capital h periods before it wears out, thus maintaining a minimum temporal commitment to the market of h periods. If TWO now enters the market with the intention of replacing ONE, TWO must suffer losses for at least h periods until ONE exits. ONE's optimal entry-barring strategy is to maximize his profits, subject to choosing h such that TWO's value of entry is never positive. In Eaton and Lipsey (1980) we show that whenever the market will not support two firms, the optimal predatory entry-barring strategy always exists and is always profitable for ONE. Such a strategy clearly involves deadweight loss, since capital is replaced before it is physically worn out.

A decrease in the rate of interest decreases costs, thereby increasing potential monopoly profits. This forces the artificial monopolist to increase h. However, as the interest rate continues to decrease, the duopoly solution will eventually offer positive profit and augmenting entry will occur. (Notice, however, that the duopolists will need to guard against predatory entry.)

3. Conclusions

■ The importance of the nature of PSC in determining entry barriers is best seen by comparing the results of the three models considered in this article. In the first, featuring immortal capital, the divisibility of production capital implies that ONE has an instrument to affect the value of TWO's entry. The infinite durability of PSC implies that ONE need only worry about augmenting entry, and that the entry-deterring problem is reducible to a static problem. To deter entry, ONE chooses a quantity of production capital (which is committed forever) so that the *flow* of profits to a new entrant is nonpositive.

We considered three possible entry equilibria: the artificial monopoly equilibrium where $k_1^* = x_1^* = B_1$; the natural monopoly equilibrium where $k_1^* = M$; and the duopoly equilibrium where $k_1^* = x_1^* = \bar{S}$. We know that at any instant, holding excess capacity ($k_1^* > N$) cannot create a commitment to use that capacity in that instant should entry occur; and since capital does not decay, excess capacity is not an entry barrier. This is Dixit's no-excess-capacity result. This implies that the artificial monopoly equilibrium (where it is possible) is socially preferred to franchise monopoly; since $k_1^* = x_1^* > M$, entry deterrence involves a transfer of some monopoly rent from the monopolist to his customers and a net increase in social rent relative to the franchise monopoly. The artificial monopoly equilibrium may or may not be socially preferable to the duopoly solution, since in the duopoly solution two units of entry capital are devoted to the market, while output need not be larger than in the monopoly solution—and where it is, the extra output may or may not be enough to compensate for the extra capital devoted to the market.

In the second model, featuring radioactive production capital, the infinite durability of entry capital again dictates that ONE need not be concerned about predatory entry, and the divisibility of production capital again implies that ONE has an instrument to affect the value of augmenting entry. However, the radioactive nature of capital implies that ONE's profit-maximizing problem can no longer be reduced to a static exercise. Whenever augmenting entry is a concern in this model, the profits in the long-run duopoly solution at T are positive. Thus ONE's entry-deterring problem is to create losses during the early stages of the adjustment process which exceed the present value of the profits earned during the later stages of the adjustment, and in the long-run equilibrium. If the duopoly solution is preferred, it converges to the symmetric Cournot solution in our model. However, the established firm still finds it profitable to impose asymmetric initial conditions and thus an asymmetric process of convergence. This process can be thought of as a dynamic von Stackelberg process. Again three equilibria are possible: a natural monopoly equilibrium with $k_1^* = x_1^* = M$; an artificial monopoly equilibrium with $x_1^* \leq k_1^*$; and the duopoly equilibrium at T.

With radioactive capital, it is apparent that artificial monopoly may or may not be preferred to franchise monopoly. Artificial monopoly involves an output which ordinarily exceeds the franchise monopoly output, and this tends to reduce the standard monopoly distortion. However, it also involves the deadweight loss associated with production capital that is excessively durable, and it may involve excess capacity as well. As in Dixit's model, holding excess capacity at any instant cannot create a commitment to use that capacity in that instant should entry occur. It does, however, increase the time at which ONE's output will remain at V_1 after TWO's entry, because it increases the time taken for ONE's capacity to decay to V_1. Excess capacity is thus a barrier to entry when capital is less than infinitely durable. It is also apparent that *artificial* monopoly may or may not be socially preferable to duopoly, since duopoly again involves an extra unit of entry capital.

The third model features indivisible, one-hoss-shay capital, which may be interpreted as either entry or production capital. The absence of divisibility implies that ONE has no instrument to affect the value of augmenting entry; and if the duopoly solution offers pure profit, then the equilibrium will be a duopoly. However, the finite durability of capital implies that predatory entry must be a concern and that premature replacement is an instrument that can prevent predatory entry. In this model, natural monopoly is impossible, and there are thus two possible equilibria: an artificial monopoly equilibrium and a duopoly equilibrium. Franchise monopoly is socially preferred to artificial monopoly, since output is the same and since the artificial monopoly involves the deadweight loss associated with premature replacement. Note that the duopoly equilibrium will also involve a deadweight loss, since the duopolists must concern themselves with predatory entry.

This review demonstrates that the properties of entry equilibrium are dependent upon the nature of PSC and apparently minor changes in the nature of PSC can produce dramatic changes in the properties of equilibrium. As a corollary, knowledge of the nature of PSC is necessary to determine whether entry deterrence is possible, is profitable, and is socially wasteful.

Seen from the vantage point of the neoclassical model, where long-run equilibrium is independent of short-run specificity of capital, giving PSC a key role in a theory of entry equilibrium appears dubious. Consideration of another model may give further insight into the significance of PSC for long-run equilibrium. Assume that there are no product-specific inputs and that the market will profitably support only one firm. Profits of the sitting firm provide an incentive for predatory entry, while the absence of PSC implies that a sitting firm has no way to protect itself against predatory attackers. The essence of entry deterrence is the creation of asymmetries between existing firms and potential new entrants, and without PSC, asymmetries are not possible. Since there is no way any sitting firm can secure a hold on the market, there is no way to stabilize the identity of the one firm that profitably serves it. The chaos of this model belongs, we believe, to the world of economic fiction, and we can be sure that if such conditions did ever exist in our world, some firm would invent a form of PSC that allowed it to create the required asymmetry. Far from being an unnecessary encumbrance, PSC is thus the stabilizing force in any world where a range of falling long-run costs makes it possible for a small number of firms to earn positive profits in a situation where the value of augmenting entry is nonpositive.

In the models we consider there are four possible market structures: natural monopoly, artificial monopoly (where the monopolist must strategically deter augmenting and/or predatory entry), natural duopoly, and artificial duopoly (where the duopolists must strategically deter predatory entry). These exhaust the possibilities in our model, since the market will not support three firms. However, the basic insights for extension of these ideas to a theory of endogenous market structure, driven by the nature of PSC, seem clear enough; and this is a task of major importance.

References

CAVES, R. AND PORTER, M. "From Entry Barriers to Mobility Barriers: Conjectural Decisions and Contrived Deterrence to New Competition." *Quarterly Journal of Economics*, Vol. 91 (May 1977), pp. 241–261.

—— AND ——. "Barriers to Exit" in R. Marson and P. Qualls, eds., *Essays in Industrial Organization in Honor of Joe Bain*, Cambridge, Mass.: Ballinger, 1976, pp. 39–70.

DIXIT, A.K. "A Model of Duopoly Suggesting a Theory of Entry Barriers." *Bell Journal of Economics*, Vol. 9 (Spring 1979), pp. 20–32.

——. "The Role of Investment in Entry Deterrence." *Economic Journal*, Vol. 90 (March 1980), pp. 95–106.

EATON, B. AND LIPSEY, R. "Spatial Monopoly, Natural Monopoly, Pure Profits, and Land Rents." Queen's University Discussion Paper No. 265, 1977.

—— AND ——. "The Theory of Market Preemption: The Persistence of Excess Capacity and Monopoly in Growing Spatial Markets." *Economica*, Vol. 46 (May 1979), pp. 149–158.

—— AND ——. "Exit Barriers Are Entry Barriers: The Durability of Capital as a Barrier to Entry." *Bell Journal of Economics*, Vol. 10 (Autumn 1980), pp. 721–729.

SCHELLING, T. "An Essay on Bargaining." *American Economic Review*, Vol. 46 (June 1956), pp. 557–583.

SCHMALENSEE, R. "Economies of Scale and Barriers to Entry." M.I.T. Working Paper No. 1130, 1980.

SPENCE, A.M. "Entry, Capacity, Investment, and Oligopolistic Pricing." *Bell Journal of Economics*, Vol. 8 (Autumn 1977), pp. 534–544.

——. "Investment Strategy and Growth in a New Market." *Bell Journal of Economics*, Vol. 9 (Spring 1979), pp. 1–19.

[12]

The Economic Journal, **92** (*March* 1982), 56–72
Printed in Great Britain

AN ECONOMIC THEORY OF CENTRAL PLACES*

B. Curtis Eaton and Richard G. Lipsey

Since the seminal work of Walter Christaller (1966) and August Lösch (1954), central place theory has become an important, perhaps the most important, theoretical tool of economic geography. No attempt seems to have been made, however, to deduce its propositions from a rigorously stated set of assumptions concerning the behaviour of buyers and sellers. Thus, existing central place theory is not really a theory of spatial economic behaviour. Instead, it is a series of brilliant conjectures about the locational configurations that will result from such behaviour. The brilliance of these conjectures is illustrated by the successful applications of the theory to such diverse phenomena as the locational patterns of retailing activity in cities and of service centres in rural areas, the size distribution of cities and the diffusion of information and diseases.[1]

In this paper, we outline an economic model of central places.[2] Our theorising has two distinct purposes. First, we wish to begin the development of a theory of central places that is based on maximising behaviour of economic agents. Any theory of economic behaviour from which central places can be derived is necessarily both difficult and cumbersome. Non-convexities in the activities of buying and selling drive the model, and thus non-differentiabilities and discontinuities abound. As one seeks more generality in such circumstances, difficulties multiply rapidly. In order to begin the job, we have used assumptions that are specific and sometimes even crude. The second purpose of our theorising is to illustrate the limitations of current central place theory by providing counter examples to some propositions commonly accepted to follow from it. For this purpose we need not worry about lack of generality in any of our counter examples. Of course we are not solely concerned to refute accepted generalisations. By doing so, we hope to make alternative possibilities apparent. What we hope to attain, therefore, is a theoretical development inspired by the extremely fruitful conjectures of existing central place theory.

---

* This paper is a revised version of Eaton and Lipsey (1979a). Preliminary work on it was done while the authors held visiting appointments at the University of Colorado at Boulder in 1974–5. We are grateful to the Killam Foundation for support, and to Gernot Kofler, David McGechie, Douglas West and Myrna Wooders for comments and suggestions.

[1] The most common, and perhaps the most successful, applications have seen studies of spatial patterns of retailing. The classic studies are those by Berry and his colleagues at the University of Chicago (see, e.g. Berry, 1958 and 1963 and Simmons, 1964 and 1966), and those by economic geographers at the University of Iowa (see, e.g. Golledge, Rushton and Clark, 1966 and Rushton, 1971). For models concerned specifically with the size distribution of cities, see Beckmann (1958) and Berry (1961). The basic paper on diffusion processes in central place systems is Hudson (1969).

[2] This paper is the third in a series dealing with the clustering of firms. In our first paper (Eaton and Lipsey, 1975) we showed that Hotelling's explanation of clustering is applicable only to duopolies. In the second paper (Eaton and Lipsey, 1979b) we showed that clustering of firms throughout the market can result from comparison shopping among firms selling similar goods. In the present paper we show that clustering can also result from scale economies for purchases of dissimilar goods. In Hotelling's model clustering is universally wasteful. In the models of comparison shopping and central places much of the clustering of firms is cost reducing and hence socially beneficial even though optimal configurations do not always result.

[56]

I. A REVIEW OF EXISTING CENTRAL PLACE THEORY

Central place theory begins with an analysis of the geographic network of trade or market areas for a single good, X_i. Consumers purchase X_i from the firm that offers the lowest delivered price. The theory asserts that in market equilibrium, producers of X_i will be located on a regular lattice of points, servicing identical hexagonal market areas and charging a common price. (Although the details of the single-industry case are still controversial, the major theoretical problems that concern us here arise only in the multi-industry case.[1]) For each good X_i, let R_i denote the size of the regular hexagonal market area that is required for a firm selling *all* of the X_i demanded within that area to be able to cover its costs. In the jargon of the theory, R_i is the 'range' of X_i. Index the n goods so that $R_1 < R_2 \ldots < R_{n-1} < R_n$.

In Christaller's analysis, the interrelationships among the locations of sellers of different goods are derived in the following manner. Let producers of X_n be located in a network with hexagonal market areas of size R_n. Since R_n exceeds R_i, $i \neq n$, Christaller argued that all n goods will be offered in these centres, central places of 'order n'. Now consider a set of central places located at the centroid of each of the equilateral triangles defined by the central places of order n. These locations, along with the original central places of order n, define a new network of hexagonal market areas of size $R_n/3$. All goods with $R_i \leqslant R_n/3$ will be offered in these new central places of order $n-1$, while all goods with $R_i > R_n/3$ will be offered only in central places of order n. Replications of this geometric argument gives rise to a system of central places which exhibits the *hierarchial principle*: any goods supplied in a central place of order i is also supplied in all central places of order $j > i$.[2]

There is no formal analysis of any economic force that causes firms in different industries to agglomerate in this fashion, nor could there be in a model that first determines the locational pattern of firms within each industry and only then considers the interrelationships among industries that are implied by each industry's locational pattern. The pattern of central places and the hierarchical principle are simply products of Christaller's geometric argument.

Analysis of the economic incentives that cause agglomeration is also absent from modern statements of the theory. For example, Dacey *et al.* (1974) give a treatment of central place theory in a one-dimensional market which has virtually no reference to purposive economic behaviour. In the statement of the theory by Alao *et al.* (1977, p. 150), the Christallerian structure is obtained by invoking 'a weak agglomeration axiom'. This axiom assumes the basic result under study rather than deducing it from a behaviourally motivated analysis of the interaction of economic agents.

---

[1] Papers dealing with the one industry locational problem in the Löschian landscape include Mills and Lav (1964), Hartwick (1973), and Eaton and Lipsey (1976).

[2] In contrast to Christaller, Lösch begins his analysis with the lowest order central place and works up. We do not review Lösch's reasoning since our paper is concerned with the retail sector of the economy and is really in the Christaller-Berry tradition.

Christaller's and Lösch's treatments contain much fruitful intuition about the economic processes that might give rise to central places.[1] Their formal analysis, however, is based on mechanistic, geometric arguments. Modern treatments have refined the mechanistic arguments, stripping away all of the discussion of behaviour that might produce agglomeration. It seems not unfair to say, therefore, that existing formal central place theory is a theory of the location and the agglomeration of firms in which no firm ever chooses its location and in which there are no economic forces that create agglomeration.

We seek to root our model in economic behaviour, and its behavioural engine arises from our answer to the basic question of agglomeration: Why do central business districts, or shopping centres, or suburban shopping districts exist? Why, in other words, do firms retailing different goods tend to cluster together? The explanation that leaps to mind is that, because the clustering of heterogeneous firms facilitates multipurpose shopping, it allows consumers to economise on shopping costs.

Direct observation reveals that the activity of 'shopping' – finding goods, purchasing, and transporting them – is constrained by some important indivisibilities that imply decreasing average total costs over some range of activity. First, there is the indivisibility of the shopper. Shoppers who combine, say, a trip to the butcher with a trip to the baker economise on the time-costs of shopping. A second indivisibility lies with the automobile. It is not 10 times as costly to transport 10 bags of groceries as it is to transport one bag; indeed, it is more accurate to regard the total costs in this example as constant. A third indivisibility relates to the goods themselves: consumer goods are usually available only in discrete units.

Abstracting from these indivisibilities greatly simplifies the analysis of shopping behaviour. If shopping were characterised by constant returns to scale, and if goods were infinitely divisible, consumers would buy and transport goods at a rate equal to the desired rate of consumption. To do otherwise would effect no

---

[1] Lösch (1954, p. 76) appears to cite multipurpose and comparison shopping as the 'first advantage of association':

'First, under any given market situation: The preference of consumers for combining small purchases or comparing various qualities of differentiated products is hardly less important for the formation of towns than for the existence of special business districts within a town and of department stores in these districts. The mere fact of their proximity not only lowers the cost of production, especially general costs, but at the same time increases the share of the demand.'

Christaller (1966, page 50) appears to have had similar insights:

'The fact that a central place is larger or smaller has an immediate influence on the range of a central good, because more types of central goods are offered at a central place of a higher order than at a central place of lower order. This means that, on the basis of a single trip (round-trip costs), one may simultaneously obtain several types of central goods. This has an effect similar to that of a general price decline of the central goods offered in the larger towns. It will be shown in the following discussion of prices that the range of a good is greater when it is offered in a smaller central place.'

But these insights are not an integral part of Christaller's or Lösch's analyses. In modern formal treatment of Dacey et al. (1974) and Alao et al. (1977), the topic of agglomeration economies receives virtually no attention. Many other modern writers have conjectures that multi-purpose shopping would provide the behavioural underpinning of a theory of central places, but none have succeeded in demonstrating this result. Bollabas and Stern (1972) give a rigorous demonstration that a hexagonal configuration of homogenous firms would be the planners solution to the locational problem in two-dimensional space. This important result has, however, no bearing on our problem: what is the market's solution to the locational problem where atomistic firms selling different kinds of products make individual locational decisions?

savings in the costs of shopping and would entail unnecessary costs of holding inventories. Furthermore, shoppers would have no incentive to engage in multipurpose shopping since this would not reduce shopping costs. Abstracting from the indivisibilities of shopping would, however, rob us of the ability to understand patterns of location. These indivisibilities imply that consumers who wish to minimise shopping costs will engage in multipurpose shopping.

Firms will then find that they can increase their profits by offering purchasers the chance to indulge in multipurpose shopping. Indeed, it is the interaction of multipurpose shopping and firms' profit-maximising behaviour that provides the core of our theory of central places.[1]

II. THE MODEL

We develop our basic theory as well as the counter examples that we require by concentrating on the two-commodity case. The first step is to set out the assumptions of our behavioural model.

(a) Households

(H-1) Households consume goods A and B at constant rates per unit of time. Units of A and B are such that their rates of consumption are unity.

(H-2) A and B are marketed in indivisible bundles of size $1/\alpha$ and $1/\beta$ units respectively.

(H-3) At regular intervals of time, each household surveys its current inventory of goods, and we choose our unit of time to be equal to this time interval. If the household's current inventory of either good is insufficient for its consumption over the next time period it makes a shopping trip.

(H-4) Households never buy more than one bundle of any good on any shopping trip. This requires the restrictions $1/\alpha, 1/\beta \geq 1$ to allow households to satisfy their consumption demands.[2]

(H-5) The time and money costs of shopping are an increasing function of distance travelled and of the number of stops the shopper must make, but they are independent of the number of commodities purchased. The cost of each stop is ϵ, which is positive but arbitrarily small.

(H-6) Shoppers minimise transport costs on each shopping trip.

(H-7) Shoppers choose randomly among alternative shopping trips that offer them equal costs.

The household behaviour required by these assumptions is as follows. At the beginning of each time interval, shoppers survey their inventories of goods. If the stock of at least one good is insufficient for consumption needs over the

---

[1] In their analyses, both Christaller and Lösch employ the assumption that transport costs are constant per unit of distance per unit of product. Although Alao *et al.* (1977, p. 94) do not assume linear transport costs, they do assume that transport costs can be independently defined as a function of distance *for each good*. These assumptions with respect to transport costs assume away the indivisibilities that drive our model, and they obviously rule out any reason for multipurpose shopping. To the extent, therefore, that multipurpose shopping plays a role in central place theory, it is used as a '*deus ex machina*', the mere mention of which justifies the formation of central places.

[2] If costs of holding inventories are sufficiently large, the household would never want to buy more than one bundle of A or B on any trip. Assumption (H-4) can then be thought of as the assumption that inventory holding costs are large.

period, a trip is made to purchase one bundle of each such good. The shopper chooses the retail shops to visit so as to minimise transport costs.

This representation of shopping behaviour catches much of the essence of multipurpose shopping while keeping the model analytically tractable. A more general treatment would formulate the household's problem as the minimisation of the sum of transport costs and costs of holding inventories of goods. Each household would then minimise the sum of transport and inventory costs, subject to the constraint that its consumption requirements be met at each point in time by choosing (1) the timing of shopping trips to purchase A only, and the quantity of A to purchase on such trips, (2) the timing of trips to purchase B only, and the quantity of B to purchase, and (3) the timing of multipurpose shopping trips and quantities of A and B to purchase on such trips. The solution would be dependent on the locations of retailers of A and B and would be different for each household. This is a mixed integer/real programming problem that is extremely difficult to solve.[1]

Assumptions (H-1) to (H-4) have a convenient implication. Consider a household's purchases of good A over a long period of time T. With a rate of consumption equal to unity, the household must purchase $T/(1/\alpha) = \alpha T$ bundles of A to meet its consumption needs, and this will require αT shopping trips since, by assumption, the household will purchase only one bundle of A on any one trip. Hence, in any one period, the probability that good A will be on the shopping list of a randomly chosen household is α. Similarly, the probability that B will be on the list is β.

(b) Firms

Since we are interested in the consequences of decisions on location taken by individual firms in two different industries, we assume that A and B are always sold by different firms. In order to concentrate on the locational aspects of our problem, we abstract from price competition. In addition, we capture the scale effects that are necessary for the very existence of firms in any spatial model by the assumption of an indivisibility in capital.

(F-1) Any firm retails A or B, but not both, and faces the following average total cost function:
$$ATC_I = K_I/Q_I + c_I, \quad I = A, B.$$

K_I is fixed costs associated with an indivisible unit of capital, Q_I is quantity retailed, and c_I is a constant marginal cost. For convenience, and without loss of generality, we assume throughout that c_I is zero.

(F-2) Goods are sold at parametric prices, P_A and P_B.

(F-3) Each firm chooses its location so as to maximise profits. Assumptions (F-1) and (F-2) imply that profit maximisation is equivalent to sales maximisation. Thus, firms choose their locations so as to maximise sales at the parametric price.

---

[1] In a path-breaking study of some agglomeration forces Bacon (1971) set up a consumer problem similar to the one just outlined. To solve the consumer's problem *given the locations of firms* he was, however, forced to rely on numerical simulation techniques. If Bacon's problem defied general analytical solution, the firm-location problem does so doubly since to choose its optimal location every firm must solve each customer's problem for each possible firm location and then aggregate these solutions to determine its demand as a function of its location.

(F-4) In choosing its location, each firm assumes that all other firms will maintain their current locations.

(F-5) For convenience, we assume that firms occupy no space and hence more than one firm can be located at the same point in space.

Assumption (F-2) is the one way in which our model is behaviourally more limited than traditional central place theory. The introduction of price formation would significantly complicate our analysis without, we believe, generating significant further insights into the phenomenon of agglomeration. If in building a theory of location and agglomeration we must choose between a behavioural theory of price and arbitrary assumptions about location on the one hand, and arbitrary assumptions on price and a behavioural theory of location on the other hand, we have no hesitation in choosing the latter combination.

Given our concerns in this paper, assumption (F-4) is convenient and, we believe, appropriate. When, however, a firm can foresee the locational reactions of other firms to its own locational choice, location becomes a strategic variable and assumption (F-4) is inappropriate. The strategic choice of location in a model of central places is an interesting theoretical problem but is beyond the scope of this paper.

(c) Completion of the Model

There is a one-dimensional market of unit length with a uniform density of households, D. Firms are numbered in ascending order from left to right along the market. The ith A firm is denoted by A_i and its location by a_i, and the jth B firm is denoted by B_j and its location by b_j. A bar over a location indicates that the location is fixed for the exercise in question, while the absence of a bar indicates that it is variable. When a shopper makes a shopping trip to buy only one good, we refer to the trip as an *A-only* or a *B-only* trip; and when a shopper makes a trip to buy A and B, we refer to the trip as an *A-with-B* trip. Sales made to shoppers on A-only trips (B-only trips) are referred to as *A-only sales* (*B-only sales*), while sales made to shoppers on *A-with-B* trips are referred to as *A-with-B sales*. A point in the market with at least one A and one B firm is called a *CP2* (for 'central place of order two'). A point with only one type of firm is called a *CP1* (for 'central place of order one'), and either a *CP1A* or *CP1B* when we wish to specify the type of firm.

III. EQUILIBRIUM CONFIGURATIONS

It is by now well known that equilibrium does not always exist in location models where the space is bounded. To keep the current paper manageable we focus only on equilibrium configurations.[1] There are three conditions that are necessary and, taken together, sufficient for an equilibrium of locations in this model.

---

[1] Non-existence is a problem in many models of location in bounded space. See Eaton and Lipsey (1975) for some examples where equilibrium does not exist, and Prescott and Visscher (1977) for a constructive response to non-existence that requires the strategic, forsightful behaviour that is ruled out of our model. In Eaton and Lipsey (1979a), we delineate the conditions in which equilibrium does and does not exist in the present model.

Equilibrium Condition (i): No existing firm can increase its sales by changing its location.

Equilibrium Condition (ii): All existing firms of type I must have revenues greater than or equal to K_I, $I = A, B$.

Equilibrium Condition (iii): At all locations, anticipated revenues for a new entrant of type I must be less than K_I, $I = A, B$. Condition (*i*) implies that no existing firm wants to change its location; condition (*ii*) implies no existing firm wants to exit; condition (*iii*) implies that no new firm wants to enter.

(a) The Necessity of Agglomeration

We begin by demonstrating that agglomeration (the existence of higher order central places) is necessarily a property of equilibrium in our model. Formally we show that Equilibrium Condition (*i*) implies

PROPOSITION 1. *In market equilibrium, (1-a) there must exist at least one CP2, and (1-b) it is impossible for a CP1A and a CP1B to be neighbours.*

To prove Proposition 1 we first show that Equilibrium Condition (*i*) implies.

PROPOSITION 2. *Scanning the market from left to right, (2-a) there must be a first CP2, and (2-b) between the left-hand market boundary and the first CP2 there can be at most one type of CP1.*

In order to avoid a tedious taxonomy, we assume that the market is large enough to support several firms of each type. Then when we scan the market from left to right, we will observe a first central place. If the first central place is a *CP2*, this does not contradict Proposition 2. If the first central place is not a *CP2*, then it must be a *CP1* and we can assume without loss of generality that it is a *CP1A*. As we continue to scan from left to right, we will eventually encounter the first B firm, B_1. If B_1 is in a *CP2*, this does not contradict Proposition 2. Accordingly, we assume that B_1 is not in a *CP2* and prove by contradiction that the market cannot be in equilibrium

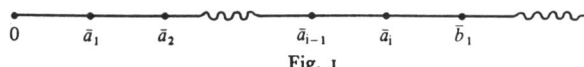

Fig. 1

Formally, assume (I) that all firms in the market satisfy equilibrium condition (*i*) and (II) that, scanning the market from left to right, we observe i *CP1A*s and then a *CP1B*. This locational configuration is illustrated in Fig. 1.

In the Appendix we show a contradiction between I and II, thus proving Proposition 2. Here we present an intuitive account of the argument. The location of A_i, a_i, is confined to the half-closed interval $[\bar{a}_{i-1}, \bar{b}_1)$ by assumption II. Observe next that a_i in the open interval $(\bar{a}_{i-1}, \bar{b}_1)$ does not satisfy assumption I. When $\bar{a}_{i-1} < a_i < \bar{b}_1$, the A-only sales of A_i are independent of a_i since the size of the market segment from which A_i attracts A-only shoppers is $(\bar{a}_{i+1} - \bar{a}_{i-1})/2$. However the A-with-B sales of A_i monotonically increase with a_i: for multipurpose shoppers to the right of a_i, the option of travelling to a_i and $\bar{b}_1$ (or some other B firm) becomes less expensive as a_i increases and accordingly the A-with-B sales of A_i from this region increase; for multipurpose shoppers located to the left of a_i, the cost of travelling to a_i and $\bar{b}_1$ is independent of a_i. Thus, for a_i in the open interval $(\bar{a}_{i-1}, \bar{b}_1)$, A_i's sales are a monotonically increasing function of a_i, and assumption I is not satisfied for a_i in this open interval.

The only possible location for A_i which could satisfy assumptions I and II is thus $\bar{a}_{i-1}$. If assumption I is to be satisfied it is, of course, necessary that A_i prefer location $\bar{a}_{i-1}$ to $\bar{b}_1$. We will argue that the conditions which ensure that A_i prefers $\bar{a}_{i-1}$ to $\bar{b}_1$ imply that A_{i-1} does not satisfy equilibrium condition (i). To do this we first ask what conditions would cause A_i to prefer $\bar{a}_{i-1}$ to $\bar{b}_1$. When $a_i = \bar{b}_1$, A_i captures all of the A-with-B business from the left of $\bar{b}_1$ since shopping at A_i and B_1 then involves only one stop, and it captures the A-only sales from a market segment equal to $(\bar{a}_{i+1} - \bar{a}_{i-1})/2$. When $a_i = \bar{a}_{i-1}$, A_i's A-with-B sales are clearly smaller than they are when $a_i = \bar{b}_1$, but its A-only sales may be

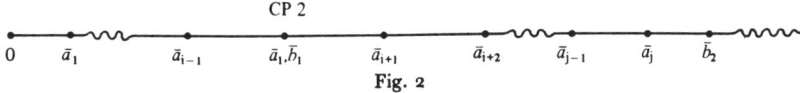

Fig. 2

larger. When $a_i = \bar{a}_{i-1}$, A_i and A_{i-1} equally share A-only sales from a market segment equal to $(\bar{a}_{i+1} - \bar{a}_{i-2})/2 = (\bar{a}_{i+1} - \bar{a}_{i-1})/2 + (\bar{a}_{i-1} - \bar{a}_{i-2})/2$. It is then clear that A_i will prefer to locate at $\bar{a}_{i-1}$ if and only if $(\bar{a}_{i-1} - \bar{a}_{i-2})/2$ is 'sufficiently large'. That is, it is the prospect of sharing A-only sales from a 'large' market segment $(\bar{a}_{i-1} - \bar{a}_{i-2})/2$ which can lead A_i to prefer $\bar{a}_{i-1}$. But in these circumstances A_{i-1} does not satisfy assumption I since it would prefer to monopolise A-only sales from this 'large' segment by moving just to the left of A_i. Thus the circumstances in which A_i would be in equilibrium at $\bar{a}_{i-1}$ (rather than $\bar{b}_1$) require that A_{i-1} not be in equilibrium. It follows that equilibrium condition (i) requires that A_i and B_1 form a $CP2$.

We can replicate the argument outlined above to prove Proposition 1. Scan the market from left to right beyond the first $CP2$. If the first central place we observe is a $CP2$, this is obviously consistent with Proposition 1. If we observe a string of $CP1$s of the same type ($CP1A$s or $CP1B$s) followed by a $CP2$, this is also consistent with Proposition 1. We must, however, demonstrate that in market equilibrium, we cannot observe a string of $CP1$s of one type followed by a $CP1$ of the other type. A proof by contradiction will establish this result. Assume (I) that all firms satisfy equilibrium condition (i) and assume, without loss of generality, (II) that we observe a string of $CP1A$s followed by a $CP1B$ (the configuration illustrated in Fig. 2). The structure of the proof follows. The location of A_j, by assumption (II), is confined to $[\bar{a}_{j-1}, \bar{b}_2)$, and the only location for A_j in this interval that satisfies assumption (I) is $a_j = \bar{a}_{j-1}$. A necessary condition for this location to satisfy assumption (I) is that $\bar{a}_{j-1} - \bar{a}_{j-2}$ be 'sufficiently' large. But when it is 'sufficiently' large, A_{j-1} would prefer to locate just to the left of A_j, and A_{j-1} does not satisfy assumption I. Hence, there can be at most one type of $CP1$ between the first and second $CP2$s. Repetition of this argument throughout the length of market establishes Proposition 1.

We have now shown that in market equilibrium, $CP1A$s and $CP1B$s cannot be adjacent to each other. In addition we have shown that in market equilibrium *CP2*s *must exist*. An immediate consequence of Propositions 1 and 2 is

PROPOSITION 3. *In market equilibrium all of the A-with-B business will be transacted in CP2s, and the firms in CP1s will serve only single-purpose shoppers.*

(b) A Taxonomy

Proposition 1 is consistent with a market served by (*a*) *CP2*s and *CP1A*s, (*b*) *CP2*s and *CP1B*s, (*c*) *CP2*s only, and (*d*) *CP1A*s and *CP1B*s in different intervals between *C2P*s. In this section we use equilibrium conditions (*ii*) and (*iii*) to eliminate case (*d*), thus establishing the hierarchial principle of our model. In addition we derive necessary and sufficient conditions for cases (*a*), (*b*) and (*c*).

Define Y, Z and λ as follows:

$$Y = K_A/(\alpha P_A D), \qquad (1)$$

$$Z = K_B/(\beta P_B D), \qquad (2)$$

$$\lambda = Z/Y. \qquad (3)$$

If an A firm could capture all of the A business from a market segment of length Y, expected revenues in any period would be $\alpha P_A DY$ since good A is on the shopping list of any shopper in any period with probability α. From (1), it is then clear that we can interpret Y as the length of a market an A firm must have in order to cover costs *if it captures all of the A business from this segment*. Z can be similarly interpreted.

We wish to prove

PROPOSITION 4. (4-*a*) *a necessary condition for the existence of CP1As in market equilibrium is that* $\lambda > 1/(1-\beta)$; (4-*b*) *a necessary condition for the existence of CP1Bs in market equilibrium is that* $\lambda < 1-\alpha$; (4-*c*) *a necessary condition for the market to be served only by CP2s is that* $(1-\alpha)/\alpha < \lambda < 2/(1-\beta)$.

In proving (4-*a*) we consider the existence of a *CP1A* in a market segment of length L bounded by *CP2*s. (The reader can verify that the necessary condition also applies to the existence of a *CP1A* in a peripheral market segment.) We begin by using equilibrium conditions (*ii*) and (*iii*) to establish bounds on L. L must be large enough so that equilibrium condition (*ii*) is satisfied for *at least one CP1A*. Proposition 3 dictates that the *CP1A* would attract only A-only shoppers. In any period the probability that any shopper will make an A-only trip is $\alpha(1-\beta)$. One *CP1A* in the segment of length L would attract the A-only shoppers from a market segment equal to $L/2$. The *CP1A*'s revenues would then be $DP_A\alpha(1-\beta)L/2$. Condition (*ii*) then implies that

$$L \geq \frac{2K_A}{DP_A\alpha(1-\beta)} = \frac{2Y}{1-\beta}, \qquad (4)$$

is necessary if *CP1A*s are to exist in market equilibrium (in the segment of length L).

Suppose we have *at least one CP1A* in the segment of length L. If a B firm were to enter this segment it would locate at a *CP1A*, forming a new *CP2*, and it would

capture all of the B business from a market segment equal to $L/2$. Its revenues would be $DP_B \beta L/2$. It is obviously necessary for the existence of $CP1As$ in market equilibrium (in the segment of length L) that a B firm *not* find the option of entering this interval attractive. That is, equilibrium condition (*iii*) dictates that
$$L < \frac{2K_B}{\beta DP_B} = 2Z, \tag{5}$$
is necessary for the existence of $CP1As$.

Inequalities (4) and (5) are necessary for the existence of $CP1As$ in market equilibrium, and if they are both to be satisfied, we require that $2Z > 2Y/(1-\beta)$, or that
$$\lambda > \frac{1}{1-\beta}. \tag{6}$$
This establishes (4-a). An exactly analogous argument establishes (4-b).

To establish (4-c) we need to find conditions which ensure that at least one firm of each type can cover costs in a $CP2$ and which ensure that neither an A nor a B firm will find it profitable to establish a $CP1$. It is convenient to proceed in stages. First assume that $\lambda > 1$, then from (4-b) we are assured that a B firm will not establish a $CP1$. Reversing inequality (4) ensures that an A firm will not establish a $CP1$:
$$L < 2Y/(1-\beta). \tag{7}$$
The firms in $CP2s$ will attract all of the business from a market segment equal to L. Viability of at least one B firm in a $CP2$ requires that $\beta P_B DL \geq K_B$ or that
$$L \geq Z. \tag{8}$$
Since $\lambda > 1$, (8) also ensures the viability of at least one A firm in a $CP2$. For (7) and (8) to hold simultaneously requires that $\lambda < 2/(1-\beta)$, the second inequality in (4-c). An analogous argument, with $\lambda < 1$, establishes the first.

The conditions in (4-a) and (4-b) cannot *simultaneously* hold. Thus we have the hierarchial principle of our model:

PROPOSITION 5. *If central places of orders one and two exist in market equilibrium, all central places of order one offer the same good.*

It is clear from Proposition 4 that equilibrium is not unique in our model; that is, the necessary conditions in Proposition 4 are not also sufficient. The following sufficient conditions are immediately implied by Proposition 4.

PROPOSITION 6. *(6-a) a sufficient condition for the existence of $CP1As$ in market equilibrium is that $\lambda \geq 2/(1-\beta)$; (6-b) a sufficient condition for the existence of $CP1Bs$ in market equilibrium is that $\lambda \leq (1-\alpha)/2$; (6-c) a sufficient condition for the market to be served only by $CP2s$ is that $(1-\alpha) \leq \lambda \leq 1/(1-\beta)$.*

One further observation on the equilibrium of our model seems worthwhile. Suppose for purposes of illustration that $1 < \lambda < (1-\beta)$ so that the market is served only by $CP2s$. Our assumption that prices are parametric implies that the number of firms of each type in each $CP2$ will be
$$\eta^A = \text{INT}[L/Y], \tag{9}$$
$$\eta^B = \text{INT}[L/Z], \tag{10}$$

where INT is the largest integer function. Using (7) and (8) we can establish bounds on η^A and η^B

$$\lambda \leqslant \eta^A < 2/(1-\beta), \qquad (11)$$

$$1 \leqslant \eta^B < 2/\lambda(1-\beta). \qquad (12)$$

It is then clear that in this case there is no upper bound on the number of firms of each type that can exist in any *CP2*.

Indeed, as we show in Eaton and Lipsey (1979a), for any value of λ it is possible to construct equilibria in which either η^A or η^B is arbitrarily large. Given our assumptions, more than one firm of either type in a *CP2* represents *pure* excess capacity – it increases the costs of retailing and does nothing to reduce the costs born by shoppers. We thus have

PROPOSITION 7. *Pure excess capacity is possible in market equilibrium.*
We comment on the possible significance of this result below.

III. SIGNIFICANCE

(a) Contrasts With Traditional Central Place Theory

In order to emphasise the contrasts between traditional central place theory and our versions of the theory we briefly compare the two in the context of an example.

Let $Z = 2Y$, or $\lambda = 2$. Our interpretation of Z and Y in section II-b means that, using the jargon of central place theory, Y is the 'range' of good A and Z is the 'range' of good B. According to traditional central place theory, we should expect a unique configuration of firms in these circumstances. There should be *CP2*s composed of one A and one B firm spaced Z units apart; there should also be a *CP1A* at the midpoint of the interval between each pair of *CP2*s.

In these circumstances, however, many equilibrium configurations are possible in our model. First, let $\beta > \frac{1}{2}$. Proposition (6-c) implies that there can be no *CP1*s, and the market will be served only by *CP2*s. The difference between the two theories arises because traditional central place theory is based solely on costs while our theory is driven by the interaction of costs and demand externalities between goods. In our model, *CP2*s impose a negative demand externality on any *CP1*s by leaving merely the A-only business to the *CP1A*s (Proposition 3). Thus, a *CP1A* requires a market segment larger than Y to survive. How much larger depends upon the magnitude of β, which can be thought of as an index of the negative demand externality between *CP2*s and *CP1A*s. When $\beta > \frac{1}{2}$, a market large enough to support a *CP1A* is large enough to invite entry of a B firm, converting the *CP1A* into a *CP2*. Thus, if we set up the market in the sequence of alternating *CP2*s and *CP1A*s suggested by central place theory, but with an interval between adjacent *CP2*s sufficient to support a *CP1A*, the isolated A firm will immediately be joined by a new B firm, and we will be left with only *CP2*s.

Secondly, let $\beta < \frac{1}{2}$ so that the condition 4-a is satisfied. Consider setting the firms down in the exact pattern suggested by central place theory – *CP2*s at intervals of Z with *CP1A*s at the midpoints between adjacent *CP2*s. The *CP1A*s will obtain the A-only business over the market segment of $Z/2$, which by the assumptions of our illustrative example is equal to Y. The revenue of each CP_1A will thus be

$$DP_A\alpha(1-\beta)Y = DP_A\alpha(1-\beta)K_A/\alpha P_A D = (1-\beta)K_A.$$

It is clear that revenues will cover costs either if $\beta = 0$, which is uninteresting since there is no second good, or *if by assumption there is no multipurpose shopping*. Thus, while traditional central place theory sometimes invokes multipurpose shopping as a justification for overlaying the locational configuration for different types of outlets developed in isolation, it is clear that the precise locational pattern that results when the range of one good is twice the range of the other is inconsistent with the existence of any multipurpose shopping. Given multipurpose shopping, we can, in this example, have CP_2s separated by some given distance and a CP_1A at the mid-point between each pair of CP_2s, but only if the CP_2s are separated by a distance larger than $Z = 2Y$ and if $\beta < \frac{1}{2}$.

The coexistence of multipurpose and single-purpose shopping follows from a rational model of household shopping behaviour. This means, however, that adjacent central places of higher order take some of the potential sales from central places of lower order. For this reason, even in something so simple as the two-good case, various patterns are possible and they depend both on costs and on the relative volumes of multipurpose and single-purpose shopping. Whatever the details of a particular case, the equilibrium configuration *can never be established* simply by finding the patterns that would exist (1) if there were only A firms and (2) if there were only B firms, and then overlaying these two patterns. This statement is true in any theory of central places where agglomeration is economically motivated. It is not dependent on the restrictive assumptions of our model.[1]

(b) Capacity Relations

Above we illustrated the possibility of substantial *pure* excess capacity in market equilibrium. Given our price and cost assumptions it is a pure social waste to have more than one firm of each type in any CP_2. Of course, if the existence of more than one firm gives rise to price competition or if we assume U-shaped cost curves, the existence of multi outlets for the same good in a CP_2 would not necessarily be a waste. Nevertheless, we believe our model generates some insight into the phenomenon of excess capacity in retailing. The demand externalities that arise from multipurpose shopping serve to create something analogous to a spaceless market in the CP_2. If a CP_2 containing one firm of each type yields pure profits other profit-seeking firms may enter the CP_2 rather than locating outside it. This is because the market for both goods from households on multipurpose shopping trips exists only in CP_2s. As long as new firms expect profits, they will enter the CP_2, and the final equilibrium will be akin to Chamberlin's – although as Kaldor (1935) long ago pointed out, the discreteness of entry due to capital indivisibilities means that existing firms may be making substantial profits while a new entrant expects losses.

[1] Some critics of traditional central place theory have obviously been aware of the problems outlined above (see Rushton (1971), Parr (1973), Clark and Rushton (1970)). The quotation from Christaller cited in Note 1 of page 58 above indicates that he was aware of these problems.

The existence of excess capacity gives rise to a second interesting possibility. Let there be a *CP2* with multiple outlets for either or both types of firms. Now let the density of customers grow. Profits of existing firms will grow, and entry of further *A* and/or *B* firms into existing *CP2*s will occur. Eventually, customer density will grow enough so that a new *CP2* will be formed between adjacent *CP2*s.[1] The market of each existing *CP2* now falls discretely, since a new entrant between adjacent *CP2*s will halve the range over which existing *CP2*s draw *A*-with-*B* business. In this case, there is a fall in the total revenues earned by all the firms in each of the original *CP2*s. If more than one firm is selling one kind of good, all may make losses. If there are N firms selling this good, then up to $N/2$ of them may be redundant after the new *CP2*s are formed. Exit will occur until the firms remaining can at least cover costs.

Thus in a market where demand is growing steadily, growth of central places may be oscillatory. First, more *A* and/or *B* firms are added to existing *CP2*s, creating Chamberlinian excess capacity. This is an equilibrium phenomenon in the sense that if demand were held constant, the excess capacity would persist indefinitely. If demand goes on expanding, however, new *CP2*s will be formed, rendering some firms in old *CP2*s redundant. Exit will occur until the firms remaining in the old *CP2*s can cover costs. Further growth of demand will then lead all *CP2*s to grow once more until a further round of entry of new *CP2*s causes the old ones to shrink in size once more.

(c) Shopping Centres as Central Places

Consider any of the *CP2*s in our model that contain more than one firm of either or both types. Now assume the central place is demolished and the developer of a shopping centre is allowed to exploit the opportunity thereby created. If we ignore the possibility of entry by independent retailers, it is obvious that, given the cost specification in our model, the developer would simply establish one *A* firm and one *B* firm in his shopping centre. Consumers would be no worse off, and the developer would quite obviously enjoy pure profits greater than those collectively earned by the independent retailers who formerly comprised the *CP2*. The shopping centre would not dissipate rents through pure excess capacity in the manner which independent retailers may do in our model.[2] This result is similar to one that comes from models of a common property resource. When there exists no mechanism to limit entry into the *CP2*, independent retailers dissipate rents in much the same fashion as independent fisherman dissipate the rents available in a fishery.[3]

---

[1] The new *CP2* can arise in either of two ways. First, if there is no *CP1A* between existing *CP2*s, then eventually it will seem profitable for a *CP1A* to be formed; the *A* firm will immediately be joined by a *B* firm, thus creating a *CP2*. Second, if the parameters are such that there is one or more *CP1A*s between existing *CP2*s, then sooner or later, as demand rises, it will pay a *B* firm to join one of the *A* firms, converting an established *CP1A* into a *CP2*.

[2] Of course, in a model (such as Eaton and Lipsey (1979b)) that allows comparison shopping, the developer might choose to have more than one outlet for the same commodity. But he never permits the dissipation of rents by having more than the joint-profit-maximising number.

[3] The classic references are Gordon (1954) and Scott (1955). Neher (1978) has recently argued that the 'common property problem' arises in many situations. One way of interpreting our arguments with respect to pure excess capacity is that the exploitation of a demand for a good in a central place is also

We have, of course, simply assumed away the potential for entry of independent retailers once the shopping centre is established. The developer can, however, effectively forestall entry by purchasing all the land within some radius of the location of the shopping centre. In this way, he can ensure that he will get all of the revenues enjoyed by the original CP_2. If he does not buy up all such land, entry will occur in the same way as it occurs in the model of independent retailers, and the rents of location will be dissipated.

V. CONCLUSIONS

The existing theory of central places is simultaneously a theory of the location and agglomeration of economic activity in which there is no force creating agglomeration, in which agglomeration serves no purpose, and in which no firm ever chooses a location. Yet this 'theory' has proved useful in interpreting the economic landscape.

To develop an economic theory of central places, we have focused on the demand externalities created by multipurpose shopping. We demonstrate that these demand externalities must give rise to higher order central places, and that equilibrium satisfies a hierarchial principle. The model differs in important respects from the traditional model, and it yields insights into the phenomenon of excess capacity in retailing, into the dynamic process of expansion of the retail sector in a growing market, and into the role played by, and the motivation behind, shopping centres.

Our model is primitive in many respects, and it can be regarded as merely a beginning. Primitive as it is, however, it demonstrates the importance of providing a behavioural economic theory of central places and it illustrates the potential pay off to such a theory in terms of understanding real world phenomena.[1]

University of Toronto
Queen's University, Kingston

Date of receipt of final typescript: September 1981

---

plagued with common property problems. The retailers can be thought of as 'fishing' for customers from a common pool – those who travel to the central place for their purchases. In the absence of a shopping centre, firms already serving the market would seem to have a very limited capacity to deter entry of competing firms.

[1] Referees and editors have asked us to investigate whether our theory has more empirical content than traditional central place theory and to show how comparative tests can be made between the two theories. In the present paper our concern is to develop a new micro behavioural underpinning for central place theory. We illustrate the importance of this by showing that our micro underpinnings produce some predictions that agree with, and others that conflict with, those of traditional central place theory. The next two urgent tasks are first to discover all of the interesting testable statements where our theory diverges from central place theory and, second, to make comparative tests of these divergent predictions. Each of these tasks is a major research project. We are pleased, therefore, that Professor D. West, who has already done empirical work on several spatial theories including some of our own (West, 1981 a, 1981 b, 1981 c) is directing his attentions to these tasks.

APPENDIX

Proof of Proposition 2

Assume (I) that all firms in the market satisfy equilibrium condition (*i*), and
(II) that, scanning the market from left to right, we observe i *CP1As* and then a *CP1B*. This locational configuration is shown in Fig. 1.

We now show a contradiction.

If $i = 1$, the contradiction is immediate since A_1 could obviously increase its sales by moving to the right (and A_1 thus does not satisfy equilibrium condition (*i*)).

Consider the case in which $i \geq 2$ and consider the location of firm A_i in $[\bar{a}_{i-1}, \bar{b}_1]$. Location anywhere in the open interval $(\bar{a}_{i-1}, \bar{b}_1)$ will generate an identical amount of *A*-only sales, given by $\frac{1}{2}D\alpha(1-\beta)(\bar{a}_{i+1} - \bar{a}_{i-1})$, and an identical amount of *A*-with-*B* trade from consumers located in the interval $[0, \bar{a}_{i-1}]$, given by $D\alpha\beta\Sigma_1$ where

$$\Sigma_1 = \frac{\bar{a}_1}{i} + \frac{\bar{a}_2 - \bar{a}_1}{i-1} + \ldots + \frac{\bar{a}_{i-1} - \bar{a}_{i-2}}{2}. \tag{1}$$

But A_i will obtain a greater share of *A*-with-*B* sales, from consumers to the right of $\bar{a}_{i-1}$ the nearer is A_i located to B_1. Thus for a_i in $(\bar{a}_{i-1}, \bar{b}_1)$, A_i's sales increase with a_i, and since the interval is open A_i cannot satisfy equilibrium condition (*i*) in it. This leaves $\bar{a}_{i-1}$ and $\bar{b}_1$ as the only locations which may be consistent with the equilibrium conditions.

(*a*) *Location at* $\bar{b}_1$. Total *A*-with-*B* sales are

$$D\alpha\beta\bar{a}_{i-1} + D\alpha\beta(\phi - \bar{a}_{i-1}), \tag{2}$$

i.e. all customers in $[0, \bar{a}_{i-1}]$ plus customers in $(\bar{a}_{i-1}, \phi)$, where ϕ is the point at which a customer would be indifferent between visiting the *CP2* at $\bar{b}_1$ and some other combination of *A* and *B* firms. Clearly $\phi > \bar{b}_1$.

(*b*) *Location at* $\bar{a}_{i-1}$. Total *A*-with-*B* sales are

$$D\alpha\beta\Sigma_1 + D\alpha\beta(\theta - \bar{a}_{i-1})/2 \tag{3}$$

i.e. a share of customers to the left of $\bar{a}_{i-1}$ plus half the customers to the right of $\bar{a}_{i-1}$ who would prefer the combination (B_1, A_i) (or (B_1, A_{i-1})) to some other combination of *A* and *B* firms. Clearly, $\theta < \phi$.

The *loss* of *A*-with-*B* sales involved in choosing location $\bar{a}_{i-1}$ in preference to $\bar{b}_1$ is:

$$L_1 = D\alpha\beta[(\bar{a}_{i-1} - \Sigma_1) + (\phi - \bar{a}_{i-1}) - \tfrac{1}{2}(\theta - \bar{a}_{i-1})] \tag{4}$$

which is positive since $\bar{a}_{i-1} > \Sigma_1, \phi > \theta$. The change in *A*-only sales is:

$$\begin{aligned} C &= D\alpha(1-\beta)\tfrac{1}{4}(\bar{a}_{i+1} - \bar{a}_{i-2}) - D\alpha(1-\beta)\tfrac{1}{2}(\bar{a}_{i+1} - \bar{a}_{i-1}) \\ &= D\alpha(1-\beta)(\tfrac{1}{2}\bar{a}_{i-1} - \tfrac{1}{4}\bar{a}_{i+1} - \tfrac{1}{4}\bar{a}_{i-2}). \end{aligned} \tag{5}$$

If assumption (II) is to be satisfied $C > L_1$ and A_i locates at $\bar{a}_{i-1}$. Now consider A_{i-1}. If A_{i-1} locates an arbitrarily small distance to the left of A_i, its *A*-with-*B* sales are given by $D\alpha\beta\Sigma_1$, i.e., it loses A-with-B sales in $[\theta - \bar{a}_{i-1}]$. The *loss* of A-with-B sales is then

$$L_2 = \tfrac{1}{2}D\alpha\beta(\theta - \bar{a}_{i-1}). \tag{6}$$

The change in A-only sales is

$$D\alpha(1-\beta)\,\tfrac{1}{2}(\bar{a}_{i-1}-\bar{a}_{i-2}) - D\alpha(1-\beta)\,\tfrac{1}{4}(\bar{a}_{i+1}-\bar{a}_{i-2})$$
$$= D\alpha(1-\beta)(\tfrac{1}{2}\bar{a}_{i-1} - \tfrac{1}{4}\bar{a}_{i+1} - \tfrac{1}{4}\bar{a}_{i-2}) = C, \tag{7}$$

which is identical to that obtained by A_i in locating at $\bar{a}_{i-1}$ rather than $\bar{b}_1$. But note that

$$L_1 - L_2 = D\alpha\beta[(\phi - \theta) + (\bar{a}_{i-1} - \Sigma_1)] > 0 \tag{8}$$

hence
$$C > L_1 > L_2. \tag{9}$$

Thus if A_i chooses location at $\bar{a}_{i-1}$, A_{i-1} would wish to change location and so cannot satisfy the equilibrium condition (i). Hence Assumption (II) leads to a contradiction.

References

Alao, N., Dacey, M., Davies, O., Denike, K., Huff, J., Parr, J. and Webber, M. (1977). *Christaller Central Place Structures: An Introductory Statement.* Evanston, Illinois: Northwestern University Studies in Geography.

Bacon, R. (1971). 'An approach to the theory of consumer shopping behavior'. *Urban Studies*, vol. 8, pp. 55–64.

Beckmann, Martin (1958). 'City hierarchies and the distribution of city size'. *Economic Development and Cultural Change*, vol. 6, pp. 243–8.

Berry, B. J. L. (1958). 'Shopping centers and the geography of urban areas'. Ph.D. Dissertation, University of Washington.

—— (1961). 'City size distributions and economic development'. *Economic Development and Cultural Change*, vol. 9, pp. 573–88.

—— (1963). 'Commercial structure and commercial blight – retail patterns and processes in the city of Chicago'. University of Chicago, Department of Geography Research Paper No. 85.

Bollobás, B., and Stern, N. (1972). 'The optimal structure of market areas'. *Journal of Economic Theory*, vol. 4, pp. 174–9.

Christaller, Walter (1966). *Central Places in Southern Germany.* Englewood Cliffs, N.J.: Prentice-Hall.

Clark, W. A. V. and Rushton, G. (1970). 'Models of intra-urban consumer behavior and their implications for central place theory'. *Economic Geography*, vol. 46, pp. 486–97.

Dacey, M., Davies, O., Flowerdew, R., Huff, J., Ko, A. and Pipkin, J. (1974). *One-Dimensional Central Place Theory.* Evanston, Illinois: North-western University Studies in Geography.

Eaton, B. C. and Lipsey, R. G. (1975). 'The principle of minimum differentiation reconsidered: some new developments in the theory of spatial competition'. *Review of Economic Studies*, vol. 42, pp. 27–49.

—— (1976). 'The non-uniqueness of equilibrium in the Löschian location model'. *American Economic Review*, vol. 66, pp. 77–93.

—— (1979a). 'Microeconomic foundations of central place theory'. Queen's Institute for Economic Research Study Paper No. 327.

—— (1979b). 'Comparison shopping and the clustering of homogeneous firms'. *Journal of Regional Science*, vol. 19, pp. 421–35.

Gordon, H. S. (1954). 'The economic theory of a common property resource: the fishery'. *Journal of Political Economy*, vol. 62, pp. 124–42.

Golledge, R. G., Rushton, G. and Clark, W. A. V. (1966). 'Some spatial characteristics of Iowa's dispersed farm population and their implications for the grouping of central place functions'. *Economic Geography*, vol. 42, pp. 261–72.

Hartwick, John (1973). 'Lösch's theorem on hexagonal market areas'. *Journal of Regional Science*, vol. 13, pp. 213–21.

Hudson, J. C. (1969). 'Diffusion in a central place system'. *Geographical Analysis*, vol. 1, pp. 45–58.

Kaldor, N. (1935). 'Market imperfection and excess capacity'. *Economica*, vol. 2, pp. 33–50.

Lösch, August (1954). *The Economics of Location.* New Haven: Yale University Press.

Mills, E. and Lav, M. (1964). 'A model of market areas with free entry'. *Journal of Political Economy*, vol. 72, pp. 278–88.

Neher, Philip A. (1978). 'The pure theory of the muggery'. *American Economic Review*, vol. 68, pp. 437–45.

Parr, John B. (1973). 'Structure and size in the urban system of Lösch'. *Economic Geography*, vol. 49, pp. 185–212.

Prescott, E. C. and Visscher, M. (1977). 'Sequential location among firms with foresight'. *The Bell Journal of Economics*, vol. 8, pp. 378–93.

Rushton, Gerard (1971). 'Postulates of central place theory and the properties of central place systems'. *Geographical Analysis*, vol. 3, pp. 140–56.

Scott, A. D. (1955). 'The fishery: the objectives of sole ownership'. *Journal of Political Economy*, vol. 63, pp. 116–24.

Simmons, James (1964). 'The changing pattern of retail location', University of Chicago, Department of Geography, Research Paper no. 92.

—— (1966). 'Toronto's changing retail complex: a study in growth and blight', University of Chicago, Department of Geography, Research Paper no. 104.

West, Douglas S. (1981 a). 'Tests of two locational implications of a theory of market pre-emption'. *The Canadian Journal of Economics*, vol. 14, pp. 313–26.

—— (1981 b). 'Testing for market preemption using sequential location data'. Forthcoming in *The Bell Journal of Economics*.

—— (1981 c). 'Market predation in a spatially extended market: theory and evidence'. Department of Economics, Purdue University, mimeograph.

[13]
Address Models of Value Theory[1]

G.C. Archibald
UNIVERSITY OF BRITISH COLUMBIA

B.C. Eaton
UNIVERSITY OF TORONTO

and

R.G. Lipsey
QUEEN'S UNIVERSITY

I INTRODUCTION

This paper presents an approach to the theory of monopolistic competition which owes a particular intellectual debt to Gorman (1980), Kaldor (1934; 1935) and Lancaster (1966). Our interest is in deriving testable hypotheses from partial equilibrium analysis. Some simple conceptual experiments, in conjunction with some awkward facts, lead us to take strong positions concerning the appropriate demand and cost primitives. The choice of primitives has important implications for the concept and the properties of equilibrium. We hope that the approach presented here is coherent; but it has to be said that the analysis has not been completed, by ourselves or anyone else. Part of our purpose is accordingly to note unsolved problems, and generate an agenda for further research. At some points we are able only to offer a conjecture as to what the results of further research may be. We confine ourselves throughout to the market for consumer goods (Chamberlin's, 1933, problem) and do not consider the markets for capital, labour or intermediate goods.

The remainder of this introduction outlines our argument.

(1) We start by inviting the reader to share in a conceptual experiment. Choose some currently produced good, X: can you specify an

3

4 Address Models

arbitrarily close substitute? To paraphrase Eddington[2] (1958, p. 119), 'Hesitate before you answer: much of modern value theory hangs in the balance'. We think that in most cases the answer must be 'yes'. (Clearly we can specify an automobile with a little more acceleration, deceleration, fuel consumption, and so on; indeed, examples are many and obvious.) A 'yes' answer has important implications. First, it would be hard to describe your specified substitute as an *arbitrarily close substitute* for an existing good without operating in some *space of product attributes or characteristics*. Second, natural notions of continuity suggest that there exists a neighbourhood around good X in the appropriate characteristics space such that all goods in the neighbourhood are close substitutes for good X. This suggests to us that the natural way to describe your preferences is in some appropriate *and continuous* characteristics space. Thus a 'yes' answer to the original question suggests that the set of goods considered by the consumer is a continuum in some appropriate characteristics space (or the union of continua in appropriate sub-spaces). Convenience suggests that the set of possible goods be described in the same space. Whether or not the set of *possible* goods should also be assumed to be a continuum is considered in Section II.

(2) Now we invite you to specify the neighbourhood in which you find close substitutes for good X, and we ask other consumers if they too regard goods in this neighbourhood to be close substitutes for X. If they answer 'yes', we conclude that they perceive goods as points in the same characteristics space. We do not expect a 'no' answer, and, indeed, it would be hard to live with: if individuals perceive different spaces, or if the characteristics are as ephemeral as automobile models themselves, we do not know how to specify tractable demand primitives. We do expect a 'yes' answer and, accordingly, adopt the characteristics approach pioneered by Baumol (1967), Quandt–Baumol (1966) and Lancaster (1966).

(3) We take as awkward facts that consumers' tastes over characteristics are diverse and that the number of produced commodities in any 'group' is small relative to the number of consumers. (The definition of a group is considered below.) We argue that product-specific capital inputs are necessary to explain the paucity of produced commodities and are sufficient to explain the range of increasing returns to outlay necessary for the very existence of firms.

(4) Specification of demand primitives in characteristics space, together with diversity of tastes and product-specificity of capital, imply that competition among firms is often localised. (The extent to which competition is localised and, indeed, the necessary conditions

for localisation itself are, however, largely unexplored issues. We return to them below.)

(5) Localised competition and product-specific capital imply the existence of a *range* of free-entry equilibria in which firms may earn profits, even in groups with large numbers of firms. At one extreme of the range, profits are zero so that exit is just avoided; at the other extreme profits are positive but just not large enough to attract entry.

(6) The existence of specific capital inputs implies that entrants into a market have something to lose if their expectations with respect to sitting firms' responses are not accurate. We argue that this rules out 'naive' expectations (for example, the assumption that sitting firms will not respond) and makes it a desirable feature that new entrants should have correct, or consistent, expectations of any equilibrium concept where specific capital is important.

(7) Consistent expectations on the part of new entrants, plus product-specific capital, make it profitable for sitting firms to engage in strategic behaviour with respect to specific inputs. The goals of such behaviour are to bar entry and/or to create asymmetric entry equilibria. Such strategic behaviour may dissipate some or all of the profits in a socially wasteful fashion.

(8) Our analysis of strategic behaviour leads us to the conjecture, contrary to much existing literature, that the market equilibrium will converge on the extreme that yields the largest profits that sitting firms can earn without attracting entry.

In Section II we discuss the set of all possible goods, and identify two distinct characterisations of that set which, we think, differ in important ways. In Section III we discuss demand primitives, and find again that a choice must be made between distinct sets of primitives. In Section IV we discuss cost-technology primitives, paying particular attention to the problems of increasing returns, indivisibility, and specificity of capital. Section V discusses free-entry equilibrium, paying particular attention to expectations and to the possibility that equilibrium profits will be strictly positive. In Section VI we endeavour to assemble results, paying particular attention to strategic behaviour. Section VII briefly considers problems of welfare economics, while in Section VIII we propose a research agenda.

II THE SET OF ALL POSSIBLE GOODS

In models of monopolistic competition, questions about firms' product selection and the optimal diversity of products naturally arise.

6 Address Models

These questions require that the set of all possible goods be larger than the set of currently-produced goods. We see two quite different characterisations of the set of possible goods.

Where goods are differentiated by 'quality' (e.g., Prescott–Visscher (1977) 'Example 3', Dorfman–Steiner (1954), Shaked–Sutton (1982)), each good is characterised by an element of a continuum in R^1 and the set of all possible goods is this set. In models of spatial competition (e.g., Hotelling (1929), Losch (1954), Eaton–Lipsey (1978), Salop (1979)), firms sell undifferentiated products but their locations are (potentially) differentiated in a continuum in R^1 or R^2. With costly transportation, undifferentiated products sold at different locations can be regarded as differentiated goods and the set of all possible goods is then a continuum in R^1 or R^2. In models of monopolistic competition in characteristics space (e.g., Baumol (1967), Archibald–Rosenbluth (1975), Lancaster (1975)), a good can be characterised by the ratio of the quantity of one characteristic embodied in a unit of that good to the quantity of a second characteristic similarly embodied (taking the two-characteristics case for illustration). In each of these illustrations, the set of all possible goods is a continuum in the real space of appropriate dimension, and there is an uncountable infinity of possible goods.

The alternative characterisation of the set of possible goods is to specify a finite, or countably infinite, list (e.g., Spence (1976), Dixit–Stiglitz (1977), Perloff–Salop (1982)). In this case the set of possible goods is obviously not a continuum. This characterisation has the obvious advantage that it is the natural extension of the set used in traditional neo-classical theory, but it imposes a severe restriction on the technology: it is discontinuous. *If brand A can be distinguished from brand B (other than merely by their labels), or if it is meaningful to ask if it is possible to produce a good arbitrarily close to brand A, there is implicitly some space of attributes, or characteristics, of goods,* however defined or measured. Then the implication of assuming that the set of possible goods is countable is that, in this space, it is not continuous.

The argument of the last paragraph in some sense replicates the conceptual experiment of sub-section I (1), except that we are now considering technological possibilities rather than consumers' perceptions. We can see no obvious *a priori* reason for assuming that production possibilities, in the appropriate characteristics space, are *not* continuous. Once again, we could obviously offer many examples. (Cost-minimising producers are clearly concerned with properties of goods for which consumers' preferences are not defined, but the analysis of demand must be carried out in the consumers' space.)

It seems to us that the vast majority of produced goods are elements from some characteristics-space continuum and that, other things equal, this is the preferred characterisation of the set of possible goods. Since analysis of such a characterisation may be difficult, we face the important question: can we successfully study behaviour in the continuum by using a countable characterisation of possible goods? We shall argue that the answer is 'no' (but we must first consider demand primitives).

Thus we see a fundamental distinction between the characterisations. The first we refer to as the *address branch*, because goods must be described by their address (co-ordinates) in some continuum. The second we refer to as the *non-address branch*, because the goods constituting the countable set are just goods.

III DEMAND PRIMITIVES

We use the address, non-address distinction to structure our discussion of demand primitives. In the non-address branch, preferences are defined over a finite or countably infinite set of goods, and in the address branch preferences are defined over the appropriate continuum.

(A) THE ADDRESS BRANCH

With some loss of generality, economists have usually analysed *either* problems in which otherwise homogeneous consumers and products are distinguished by their locations in physical space, *or* problems in which consumers are not homogeneous and goods are distinguished by their locations in characteristics space. In this section we consider these two approaches and the sense in which they may be analogous.

(1) Geographic Models

(i) In these models, firms sell products with identical characteristics bundles, but firms and consumers are distinguished by addresses in the continuum of geographic space. For simplicity, we examine the consumer's problem in a one-dimensional geographic continuum, assuming that the prices he faces are simply mill-prices plus transport costs. Define his preferences over quantity of the 'group' good, y, and quantity of a composite good, x, with representation $U = U(y, x)$,

8 *Address Models*

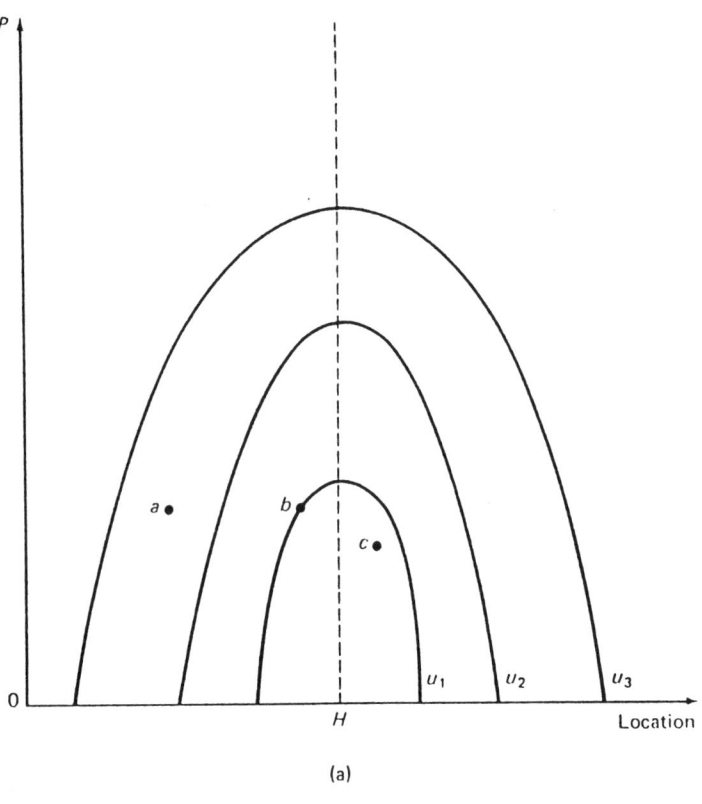

(a)

Fig. 1.1(a)

having the standard properties. Let H and L denote respectively the consumer's and a firm's location in the continuum, and let $t(L, H)$ denote the cost to the consumer of transporting a unit of y from L to H. To ensure that competition is localised we assume now that $t(L, H)$ is an increasing and convex function of $|L - H|$. Then we can define an indirect representation of the consumer's preferences:

$$W(L, p) = \max_{y, x} \{U(y, x) \quad \text{subject to } [p + t(L, H)]y + x = B\},$$

where p is price at the mill, and the price of the composite good is normalised to be 1. Figure 1.1(a) presents level surfaces of $W(L, p)$. These level surfaces are necessarily vertical translates of one another, and intersect the horizontal axis as illustrated. Clearly W is decreasing in p.

Goods can then be characterised by points in (L, p) space. The consumer will obviously choose to purchase the good which maximises $W(L, p)$: e.g., good c in Figure 1.1(a).

(ii) From this representation of the problem, it follows immediately that the consumer's cross-price elasticities among goods are discontinuous: they are infinite at crucial prices and zero at all others. The consumer typically purchases a positive amount of only one (or at most two) of the many goods.

(iii) Assume that there is a continuum of consumers along the geographic space. Then competition is localised: cross-price elasticities between a good and its neighbouring goods (of which there are only two in our linear market) are non-zero, but between that good and all others they are zero. (We consider the conditions under which competition is localised in this sense in Section (4) below.)

(2) Characteristics Models

(i) In these models consumers' preferences are defined over characteristics, which are embodied in goods. Either all production and consumption implicitly takes place at one point in geographic space, or transportation is costless. For simplicity, we consider the case in which the goods in a group embody two characteristics. Define the utility of a consumer over the quantity of the two characteristics, z_1 and z_2, and the quantity of a composite good, x (which embodies neither z_1 nor z_2), with the representation $U = U(z_1, z_2, x)$ having standard properties.

For easy comparison with models in geographic space, we again derive an indirect representation of the consumer's preferences. To do so, we need a convention for defining units of 'group' goods. Let L be the angle between a ray through the origin in (z_1, z_2) space and the z_1 axis. For any given L, the functions $g(\cdot)$ and $h(\cdot)$ define the amount of each characteristic in a unit of the specific group good described by that value of L. Now we define the indirect utility function

$$W(L, p) = \max_{y, x} \{U(yg(L), yh(L), x) \quad \text{subject to } (py + x = B)\},$$

where y is the quantity of the group good. Of course, $g(L)$ and $h(L)$ are simply a parametric representation of a line in (z_1, z_2) space. If we choose $g(L)$ and $h(L)$ appropriately, $W(L, p)$ is quasi-concave and we have the level surfaces shown in Figures 1.1(b) and 1.1(c). L is, of course, defined on the interval $[0, \pi/2]$. If the indifference curves of $U(z_1, z_2, x)$ in z_1-z_2 space are asymptotic to the axes, the level surfaces of $W(L, p)$ are as illustrated. If the indifference curves

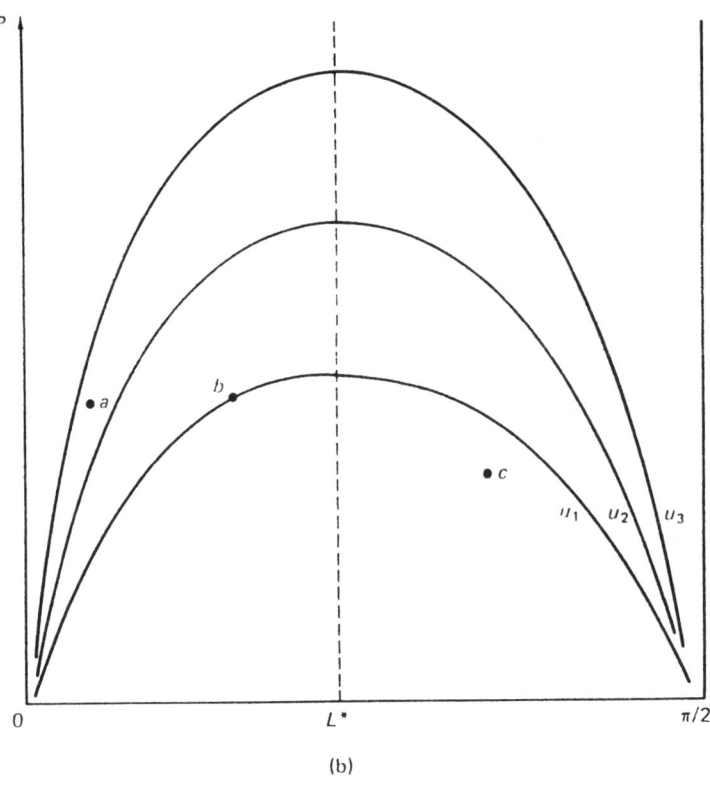

(b)

Fig. 1.1(b)

intersect one or both axes, the level surfaces intersect one or both of the vertical axes in Figure 1.1(b) and 1.1(c). Unlike the level surfaces of Figure 1.1(a), these level surfaces *cannot* intersect the horizontal axis if the indifference curves have throughout a negative slope in characteristics space (see Note 5), and, of course, cannot be vertical translates. Again W is decreasing in p. If z_1 and z_2 are homothetically separable from x in U, then the consumer has a most-preferred L, L^* in Figure 1.1(b). L^* is clearly analogous to the consumer's location, H, in Figure 1.1(a). The consumer is 'located' at L^* in the continuum of possible goods in the sense that L^* defines his 'most preferred good'. Marketed goods can obviously be characterised by points in (L, p) space, such as points a, b and c in the Figure. If we do not have homothetic separability (Figure 1.1(c)), we cannot define a 'most preferred good' and there is no direct analogy between *location* in geographic and in characteristic space.

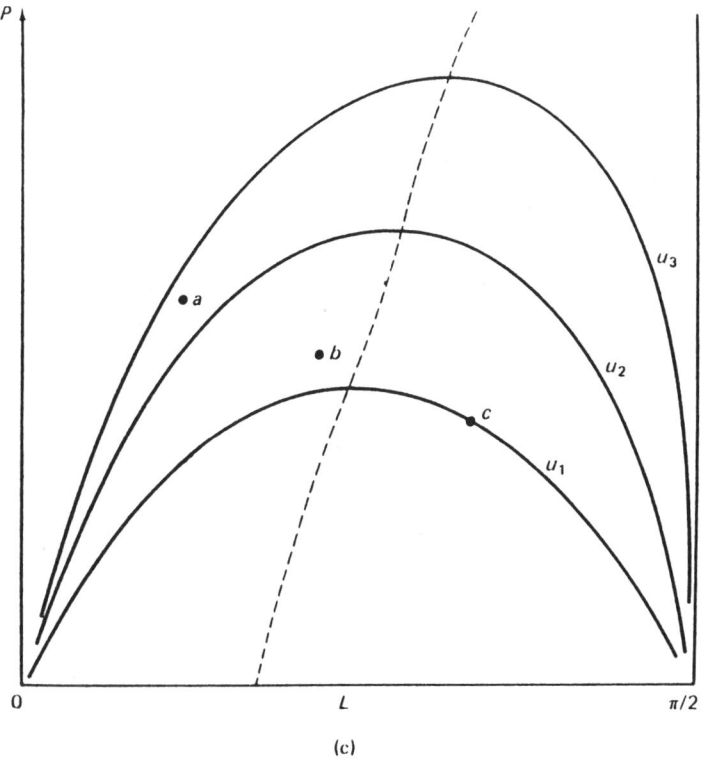

FIG. 1.1(c)

(ii) We have to decide a question about the consumer's technological possibilities: can he combine goods in order to produce characteristic combinations not embodied in any single, marketed good? At the two extremes, combining may be physically impossible or combining may be possible at zero cost. In the latter case, any convex combination of the mixes of characteristics provided by the separate goods is available. In between, combining may be possible at some (objective and/or psychological) cost. We consider the combining and non-combining cases separately (but omit intermediate cases of costly combination).

(iii) In the non-combining case, the choice set which the consumer faces is just the set of points in (L, p) space which describe marketed goods (and good c is the preferred good in Figures 1.1(b) and 1.1(c)). As in the geographic model, each consumer's cross-price elasticities are discontinuous: infinite at crucial prices and zero at all others. The consumer typically will purchase a positive amount of only one marketed good in the group.

(iv) In the combining case, the consumer never needs to consume more goods than there are characteristics (Lancaster, 1966). If there are more goods than characteristics, then the consumer's cross-price elasticities among goods are again discontinuous.

(v) Localised competition is possible in characteristics space just as it is geographic space. In the combining case, every commodity can be in competition only with its immediate neighbours[3] which obviously cannot exceed two in two-space. Archibald–Rosenbluth (1975) show that the *average* number of neighbours that goods may have in the three characteristics case cannot exceed six, no matter how large the number of goods, n, may be, whereas in the four-characteristics case the average may approach $n/2$, as n gets large.

(vi) In the non-combining case, matters are more complicated. The simple 'dominance' argument for convexity of the market-opportunity frontier (Lancaster, (1966) does not apply. We conjecture that if it is 'convex',[4] the Archibald–Rosenbluth argument goes through, but we have not established it. We take up the problem of 'non-convexity' in (4) below.

(3) The Analogy

There are some obvious differences between market spaces in geographic and characteristic models. First, the finite, unbounded and, closed geographic space that results when an n dimensional space is curved back on itself in the $(n + 1)$th dimension has few, if any, analogies in characteristics space. Thus we cannot in characteristics space avoid the problems associated with boundaries. Second, the obvious restriction on the dimensionality of geographic space does not apply to characteristics space: it is easy to think of a group of commodities sharing a very large number of characteristics. (On the other hand, we can readily increase the dimensionality of geographical models by adding non-spatial characteristics such as the product range and service quality of stores.)

We have so far taken the group or 'market area' as a primitive which is, of course, essential if we are to engage in partial-equilibrium analysis. In geographic models the market area, defined as the space over which potential customers are distributed, may be taken as a primitive without much difficulty. (The distribution of customers is often taken as exogenous. In the most general models it is, of course, endogenous.)

In characteristics space the problem is more complex. We unambiguously have a group if: (1) we can identify a set of produced goods, each of which embodies non-negative amounts of the same list of characteristics (at least one amount must be positive), and none of which embodies positive amounts of any other characteristic; and (2) no other goods outside the group embody the characteristics supplied by the group. Whether these conditions are satisfied, and thus whether we have an unambiguous group, is in the long run endogenous: it is determined by tastes and technology. We have very little more to say about this interesting problem. It does, however, raise two further questions. To what extent can these conditions be violated while still preserving some useful concept of a group? And, assuming the conditions are violated, to what extent may we still have localised competition between goods? This last question seems to us to be of fundamental importance.

(4) Localised competition

In the previous paragraph we encountered Triffin's problem: is there a meaningful unit of economic activity between the firm and the whole economy? If there is not, of course competition cannot be localised. Much recent literature has been addressed to localised competition; but we need a more careful analysis of the determinants of the extent of localisation. We know sufficient conditions for localisation, and were careful to employ them in (1) and (2) above; but we do not know the necessary conditions, as we may now see.

Consider first geographic address models. If transportation costs are identical for all consumers and convex in distance, then competition is clearly local in nature. Thus in one-dimensional models, each firm is in direct competition with at most two other firms. Suppose, however, that transportation costs are subjective and differ among consumers. Then a low-price firm could be in direct competition with a large number of high-price firms selling identical products. Its market area would no longer be a connected subset of the entire market, and competition would not be localised to the same extent. The analogous problem obviously arises in characteristics space. Lancaster (1975) refers to this phenomenon as 'cross over', and makes assumptions sufficient to rule it out.[5] In the non-combining case, it is possible that the consumer's choice set is not 'd-convex' (see Note 4) so that cross-over, as in the spatial example, is an obvious possibility. Suppose now that in the spatial model transport costs are a concave function of distance and identical for all consumers. Again, it is possible that a low-price firm may be in competition with several high-priced ones, diminishing the extent to which competition is localised. Indeed, the use of delivered pricing systems clearly raises the possibility that, in some geographical markets, competition is not localised at all. We have to ask what determines the choice of pricing mode in geographic markets, and what are the effects of delivered pricing modes on the extent to which competition is localised.

In the characteristics model the dimensionality of the space itself may be an important determinant of the extent to which competition is localised. Apart from the Archibald–Rosenbluth results, however, we know virtually nothing about how these possibilities may affect the properties of equilibrium. We think that there is an obvious research task here. We should also bear in mind that in more-general models goods would have addresses in both spaces: in characteristics space for the reasons we have argued; and in physical space whenever transport costs are non-zero. At this stage, it can be a conjecture only that in such a model we should find a high degree of localisation to be the most plausible configuration.

(B) THE NON-ADDRESS BRANCH

The seminal papers in this tradition are Dixit–Stiglitz (1977), which can be regarded as a formalisation of Chamberlin's large group case, and Spence (1976). In these models, the set of possible goods is countable. Fixed costs of production, associated with each good, dictate that only a subset of possible goods will be produced.

The demand primitive is a well-behaved utility function of a representative consumer, defined over the set of all possible goods. The representative consumer's problem is the standard choice problem: given prices, he chooses quantities to maximise utility. In any equilibrium, the representative consumer necessarily consumes a non-zero quantity of each of the goods produced, and the cross-price elasticity of demand between any pair of marketed goods is non-zero: competition is not localised.

If we take the notion of a representative consumer literally, then we ignore an important and obvious source of product diversity,

diversity in consumers' tastes. For reasons suggested in sub-section I(3), this approach is not appealing to us. If, instead, we regard the utility function as an aggregate preference relation, we are forced to ask what the implied restrictions on individual's preferences are.

Given our view of monopolistic competition, we accordingly must ask if the utility function of the representative consumer could be derived from some aggregation of individual preferences, drawn from the address branch. In general, the answer is no. In the combining case of the characteristics model, where localised competition is a certainty in the two-characteristics case, every consumer who buys some of commodity L_i buys at most one other commodity. Thus no matter how diverse are the tastes of individual consumers, the cross-elasticity between L_i and all but two other goods in the group must be zero. Thus the representative consumer, with positive cross-elasticities for all goods in the group, cannot be taken as representing the aggregate behaviour of market demand when tastes are defined over characteristics. In the non-combining case, non-localised competition becomes possible. It is then important to know if there exists *some* specification of demand primitives in the address branch which could be aggregated to yield well-behaved preferences of a representative consumer. The model of Perloff–Salop (1982) allows them to aggregate, in order to obtain a representative preference-relation which is symmetric over goods, thus satisfying the necessary condition for a Chamberlinian equilibrium. We think their approach is illuminating, but unsatisfactory.

To see why, recall the question of whether consumers' perceptions of relevant characteristics differ, so that we cannot define demand primitives over a *common* characteristics space or proceed with the characteristics approach as outlined above. We suggested an experiment designed to answer this question in Section I(2), and need not repeat it. If the characteristics space is specific to the consumer (which, although possible, is not what we expect), then tractability may require that we define individual preferences over a countable set of goods.

Perloff and Salop do this. They assume that there is a finite number, n, of differentiated brands available in a given product-class.[6] Each consumer '. . . attaches relative values to these brands according to his *preference vector* . . .' (p. 3) $\theta = (\theta_1, \theta_2, \ldots, \theta_n)$ and each chooses the brand which maximises his surplus, $\theta_i - p_i$ (p. 4) (and consumes zero of $n - 1$ goods).[7] *Diversity is then obtained by the random assignment of θs to consumers.* In the symmetric case, aggregate preferences for each brand are independent and identically distributed: each brand is the best-buy for an equal share of consumers, and all firms' demand curves are identical. It also follows that all consumers who agree that good i is the best buy have their second choice uniformly distributed over the remaining $n - 1$ goods (with obvious implications for non-localised competition).

Perloff and Salop argue that their approach is, in some sense, a synthesis of what we have called the address and non-address approaches to the problem. Although they do capture the address branch phenomenon – that consumers are in corner solutions with respect to most goods in the group – they do this at the cost of implying consumer-specific characteristic spaces. It is not clear what the appropriate primitives are in this approach.

Our rejection of this approach leads us to conclude that a clear *choice* of demand primitives must be made in the study of monopolistic competition. The choice is between the usual goods-approach exploited by Dixit–Stiglitz, and Spence, and the characteristics-approach. This choice must be determined, at least in part, by how we think we should try to account for the diversity of produced goods that we observe. If we take the goods approach, the representative consumer buys at least some amount of everything. Given some initial range of falling costs in production, diversity of produced goods increases as his endowment increases. If we want to account for the observation that most consumers buy a zero quantity of most goods produced, we must proceed otherwise. Diversity of produced goods now follows from the diversity among consumers themselves, and production-diversity increases as this consumer-diversity is increased (more non-identical consumers are added to the model). It seems to us that the characteristics approach accounts satisfactorily for this sort of diversity. Whether or not it 'works', in the sense that consumers do consider the same short list of characteristics to be relevant, is an empirical question not yet resolved.

Also, there is much yet to be done in the way of formulating and testing restrictions on the distribution of preferences. We argued in Section I(2) that agreement on what is a close substitute implies the existence of some common space of characteristics on which preferences are defined. In any case, to avoid making undesirable or even absurd implicit assumptions on the basic primitives, it is imperative to ask what restrictions on tastes in characteristic space are implied by even seemingly very reasonable restrictions on tastes defined over goods.

IV COST-TECHNOLOGY PRIMITIVES

(1) AWKWARD FACTS

It is generally agreed that *in the absence of a range of increasing returns to outlay, or decreasing unit costs of production,* any good for which there is positive demand at minimum unit cost of production (given all other prices) will be produced. First, suppose that each consumer has a unique 'most-preferred good' in the continuum of possible goods. Then, if that good is not offered by some producer at minimum unit cost of production, the consumer can and will produce that good for himself. (There are, in this case, no compelling reasons for the existence of firms.) Second, suppose that there is a continuum of most-preferred goods. There will then be a continuum of produced goods.

Given that the set of possible goods is a continuum (in some space), the awkward fact which we must confront is that the set of produced goods is small relative to the set of consumers. But although the phenomenon of increasing returns to outlay is necessary to explain the awkward fact, it is not sufficient. Imagine, for example, that the production function for a good, written in terms of flows of inputs and output, exhibits an initial range of increasing returns to scale, and that all inputs are perfectly divisible, i.e., can be purchased as flows. Then, again, each consumer has the option of producing his most-preferred good at its minimum unit cost of production. This is because production of an arbitrarily small quantity at minimum unit cost can be achieved by producing at minimum efficient scale for an arbitrarily short period of time.[8] Again, there is no compelling reason for the existence of firms and if there is a continuum of most-preferred goods, there will be a continuum of produced goods.

To sum up, the existence of some degree of increase in returns is not sufficient to explain the awkward facts, so long as that increase is associated only with the flow-rate of output. If it is, an arbitrarily small output can be had at minimum cost by producing at as fast a rate as is needed, for an arbitrarily short interval. Thus, to explain the awkward facts there must be some property of the technology that prevents us from 'getting round' the non-convexity in this way. We think there is; and we shall sketch a model in Section (2). Suppose that there do exist product-specific capital inputs which cannot be dispensed with.[9] Suppose further that they are 'lumpy' in the sense that, once constructed, they embody a *stock* of capital services to be used up over time, and that this lumpiness sets a (strictly positive) lower bound to the total quantity of output that must be produced in order to attain minimum unit cost of production. Now, if there is any positive cost of waiting (an interest rate) it is cheaper to use up the stock of services embodied in the capital good sooner rather than later. It follows that 'home production' at high speed for short intervals is not as cheap as is continuous 'mass production' at high speed: there is a reason for the existence of production-points (firms) selling to many consumers. It also and obviously follows that the existence of such lumpy inputs implies that the existence of a continuum of goods would violate the scarcity constraint.

Production functions for final goods, defined by the flow inputs of capital services and of labour, may exhibit constant returns to scale. Indeed, we shall assume that they do. Even so, the existence of product-specific lumpy capital goods implies increasing returns to outlay. This in turn explains both the existence of firms and the fact that the number of products is small (relative to both the number of consumers and, we conjecture, the diversity of their 'most-preferred goods'). As we shall see specific, lumpy capital is also the vehicle for commitment and thus essential to strategic behaviour.

(2) SPECIFICITY AND INDIVISIBILITY

We confine our attention to the extreme case where the meaning of the product-specificity of capital goods is unambiguous: product-specific capital goods are ones that are useful in the production of a particular good and which have no alternative uses. Although the definition of partial-specificity poses some difficult conceptual issues,[10] it is obvious that transactions costs, set-up costs, re-location costs and costs of training specialised labour contribute significantly to specificity.

We now turn to a simple demonstration that product-specific capital inputs imply increasing returns to outlay in the production of final goods. The presentation is an intuitive but, we hope, comprehensible account of the basic argument made in a forthcoming paper by Eaton and Lipsey.

Suppose that good X can be produced as a flow, using a flow of labour, n, and a flow of product specific capital services, according to

$$x = f(n, v). \tag{1}$$

Assume that $f(\cdot)$ exhibits constant returns to scale (and is quasi-concave) and that the flow of specific capital services, v, is obtained from a capital good which embodies a stock of specific capital services.

We adopt the simplest possible characterisation of the specific capital good: it is characterised completely by the number S which is the stock of specific capital services embodied in the *indivisible* good.[11] Initially we assume that $S = \bar{S}$ and is not subject to choice. Define $C(v)$ as the present discounted cost of obtaining a constant positive flow of capital services, v, over an infinite horizon. Assume for convenience a time-invariant rate of interest, r. We then have

$$C(v) = \frac{\bar{c}}{1 - e^{-rT}}, \quad T = \bar{S}/v, \qquad (2)$$

where $\bar{c}$ is the cost of the capital good. $C(v)$ is simply the present discounted-cost of buying the stock $\bar{S}$ every $T = \bar{S}/v$ periods (evaluated at a point in time at which a unit is purchased). The following results can be shown, and are in any case intuitively obvious:

$$C'(v) > 0, \; C''(v) > 0, \quad \lim_{v \to \infty} C'(v) = \bar{c}/\bar{S}r, \qquad (3)$$

$$\lim_{v \to 0} C'(v) = 0, \quad \lim_{v \to \infty} \frac{C(v)}{v} = \bar{c}/\bar{S}r.$$

Thus $C(v)$ and $C(v)/v$ are as illustrated in Figure 1.2(a) and (b).

Now consider minimising the present discounted-cost of producing a flow of output, x^1, over an infinite horizon, and let $V(x)$ denote that minimised cost. Let W be the present discounted-cost of obtaining a flow of one unit of labour over an infinite horizon. Let v^1 and n^1 solve the cost-minimisation problem for x^1, and assume that we have an interior solution ($v^1 > 0$, $n^1 > 0$). Consider, now, producing some larger level of output αx^1, $\alpha > 1$. Then we have

$$V(\alpha x^1) < C(\alpha v^1) + \alpha W n^1 < \alpha C(v^1) + \alpha W n^1 = \alpha V(x^1). \qquad (4)$$

The first inequality follows from the assumption that f is homogeneous of degree 1 and the fact that, although $(\alpha n^1, \alpha v^1)$ will produce αx^1, it is not the cost-minimising input combination.[12] The second inequality follows from the properties of $C(\cdot)$ given in (3): $C(\alpha v) < \alpha C(v)$. Thus the indivisibility of specific capital implies increasing returns to outlay.[13] The general shape of $V(x)$ and $V(x)/x$ will mirror the shapes of $C(v)$ and $C(v)/v$ in Figure 1.2(a) and (b).

(3) CHOICE OF INDIVISIBILITY

These results are based on our assumption that the capital good is indivisible. Let us then enquire into the conditions which might lead

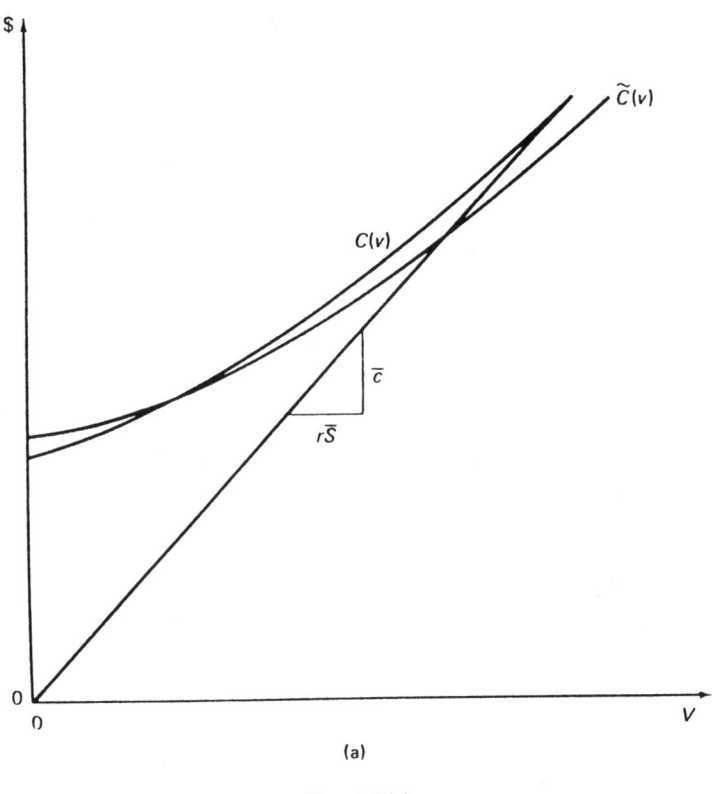

FIG. 1.2(a)

firms to create such indivisibilities. Suppose that the quantity (S) of capital services is produced by embodying a quantity of labour (L) and a quantity of materials (M) into a good according to

$$S = g(L, M), \qquad (5)$$

and that L and M are purchased on competitive markets. Let (g) be homogeneous of degree λ, and define $H(S)$ to be the minimum cost of embodying (S) units of capital services in a capital good. Now consider,

$$\bar{C}(v) = \min_{S}\left(\frac{H(S)}{1 - e^{-rT}}\right), \quad T = S/v. \qquad (6)$$

$\bar{C}(v)$ is the minimum cost of obtaining (v) units of capital services forever, when we choose the magnitude of the indivisibility (S). It is

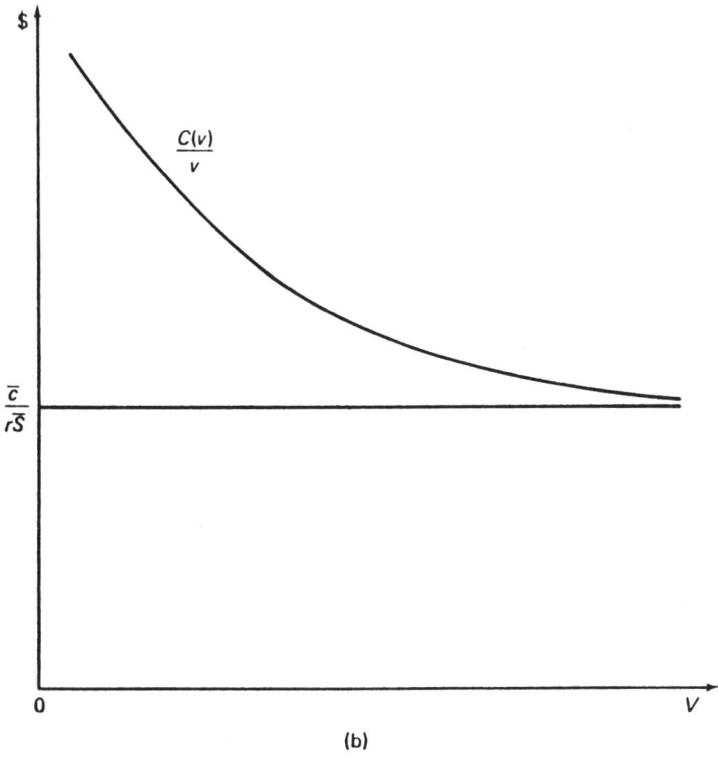

FIG. 1.2(b)

easy to show, and is intuitively obvious, that the solution to the minimisation problem is degenerate, in the sense that S goes to zero, if $\lambda < 1$. Thus, if we rule out God-given indivisibilities, man-made indivisibilities (capital goods) arise because there are increasing returns to scale (or outlay) in the embodiment of capital services in goods.[14]

According, let $\lambda > 1$. Then $\bar{C}(v)$ is the envelope of $C(v)$ (defined in equation (2)) as S varies. $\bar{C}(v)$ has the same general properties as $C(v)$, and our conclusion that God-given indivisibilities imply increasing returns to outlay is obviously strengthened when we allow for man-made indivisibilities.[15] Thus the age-old question of why there should be scale effects when combining pure flows of input services is answered 'there do not have to be'. The range of falling costs needed to explain the existence of a finite number of firms and products requires only that there be increasing returns in embodying a flow of (capital) services in a (capital) good with the dimension of a stock.

V FREE-ENTRY EQUILIBRIUM

(A) EQUILIBRIUM CONCEPTS

Given some specification of demand and technology-cost primitives, the fundamental analytical problem in monopolistic competition is the characterisation of free-entry equilibrium (FEE) as: (i) no existing firm *perceives* that a change in any of the variables under its control, such as prices, quantities, and range of products (including the option of exit) will increase profits; (ii) no potential entrant *perceives* that entry is profitable.

We consider condition (ii) first. Here, the key problem is how the potential new entrant predicts his post-entry profits. In particular does he take current prices, quantities, etc. as given? The principal determinants of the answer are capital specificity and size of group.

In the complete absence of capital specificity (as in Baumol, 1982), the potential entrant can enter or leave without cost. Thus there is no penalty for mistakes, and it is possible to produce an arbitrarily small output without cost penalty merely by producing it at the appropriate rate for a sufficiently short interval of time. In these circumstances, profits earned by existing firms signal the opportunity for profits to a new entrant. The FEE will then display zero profit and will hold at all points in time.

Now consider the case of specific, lumpy capital in the non-address branch. Here we encounter the well-known *integer problem*. Suppose that market demand is such that n firms make positive profits while $n + 1$ firms would make losses. In the large number case, this problem may not be of great practical significance, but it does raise theoretical issues.[16] When n is small, say 1 for purposes of illustration, a rational, potential new entrant will not take the sitting firm's data as given. A potential entrant who did take the monopolist's price as given would enter and undercut this price, expecting to usurp virtually all the sitting monopolist's pure profits. But the sitting monopolist will prefer to supply a positive output at any price not less than his minimum average variable cost than to shut down. By asking himself what he would do if he were in the sitting monopolist's position, the potential entrant can foresee that result: he cannot take the sitting monopolist's price as given. If we accept the notion that the potential entrant expects the post-entry equilibrium to be symmetric, then we infer that entry will not occur (since, by hypothesis, there exists no price at which $n + 1$ firms can cover costs of production). Thus if entrants are rational, pure profit does not necessarily invite entry: potential entrants do not naively take existing market data as given, at least in small-group situations.

This much foresight is a necessary condition for small-group FEE to exist (and is sufficient for it to exhibit positive profit). It seems imperative therefore to impose some form of rationality on the entrants' expectations. We adopt what we call *consistent expectations:* the new entrants' expectations are consistent with realisations. (The concept of consistent expectations is distinct from that of consistent conjectural variations.)

Now consider condition (i) of our FEE definition. To give (i) meaning requires an equilibrium concept. The Nash concept seems the acceptable one for the non-address, large-group case. But in the small-group cases, in both the address and non-address branch, where we necessarily have localised competition, the choice of an equilibrium concept is more problematic. The argument against the Nash concept is that rational firms in small-group competition know that their competitors will respond to any initiative that they take. Choice of the most plausible concepts will, of course, have to be made in the end on empirical grounds.

In the meantime *we take some equilibrium concept for (i) as given and assume that an equilibrium actually exists.* Consistent expectations then requires the potential new entrant to calculate the post-entry equilibrium and to base his entry decision on the profits or losses that he would then earn.[17]

Consistency of expectations leads logically to the strategic use of specific capital. This appears to us to be one of the key conceptual innovations in the recent literature on imperfect competition. If the post-entry equilibrium is influenced by the quantity of specific capital held by firms, then existing firms can influence the value of entry. They may find it in their interest to deter entry (as in Eaton–Lipsey, 1979, 1980b; Dixit, 1980; Schmalensee, 1978; Salop, 1979a) or to impose asymmetric post-entry equilibria (as in Prescott–Visscher, 1977; Dixit, 1980; Eaton–Lipsey, 1981).

What has emerged over the past few years in the literature on imperfect competition is what might be called a paradigm of *strategic free-entry equilibrium*. The essentials of this approach are the existence of firm-specific capital and the assumption that all actors know the manner in which prices and quantities are determined, given the commitments of specific capital to the market. This assumption allows all actors, existing firms as well as potential entrants, to assess accurately the consequences associated with the commitment of new specific capital to a product group.

The paradigm seems to have evolved in two bodies of literature. One line of evolution arose from misgivings about the limit-quantity (or limit-price) model of oligopoly. The credibility of the implied threat to maintain output in the face of entry was questioned. Spence (1977), drawing on Schelling's (1956) distinction between threats and commitments, observed that it is the *ability* to produce the limit output after entry has occurred (the holding of 'limit capacity'), and not actually producing that output before entry, which influences the credibility of the threat. Dixit (1979) observed that, even if the threat were credible, the entry-deterrence strategy might not be preferred, thus making endogenous the decision whether or not to deter entry. Dixit (1980) imposed consistent expectations by invoking the assumption of 'known rules of the game', which allowed him to assess the credibility of the limit-output threat: the threat is credible if and only if the solution to the post-entry game has the established firm producing at least the limit output. Eaton–Lipsey (1980a) invoked known rules of the game and employed Schelling's distinction. They thereby determine the optimal strategy by which a natural monopolist would deter *predatory* entry, entry with the objective of driving the monopolist out of the market when committed capital was not infinitely durable.

In the literature on differentiated products and spatial competition, Archibald–Rosenbluth (1975) raise the possibility of market preemption (entry deterrence) through product proliferation. Peles (1974), in a model with parametric prices, raises the possibility of entry deterrence by plant proliferation. Prescott–Visscher (1977) invoke known rules of the game, again with parametric prices, to analyse asymmetric market solutions and clearly raise the possibility of entry deterrence through plant proliferation. Schmalensee (1978) uses the notion of brand proliferation to understand the ready-to-eat cereals industry. Eaton and Lipsey (1979) invoke consistent expectations to analyse entry deterrence in a 'small' spatial market.

Another implication of the use of specific capital to deter entry is that capital may be used wastefully in the sense that more than the socially optimal amount may be committed to the industry. Such possibilities are raised in most of the works cited in the previous two paragraphs. Similar results are obtained in the literature on technological change (see, e.g., the chapter by Dasgupta in this volume, and Gilbert–Newbery (1982)).

(B) EXISTENCE

The discussion so far has avoided the troublesome problem of existence of equilibrium, which is particularly difficult in the address models. Suppose we adopt *price-taking behaviour* as our equilibrium concept. Then, as d'Aspremont–Gabszewicz–Thisse (1979 and 1981) demonstrate,[18] price equilibrium does not exist in Hotelling's model if the two firms are too close together. Indeed, this is a general problem in one-dimensional models of spatial competition where transport costs are linear. The source of non-existence is a discontinuity in the firms' (perceived) demand functions. In Salop's (1979) terminology, there exist 'zap prices'. (Let p_1 and p_2 be the mill prices of the two firms, $a < b$ be their locations on the unit line, and t be unit transport cost; then Firm 1's demand function is discontinuous at $p_1 = p_2 - t(b - a)$.) Archibald–Rosenbluth (1975) observe that 'zap' prices exist in characteristics space, at least in the combining case.[19]

Hotelling, who clearly foresaw this problem, appears to invoke what Eaton–Lipsey call the 'no mill-price undercutting' assumption to remove the problem (see Hotelling, 1929, p. 48). Eaton (1972) explicitly invokes this assumption. Archibald–Rosenbluth dismissed as absurd the idea that firm i would assume it could drive firm j out of the market, when j had the option of cutting its own price and thus continuing to sell goods profitably. Eaton–Lipsey (1976; 1978) argue that the most elementary foresight will allow any firm to conclude that it cannot drive a competitor out of the market by charging a price marginally-lower than the zap price, as long as the competitor has the option of selling a positive quantity at a price in excess of unit *avoidable* costs. They therefore introduce the 'no mill-price undercutting assumption'. This can be thought of as an attempt to rule out obviously inconsistent expectations by 'doctoring' the equilibrium concept.[20] Indeed, Novshek (1980) argues that, in the absence of this restriction, FEE will ordinarily not exist in address models.

We would not argue that this is necessarily the correct solution to the problem. We would, however, argue that where the source of non-existence of price equilibrium arises from assumptions about competitors' responses which are grossly inconsistent with competitors' profit maximising responses, and where elementary foresight reveals this inconsistency, the problem is not in any empirically-relevant sense one of the non-existence of equilibrium. The problem is that we have attributed foolish beliefs to economic agents.

(C). SPECIFICITY, COMMITMENT AND LUMPINESS

In our discussion of free-entry equilibrium, we simply assumed that product-specific capital was also firm-specific. Product-specific capital is firm-specific *if there exists no other use for such capital that will increase the value of the firm*. This view of firm specificity is a direct consequence of Schelling's notion of commitment and the view, implicit in our discussion of FEE, that commitments, but *not threats*, are credible. As we saw in Section (A), the importance of specificity is well understood in recent literature on industrial organisation. We wish to argue that specificity must be considered in conjunction with indivisibility and, in particular, that the extent to which product-specific capital is firm-specific depends on its lumpiness. We shall illustrate this argument by examining Dixit's (1980) formulation of the undifferentiated duopoly problem. We shall show that the effect of assuming divisibility is to make product-specific capital non-firm-specific; and, indeed, the possibility that one firm may sell some (necessarily divisible) capital to the other opens up a set of possible solutions which would not be feasible in the indivisible case. (We could make the same point by adapting the Eaton–Lipsey (1981) model in which capital is subject to radioactive decay; but it is seen more easily in Dixit's model in which capital is infinitely durable.)

In Dixit's model, the 'rules of the (post-entry) game' are Nash rules for quantities, based on *avoidable costs*. It is assumed that there are two types of product-specific capital. The first entails a once-for-all 'set-up cost', f, on entry. *Each unit* of output per unit time also requires *one unit* of 'production capital' (k) Choice of (k) thus sets an upper bound to output. Average variable costs are assumed to be constant. Both entry capital and production-capital are completely product specific and infinitely durable. Production capital is perfectly divisible. We assume, for simplicity, that costs are identical for both firms and that both would earn profits in the symmetric Nash equilibrium. Dixit shows that the incumbent firm (first mover) is able to impose asymmetric solutions by his choice of (k), which determines his own avoidable cost reaction function and therefore the post-entry equilibrium.

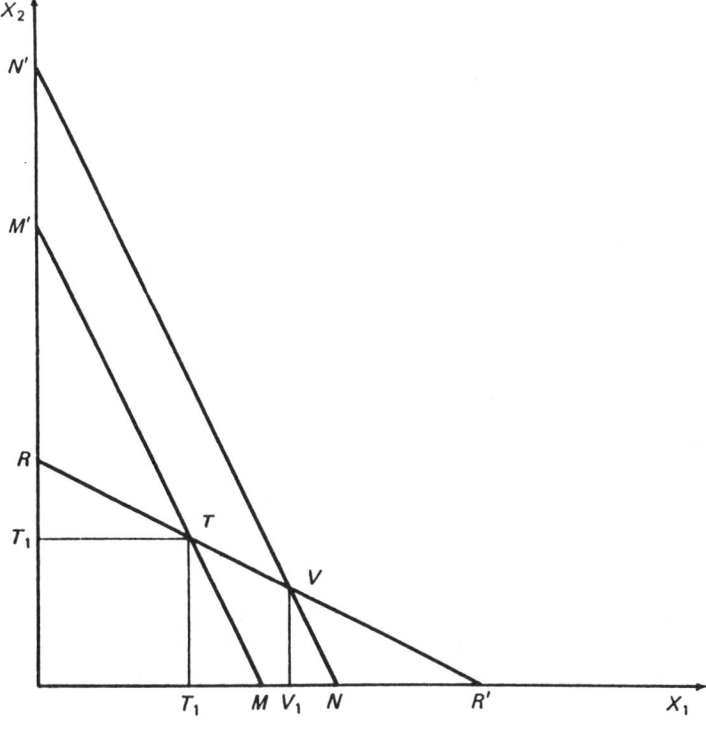

Fig. 1.3

For the incumbent (Firm 1) Dixit defines three reaction functions. The first is the 'full-cost' reaction function, i.e., it takes into account the cost of the capacity k_1 required to produce x_1, as well as the (constant) variable cost. It is illustrated by MM' in Figure 1.3. The second is the avoidable-cost reaction function which takes into account only the constant variable cost. It is illustrated by NN' in Figure 1.3. The third, or 'effective', reaction function, which we will write $g_1(x_2 \mid \bar{k}_1)$, is conditional on 1's choice of capacity, $\bar{k}_1$. For a given $\bar{k}_1$, it is NN' for $x_1 < \bar{k}_1$ (spare capacity) and MM' for $x_1 > \bar{k}_1$ (expansion costs). The potential entrant (Firm 2) has no prior commitments, and accordingly has the full-cost reaction function shown as RR' in Figure 1.3 (where the stable, Cournot case is assumed).

Now Firm 1 chooses k_1 and thus the reaction function $x_1 = g_1(x_2 \mid \bar{k}_1)$ that it will present to Firm 2 in the event of entry. The locus of possible equilibria is illustrated by TV in Figure 1.3. We take the case in which the set-up cost (f) is small enough for entry deterrence to be impossible. Suppose, for the purpose of argument, that Firm 1 chooses $\bar{k}_1$ so as to impose the asymmetric duopoly solution at V. Its capacity is then V_1. If production capital were indivisible once created, or if there was no market in second-hand capital, this would be a completely successful strategy: the choice of capacity determines Firm 1's effective reaction function $N'VV_1$, and thus commits it to the Cournot–Nash duopoly solution, at V.

To show the importance of the assumption that production capital is perfectly divisible (as well as product-specific), suppose that Firm 2 had the option of buying some of Firm 1's production capital. (For simplicity, we assume 1's capital V_1 is less than the total capital $2T_1$ that would be employed at the symmetric Nash-equilibrium point.) If Firm 2 bought $V_1 - T_1$ of Firm 1's capacity (and added $2T_1 - V_1$ itself) it could force the symmetric duopoly solution at T. Firm 1 may, however, be better off at T than at V (and must be if the sale of capacity is to be voluntary). Joint profit is maximised at T, and exceeds joint profit at V. At T, Firm 1 receives his half of the joint profit *plus* any share less than unity of Firm 2's half. This share will be determined by the price paid by Firm 2 for the quantity $V_1 - T_1$ of 1's productive capacity. There is an obvious bilateral bargaining problem between 1 and 2 (or any potential Firm 2), with which we are not here concerned. The point is that, by purchasing some of Firm 1's 'entry-deterring' capital, 2 can, in fact, force the duopoly solution at T on terms advantageous to both. Thus 1's original strategy is not successful, but may be more profitable to 1 than non-strategic behaviour, i.e., the failure to use incumbent advantage and instead, meek acceptance of the symmetric solution, by building T_1 capital in the first place.

Our purpose in exploring this variation in Dixit's model is to show that product-specific capital is not necessarily a vehicle for commitment in a model of undifferentiated oligopoly, if it is *divisible*. If production-capital could be made indivisible after its construction, then 1's choice of capacity, V_1, would be irreversible, and would block entry.

In the address branch, entrants usually choose to differentiate their products from those of existing firms. Product-specific capital is then firm-specific capital – although group-specific capital is not. Thus, in an address model, product-specific capital is a vehicle for commitment regardless of its divisibility, while group-specific capital needs to be lumpy if it is to act as an entry deterrent.[21]

VI SOME RESULTS

The analysis of strategic behaviour is essentially the analysis of rent-seeking behaviour. In our view the most significant difference between the address and non-address branches is that, in the address branch, there is a presumption that rents will exist in free-entry equilibrium even if firms behave non-strategically: while there is no such presumption in the non-address branch. We must then expect firms to behave strategically, as they attempt to capture such rents. (Firms may, of course, dissipate some or all of these potential rents in their attempts to capture them.) We first consider non-strategic behaviour and then turn to strategic behaviour.

(A) PROFIT IN NON-STRATEGIC FEE

(1) The Non-Address Branch

Consider first an industry in which firms sell undifferentiated products. The potential for pure profit is then essentially determined by the ratio of minimum efficient scale to market demand. If this ratio is large, we have an undifferentiated oligopoly and there exists some potential for pure profit. As this ratio becomes small, the non-strategic equilibrium rapidly approaches the competitive equilibrium.

Now consider the case of monopolistic competition, in which there is a finite or countably-infinite number of goods. In the absence of further restrictions, each product will attract entrants as long as entry promises some profit. The crucial feature is again the ratio of minimum efficient scale to market demand. If it is arbitrarily assumed that one product can only have one producer (say, in an attempt to catch the 'essence' of monopolistic competition in a non-address branch formulation), then other results are possible. If every good in the group is made a symmetrical substitute for every other good, as in Dixit–Stiglitz (1977), then a Chamberlinian tangency solution is possible. If this symmetry is not assumed, then positive profits can be earned by some firms, since their positions can be assailed only by producing the nearest permissible substitute (as in Spence, (1976). Then, while the marginal entrant earns approximately zero profits, other firms may earn positive profits. But this result seem to us to be an artefact of the arbitrary restriction on the number of producers of each good.

(2) The Address Branch

First, consider geographical location models in which existing firms behave non-strategically with respect to entry. In Eaton–Lipsey (1976 and 1978, Section VI) entrants' profit expectations are consistent, and existing firms can earn a rate of return on specific capital which is up to twice the competitive rate of return. In Eaton (1976), the main model of Eaton–Lipsey (1978), and Novshek (1980), entrants' profit expectations are inconsistent, since they expect existing firms to maintain price. Since existing firms respond to entry by reducing price, their profit expectations are overly optimistic. Despite this, FEE is consistent with pure profit, which may be substantial. In Eaton (1976), the rate of return on specific capital is up to 16/9 times the competitive rate of return.

What is the source of these positive profits in FEE? First, the source is *not* the integer problem. The integer problem arises in a locational model when existing plants (or products) can be costlessly relocated. Then their number can be augmented one at a time, while all relocate to remain in the middle of equally-sized markets. Under such circumstances (in finite-sized markets such as the boundary of a circle) positive profits in FEE depend only on the integer problem. Note, however, that if firms really could relocate costlessly (in money and in time) they would move continuously, producing at each point in space since there would be no reason to transport goods costfully, if firms themselves could be transported costlessly. *Absence of relocation costs in a spatial market implies a continuum of production over that market.*[22]

The source of positive pure profits in FEE is specific, lumpy capital that must take on a specific address, which means fitting this into a slot among existing firms. Thus if, for example, a new entrant expects to be charging the same price as his neighbours, he expects to obtain a market that is discretely smaller than those they enjoyed before his entry. In a one-dimensional market, the ratio of the new entrant's expected market length to the market lengths of existing plants before entry is 1/2, regardless of the number of plants in the market. In a two-dimensional spatial model with some symmetric configuration of plants throughout the market, the ratio is on the order of 1/2 (see Eaton–Lipsey, 1976), and is again independent of the number of plants in the market. In these spatial models, the market structure is one of overlapping oligopolies.

Now consider characteristics models. Lane (1980), develops a model in which FEE is consistent with substantial pure profits. Where the number of characteristics is small, the reason for positive profits in FEE is the same as in geographic models: any new product must fit into a slot in characteristic space between a small number of neighbours, the number of neighbours remaining small even as the number of products increases indefinitely. That a new product must fit into a slot between existing products and therefore expect a significantly smaller market area than that enjoyed by its neighbours before entry, is independent of whether or not products are combined to obtain characteristic mixes not available in any single product.

Shaked–Sutton (1982), drawing on Gabszewicz–Thisse (1980), develop a model in which goods are differentiated by quality. They identify quite plausible cases in which there is an upper bound to the number of firms which can attract a positive market share in equilibrium. Suppose, for purposes of illustration, that a 'large' number of firms have committed specific capital to such a market. Their result says that only a limited number of these firms will make non-zero sales in the non-cooperative price equilibrium. In the terminology of Shaked–Sutton, we have a 'natural oligopoly' and substantial pure profit is clearly possible in FEE.

In spite of these results, a great deal of the literature in the address branch (particularly in geographical-location models) imposes a zero-profit equilibrium condition with, as far as we can see, *no behavioural justification whatsoever*. There seems to be an intuitive feeling that the non-specificity of capital in the long run should lead to a zero-profit result. Some people have envisaged a tatonnement process in which no specific capital is committed to the market until equilibrium is reached.[23] But the real world does not duplicate this 'empty-plain experiment'. For the market as a whole, the closest we get to such a long-run experiment is a *mixed long-run case*. Here, one firm makes a long-run decision (e.g., to replace a depreciated plant or to create a new plant) in a situation in which some specific capital is currently committed to the market.[24]

To see that such mixed long-run decisions do not necessarily lead to a zero-profit equilibrium, consider the following example. Imagine a circular market, one unit in length, with a uniform density of demand of one unit of demand per unit distance (which is independent of delivered price). Let price be parametric at a value of one (resale price maintenance). Firms enter the market by locating an immovable plant, which produces any desired output at a fixed total cost of (K) per unit of time for as long as it exists. Each firm can own

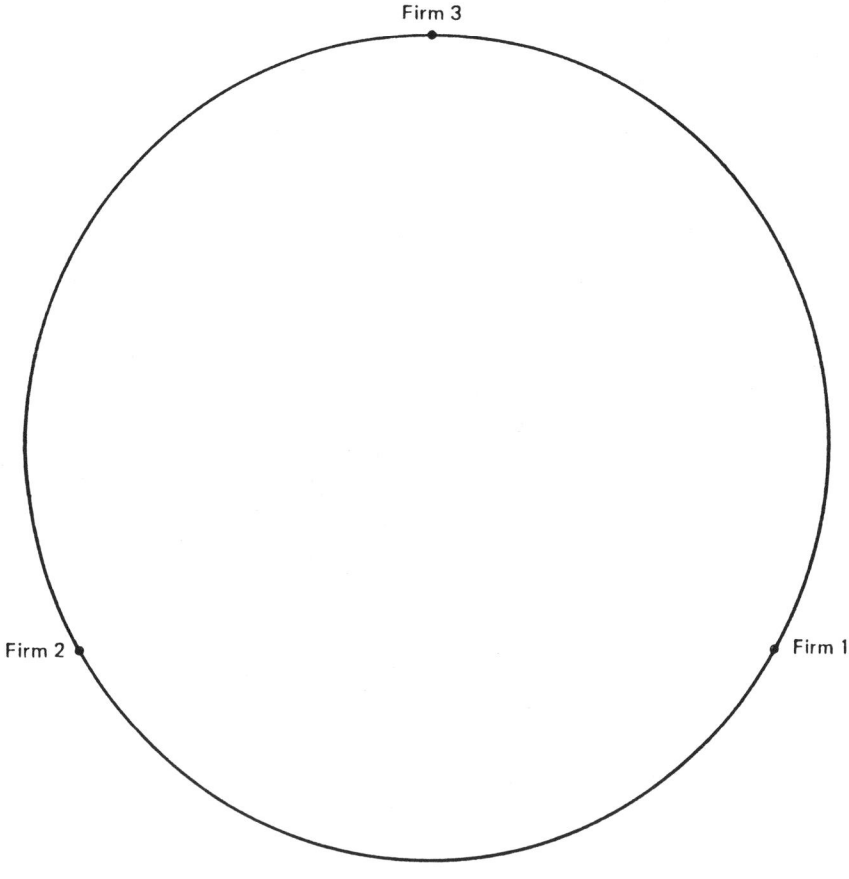

FIG. 1.4

only one plant and all plants are subject to random expiry. If a firm's capital expires, this information is available first to the firm itself so that it can maintain its hold on the market by immediately replacing it. Capital having expired, there is a non-zero but 'small' cost of choosing a different location for the new plant.

Initially, let there be three firms equally spaced around the circular market, as shown in Figure 1.4, and let $1/5 > K > 1/6$ so that the market could sustain four or five equally spaced firms. If existing firms behave *non-strategically*, they will simply replicate their locations when their plant expires. Further, a new entrant must anticipate a market of size $1/6$, but requires a market of K, which is greater than

1/6, to cover costs The three-firm locational configuration is thus a FEE when firms behave non-strategically, and there is no tendency for profits to be driven towards zero. A second point is also obvious from this example. If we take as an initial condition four or five equally-spaced firms, we conclude that these are also free-entry equilibria when firms behave non-strategically: FEE is not unique. Thus history, in the form of the specific capital that is in place, affects the mixed long-run decisions taken by each firm, and thus the convergent FEE. (We consider strategic behaviour in this model in Section (B).)

In the address branch, there is a strong presumption that rents do exist in free-entry equilibrium when firms behave non-strategically. These rents will, however, induce firms to behave strategically with respect to specific capital.

(B) STRATEGIC BEHAVIOUR: DEMAND PRIMITIVES AND MARKET STRUCTURE

In the non-address branch, the fundamental determinant of the extent to which FEE is consistent with pure profit and, therefore, the extent to which firms are able and willing to create asymmetry through strategic behaviour is, roughly speaking, the size of the market relative to MES. Schmalensee (1981) argues that strategic behaviour in non-address models is a trivial issue when the market can support even a few firms. His arguments suggest 'the general unimportance of entry barriers erected by economies of scale' (p. 1228) (see also Gilbert's chapter in this volume).

Although the paradigm of strategic, free-entry equilibrium discussed above has not yet been systematically applied to the address branch, the existing literature suggests that the problem is fundamentally different in this branch.

Prescott–Visscher (1977), Hay (1976) and Rothschild (1976) investigate the problem in models of spatial competition in which price is parametric, and the artificial one-plant, one-firm restriction is imposed. The initial conditions are that the market is unserved, and that firms enter sequentially. Lane (1980) extends the sequential entry paradigm to a characteristics model in which price is endogenous. In these models, the convergent FEE is unique: it is the FEE which yields, for sitting firms, the largest profits that will not attract entry.

Schmalensee (1978) analyses the problem of product selection in a model of spatial competition in which the density of demand is growing over time, price formation is co-operative, and the artificial one-plant, one-firm restriction is removed. Given an initial selection of products (or brands) he concludes that existing firms always have an incentive to pre-empt entry by proliferating brands and also that the unique FEE is that FEE which yields, for sitting firms, the largest profits that will not attract entry. Eaton–Lipsey (1979) arrive at the same conclusions in a somewhat more general model.

Two important questions arise from this literature.

(1) Given an unserved market and sequential entry, is monopoly pre-emption always to be expected? (If initial conditions have more then one firm serving the market, some closely related questions arise. When the growth of demand is foreseen, will strategic behaviour by existing firms prevent the subsequent entry of other firms? Do there exist incentives for the whole market to be monopolised?)
(2) Is the result *that the convergent FEE (in the presence of strategic behaviour) yields the maximum profit that sitting firms can earn without attracting entry* independent of initial conditions?

We address these questions sequentially. (The argument in the next two paragraphs is based on a forthcoming paper by Eaton.)

Suppose we have some market in the address branch which is unserved, and consider the problem facing a first mover. Given the equilibrium concept which determines prices (given a vector of products), the first mover could contemplate establishing a sufficient number of products in the continuum to deter entry. It is not obvious that such a 'sufficient number' even exists. What is, however, obvious is that if the equilibrium concept is non-cooperative (in the broad sense that it does not maximise profit given the number of products), the number of products which the monopolist would have to establish to deter entry is larger than the number of products which would deter entry if they were owned by independent firms (since equilibrium prices will be lower when three firms are in the market than when there are only two). This raises the important point that monopoly pre-emption in this circumstance is not necessarily the most profitable option facing the initial mover.

In spite of the above, we must nevertheless expect substantial concentration in this market when we allow a first mover to enter an unserved market. Suppose, for example, that the equilibrium concept is Nash in prices, subject to the no-mill-price-undercutting assumption. Identify the minimum number of one-product firms (n) which will deter entry in a one-dimensional market. The first mover has the option of establishing $n/2$ products, alternating over the continuum, knowing that the second mover will also establish $n/2$ products to deter entry. We then have 'duopoly pre-emption'. Notice that, given this equilibrium concept, *the first mover can do no worse than to adopt this duopoly–pre-emption solution.* Three observations then follow. First, we must always expect substantial concentration to emerge in this first-mover experiment. Second, any measure of this concentration is not easily interpreted. Suppose the first mover chooses the duopoly solution. Then, from an economic point of view, this solution is indistinguishable from the solution which would emerge if we conducted the corresponding sequential-entry experiment with the one-product, one-firm restriction. Yet, in one case, measured concentration is insignificant (assuming n to be large) and in the other the two-firm concentration ratio is 1. The point is obvious (and well known): we must be very careful to define 'markets' in an economically meaningful sense. What is, however, not so obvious is just how difficult this may be in the address branch. Third, the possibility that the first entrant might prefer to create the conditions for a multi-plant duopoly rather than a multi-plant monopoly may be the answer to the worry expressed by many theorists: why do not we see monopoly everywhere that addresses matter? (See, e.g., Prescott–Visscher (1977, pp. 391–2) and Eaton–Lipsey (1979, p. 157).)

The above discussion is clearly related to Markham's (1966) observation that the standard, monopolistically-competitive case seems to comprise a few firms, each producing a wide range of differentiated products. This phenomenon is, we think, more easily understood in the address branch.

We turn now to the second question. Impose the one-product, one-firm restriction. Independent of initial conditions, is the convergent FEE, when firms behave strategically, always the equilibrium which yields the maximal profit which sitting firms can earn without attracting entry? We do not provide a general answer to this question. We simply present a simple example, in which the answer is 'yes'.

Consider the model introduced in the previous section and illustrated in Figure 1.4. We make one alteration: $1/4 < K < 1/3$. Now the market: (i) will not support four firms; (ii) will support three or two firms with positive profit in FEE; and (iii) will not be in FEE with only one firm (since a new entrant could then expect a market of $1/2$).

Now, starting with three firms, suppose Firm 1's capital expires first, and consider the available strategic options. If Firm 1 chooses to relocate at $1/3$, it must expect to serve $1/3$ of the market. If it chooses to locate at 1/2, it will again expect to serve 1/3 of the market until another firm's capital expires. Suppose Firm 1 makes the latter choice. If Firm 2's capital expires second, then Firm 2 will exit, leaving Firm 1 and Firm 3 to serve the market. In this case, Firm 1's 'squeeze play' is obviously successful. If Firm 3's capital expires second, Firm 3 cannot move left, since that would invite entry. Nor will he attempt to squeeze 1, since there is a small added-cost of replacing 1's plant at a different location. Thus Firm 3 sits tight. Eventually Firm 2's capital will expire. Firm 2 then exits, and we again end up with just two firms serving the market.

The above is, if nothing else, a counter-example to the commonly-expressed idea about positive profits in equilibrium of address models. This idea is that it is a result of capital fixity and that, in the long run, when all capital is variable, profits must tend to zero. What is wrong with this idea is, of course, that in the long run all capital does not become *simultaneously* variable.

There remains the question of asymptotic properties: do small groups become large groups as the market grows, and, particularly, is the equilibrium configuration competitive in the limit? In the non-address branch, the answer given has usually been 'yes' (see Hart, 1979). It is easy to see intuitively that a growing demand for a finite number of goods must create a market for each of them in which MES can be made as small as we like, relative to demand. In such a market there is, as we have seen, little room for strategic behaviour. It is our conjecture that, in the address branch, the asymptotic results are, in general, *not* competitive. In this branch, the interesting replication experiment is not cloning the representative consumer, but increasing the diversity of tastes: introducing new utility functions (perhaps 'between' the initial ones in some appropriate, i.e., continuous, function space) or new locations (more consumers between the initial ones in physical space). As we saw in Section III (A)(4), we do not know the sufficient conditions for competition to be localised in address-branch models. Suppose, however, that the necessary conditions are satisfied. It is not then obvious that this replication experiment will reduce the degree of localisation or ensure that pure profit in FEE is zero.

(C) CHOICE OF SPECIFICITY

We observed above that indivisibility of capital goods is not God-given, but is subject to technologically-constrained choice. An analogous observation applies to specificity: it is subject to technologically-constrained choice. In the address branch, which we take to be the 'standard' case, specificity of capital implies the possibility of profits in strategic free-entry equilibrium. This implies that firms have some incentive to create more specificity than cost-minimisation requires.

It is this observation which leads us to be sceptical of the theory of contestable markets (see Baumol (1982) and chapter by Baumol, Panzar and Willig in this volume) as a positive theory of market structure. Although the *sine qua non* of a contestable market is the absence of specificity, firms engaged in strategic behaviour have incentives to create specificity even where cost-minimisation requires none. Our view is that a positive theory of market structure must be driven, on the cost side, by specificity.

This force opposes another well-known force acting on the firm: *ceteris paribus*, in an uncertain world, it is wise to keep one's options open. The discussion of 'flexibility' in Stigler's (1939) classic is addressed to this proposition. Uncertainty provides an incentive for firms to choose less specificity than cost-minimisation requires. There is thus an important unexplored margin: non-specificity has value because it maintains options, while specificity has strategic value precisely because it limits options (it is the vehicle for commitment).

A theory of endogenous market structure must therefore take into consideration the firm's choice of specificity. Are the incentives to create specificity for strategic purposes swamped by the inherent uncertainty of our world? This would seem to be a very important research topic.

(D) THE ANALOGY BETWEEN SPATIAL AND CHARACTERISTICS MODELS

In Sections III (A)(3) and (4), we noted some obvious similarities and dissimilarities between spatial and characteristics models. We make only a further brief remark (since the forthcoming Archibald–Eaton paper is addressed to the subject). From what has been said, it is clear that a pair of models *can* be specified in such a fashion that they are very close (perhaps isomorphic), but they need not be. The models may differ in several ways, among which are: (i) the dimensions of the space, (ii) the existence of boundaries; (iii) the uniqueness of a consumer's address. Further, in the characteristics case, the consumer's choice-set may be continuous or discrete and, if discrete, may not be 'd-convex'. Similarly, the possibility of 'cross-over' arises in the spatial model, if consumers perceive 'distance' differently or the transport-cost function is concave. Thus we cannot agree with Schmalensee (1983) when he writes

> As the analyses of Baumol (1967), Lancaster (1975) and Salop (1979) have shown, the formal correspondence between Lancastrian models with two characteristics and one-dimensional spatial models is almost exact. In particular the same localization of competition is preseved.

It is, of course, *possible* to put sufficient restrictions on a characteristics model to reduce it effectively to the simplest spatial model, as Lancaster attempted[25] in the reference quoted by Schmalensee; but it is false to assume that any characteristics model necessarily 'twins' with all, or indeed any, spatial model, or vice versa. Further, only sufficient conditions for the localisation of competition in these models are presently known.

VII WELFARE

Many investigators have made welfare comparisons of alternative states within address models, by summing consumers' surpluses or using other similar techniques. We are sceptical of all existing attempts, for at least the following reasons.

(1) Even the partial-equilibrium analysis of single markets seems to pose difficult second-best problems. The positive model is one of overlapping oligopolies in which marginal cost does not equal price.

(2) The theory of contestable markets provides one benchmark against which the performance of real markets may be compared. It may be of interest to know how much worse is the performance of some real market than that of a perfect but unattainable market. For policy purposes, however, it seems to us that it is more interesting to compare the performance of some existing market with the best-attainable alternative market structure. This requires that we first have a theory of attainable market structures.

(3) It is at least possible that markets for factors and intermediate goods are fragmented for the same reasons that tend to confine competition to a few neighbours in the address-branch models for final goods considered here. In that case, it cannot be assumed that transactions prices reflect opportunity costs, so that the status of any

partial-equilibrium welfare economics becomes dubious. The implications for general equilibrium theory of an address view of the world have yet to be studied.

(4) Once it is agreed that, thanks to scale effects, only a small subset of the set of possible goods will be produced, the question of which ones should be produced becomes urgent. Lancaster (1975; 1979) has seen correctly that the implication of scale effects, given diversity of tastes, is that efficiency and distributional considerations are inextricably mixed here.[26] The old 'overhead-cost problem', which was thought to be peculiar to the public utilities (the natural monopolies) becomes ubiquitous in the address branch and, we therefore think, in the real world. The problem of the optimal product range is yet to be solved.

(5) Another urgent question follows. If we knew how to characterise the optimal product range, what institutions (market structure) would deliver it? It seems at least a plausible conjecture that the sort of market structure which we expect in the address branch (Kaldorean chains of overlapping oligopolies; positive profit in FEE; pre-emptive proliferation of stores, plants, and products) delivers nothing of the kind. The whole policy problem here awaits exploration.

VIII SOME OUTSTANDING PROBLEMS AND RESEARCH NEEDS

(1) A systematic application of the paradigm of strategic FEE to address models is, we think, an important research task. We suspect that it will produce a theoretical understanding of what seems to us to be the empirically relevant case for monopolistic competition: a multitude of differentiated products produced by a few oligopolistic competitors.

(2) Most of the address-branch modelling has worked with spaces of low dimensionality. This is perhaps not too restrictive in geographic space, but in characteristics space there is no *a priori* restriction on the dimensionality of the space, and we need some empirical work.[27]

Archibald–Rosenbluth have argued that, in the combining case, if there are more than three characteristics, the average number of neighbours which a product may have approaches $n/2$, where n is the total number of products in the group. For us, this raises two key issues. First, does the large number of neighbours of a new entrant mean that the loss of market by each neighbour is small enough, and diffuse enough, so that something analogous to Chamberlin's symmetry assumption will apply? Second, will the new entrant's market be of approximately the same size as (say only $1/n$ smaller than) the pre-entry markets of its neighbours, or will it be discretely smaller (say one-half the size)? Note that the new entrant can have a very diffuse effect on its (large number of) neighbours' markets, while itself picking up only a total market on the order of one-half the size of the pre-entry markets of its neighbours. We suspect that the discreteness of entry will in fact produce this result even when the number of neighbours is large, *thus preserving the possibility of substantial positive profits in FEE.*

(3) Virtually all of the characteristics models of which we are aware make assumptions designed to localise competition completely. Yet we know of nothing to suggest that 'cross over' is unimportant, empirically.

(4) In many ways, the most interesting and potentially rewarding research task is to develop a theory of endogenous market structure. We have explained above why we think that the theory of contestable markets will not do the job. To us market structure is a battle between attacking potential entrants and defending sitting firms. Entry and entry prevention seems to us to be driven by the nature of firm-, product-, and group-specific capital. Thus another potentially-fruitful research programme seems to be the development of a theory of endogenous market structure based to a large extent on the nature (which is itself partly endogenous and partly exogenous) of lumpy, specific, sunk capital (see Eaton–Lipsey, 1981, Section III for some discussion).

As one possibility for a theory of endogenous market structure, we conjecture that the results of several studies we have reviewed will turn out to be illustrative of a generalization: the FEE consistent with rational, strategic behaviour and foresighted entry decisions will be the one that produces the largest profits which sitting firms can earn without attracting entry.

NOTES

1. The first and third authors are indebted to the Canada Council for the opportunity provided by Killam Fellowships in various years. All three authors are indebted to the Social Sciences and Humanities Research Council of Canada for research support. We are also indebted to Simon

Anderson, Mukesh Eswaran, David McGechie and Gernot Kofler for comments and suggestions.
2. The full quotation is 'Is the bunghole of a barrel part of the barrel? Think well before you answer; because the whole structure of theoretical physics is trembling in the balance'.
3. Since, in some cases to be considered, firms may be in competition with firms that are not their immediate neighbours in the physical sense, we need a potentially wider definition of 'economic neighbours'. We say that two goods are neighbours, at given prices, if it is possible that a consumer with convex indifference curves (in characteristics space) could be indifferent between them and that there exists no intermediate good (mixing their characteristics) which he prefers.
4. The Market Opportunity Frontier in characteristics space is determined, for any consumer, by the set of produced goods, their prices, and his budget. In the combining case, an interior good would be dominated by a convex combination of neighbouring goods and be unsaleable. This does not necessarily follow in the non-combining case. The 'MOF' is a discrete point set. We construct the free-disposal convex hull of this set. If every attainable point lies within the boundary of the convex hull, we say that the set is 'd-convex'. An interior good is not, however, dominated by an (unattainable) convex combination of neighbouring goods (it may be the 'best buy' for some individuals) so that the set is not necessarily d-convex.
5. Lancaster (1979) does this by placing restrictions – symmetry and mutuality – directly on his derived compensating functions. He does not investigate the implied restrictions on his primitives and it seems to us that these are unacceptable – e.g., if the consumer whose most-preferred good is 1/2 has indifference curves that are asymptotic to both characteristic axes, other consumers must have indifference curves that slope upwards over part of their range.
6. 'Product class' is not, in fact, defined; and it is not clear that a useful definition could be formulated in this approach when each consumer perceives a different characteristics space. Also note that, in this approach, 'tastes' cannot be represented as continuous and that the problem of modelling changes in the vector of available goods, so easily dealt with in Lancaster's approach, remains awkward.
7. The preference vector θ is a vector of reservation prices. This, as it stands, means that the demand 'primitives' are not independent of the budget set, which must be known to the consumer before he can compute reservation *prices*.
8. The argument applies only to goods and does not carry over to services that must be consumed at their rate of production. If the consumer's desired rate of consumption of a service is less than the minimum-cost production rate, he is not indifferent between producing it for himself and buying it from a firm that is operating at its minimum efficient scale. Since writing our paper, we have discovered that a similar argument is most lucidly made by Weitzman (1983). Whereas we restrict our argument to goods, he seems to imply it is also applicable to services.

9. There are some interesting issues with respect to product- and group-specific capital that we do not go into here. The identical capital may be able to produce some variations of breakfast cereals or of chocolates, but be unable to produce equally well over the whole range of group characteristics. Experience thus suggests a rich range of product-, subgroup- and group-specific capital. What we need for the argument of the text, however, is that there be some product specificity to the capital; otherwise there would be a continuum of goods produced over the characteristics space that defines the group.
10. Eaton–Lipsey (1981) suggest that the index $1 - R$, where R is the ratio of the value of a capital good, in its best alternative use, to its reproduction cost, is a useful index of specificity. 'Value in best alternative use, presumes, however, at least known properties of equilibrium and perhaps even the equilibrium concept itself, whence the index is not a technological primitive. Moreover, our attempts to define an index of specificity convince us that, except in the extreme case used in the text, any appealing index uses market data and therefore implicitly involves some properties of equilibrium. We cannot now offer a satisfactory technological measure of specificity. None the less, we shall argue that specific inputs can be used strategically and that they are therefore determinants of the properties of equilibrium, so that it seems unwise to use value in alternative use to devise an index of specificity. Moreover, as we argue below, some interesting puzzles involving the equilibrium concept, and the possible use of specific capital as a vehicle for commitment, arise even when capital is completely product-specific.
11. Imposing an upper bound on the rate of which capital services can be extracted from the capital good does not change the *fundamental* result: specific capital implies increasing returns to outlay over some initial range of output.
12. The first order condition for an interior solution to this cost minimisation problem is

$$\frac{W}{C'(v)} = \frac{f_1(n, v)}{f_2(n, v)}$$

Since $C'(v)$ is not constant, it is clear that n/v depends on x. Indeed n/v increases as x increases. A corner solution with $v = 0$ is clearly possible for low levels of output, since the unit cost of (v) goes to infinity as (v) goes to zero.
13. If there is an upper bound on the rate at which capital services can be extracted from the capital good, then we clearly have increasing returns to outlay up to the level of output at which the optimal rate of extraction is equal to this upper bound.
14. The demonstration that the existence of man-made capital goods requires some non-convexity can be thought of as an illustration of the 'round-aboutness' of production in time: we embody capital services today for use in the future. There is, however, another interpretation of 'round-aboutness' which centres on the question: why does production involve specialised inputs (some of which may be capital services)? This

interpretation focuses on the number of arguments in the production function. These are quite separate issues.
15. This analysis implicitly assumes that the firm itself purchases the indivisible capital good. The indivisibility of the good will, in many circumstances, require this. It is, however, conceivable that the capital good could simultaneously yield services to many firms, i.e. although product-specific it is not firm-specific. We can then imagine many final-goods-producing firms purchasing specific capital services from firms which own capital goods. In this, case individual firms in the X industry will be price takers for capital services and they will have constant returns to outlay in X production.
16. There are two approaches to equilibrium in this circumstance. First, assume that potential entrants take existing market data as given. Given n firms, one firm will enter, creating losses for all. As specific capital of firms expires, one firm will leave, creating positive profits for the remainder and the incentive for yet another to enter. We have approximate equilibrium (n firms, $n + 1$ firms, n firms,...), and price is approximately the competitive price. Moreover, although entrants' expectations about profits are incorrect, they are approximately correct. Second, assume that each potential entrant, *knowing how each firm chooses quantity*, calculates the post-entry equilibrium and enters only if its profits in the post-entry equilibrium are positive. Then the FEE is unique (n firms) and is also approximately the competitive equilibrium.
17. This view of the entrant's problem dates at least as far back as Hotelling (1929). The mobile firm in Hotelling (which could just as well be considered to be a new entrant as a relocating existing firm) uses the rules of the game, which are Nash in prices, to calculate its equilibrium profits in each possible location. The choice of location is that which yields the highest post-relocation equilibrium profits.
18. Although they were the first to demonstrate this rigorously, many earlier writers, including Hotelling himself, have noted the possibility. See, e.g., Hotelling (1929), p. 48; Eaton (1972), p. 269, and Prescott–Visscher (1977), p. 380–1.
19. As d'Aspremont–Gabszewicz–Thisse demonstrate, the non-existence problem does not arise when transport costs are quadratic, nor does it arise in a two-dimensional market when the metric is Euclidean. However, the problem remains with the 'block metric' in two space (Eaton–Lipsey, 1980a).
20. Notice that this also rules out Bertrand's price-taking assumption. It was argued to us in the conference that our no mill-price undercutting assumption was inconsistent with the common observation that *ceteris paribus* the more distant is a firm's nearest competitor the higher is its price. We do not see, however, that the irrational behaviour implied by mill-price undercutting is necessary for this result.
21. Although we have not needed the concept of group-specific capital here, it is clearly needed for a more general treatment. Group-specific capital is committed to the group (cars or popsicles) but not to the firm (GM or General Foods).

22. This argument applies to goods, but not necessarily to services. See note 8 above.
23. For example, Mills–Lav write (1964, p. 283, footnote 6)

> It should be emphasised that we consider only static industry equilibriums in this paper. We do not consider adjustment processes, and we make no attempt to ascertain whether any adjustment process will converge to industry equilibrium . . . One way to envisage the adjustment is to assume a *tatonnement* process in which no plants are actually built until equilibrium is reached.

We doubt that such a tatonnement process would converge on a long-run equilibrium. In any case, the experiment is inappropriate: the relevant experiment relates to the mixed long-run case.

24. When commitment to the market matters and firms make strategic decisions, the behaviour of firms will ensure that all long-run decisions are 'mixed', since firms will choose to replace their capital before it is economically worthless (Eaton–Lipsey, 1980).
25. But cf. Note 5 above.
26. Space prevents us from exploring here the properties of Lancaster's compensation function, or of the distance functions that may be defined by characteristics space. It is in fact possible to define a precise and 'reasonable' measure of the distance between two goods in a group, i.e. to metrise the MOF. This is discussed in a forthcoming paper by Archibald–Eaton.
27. Successful empirical applications have, however, made do with very few characteristics. See, e.g., Quandt–Baumol (1966), Lancaster (1971) and Morey (1981).

REFERENCES

Archibald, G. C. and Rosenbluth, G. (1975) 'The "New" Theory of Consumer Demand and Monopolistic Competition', *Quarterly Journal of Economics*, vol. 80, pp. 569–90.

d'Aspremont, C., Gabszewicz, J. J. and Thisse, J. F. (1979) 'On "Hotelling's Stability in Competition"', *Econometrica*, vol. 47, pp. 1145–50.

Baumol, W. J. (1967), 'Calculation of Optimal Product and Retailer Characteristics: The Abstract Product Approach', *Journal of Political Economy*, vol. 75, pp. 674–85.

Baumol, W. J. (1982) 'Contestable Markets: An Uprising in the Theory of Industry Structure', *American Economic Review*, vol. 72, pp. 1–15.

Chamberlin, E. (1933) *The Theory of Monopolistic Competition*, (Cambridge, Mass.: Harvard University Press).

Dorfman, R. and Steiner, P. O. (1954) 'Optimal Advertising and Optimal Quality', *American Economic Review*, vol. 44, pp. 826–36.

Dixit, A. (1979) 'A Model of Duopoly Suggesting a Theory of Entry Barriers', *Bell Journal of Economics*, vol. 10, pp. 20–32.

Dixit, A. (1980) 'The Role of Investment in Entry-Deterrence', *The Economic Journal*, vol. 90, 95–106.

Dixit, A. K. and Stiglitz, J. E. (1977) 'Monopolistic Competition and Optimum Product Diversity', *American Economic Review*, vol. 67, pp. 297–308.

Eaton, B. C. (1972) 'Spatial Competition Revisited', *Canadian Journal of Economics*, vol. 5, pp. 268–78.

Eaton, B. C. (1976) 'Free Entry in One Dimensional Models: Pure Profits and Multiple Equilibria', *Journal of Regional Science*, vol. 16, pp. 21–33.

Eaton, B. C. and Lipsey, R. G. (1975) 'The Principle of Minimum Differentiation Reconsidered: Some New Developments in the Theory of Spatial Competition', *Review of Economic Studies*, vol. 42, pp. 27–49.

Eaton, B.C. and Lipsey, R. G. (1976) 'The Non-Uniqueness of Equilibrium in the Loschian Location Model', *American Economic Review*, vol. 66, pp. 77–93.

Eaton, B. C. and Lipsey, R. G. (1977) 'The Introduction of Space into the Neo-Classical Model of Value Theory', in *Studies in Modern Economic Analysis*, M. J. Artis and A. R. Nobay, (eds) (Oxford: Basil Blackwell), pp. 59–96.

Eaton, B. C. and Lipsey, R. G. (1978) 'Freedom of Entry and the Existence of Pure Profit', *Economic Journal*, vol. 88, pp. 455–69.

Eaton, B. C. and Lipsey, R. G. (1979) 'The Theory of Market Preemption: the Persistence of Excess Capacity and Monopoly in Growing spatial Markets', *Economica*, vol. 46, pp. 149–58.

Eaton, B. C. and Lipsey, R. G. (1980a) 'Block Metric and the Law of Markets', *Journal of Urban Economics*, vol. 7, pp. 337–47.

Eaton, B. C. and Lipsey, R. G. (1980b) 'Exit Barriers are Entry Barriers: the Durability of Capital as a Barrier to Entry', *The Bell Journal of Economics*, vol. 11, pp. 721–9.

Eaton, B. C. and Lipsey, R. G. (1981) 'Capital, Commitment and Entry Equilibrium', *Bell Journal of Economics*, vol. 12, pp. 593–604.

Eddington, Sir A. (1958) *The Philosophy of Physical Science* (Ann Arbor: University of Michigan Press).

Gabszewicz, J. J. and Thisse, J. F. (1980) 'Entry (and Exit) in a Differentiated Industry', *Journal of Economic Theory*, vol. 22, pp. 327–38.

Gilbert, R. J. and Newbery, D. M. G. (1982) 'Preemptive Patenting and the Persistence of Monopoly', *American Economic Review*, forthcoming.

Gorman, W. M. (1980) 'A Possible Procedure for Analyzing Quality Differentials in the Egg Market', *Review of Economic Studies*, vol. 47, pp. 843–56.

Hart, O. (1979) 'Monopolistic Competition in a Large Economy with Differentiated Commodities', *Review of Economic Studies*, vol. 46, pp. 1–30.

Hay, D. A. (1976) 'Sequential Entry and Entry-Deterring Strategies in Spatial Competition', *Oxford Economic Papers*, vol. 28, pp. 240–57.

Hotelling, H. (1929) 'Stability in Competition', *Economic Journal*, vol. 39, pp. 41–57.

Kaldor, N. (1934) 'Mrs. Robinson's "Economics of Imperfect Competition"' *Economica*, vol. 1, pp. 335–41.

Kaldor, N. (1935) 'Market Imperfections and Excess Capacity', *Economica*, vol. 2, pp. 33–50.

Lancaster, K. J. (1966) 'A New Approach to Consumer Theory', *Journal of Political Economy*, vol. 74, pp. 132–57.

Lancaster, K. J. (1971) *Consumer Demand: A New Approach* (New York; Columbia University Press).

Lancaster, K. J. (1975) 'Socially Optimal Product Differentiation', *American Economic Review*, vol. 65, pp. 567–85.

Lancaster, K. J. (1979) *Variety, Equity, and Efficiency* (New York; Columbia University Press).

Lane, W. (1980) 'Product Differentiation in a Market with Endogenous Sequential Entry', *Bell Journal of Economics*, vol. 11, pp. 237–60.

Losch, A. (1954) *The Economics of Location* (New Haven: Yale University Press).

Markham, J. W. (1964) 'The Theory of Monopolistic Competition After Thirty Years', *American Economic Review*, vol. 54, pp. 53–5.

Mills, E. S. and Lav, M. R. (1964) 'A Model of Market Areas with Free Entry', *Journal of Political Economy*, vol. 72, pp. 278–88.

Morey, Edward R. (1981) 'The Demand for Site-Specific Recreational Activities: A Characteristics Approach', *Journal of Environmental Economics and Management*, vol. 8, pp. 345–71.

Novshek, W. (1980) 'Equilibrium in Simple Spatial (or Differentiated Product) Models', *Journal of Economic Theory*, vol. 22, pp. 313–26.

Peles, Y. (1974) 'A Note on Equilibrium in Monopolistic Competition', *Journal of Political Economy*, vol. 82, pp. 626–30.

Perloff, J. M. and Salop, S. C. (1982) 'Equilibrium with Product Differentiation', Gianini Foundation for Agricultural Economics, Working Paper, no. 179.

Prescott, E. C. and Visscher, M. (1977) 'Sequential Location Among Firms with Foresight', *Bell Journal of Economics*, vol. 8, pp. 378–93.

Quandt, R. E. and Baumol, W. J. (1966) 'The Demand for Abstract Transport Modes: Theory and Measurement', *Journal of Regional Science*, vol. 6, pp. 13–26.

Rothschild, R. (1976) 'A Note on the Effect of Sequential Entry on Choice of Location', *Journal of Industrial Economics*, vol. 24, pp. 313–20.

Salop, S. (1979) 'Monopolistic Competition with Outside Goods', *Bell Journal of Economics*, vol. 10, pp. 141–56.

Salop, S. (1979a) 'Strategic Entry Deterrence', *American Economic Review*, vol. 69, pp. 335–8.

Schelling, T. C. (1956) 'An Essay on Bargaining', *American Economic Review*, vol. 46, pp. 281–306.

Schmalensee, R. (1978) 'Entry Deterrence in the Ready-to-Eat Breakfast Cereal Industry', *Bell Journal of Economics*, vol. 9, pp. 305–27.

Schmalensee, R. (1981) 'Economies of Scale and Barriers to Entry', *Journal of Political Economy*, vol. 89, pp. 1228–38.

Schmalensee, R. (1982) 'The New Industrial Organization and the Economic Analysis of Modern Markets', in W. Hildenbrand (ed.), *Advances in Economic Theory* (Cambridge: Cambridge University Press).

Shaked, A. and Sutton, J. (1982) 'Natural Oligopolies', unpublished manuscript, London School of Economics.

Spence, A. M. (1976) 'Product Selection, Fixed Costs, and Monopolistic Competition', *Review of Economic Studies*, vol. 43, pp. 217–35.

Spence, A. M. (1977) 'Entry, Capacity, Investment and Oligopolistic Pricing', *Bell Journal of Economics*, vol. 8, pp. 534–44.

Stigler, George J. (1939) 'Production and Distribution in the Short Run', *Journal of Political Economy*, 47, pp. 305–27.

Weitzman, Martin L. (1983) 'Constestable Markets: An uprising in the Theory of Industry Structure: Comment', *American Economic Review*, 73, pp. 486–7.

[14]

1. Introduction

In a loose sense, any set of commodities closely related in consumption and/or in production may be regarded as differentiated products. Close relation in consumption depends on consumers' tastes. Do consumers perceive two products to be close substitutes for each other? Close relation in production concerns economies of scope. Is there any cost economy in having two products produced by one firm rather than two? The same set of products may be closely related in both production and consumption, as with yellow and orange tennis balls, in the former but not the latter, as with size 12 and size 8 shoes, or in the latter but not the former, as with coffee and tea.

We follow most of the existing literature in dealing with industries producing a large number of products that are closely related in consumption, while ignoring the interesting issues that arise from the presence of scope economies. We also ignore issues arising out of consumption complimentarities, e.g. should IBM produce software as well as hardware?

1.1. The awkward facts

Elementary scientific methodology tells us that theories aspiring to empirical relevance must be consistent with the observed facts. For this reason, awkward facts are to be welcomed; indeed, the more awkward they are, the greater are the constraints that they place on our theorizing.

Seven of the most important awkward facts that are available to constrain theorizing about product differentiation are listed below.

(1) Many industries, including most that produce consumers' goods, produce a large number of similar but differentiated products. Observe, for example, the variety of cars and bicycles on the streets of any moderately sized city.

(2) The consumers' goods produced by different firms in the same industry are differentiated from each other so that two products produced by two different firms are rarely, if ever, identical. Consider, for example, the differences between the competing middle-priced cars produced by GM, Ford and Chrysler.

(3) The set of products made by the firms in any one industry is a small subset of the set of possible products. Consider, for example, all of the different cars that could be produced by marginally varying the characteristics of existing cars one way or the other – e.g. a bit more or less acceleration, or braking power, or fuel consumption.

(4) In most industries each firm produces a range of differentiated products; indeed, a typical pattern in consumers' goods industries is for a large number of differentiated products to be produced by quite a small number of firms. For example, most of the many soaps, cleansers and detergents on sale in the United States today are produced by two firms.

(5) Any one consumer purchases only a small subset of the products that are available from any one industry. For example, how many brands of toothpaste has the reader purchased in the recent past?

(6) Consumers perceive the differences among differentiated products to be real and there is often approximate agreement on which ones are, and are not, close substitutes. Consider how many loyal supporters there are for different brands of cigarettes, cars and cameras. Also consider how much agreement there is that different brands of low-tar cigarettes are closer substitutes for each other than for any high-tar cigarette, and that different types of subcompact cars are closer substitutes for each other than for any full-sized car.

(7) Tastes are revealed to vary among consumers because different consumers purchase different bundles of differentiated commodities and these differences cannot be fully accounted for by differences in their incomes. For example, look into different houses inhabited by people of roughly similar incomes and observe that while each has a car, a refrigerator, a TV, a hi-fi, a tape deck, a video recorder, a camera, a stove, and so on, each has a different mix of brands, styles and types of these generic products.

The literature on product differentiation can be seen as a search for answers to three basic questions that arise out of the above awkward facts. What are the processes that give rise to these facts? What are their positive implications? What can be said about their normative implications?

The models used to study these problems are standard in their broad outline, although not in many substantial details. Most employ equilibrium techniques and use comparative statics to derive their predictions. From among the possibilities open to them, firms are assumed to choose the alternatives that will maximize profits.

A complete model of product differentiation would specify (i) the set of possible products, (ii) the technology associated with each product, (iii) the tastes of consumers over the set of possible products, and (iv) an equilibrium concept. At any significant level of generality such a model seems intractable. Hence, most of the literature involves strong simplifying assumptions of one sort or another.

1.2. Technology

There is little debate over the cost aspects of relevant models. Of the assumptions that are typically made, some are needed to accommodate one or another of the awkward facts, while others are employed merely for analytical convenience. Awkward fact (3), that the number of produced products is a small subset of the number of possible products, would seem to have two main lines of possible explanation.

(i) *Demand side explanations.* Given linearly homogeneous production functions, the explanation must come from the demand side. The explanation would be that consumers wish to consume only the subset of products currently being produced. This could be understood in terms of a representative consumer, or in terms of consumers with tastes that differ but are concentrated on the subset of produced goods.

(ii) *Supply side explanations.* Now let there be a diversity of tastes such that every differentiated product would be demanded by some consumers if all were priced at minimum average cost. Given linearly homogeneous production functions, all possible products would then be produced. For example, if there were a continuum of consumers' preferences over some set of product characteristics, there would be a continuum of products produced to satisfy these tastes. In these circumstances the limitation on the number of produced products must come from the supply side. The explanation of awkward fact (3) is then provided by production non-convexities, which result from such things as product development costs, and indivisibilities of fixed capital, and which imply decreasing average costs over an initial range of output. This explanation is the one that we accept, along with most of the writers in the field.

These non-convexities are commonly captured by the assumption of a simple cost function with a fixed cost of entry and (for convenience) a constant marginal cost of production that may or may not be subject to a capacity constraint. (Of course the cost function may be product specific.)

1.3. Two approaches to consumers' preferences

A basic requirement on the demand side of the problem is to have a model that accommodates awkward fact (1) – many differentiated products are produced and consumed in the typical consumer good industry.

1.3.1. The address branch

One branch of the literature captures awkward fact (1) by positing a distribution of consumers' tastes over some continuous space of parameters describing the nature of products. Different consumers have different most preferred locations in this space and thus can be thought of as having different *addresses* in that space. Products are also defined by their addresses in the space, and this makes the set of all possible products infinite.

This approach follows Hotelling's (1929) seminal paper and we refer to it as the *address branch*. Tractability demands a relatively simple parameterization of tastes. A major issue here is whether the parameterization of preferences is sufficiently rich to approximate the real diversity of consumers' tastes.

1.3.2. The non-address branch

The other branch follows traditional value theory in assuming that consumers' preferences for differentiated goods are defined over a predetermined set of all possible goods, which set may be finite or countably infinite. For obvious reasons we call this the *goods-are-goods* or the *non-address* branch. Chamberlin's original vision of monopolistic competition lies in this branch of the literature. Once again, tractability requires parameterization of tastes.

Within this branch, there are two possible ways of accounting for the purchase of many differentiated commodities. The first assumes that the aggregated preferences for differentiated goods can be captured by the fiction of a representative consumer. Since the problem of aggregating tastes over diverse consumers is ignored, the approach is more flexible in some important respects than the address approach.

It should be clear, however, that this approach does not directly incorporate awkward facts (5), (6) and (7), which relate to differences among consumers. This raises the question: Can the representative consumer's utility function be derived from a model which does allow for these awkward facts?

The second approach is to assume differences in individual tastes and deduce aggregate behavior from individual motivations. All models that have taken this approach so far have used some variant of Chamberlin's symmetry assumption which, loosely interpreted, means that all products are in equal competition with all other products. (This is discussed in more detail below.)

In the next section we consider the non-address branch and in subsequent sections the address branch.

2. Non-address branch

2.1. The representative consumer approach

The seminal papers are Spence (1976a, 1976b) and Dixit and Stiglitz (1977). In these models there is a large number of possible products in the sector or industry of interest. Product demands arise from the utility maximizing decisions of a representative consumer with a strictly quasi-concave utility function:

$$u = U(y, x_1, \ldots, x_n),$$

where y is quantity of a composite commodity, which is produced under conditions of constant returns to scale, and x_i is quantity of the ith sectoral good. Cost functions, $C_i(x_i)$, are potentially product specific, and ordinarily take the following convenient form:

$$C_i(x_i) = K_i + c_i x_i,$$

where K_i is a fixed cost, associated with product development or indivisible capital, and c_i is a constant marginal cost. Prices are normalized so that the price of the composite commodity is $1, and costs are denominated in dollars or units of the composite commodity.

In the basic models, each product is produced by at most one firm, and, when the number of possible products is sufficiently large, not all products will be produced. Given any set of produced products, the equilibrium is (ordinarily) a Cournot equilibrium – firms choose quantities to maximize profit. [Koenker and Perry (1981) use conjectural variations to generalize this aspect of the basic model.] In free-entry equilibrium all products which are produced earn non-negative profit, and entry of any additional product is not profitable. That is, there exists no non-produced product which could cover its costs in the Cournot equilibrium which would result if the product were produced.

This sort of model is obviously quite flexible and well adapted to welfare analysis. One can create a variety of tractable models by choosing appropriate functional forms for the utility function. Since profit can be measured in units of the composite commodity, welfare analysis is relatively easy. Supposing that profits accrue to the representative consumer, welfare comparisons merely involve comparisons of the representative consumer's utility in alternative situations. If utility is linear in the composite commodity [as in Spence (1976a)] an equivalent welfare criterion is maximization of total surplus.

Two sorts of normative questions have been addressed in these models. The first concerns possible biases in the set of produced products, and is discussed in the following section. The second concerns possible biases in the number of products produced, and is best discussed in the context of Chamberlin's vision of monopolistic competition.

Product selection bias

Given the number of products produced in equilibrium, are some products produced which should not be, and others not produced which should be? We can convey the basic insights regarding possible biases in product selection by adapting the model used in Spence (1976b). Let the utility function take the following form:

$$u = y + a_1 x_1 + a_2 x_2 - 1/2 \left(b_1 x_1^2 + 2d x_1 x_2 + b_2 x_2^2 \right),$$

where the parameters a_i, b_i and d are positive and $d < b_i$, $i = 1, 2$. To focus on product selection bias, we suppose that both products cannot profitably be produced in a Cournot equilibrium, and ask which one will be produced and which one should be produced. Since utility is linear in y we use the total surplus optimality criterion.

In the monopoly equilibrium the gross profit of firm i (total profit plus K_i) is

$$\Pi_i = \theta_i^2 / 4b_i,$$

and the gross surplus generated by product i (total surplus plus K_i) is

$$S_i = 3\theta_i^2 / 8b_i,$$

where $\theta_i = a_i - c_i$. Thus, firm i captures two-thirds of the gross surplus generated by its product. There is a selection bias if the product which produces the larger total surplus is not produced in equilibrium.

To illustrate the possibility of a selection bias, suppose that $K_1 > K_2$ and that $\Pi_2 - K_2 > 0$, or equivalently, that $S_2 > 3K_2/2$ (the second product is profitable). In this case there is inevitably a selection bias if product 1 generates the larger total surplus ($S_1 - K_1 > S_2 - K_2$) but does not generate positive profit ($S_1 < 3K_1/2$), and hence will not be produced. Note also that if $K_i > 3S_i/2$ for $i = 1, 2$, either product is viable by itself, but, by hypothesis, both are not. Hence, multiple equilibria are possible.

To see the forces which tend to generate a selection bias, suppose initially that $S_i = 3K_i/2$, $i = 1, 2$, so that either product would earn zero profit, and that $K_1 > K_2$. Either product is then viable, but the first generates a discretely larger surplus. Then a small increase in K_1 or b_1 or a small decrease in θ_1 (equal to $a_1 - c_1$) renders product 1 unprofitable, even though it still generates the larger surplus. Thus, among other things, large product development costs and price inelastic demand functions tend to produce a selection bias. This point is developed more fully in Spence (1976a, 1976b).

A standard result in welfare economics is that price discrimination may be welfare improving if there are significant product development costs or economies of scale. This is because a non-discriminating monopolist cannot capture all the surplus it creates. In the model developed here it is easy to show that if firms can perfectly discriminate (that is, capture all the surplus they create), there is no selection bias and the first best optimum is achieved. Spence (1976a) develops this result in a more general context.

It is also worth noting that when $d < 0$, making the products complements, it is possible that neither product by itself is profitable, but that, as a package, they are profitable. In this case, one expects *one* firm to produce both products.

2.2. Monopolistic competition and the representative consumer

A major contribution of the non-address branch is the formalization of Chamberlin's model of monopolistic competition. Hart (1985) is especially interesting in this regard. The representative consumer approach can be used to construct a Chamberlinian model of monopolistic competition as follows. Write the utility function as:

$$u = U(y, V(x_1, \ldots, x_n)),$$

and assume that $V(\cdot)$ is a symmetric function. [Dixit and Stiglitz (1977), for example, use a symmetric CES specification.] Similarly, assume that the cost functions are identical, so that $c_i = c$ and $K_i = K$ for all i. This generates a Chamberlin model because the demand functions inherit the symmetry of $V(x_1, \ldots, x_n)$.

The major issue in this case is whether there are too few or too many products in equilibrium. Dixit and Stiglitz (1977) provide an interesting analysis of this problem. In the unconstrained optimum, prices of all produced goods must equal c, an impossibility in the Chamberlin equilibrium. A constrained optimality criterion is therefore appropriate – the constraint being that all firms must cover their costs of production. They discover cases in which the equilibrium is a constrained optimum and cases in which there are too few and too many products in equilibrium, relative to the constrained optimum. Hence, there is no presumption that the number of products is optimal in Chamberlin's model of monopolistic competition.

An important question that arises with the model of the representative consumer is what lies behind the assumed utility function. Of course, one answer is that all individual's preferences are identical. This answer is, however, inconsistent with awkward facts (5), that each consumer buys only a small subset of the available commodities, and (7), that tastes are revealed to differ among individuals. Hence, a number of authors have investigated the micro foundations of the Chamberlin model.

2.3. Chamberlin's model and diversity of tastes

A number of papers derive the symmetric demand functions of Chamberlin's models from diverse consumer tastes. See, especially, Anderson et al. (1988), Ferguson (1983), Hart (1985), Perloff and Salop (1985) and Sattinger (1984). We will develop the Perloff and Salop model as a way of illustrating the type of preferences that are required for symmetry. Although we will not develop the point, these models are interesting for another reason as well: implicit in them is a way to develop models that are hybrids of the address and non-address approaches. See, especially, Deneckere and Rothschild (1986).

There is a large number, N, of consumers and an infinite number of possible products. Any consumer buys at most one product, and if he buys a product he buys exactly one unit of it. Given n produced goods, a consumer's preferences over the n goods are described by $(B\theta_1, \ldots, B\theta_n)$. $B\theta_i$ is the value (in units of a composite commodity) that the consumer attaches to one unit of good i. For all consumers, θ_i is a random drawing from a differentiable density function, $f(\theta)$, with finite support, and B is a parameter that captures preference intensity.[1]

Consider two products with prices p_i and p_j. Product i is preferred to product j if $B\theta_i - p_i > B\theta_j - p_j$ or if $\theta_j < \theta_i + p_j/B - p_i/B$. Since θ_i and θ_j are independent drawings from $f(\theta)$, we can compute the probability that any consumer prefers product i to product j. Given p_i, p_j and (for the moment) θ_i, the probability that i is preferred to j is $F(\theta_i + p_j/B - p_i/B)$, where $F(\cdot)$ is the cumulative density function associated with $f(\cdot)$. But θ_i is also a random variable and hence the probability that any consumer prefers i to j is

$$\int F(\theta_i + p_j/B - p_i/B) f(\theta_i) \, d\theta_i.$$

Given n produced goods, the probability that any consumer prefers i to all other produced products is

$$H_i(p_i, \bar{p}, n) = \prod_{j \neq i} \int F(\theta_i + p_j/B - p_i/B) f(\theta_i) \, d\theta_i,$$

where $\bar{p}$ is the vector of prices, p_j, $j \neq i$. Assuming that there is at least one good for which $B\theta > p$ for each consumer, the (expected) demand function for good i is

$$Q_i(p_i, \bar{p}, n) = NH_i(p_i, \bar{p}, n).$$

These demand functions exhibit some obvious symmetry properties. First, $Q_i(p_i, \bar{p}, n)$ is symmetric in the prices p_j, $j \neq i$. For example, if $n = 3$, then

$$Q_1(p_1, p_2, p_3, 3) = Q_1(p_1, p_3, p_2, 3).$$

Furthermore, if all prices are identical, as they are in equilibrium, quantities demanded from each firm are identical and equal to N/n.

---

[1] It is not necessary for symmetry that different consumers' θ's are drawn from the *same* density function. What is necessary is that any consumer's θ's be *independent* drawings from some density function. The way to construct hybrid models is to fix the number of possible products and let any consumer's $(\theta_1, \ldots, \theta_n)$ be a drawing from some *joint* density function.

Now let us characterize the symmetric equilibrium of this model. For concreteness, it is useful to consider the case in which $f(\theta)$ has uniform density on $[u, v]$. To characterize the equilibrium price given n, $p(n)$, set all prices but the ith price equal to a common value, p. Then the ith firm's profit is a function of p_i, p and n. Setting the partial derivative of its profit function with respect to p_i equal to zero, and all prices equal to $p(n)$, we obtain:

$$p(n) = c + B(v - u)/n.$$

As n increases without bound, $p(n)$ approaches c. As preference intensity, B, goes to zero, all goods become perfect substitutes and $p(n)$ approaches c. This reflects the fact that this model is just the Bertrand model in the limit where $B = 0$.

To characterize the free-entry equilibrium, we use the zero-profit condition. In free-entry equilibrium the equilibrium number of firms, $\bar{n}$, is such that each firm earns zero profit. The zero-profit condition implies that

$$\bar{n} = [BN(v - u)/K]^{1/2}.$$

It is also easy to determine the optimal number of firms in free-entry equilibrium. Given n, the expected maximum value of $B\theta_i$, $M(n)$, is

$$M(n) = B(nv + u)/(n + 1).$$

The expected value of total surplus, when all goods are sold at a common price, is then $N[M(n) - c] - nK$.

The optimal number of products, n^*, maximizes total surplus:

$$n^* = [BN(v - u)/K]^{1/2} - 1.$$

Observe that n^* is $\bar{n} - 1$: in free-entry equilibrium, the number of firms is approximately the optimal number.

Because, by assumption, each firm produces at most one product, the Chamberlinian equilibrium is inconsistent with awkward fact (4). This raises an interesting question: If firms were allowed to produce more than one product in a Chamberlin model, would they choose to do so? That is to say, is the equilibrium of such a model consistent with awkward fact (4), when the one-firm, one-product assumption is relaxed?

Two key characteristics of this model are now apparent. First, the zero-profit condition that we used above is appropriate only because of symmetry. There is an integer problem (see Section 5 below) in that n firms might make small profits while $n + 1$ firms would make losses. But within the limits of this integer problem (which is trivial when n is at all large) zero profit is appropriate because a new entrant takes customers equally from all existing products. We shall see below that because symmetry is not a property of address models, the zero-profit condition for entry equilibrium does not apply to them.

Second, symmetry arises because the θ's for each consumer are independent random drawings from some density function. It follows that if one good i were removed from the choice set of n differentiated goods, all those consumers who were purchasing i would redistribute themselves uniformly over the other $n-1$ goods. This property is an appealing one where differentiation is spurious. If all soaps were identical so that perceived differences were solely a product of brand-image advertising, the removal of one soap might lead to this symmetric redistribution of purchases.

This property would not be found, however, where consumers agree on what differentiated products are, and are not, close substitutes for each other, and, in such cases, it conflicts with awkward fact (6). For example, the removal of one low-tar brand of cigarette would lead mainly to increases in the demands for other low-tar products, and not to symmetric increases in the demands for low-tar, medium-tar and high-tar cigarettes. Since the properties of equilibrium in models which do allow for such agreement among consumers are significantly different for those that do not, the propositions that follow from the Chamberlin model must be suspect in those cases where agreement exists. [For further discussion, see Archibald, Eaton and Lipsey (1986).]

3. The address approach

A key aspect of the address approach is that it allows for diversity of consumers' tastes while making the closeness of substitutability among goods at least partially an objective phenomenon. In all consumers' minds, two low-tar cigarettes will be closer substitutes than a low- and a high-tar cigarette; two subcompact cars will be closer substitutes than a subcompact and a stretch limousine; two adjacent drugstores will be closer substitutes than two drugstores at the opposite ends of town.

3.1. Describing a good

In the address branch, a good is described by (θ, p), where p is its price and θ is its "address", some relevant physical description of the good. The address can either be a scalar or a vector and the descriptor, θ, can have many different interpretations. Here are the most common:
- θ may be the location of a firm in some physical space. On a line, it is one number; on a plane, two.

- θ may be the description of the good in some other "spectrum"; for example, the spectrum of color, or a "quality" spectrum.
- θ may be the time at which a service is delivered as, for example, with airline or TV scheduling.
- In Lancaster's characteristics model, a specific good embodies characteristics, z, in fixed proportions. Thus, in the two-characteristics case, we can describe goods by one number, for example, $\theta = z_1/z_2$, where z_1/z_2 is the fixed proportion of the quantity of characteristic one to the quantity of characteristic two.

3.2. Consumers' preferences

Consider first the usual model of spatial competition where firms and consumers are distributed over some geographic space. Any consumer's preferences can be described by a standard utility function, $U(x, y)$, where x is quantity of the good sold by spatially differentiated firms and y is quantity of a composite commodity. Let $\bar{\theta}$ be the consumer's address in the physical space, θ_i the address of firm i, and $T(\theta_i, \bar{\theta})$ the cost of transporting a unit of x from θ_i to $\bar{\theta}$, and assume that consumers bear transport costs. The consumer will, of course, buy x from the firm with the lowest delivered price, $p_i + T(\theta_i, \bar{\theta})$. Thus, awkward fact (5), that each consumer buys only a small number of the goods available, is a theorem in this address model. (As we will see it is also a theorem in Lancaster's characteristics model.)

To emphasize the common features of all address models, it is useful to represent the consumer's preferences in the model of spatial competition indirectly:

$$W(\theta, p, \bar{\theta}) = \max_{x, y} \left\{ U(x, y) \text{ s.t. } [p + T(\theta, \bar{\theta})] x + y = 1 \right\}.$$

The level surfaces of the indirect utility function $W(\theta, p, \bar{\theta})$ in a one-dimensional physical space when transport costs are a linear function of distance are illustrated in Figure 12.1. They are linear tents centered on the consumers location, $\bar{\theta}$.

In Lancaster's characteristics model any good embodies characteristics in fixed proportions, and quantities of the characteristics are arguments of consumer's utility functions. In the primal space with two characteristics the utility function is $U(g(z_1, z_2), y)$, where $g(z_1, z_2)$ is a utility aggregator, z_1 and z_2 are the quantities of characteristics embodied in group goods, and y is the quantity of a composite commodity. If goods are combinable, so that aggregate quantities of z_1 and z_2 obtained by a consumer are simply the sums of the quantities of characteristics embodied in the bundle of goods he purchases, the utility-maximizing consumer needs to purchase no more goods than there are character-

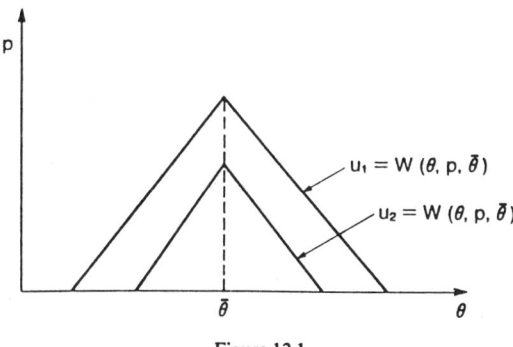

Figure 12.1

istics. Hence, when the number of characteristics embodied in a group of goods is small relative to the number of goods embodying them, awkward fact (5) is again a theorem. See Lancaster (1966).

The recent literature on Lancaster's characteristics model has assumed that each consumer purchases at most one out of a group of differentiated goods, arguing that for technological or other reasons, goods are not combinable. [See Lancaster (1979) and Archibald and Eaton (1987) for a consideration of the very thorny issues concerning combinability.] In this case it is again convenient to derive an indirect representation of the consumer's preferences. A good may be described by the quantities of characteristics, z_1 and z_2, embodied in a unit of that good. The unit in which we measure quantity of the good is, of course, arbitrary. If the good is some brand of cigarettes and the initial unit is a pack of cigarettes, then $(10z_1, 10z_2)$ describes the good when the unit is a carton containing 10 packs. Of course, in any description of the good, z_1/z_2 is fixed.

Thus, we have a degree of freedom that we can use to simplify the way in which goods are described. We illustrate by considering one convenient *units convention*. The good is described by the angle, θ, whose tangent is the (fixed) ratio of z_1 to z_2. The units convention is a quarter circle in the (z_1, z_2) space – the line $z_1^2 + z_2^2 = 1$. The parametric (on θ) representation of this convention is

$$z_1 = \cos \theta, \qquad z_2 = \sin \theta.$$

The indirect utility function is then defined as

$$W(\theta, p) = \max_{x, y} \{ U(g(x \cos \theta, x \sin \theta), y) \text{ s.t. } px + y = 1 \}.$$

Product Differentiation

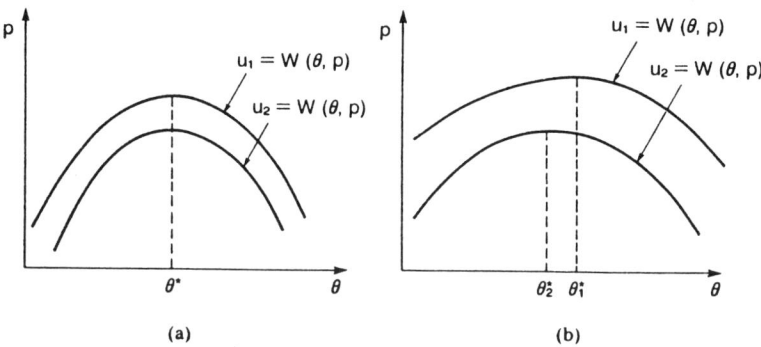

Figure 12.2

The level surfaces of the associated indirect utility function, when z_1 and z_2 are goods, are illustrated in Figure 12.2. When $g(z_1, z_2)$ is homothetic, as it is in Figure 12.2(a), the consumer has a well-defined address, θ^*: for all p, θ^* is the most preferred good. When this is not so, the consumer's address depends on his or her utility level, as illustrated in Figure 12.2(b).

With three characteristics, any units convention involves two θ's. For example, θ_1 might be the ratio z_1/z_2, and θ_2 the ratio z_1/z_3. In general, the choice of a units convention in an n characteristic model requires $n - 1$ θ's.

At a more general level, a consumer's preferences in an address model are described by an indirect utility function, $W(\theta, p)$, where θ is the description of a good in θ space. If θ is interpreted as quality – anything of which more is better – level surfaces will be upward-sloping. In the color-spectrum example shown in Figure 12.3, there are no apparent constraints on the shape of the level surfaces. A consumer could, for example, have strong preferences for the three primary colors and not be attracted to intermediate shades

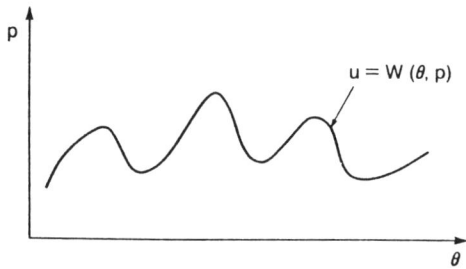

Figure 12.3

3.3. Aspects of an address model

The purpose of address models of product differentiation is to explain observed product diversity by reference to technology and diversity of tastes. Any such model requires the specification of diverse preferences, technology and an equilibrium concept.

Diversity of tastes is ordinarily captured by specifying a continuum of preferences in some appropriate space. In the one-dimensional model of spatial competition diversity is captured by specifying a density of consumers' addresses. Lane (1980) analyzes a two-characteristic model. He uses a Cobb–Douglas specification for $g(z_1, z_2)$, and captures diversity by assuming that the parameter of the Cobb–Douglas function is uniformly distributed on $[0, 1]$.

Technology is ordinarily described by a cost function, $C(\theta, q)$, which specifies the cost of producing q units of a good with description θ. In most models the cost function takes the familiar form:

$$C(\theta, q) = K(\theta) + C(\theta)q.$$

The fixed cost, $K(\theta)$, is often associated with product development or with some other product-specific capital input, and is, therefore, a sunk cost.

Recent address models use subgame perfection in some form as the equilibrium concept. In the simplest case, to characterize free-entry equilibrium potential entrants are treated as players in a game of perfect information. In more complex models, the entire industry structure is generated by an extensive form game of sequential entry. Where sunk costs are an important aspect of the technology, any rational theory of product diversity would seem to require subgame perfection. Sunk costs imply that firms have something to lose if their profit expectations are incorrect. Subgame perfection forces these expectations to be correct.

Two important questions now arise. First (for all consumers) is $W(\theta, p)$ continuous in θ and p? We believe that for the vast majority of cases, the answer is "yes". Second, are the level surfaces of $W(\theta, p)$ single peaked? In many cases the answer is clearly "yes" – e.g. where goods are differentiated by location, by quality, or by the fixed ratio of one Lancastrian characteristic to another. In other cases it is clearly possible that the answer is "no" – e.g. when goods are differentiated by color.

If the answer to both questions is "yes", we are in a world that is quite different from the "goods-are-goods" world of the non-address branch. Given a large set of available products, n, suppose we identify all consumers who buy product A. Now eliminate A from the set of available products. The fact that level surfaces are single peaked implies that the second choices of the consumers who bought A will be distributed over a small subset of the remaining products.

Now suppose that we perturb the price of A slightly. Then quantities demanded of a small subset of products will change. That is, the price of A will be an argument of a small subset of the product demand functions. Hence, the Chamberlin symmetry assumptions are violated. Moreover, aggregate choice behavior cannot be captured by the fiction of a representative consumer with a strictly quasi-concave utility function. For any strictly quasi-concave utility function, there is a non-empty set of prices ($p_1, \ldots, p_n$) such that all n prices enter all n demand functions in a non-trivial way.

If level surfaces of $W(\theta, p)$ have many peaks (and tastes differ among consumers), then it is conceivable that second choices will be (uniformly) distributed over the remaining products and that the price of A is an argument of all demand functions. In this case there is no necessary conflict between the representative consumer and the address approaches to product differentiation.

4. An illustrative address model

We begin by developing an extremely simple model in which addresses are the only endogenous variables. That is, the model focuses exclusively on competition in addresses. It illustrates a number of important and robust propositions that arise in a wide range of address models. Having developed the simple model, we consider the robustness of the results in Section 5.

4.1. Competition in addresses

The space in which goods are differentiated is a segment of the real line of unit length. We refer to the good with address θ_i as good i. In general, the space may be interpreted as a geographic space – a main street, for example – or as some more general charactistics space. Lancaster (1979) and Salop (1979) carefully develop the characteristic interpretation in this type of model.

The cost function, which is independent of the good's address, is

$$C(q) = K + cq,$$

where q is output, c is a constant marginal cost – which, without loss of generality, we take to be zero – and K is a sunk cost associated with an address-specific, and infinitely durable investment, I. Thus, $K = rI$, where r is the rate of interest reflecting the opportunity cost of investing in this industry. The cost I may be thought of either as a product development cost or as the cost of some type of physical capital of which only one indivisible unit is needed. To focus exclusively on competition in addresses, we assume that prices of all goods are exogenous and equal to one. To focus on non-collusive free-entry equilibrium, we assume that each good is produced by a separate firm and that there is an arbitrarily large number of potential entrants.

Let $\bar{\theta}$ be the address of some consumer in the characteristics space. Let good i, with address θ_i, be the good nearest to $\bar{\theta}$. The consumer's utility function is

$$U(x, y, \bar{\theta}, \theta_i) = \begin{cases} y, & \text{if } x < 1, \\ y + R - T(D), & \text{if } x \geq 1, \end{cases}$$

where D is the distance from $\bar{\theta}$ to θ_i (that is, $D = |\bar{\theta} - \theta_i|$), y is the quantity of a composite commodity, and x is the quantity of good i. We assume that $R - T(D)$, the consumer's reservation price for good i, exceeds 1 (the exogenous price of good i) for all θ_i and $\bar{\theta}$ in the unit interval, which implies that the consumer demands one unit of good i. We assume that $T'(D) > 0$, which allows us to interpret $\bar{\theta}$ as this consumer's most preferred good since the consumer's utility is maximal when $\theta_i = \bar{\theta}$. We capture diversity of consumers' tastes by assuming that $\bar{\theta}$ is uniformly distributed on the unit interval with unit density. Notice that consumers differ only with respect to their most preferred good.

In a model of spatial competition $T(D)$ is the cost of transporting one unit of the good a distance D. In a more general characteristics framework, $T(D)$ is a utility cost (measured in units of the composite commodity) associated with the distance from θ_i to $\bar{\theta}$, the consumer's most preferred good. For concreteness and clarity we will use the spatial competition interpretation of the model.

4.2. Free-entry equilibrium

It is a simple matter to characterize the free-entry equilibrium of this model. Let w denote the length of any interval between any two adjacent goods. We call any such interval an *interior interval*. We assume that potential entrants play a game of perfect information. Given our assumption that I is an address-specific, infinitely durable investment, the potential entrant knows that the addresses of the two goods at either end of the interval of length w are fixed, which, given our other assumptions, allows the entrant to calculate its post-entry profit. For any address in this interval, the entrant would attract the custom of half of the customers in the interval. Its gross profit, total profit plus K, would then be $w/2$, and it would *not* enter if and only if

$$w \leq 2K,$$

which is the no-entry condition for any interior interval. (We assume for convenience that zero profit does not induce entry.)

Let v denote the length of the interval between either boundary of the space and the good nearest that boundary, the peripheral good. The entrant's best address in either peripheral segment is adjacent to the peripheral good, where it obtains the purchases of all of the customers in the peripheral segment. So, the no-entry condition for either peripheral segment is

$v \leq K.$

These two conditions completely determine the free-entry equilibrium of this simple model. Interior segments can be no larger than $2K$, and the peripheral segments can be no larger than K. Some important, and we stress *robust*, features of free-entry equilibrium in this model deserve attention.

4.3. Pure profit in free-entry equilibrium

The profit any existing good earns is obviously directly proportional to its market. To maximize the profit of an interior good in free-entry equilibrium, denoted by Π^i, we simply maximize the size of the interior segments on either side of the good. Setting each of these segments equal to $2K$, we see that the good's market is $2K$ since it attracts half of the custom from each of these two segments. Maximal pure profit in free-entry equilibrium is then K, which implies that the maximum rate of return an interior good can earn on its specific investment, I, is $2r$. The maximal pure profit of a peripheral good in free-entry equilibrium is also K.

4.4. Non-uniqueness of free-entry equilibrium

Another obvious consequence of the no-entry conditions is that free-entry equilibrium is not unique. Any configuration of addresses satisfying these conditions is a free-entry equilibrium.

4.5. No invisible hand

Any configuration of addresses is Pareto optimal in this model because any relocation of any firm must make some people worse off. Hence, Pareto optimality is not a useful welfare criterion for the model. To consider optimality, some form of aggregation of gains and losses is essential in address models. In the spatial interpretation of the model, the obvious criterion is the minimization of the total resource cost of serving the market, which is equivalent to maximizing the sum of producers' and consumers' surplus. Since consumers' demands are perfectly price inelastic in this model, the only welfare issue concerns the optimal amount of diversity. That is to say, the failure of price to be equal to marginal cost is not indicative of market failure since demand is not responsive to price.

There are two resource costs in this model: costs associated with goods, K per good, and transport costs. If $T''(D) \geq 0$, it is intuitive and easily proven that the configuration of addresses which minimizes transport costs, given n goods, is $(1/2n, 3/2n, \ldots, 1 - 1/2n)$. In this configuration, the total resource cost, $R(n)$, is

$$R(n) = n\left[K + 2\int_0^{n/2} T(D)\,\mathrm{d}D\right].$$

The second term in the brackets is transport costs borne by a representative good's customers, and K is, of course, the cost associated with the good. Ignoring the obvious integer problem, the optimal number of goods, n^*, is characterized by $R'(n^*) = 0$.

It is now easy to see that there is no invisible hand at work in this model. To characterize free-entry equilibrium we needed to know nothing about $T(D)$, whereas we do need to know $T(D)$ to determine n^*. It follows that there may be too much, too little, or just the right amount of diversity in free-entry equilibrium.

There are two intuitive ways to see this. First, suppose that the optimal configuration, $(1/2n^*, 3/2n^*, \ldots, 1 - 1/2n^*)$, is a free-entry equilibrium. Since free-entry equilibrium is not unique, there are any number of non-optimal free-entry equilibria. But the optimal configuration is not necessarily a free-entry equilibrium. Suppose, for concreteness, that $T(D) = tD$. In this case n^* is an increasing function of t. Then if t is sufficiently small, n^* will be so small that the no-entry conditions will not be satisfied in the optimal configuration. In this case, there is too much diversity in any free-entry equilibrium. Furthermore, if t is sufficiently large, n^* will be so large that each good in the optimal configuration could not cover its costs. In this case, although the optimal configuration is a free-entry equilibrium, it is difficult to imagine an entry process that would give rise to it. That is to say, if we insist that goods cover their costs, there will be too little diversity in free-entry equilibrium when t is large.

4.6. Foresighted entry

Is any one of the many free-entry equilibria which are possible in this model a salient equilibrium – one we would expect to see? Prescott and Visscher (1977) ask this question in this model when entry is sequential. [Hay (1976) examines sequential entry in a model with endogenous prices. See Baumol (1967, n. 4. p. 679) for an extremely insightful early discussion of the issue of entry in an address model.] Each firm is constrained to own at most one good, the market is initially unserved, and the order in which firms confront the entry decision is predetermined. The sequential entry process is modelled as a game of perfect information and hence the equilibrium they derive is subgame perfect.

We know from our earlier discussion that $w = K$ is the size of market which produces zero pure profit for one good. Let $\underline{n}$ be the smallest integer, n, such that $n \geq 1/2\underline{w}$, and consider the following configuration of $\underline{n}$ firms: $[1/2\underline{n}, 3/2\underline{n}, \ldots, 1 - (1/2\underline{n})]$. As you can easily verify, this configuration deters entry, and any configuration with fewer than $\underline{n}$ firms does not. Thus, this configuration is a free-entry equilibrium that maximizes the pure profit that can be extracted from the market. As you can also verify, if $1/2\underline{w}$ is not an integer, there are other configurations of $\underline{n}$ firms that satisfy the no-entry conditions.

To see the nature of the Prescott–Visscher equilibrium, suppose that $1/2\underline{w}$ is an integer. In this case

$$[1/2\underline{n}, 3/2\underline{n}, \ldots, 1 - (1/2\underline{n})]$$

is the only configuration of $\underline{n}$ firms which deters further entry, and in this configuration each firm earns pure profit K, the maximum possible profit in free-entry equilibrium. This configuration is the unique perfect equilibrium configuration of the sequential entry game, although any firm in the sequence can be located at any of the $\underline{n}$ locations in the configuration. To see that it is a perfect equilibrium, consider the sequence in which firm 1 locates at $1/2\underline{n}$, firm 2 at $3/2\underline{n}$, firm three at $5/2\underline{n}$, and so on. It is clear that the $\underline{n}$th firm would choose to locate at $1 - (1/2\underline{n})$ if the first $\underline{n} - 1$ chose to locate at $(1/2\underline{n}, \ldots, 1 - 3/2\underline{n})$ since by choosing $1 - (1/2\underline{n})$, it gets the maximum possible profit in free-entry equilibrium, K, and since any other location would induce entry of an additional firm which would leave firm $\underline{n}$ with a profit less than K. Knowing this, firm $\underline{n} - 1$ will choose to locate at $1 - 3/2\underline{n}$ if firms 1 through $\underline{n} - 2$ locate at $(1/2\underline{n}, \ldots, 1 - 5/2\underline{n})$, because only this location offers $\underline{n} - 1$ the maximum possible profit in free-entry equilibrium. Replicating this argument for firms $\underline{n} - 2, \ldots,$ and 1, we see that this sequence is subgame perfect because it offers each firm the maximum possible profit in free-entry equilibrium.

Notice that awkward fact (2), that firms rarely produce identical products, is a theorem in this model with foresighted entry. Each firm in the sequence (except the first) has the option of producing a product identical to its predecessor's, but it chooses to maximally differentiate its product from its predecessor's, subject to entry being unprofitable in the interval between the two products.

When $1/2\underline{w}$ is not an integer, the problem is more complex. Prescott and Visscher argue that the following sequence is subgame perfect: firm 1 enters at $\underline{w}$,

2 at $1 - \underline{w}$, 3 at $3\underline{w}$, 4 at $1 - 3\underline{w}$,..., and firm $\underline{n}$ anywhere in the segment between firms $\underline{n} - 1$ and $\underline{n} - 2$ that does not leave a market larger than $2\underline{w}$ on either side of it. In this sequence, the first $n - 3$ firms earn pure profit equal to K and the last 3 firms pure profit greater than zero and less than K.

Suppose now that we drop the restriction that each firm owns at most one address. Then the perfect equilibrium exhibits *monopoly preemption*: the first firm preempts the entire market by locating $\underline{n}$ plants in such a way that no interior segment exceeds $2\underline{w}$ and neither peripheral segment exceeds $\underline{w}$. Observe that from a resource cost, or total surplus, perspective the two solutions are essentially the same (they are necessarily identical when $1/2\underline{w}$ is an integer), despite the fact that the first industry structure is unconcentrated and the second exhibits maximal concentration.[2] The only significant difference between the two is distributional – all of the profit is captured by one firm in the monopoly preemption case. Thus, in this model, awkward fact (4), that a few firms produce many products, is a theorem where entry of firms is sequential. (As we will see in Section 7, when prices and/or quantities are endogenous, *monopoly* preemption is not an implication of sequential entry.)

4.7. History matters

The non-uniqueness of equilibrium implies that the present characteristics of markets may not depend solely on their current demand and cost conditions. Their past histories can matter in important ways. This can easily be illustrated using the Prescott–Visscher model when $1/2\underline{w}$ is an integer.

Consider two markets, A and B. Market A displays all of the features described in the previous section, so that in sequential equilibrium there are $\underline{n}$ firms in the market and each firm is earning a pure profit of K. Market B, however, has a past history that differs from A in one key respect. When the sequence of entry occurred in B, the density of customers was two instead of one. The result was $2\underline{n}$ plants, each earning pure profits of K. After entry, however, there was an unanticipated fall in consumer density to one. The two markets are now identical in terms of demand and cost conditions. Market B will, however, continue to have twice the number of firms as market A and the firms in B will earn zero pure profits while those in A will earn pure profits of K.

If we looked only at the present conditions in these markets, we would be unable to explain their differences. Only a knowledge of their past histories provides the correct explanation – as must generally be the case whenever equilibrium is not unique.

---

[2] They are not identical when $1/2\underline{w}$ is not an integer. The monopolist need not locate the first and last plants at $1/2\underline{w}$ and $1 - 1/2\underline{w}$, but when each firm chooses one location, the first and last plants will be so located.

5. Pure profit reconsidered

The possibility of pure profit in free-entry equilibrium is clearly a crucial aspect of this and other address models. It is crucial to the non-uniqueness of equilibrium and to the strategic behavior in the context of foresighted entry. Because it is so important and so often misunderstood, we consider the genesis of pure profit at length.

5.1. The importance of sunk costs

In spatial models a continuum of firms would allow all production to occur at the point of consumption so reducing transport costs to zero. In characteristics models a continuum of products would allow everyone to consume their own most preferred good.

The geographic concentration of production in firms located at discrete addresses is an obvious characteristic of the real world. To explain this along with awkward fact (3), that the number of products produced is much less than the number of possible products, some source of increasing returns to scale, or its cost equivalent, is necessary. In our simple model the cost I is the source of decreasing average total costs.

The address-specificity of I is at the heart of the pure-profit result since it is the sunk nature of this cost at any address which forces the entrant to regard addresses as fixed. It is, of course, entirely possible that this cost is not completely address specific. To the extent that it is not, the magnitude of pure profit possible in free-entry equilibrium is altered.

We can briefly consider this possibility by using a simplified version of the analysis in Eaton and Lipsey (1978) supposing that a portion s of I is address specific and therefore that $(1 - s)$ is not. Consider a symmetric configuration of many addresses in which the interior segments are of length w and peripheral segments are of length $w/2$, and each firm occupies only one address. Now ask under what circumstances one existing firm would change its address in response to entry. Suppose that the entrant locates just next to an existing firm and so takes one-half of that firm's market. Any rational relocation decision is obviously quite complex since the existing firm must itself ask whether or not it must take the addresses of other firms, including the entrant's, as given and, if not, it must solve their relocation problems. To avoid solving this problem and to maximize the existing firm's perceived incentive to relocate, suppose that the existing firm believes (or more properly that the entrant believes that the existing firm believes) that by relocating it will touch off a series of instantaneous relocations that would leave it and the entrant with a market identical to its pre-entry market – a market of length w. Given this belief, the existing firm will relocate if and only if

$w - sK > w/2$, since its anticipated market, if it relocates, is w and only $w/2$ if it does not. This inequality implies that the existing firm will not relocate if $w \leq 2sK$.

If the entrant foresees this result (notice that it could not be more optimistic about the possibility of relocation), it will not enter if $w \leq 2sK$ since its post-entry market would be $w/2$, which is not large enough to cover its costs. That is, $w/2 - K < 0$ when $w < 2sK$. This result in turn implies that the maximum pure profit in free-entry equilibrium is sK. Thus, if s is greater than 0, the magnitude, but not the existence of profit, is an issue.

5.2. The durability of sunk capital, predatory entry and profit dissipation

To focus on the influence of durability, we return to the case in which sunk capital is completely address specific. Infinitely durable, address-specific, sunk capital commits any plant to remain at its present address forever – it creates in essence a property right to the flow of pure profits available in free-entry equilibrium. As a result, the only sort of entry which is possible is *augmenting entry* – entry that increases the number of addresses.

When sunk capital is not infinitely durable, a second type of entry becomes a possibility. This is *predatory entry* – entry that causes an existing address to be abandoned when its associated capital expires. In these circumstances, a property right to some, but not all, of the pure profit that would be available if augmenting entry were the only possibility can be created by premature replacement of sunk capital in the market. As we show, this behavior tends to dissipate profit.

To see what is involved, we use a simplified version of the analysis in Eaton and Lipsey (1980). We suppose that sunk capital, which again costs I, has a durability of H periods. When unconcerned about predatory entry, a sitting firm replaces its plant every H periods. But a new entrant could establish its plant at the same location just as the sitting firm was about to replace its own capital. The market would then "belong" to the new entrant. But foreseeing that strategy, the sitting firm could renew its capital at some earlier date. We want to find the optimal premature replacement strategy.

To set the stage for a consideration of predatory entry, and its preemption by the early renewal of address-specific capital, we first derive a constraint on the size of intervals between plants which is implied by the possibility of augmenting entry. The constraint is analogous to the no-entry conditions derived in Subsection 4.2. Consider entry into an interior segment of length w. (For simplicity we ignore peripheral segments.) The present value of augmenting entry, discounted over an infinite time horizon and evaluated at the instant of entry, is

$$w/2r - I/[1 - E(rH)],$$

where $E(x) \equiv e^{-x}$. The first term is the present value of the entrant's revenues and the second the present value of its costs. The condition for augmenting entry to be unprofitable is

$$w \le 2rI/[1 - E(rH)] \equiv M.$$

For simplicity we suppose that $w = M$ so that firms are separated by the maximum distance consistent with no augmenting entry. We once again assume that each existing firm owns only one address. We wish to find a premature replacement strategy that deters predatory entry. The strategy we consider is for each firm to replace its address-specific capital δ periods prematurely. Thus, each firm incurs the cost I every $H - \delta$ periods and hence never has a commitment to the market less than δ periods.

At the instant in time when capital is replaced, the present value of any existing firm, if the strategy deters predatory entry, is

$$V(\delta) = M/r - I/[1 - E(r(H - \delta))],$$

which is obviously decreasing in δ. Thus, the problem is to find the minimum value of δ, which we denote by δ^*, that deters predatory entry. Think of δ^* as the optimal entry deterring strategy.

The point in time at which predatory entry is most attractive is the instant before an existing firm replaces its capital. At this point, the present value of a predatory entrant which adopts the address of an existing firm, and itself uses the optimal entry deterring strategy, δ^*, is

$$U(\delta, \delta^*) = -I + [M/2][1 - E(r\delta)] + M[E(r\delta) - E(r(H - \delta^*))]$$
$$+ V(\delta^*)E(r(H - \delta^*)).$$

The second term reflects the power of premature replacement as an entry deterrent – the successful predatory entrant must contend with the existing firm for δ periods, and its sales over this interval of time are only $M/2$ per period.

The existing firm's strategy, δ, will deter entry if $U(\delta, \delta^*) \le 0$. Since $V(\delta)$ is decreasing in δ, δ^* is the value of δ such that $U(\delta, \delta^*) = 0$. That is, δ^* is defined by $U(\delta^*, \delta^*) = 0$. As the reader can verify, $\delta^* = H/2$.

If augmenting entry were the only issue, δ would be zero, and any existing firm's present value at time of replacement would be $V(0) = I/(1 - E(rH))$, which is identical to the present value of the firm's address-specific capital cost. But predatory entry is an issue, and the maximum present value of the firm is only $V(\delta^*) = I/[1 - E(rH/2)]$. As H gets large, $V(\delta^*)$ approaches $V(0)$ and as H gets small, $V(\delta^*)$ goes to zero. In the latter limit all of the potential profit is dissipated by premature replacement.

Profit dissipation also arises in the context of *foreseen* market growth. [See Eaton and Lipsey (1979).] In a growing market, entry itself is premature since only by prematurely entering can a firm create the necessary property right to appropriate the profit available in free-entry equilibrium. Indeed, with many potential entrants and parametric prices, all of the profit is dissipated by premature entry – that is, entry occurs when the present value of entry is zero.

These dissipation results are, of course, in no way inconsistent with the existence of flows of pure profit in static free-entry equilibrium. Indeed, it is this possibility that drives the premature entry and/or capital replacement which itself is partially or totally profit dissipating. And, of course, these results are not (necessarily) welfare improving. For example, the premature replacement of capital to deter predatory entry is associated with a pure deadweight welfare loss.

5.3. Endogenous prices

To articulate in the simplest possible way what we think are the essential issues peculiar to address models, we have assumed that prices are exogenous. In this subsection we discuss some thorny problems that arise when prices are endogenous, and we ask if the basic properties of free-entry equilibrium found in our simple model are robust with respect to endogenous prices. We continue to assume that any firm occupies at most one address. We add the assumption that the configuration of addresses is symmetric on a circular market (which avoids boundary problems) as in Salop (1979). Let $p(n)$ be the symmetric Nash equilibrium price in this circular model with n firms.

If we suppose that entrants are price takers – that entrants believe that the post-entry prices of existing firms will be $p(n)$ – then pure profit is impossible in free-entry equilibrium. For example, an entrant that adopted some existing firm's address and charged a price just lower than $p(n)$ would anticipate positive profit as long as the existing firm was earning positive profit. Hence, zero profit is not a property of free-entry equilibrium if entrants assume that they are price takers.

But in a model where existing firms have sunk costs which commit them to the market, foresighted entrants will not take price as given. The existing firm, which would be wiped out by the price-cutting entrant, will not maintain price. Rather, it will respond by reducing price, and the entrant can foresee that it will. For this reason, Eaton and Lipsey (1978) and Novshek (1980) impose a no-mill-price-undercutting restriction. They do not allow any entrant (or any existing firm) to believe that it can adopt a price which would reduce an existing firm's sales to zero without any reaction. The resulting free-entry equilibrium – where the prices of existing firms are Nash equilibrium prices subject to this restriction, and where entrants take established firms' prices as given but do not consider undercutting – exhibits pure profits.

The no-mill-price-undercutting restriction can be seen as an attempt to rule out an entrant's profit expectations which are wildly inconsistent with its post-entry profit realization. Consider again the price-cutting entrant which expects to appropriate virtually all of an existing firm's profits by replicating its address and undercutting its price. If, given addresses, the price equilibrium is a Nash price equilibrium, then the post-entry prices of the entrant and its intended victim will be equal to marginal cost, and the entrant's profit expectations will not be fulfilled. The entrant is a victim of its own myopic profit expectation. If the entrant must incur address-specific sunk costs, then it will not take the prices of existing firms as given. Instead, it will attempt to anticipate the post-entry price equilibrium. This, of course, suggests that the appropriate equilibrium concept for the subgame in which a potential entrant makes its entry decision is subgame perfection.

Eaton and Wooders (1985) use this approach to characterize the symmetric free-entry equilibria of a model similar to our basic model, in which the price equilibrium in both the pre- and post-entry games is a Nash equilibrium in pure price strategies, and in which each firm owns one address. Their free-entry equilibria exhibit the two fundamental features of our basic model: the maximum rate of return on sunk capital is $3.33r$, and there may be too much, too little, or the optimal degree of product diversity in equilibrium. (Relative to our basic model, the maximum profit in equilibrium is larger because existing firms respond to entry by reducing price, a result which entrants foresee.) This establishes that parametric prices are not a necessary condition for the basic characteristics of the model discussed in Section 3.

There is, in addition, a potential problem of non-existence of price equilibrium associated with price undercutting. The problem is articulated by d'Aspremont, Gabszewicz and Thisse (1979). If, for example, transportation costs in our basic model are linear in distance, then the Nash price equilibrium (for given addresses) does not always exist. If, on the other hand, transportation costs are quadratic in distance (as in the model proposed by d'Aspremont, Gabszewicz and Thisse and employed by Eaton and Wooders), then the price equilibrium does exist.

5.4. The integer problem, balkanization and localized competition

The pure-profit result in address models is sometimes *wrongly* attributed to what we call the integer problem. The integer problem, which we brushed aside in our discussion of the Chamberlin model, occurs in non-address models when n firms can make a profit and $n + 1$ firms cannot, and its source is increasing returns to scale or its cost equivalent. As a result, n firms can earn profit in a non-address model that is in equilibrium with respect to foresightful entry. The same problem arises in an address model in which we *arbitrarily assume* that the number of firms is maximized, subject to the constraint that no firm incurs losses.

In either case – and assuming for convenience that sunk costs per period are K, marginal cost is constant, and price parametric – the maximum pure profit consistent with entry equilibrium is K/n. So, for example, one firm can earn up to twice the normal rate of return on its sunk capital ($2r$), two up to $1.5r$, and 10 up to $1.1r$. The integer problem can thus account for substantial long-run profits in industries where demand is sufficient to sustain only a few firms – natural monopolies and natural oligopolies – but as more and more firms can be supported by the market, the excess profit attributable to the integer problem rapidly diminishes.

But in address models, the location of existing goods or products balkanizes the market into a number of overlapping submarkets. As a result, competition is localized – each good has only a few neighboring goods with which it competes directly, regardless of the number of goods serving the entire market. This localized competition imparts a natural oligopoly characteristic to address models – indeed, this is what Kaldor (1935) intended by the phrase "overlapping oligopolies". It also allows the maximum profit consistent with free-entry equilibrium to remain constant as the number of firms in the market is increased. For example, let the density of customers grow in the model considered above. The minimum number of goods consistent with free-entry equilibrium will now grow, and the distance between goods will diminish but each good will continue to have only two neighbors and the maximum profit consistent with free-entry equilibrium will remain at $2r$. [See Eaton and Wooders (1985) for an illustration of this result when price is endogenous.]

The driving feature of these results is that the expected size of the market for a new entrant, R^e, is significantly smaller than the market enjoyed before entry by the firms which will be the entrant's neighbors, R^a (given identical prices). In our simple model R^e/R^a is one-half, and, hence, existing firms can earn up to twice the normal return on capital without attracting entry.

5.5. How robust is balkanization?

What happens to balkanization and its implication of localized competition when our restrictive assumptions are relaxed? We discuss models of spatial competition first.

A key assumption concerns transportation costs. If these are identical for all consumers and convex in distance, then competition is clearly local in nature. Thus, in one-dimensional models, each firm is in direct competition with at most two others.

Suppose, however, that transport costs are a concave function of distance and identical for all consumers. It is now possible that a low-price firm may be in competition with several high-priced ones, diminishing the extent to which competition is localized.

Another way in which this result can occur is if "transportation costs" are subjective and differ among consumers. Again, a low-price firm could be in direct competition with a number of high-price firms selling identical products from different addresses. In both of the above cases a firm's market area is no longer a connected subset of the entire market, and competition is not localized to the same extent. Analogous possibilities arise in characteristics models – a phenomenon referred to as "cross-over" by Lancaster (1979).

Notice that in both of the above cases there is still some balkanization of the market in that the entry of either one low-priced or one high-priced firm at a specific address will not take sales in one set of *equal* increments from all existing low-priced firms and another set of equal increments from all existing high-priced firms.

Another issue relevant to balkanization concerns the dimensionality of the space itself. Models of spatial competition in a two-dimensional space exhibit the key properties of equilibrium in our simple one-dimensional model. In particular, competition is localized and plants can earn substantial pure profit in entry equilibrium. For example, in a two-dimensional model analogous to the one-dimensional model developed here, Eaton and Lipsey (1976) show that the pure profit of all plants in free-entry equilibrium can be as large as $0.96K$.

In the characteristics model, the number of characteristics embodied in goods, and hence the dimensionality of the space, may be an important determinant of the extent to which competition is localized. Archibald and Rosenbluth (1975) consider the number of neighbors a firm can have in the case where goods are combinable. With two characteristics, each good can be in direct competition with at most two neighboring goods and in the case of three characteristics, the average number of neighbors cannot exceed 6. However, with four characteristics, the average number of neighbors can be as large as $n/2$, where n is the number of goods. Apart from the Archibald–Rosenbluth results for the combining case, we know virtually nothing about how the number of characteristics affects the number of neighbors.

Archibald and Rosenbluth focus on the average number of neighbors a firm can have. This does not seem to us to be the important question. Instead, what matters is whether or not R^e is bounded away from R^a. We suspect this is a characteristic that will be robust to increasing the number of dimensions.

Schmalansee (1983) observes quite rightly that the extent to which competition is localized cannot be resolved by the theorists' paper and pencil. It is at root an empirical question. He develops some empirical tests for localization. The payoff to careful empirical work in this area is, we think, immense.

6. Vertical differentiation and natural oligopoly

In a model of vertical differentiation goods are differentiated in a one-dimensional space but, in contrast to the illustrative model discussed above, the characteristic θ that describes a vertically differentiated good is something of which more is better from every consumer's perspective. In contrast, the earlier model in which consumer's had different preferred θ's can be called one of horizontal differentiation.

There are at least two ways in which vertical differentiation can arise. First, the technology might be such that the product only contained one variable characteristic. Say it is quality, which we assume can vary over the range $0 < \theta < 1$. Second, consumers might live at points θ on a one-dimensional housing estate occupying the range $1 < \theta < 2$, while retail stores were constrained by zoning laws to locate at points $\theta < 1$. The first case is driven solely by technology and the second by institutional arrangements. [Notice in the second case, which is due to Gabszewicz and Thisse (1986), the estate must be one-dimensional and the stores must be constrained to locate on only one side of it.]

Vertical differentiation is an address model but the fact that everyone agrees on the most preferred address for the good or store gives it some special characteristics. One issue that has attracted attention in recent years concerns the circumstances under which the model produces a *natural oligopoly*. In this section we outline the results obtained in a simple model which is designed to illustrate some of the arguments developed by Gabszewicz and Thisse (1979, 1980, 1986) and Shaked and Sutton (1982, 1983).

In this model θ is interpreted as a measure of quality and we assume that the feasible quality range is $0 \leq \theta \leq 1$. Each consumer buys one unit of his or her most preferred good, given the prices and θ's of the available goods. The indirect indifference curves for each consumer have the following form:

$$\bar{u} = m\theta - p,$$

where θ and p are quality and price, and m is the willingness of consumers to trade off quality against price. We capture diversity by assuming that m is uniformly distributed on $[a, b]$ with density D, where $b > a > 0$.

Now consider a consumer's choice between two goods, (θ_1, p_1) and (θ_2, p_2), with $\theta_1 > \theta_2$. If $p_2 > p_1$, all consumers prefer good one, so suppose that $p_2 < p_1$. The "market boundary" in θ space, $\bar{m}$, satisfies:

$$\bar{m}\theta_1 - p_1 = \bar{m}\theta_2 - p_2$$

or

$$\overline{m} = (p_1 - p_2)/(\theta_1 - \theta_2).$$

For $m > \overline{m}$, (θ_1, p_1) is preferred to (θ_2, p_2), and for $m < \overline{m}$, the opposite is true. From this, we see that the demand functions are:

$$D_1(\theta, p) = D(b - \overline{m}),$$

$$D_2(\theta, p) = D(\overline{m} - a).$$

We assume that the only cost of production is K, a sunk cost which is independent of θ. Hence, the marginal cost of producing a higher quality good is zero. The property that is necessary and sufficient for the natural oligopoly result is that the marginal cost of producing higher quality be less than a.

Firms choose price non-cooperatively. If one firm enters it will choose $\theta = 1$, since it will be profitable to produce all the quality possible when people are more than willing to pay its marginal cost. Now let a second firm enter. If it also chooses $\theta = 1$, competition will drive price to zero so that sunk costs will not be covered.

This parallels the natural monopoly result in the undifferentiated Bertrand model. With foresighted entry and constant marginal costs, a second firm will never enter no matter how large the market. But unlike the spaceless model with a homogeneous good, the second firm has the option of building a worse mouse trap (or purposely polluting its mineral spring!). This allows it to differentiate itself from the first firm and so avoid ruinous price competition. It will pay a second firm to enter with a poorer product, if consumers' tastes are diverse enough. Specifically, for $\theta_2 < 1$ the second firm commands a positive market share in the non-cooperative price equilibrium if and only if $b > 2a$. Hence, if $b > 2a$, and K is not too large, there will be at least two firms in this market. Will there be three? It again depends on diversity of consumers' tastes. If they are not too diverse (if $b < 4a$), and if there are three firms, then the one with the smallest θ does not command a positive market share in the non-cooperative price equilibrium. Hence, if $4a > b > 2a$, and if K is not too large, we will have natural duopoly. Notice that the market share conditions for natural duopoly do not depend on the density of consumers, D. With more diversity of tastes we can have more firms, but there is always a maximum number of firms that can coexist in a non-cooperative price equilibrium, and the maximum is independent of D.

Let us now consider sequential entry in the natural duopoly case. What may not be immediately obvious is that, if the second firm does not fear entry from a third firm, it will go all the way to shoddy quality and choose $\theta_2 = 0$. If, however, firm 2 foresees the possibility of entry by a third firm, it will choose a θ_2^* sufficiently close to 1 so that a third firm does not anticipate positive profits at any θ_3.

Now let the density of customers, D, or the size of the fixed costs, K, vary. As D goes to infinity or K goes to zero, θ_2^* goes to 1, while prices go to zero. These results reflect asymptotic optimality. The common sense of the result is that, as the size of the sales to be obtained from a third firm locating between $\theta_1 = 1$ and θ_2 rises, or as the sunk cost K declines, firm 2 must choose its θ closer and closer to θ_1 in order to keep a third firm out. In the limit the two firms select $\theta = 1$ and price is equal to zero. But since fixed cost per unit of output approaches zero in either limit, the two firms will remain profitable.

These results reflect the more general result in this type of model. As long as every consumer would choose maximal quality if asked to pay the marginal cost of producing it, the number of firms is bounded above, and is independent of customer density.

Given the assumptions about tastes for and costs of added quality, the results are driven by the destructiveness of price competition. As in the spaceless model, a second firm would never enter if it had to produce an identical product but, if consumers' tastes are sufficiently diverse, entry with a worse mouse trap is profitable.

In the spaceless model, the natural monopoly result does not hold when competition is in quantities instead of prices. The number of firms in a subgame perfect sequential entry exercise then varies positively with the size of the market. An analogous result occurs in the model of quality competition outlined here. Because individual demand is price inelastic – total quantity demanded is $(b - a)D$ regardless of the prices and θ's of firms – there are many non-cooperative quantity equilibria in the model. To make the quantity setting equilibrium more interesting, assume that each consumer's demand function for the consumer's most preferred good is $1 - p$.

Some tedious manipulation then shows that in the sequential entry game with two firms, the first firm chooses $\theta_1 = 1$ and the second chooses $\theta_2 = 1$. That is to say, although firm 2 could choose to differentiate its product, it will not choose to do so when competition is in quantities instead of prices. Just as the natural monopoly feature of the Bertrand model vanishes when we suppose that competition is in quantities instead of prices, so does the natural oligopoly feature of this model vanish when we switch to quantity competition. No firm will ever choose θ less than one when competition is in quantities, and hence the model is, in essence, now an undifferentiated Cournot model. [Bonanno (1986) derives the same result in a slightly different model.]

We conclude that the natural oligopoly result in an address model with vertical differentiation is driven by the assumption that price is the strategic variable, as well as certain necessary taste and cost assumptions. It is also worth noting that cases in which commodities can be differentiated by only a single characteristic are few in number.

7. Price versus quantity competition

Most address models in which prices are endogenous are based on the presumption that competition is in prices. One reason for this modelling choice is analytical convenience – when one aggregates demand in an address model the natural way to proceed is to derive demand functions. The resulting functions are frequently quite difficult to invert – with n firms one must invert an n-equation system. Thus, it is more convenient to assume that competition is in prices.

Obviously, analytical convenience is not a sufficient reason for assuming that competition is in prices since, as the following examples illustrate, there are significant differences between address models in which competition is in prices and those in which competition is in quantities. (The circumstances in which oligopolists may play either a pricing or a quantity game are discussed by Carl Shapiro in Chapter 6 of this Handbook, so we make only a few points of special relevance to address models.)

We saw in the discussion of natural oligopoly that the very nature of the equilibrium is different: with price competition, products are differentiated; with quantity competition, they are not.

Deneckere and Davidson (1985) show that in a model of differentiated products and many firms, when entry is not a concern, any sort of merger is profitable if competition is in prices, whereas mergers are only rarely profitable if competition is in quantities.

d'Aspremont, Gabszewicz and Thisse (1979) have shown that the very existence of price equilibrium is in question in address models that do not invoke the no-mill-price-undercutting assumption. One source of non-existence in these models is the temptation to undercut, which requires that price be the strategic variable. Salant (1986) shows that the undercutting temptation is removed when competition is in quantities and goes on to prove the existence of quantity equilibrium in one-dimensional address models in a fairly general setting.

One argument for the appropriateness of price competition is that firms must announce price in an address model. Given cost and demand conditions, impersonal market forces cannot give rise to market-clearing prices in differentiated products as they can with undifferentiated products. But this fact does not necessarily mean that prices are the strategic variable.

Salant (1986), for example, argues that in many industries there are long lags in production – the next period's output is committed by this period's production decisions. In this case firms' quantity decisions precede their price decisions. Such firms are forced to ask at what price tomorrow can today's production be marketed? That is, they are forced to make conjectures concerning market-clearing prices for their quantities. In these circumstances, it seems appropriate to model competition in quantities.

In an analysis of undifferentiated products that is clearly also applicable to differentiated ones, Kreps and Scheinkman (1983) consider a two-stage model in which duopolists simultaneously choose quantities in stage 1 and prices in stage 2. The subgame perfect equilibrium in their model is identical to a Cournot equilibrium in spite of competition being in prices in stage 2. The intuition is that firms recognize the destructiveness of Bertrand competition and commit themselves in advance to curbing their non-cooperative pricing behavior by choosing a limited quantity. Where this model applies, we would expect Cournot results when demand is correctly predicted, but Bertrand-style price wars whenever unexpectedly low demand occurs.

Singh and Vives (1984) consider a two-stage game in which each firm first selects price or quantity as its strategic variable and then competes according to its selected variable in the second stage. In their model the dominant strategy is to select quantity, and this leads to the Cournot equilibrium.

These studies convince us that there is likely to be a range of real circumstances in which quantity, rather than price, will be chosen as the strategic variable. This in turn suggests a research agenda: rework address models using quantity competition. Here is one obvious example. In response to non-existence of price equilibrium in Hotelling's model, d'Aspremont, Gabszewicz and Thisse (1979) present a modified version of Hotelling's model in which the sequential equilibrium exhibits *maximum* differentiation. Is this result robust to competition in quantities? Will differentiation be less than optimal if competition is in quantities? We suspect the answers are "no" to the first question and "yes" to the second.

8. Multi-address firms

The great bulk of the literature on product differentiation in both large- and small-group situations has used the simplifying assumption of one-address firms. On a research agenda of tackling the easiest problems first, this is understandable. But awkward fact (4) states that the vast majority of real-world firms are multi-address, both in characteristic and geographic space. This is obvious in the consumers' goods sector – toiletries, tobacco products, refrigerators, automobiles, etc. The growth of retail chains has spread the same effect to the retail sector. For example, many single-outlet restaurants, which were the dominant form within living memory, have given way in the lower price range to such chains as

Macdonald's, Kentucky Fried Chicken, and the Dutch Oven. To come to grips with reality, the model needs to be extended to analyze multi-address firms.

One valuable step in this direction, using the non-address approach, has recently been taken by Brander and Eaton (1984). They deal with a model of four products. The pairs (1, 2) and (3,4) are close substitutes, while the pairs (1, 3), (1, 4), (2, 3), and (2, 4) are more distant substitutes as defined by cross-elasticities of demand. Because they use the goods-are-goods approach, they are able to use competition in quantities without difficulty.

The results are driven by the property that when two single-product firms compete, profits in equilibrium are lower the more substitutable are the two goods. As a result, a *segmented market structure*, with one firm producing products 1 and 2 and the other firm producing products 3 and 4, yields higher profits than an *interlaced market structure*, where each firm produces one good from the pair (1, 2) and one good from the pair (3, 4).

It follows immediately that when two firms enter the market sequentially choosing (by assumption) two products each, and knowing that no other firms will enter, the segmented structure will result. One firm will choose the pair (1, 2) while the other chooses (3, 4), thus minimizing the profit-reducing competition between them.

If firms are also allowed to choose the number of products they produce, the above result holds only for some intermediate levels of demand. At one extreme, demand may be so low that, if one firm chooses any one of the four products, the other would choose not to enter. This is a natural monopoly. At the other extreme, demand may be so great that, even if one firm chooses all four products, the other firm would still choose to enter. This will lead to an overlapping market structure. Only for intermediate levels of demand is segmentation the unique subgame perfect equilibrium.

Finally, if the two firms fear further entry, they may be led to select an interlaced, rather than a segmented, market structure. Since the interlaced market structure is more competitive and therefore discourages entry, it may result in higher duopoly profits than would result from the oligopoly that would evolve if the two firms encouraged entry by selecting a segmented structure. The general insight is that creating a more competitive n-firm situation may deter entry and result in higher profits for the n firms than the profit they would earn in any $n + 1$-firm free-entry equilibrium. Brander and Eaton's analysis leads to the conjecture that in a growing market, the natural evolution may be from monopoly, to a segmented duopoly, to an interlaced oligopoly.

Two earlier studies of multi-unit firms in address models are Schmalensee (1978) and Eaton and Lipsey (1979). Schmalensee studied a situation where a firm could deter entry by proliferating differentiated products so as to avoid presenting a new entrant with a market niche large enough to be profitable. The monopoly preemption result in our basic model of horizontal differentiation is a simple illustration of Schmalensee's argument.

Eaton and Lipsey analyzed a growing market initially large enough to support production at just one address. If the incumbent firm does not preempt the market, and if there are many potential entrants, then entry at a new address will occur at the point in time, T, when the present value of entry is zero. But the incumbent firm can deter entry by itself choosing a new address an instant before T. If the incumbent chooses the new address, the profit generated by the whole market will be larger (than if an entrant chooses the new address) for the simple reason that the incumbent will choose the new address, and the two prices, to maximize total profit. This implies that the incumbent will choose to deter entry. (The argument is similar to the one we used above in discussing the deterrence of predatory entry by premature replacement of sunk capital.)

Judd (1985) has pointed out that these preemption arguments neglect to consider the possibility that a new entrant, who would find entry unprofitable *given* the existing occupied addresses, might still be able to enter by inducing the incumbent to vacate one or more addresses – a strategy of predatory entry.

To see what is involved, consider a market of unit length with uniform customer density. Suppose that if firm 1 were to locate at two addresses, 1/4 and 3/4, an entrant which took these locations as given could not cover its costs, which are composed of a constant marginal cost and a cost of entry. Suppose also that two firms could cover their costs if one of them was located at 1/4 and the other at 3/4.

Now suppose that a first firm considering entering at locations 1/4 and 3/4 anticipates the possibility of predatory entry. We consider three cases in which the original firm is at 1/4 and 3/4 and the new firm at 1/4.

Case 1: Competition in prices. Competition in prices would drive price down to marginal cost at 1/4, and the incumbent would earn zero gross profit from his address at 1/4. Price would, of course, exceed marginal cost at 3/4 and the market boundary would be at some point to the right of 1/2. If firm 1 were to abandon its address at 1/4, the prices at 1/4 and 3/4 would both rise and the market boundary would be at 1/2. Hence, firm 1's profit would increase. Foreseeing this result, one would not attempt the (1/4, 3/4) preemption strategy.

Case 2: Cooperative pricing. Now suppose that post-entry pricing is cooperative. (Firm 1 could induce cooperative pricing if it could credibly announce a price-following strategy – "we will not knowingly be undersold" is, for example, a stated policy of some well-known retailers.) The prices at 1/4 and 3/4 are now identical regardless of whether there are two or one plants at address 1/4. In this case, firm 1 would not abandon address 1/4. Knowing this, there would be no predatory entry and the (1/4, 3/4) preemption strategy works.

Case 3: Competition in quantities. In this case, the predatory entry strategy might or might not induce firm 1 to abandon address 1/4. If the cross-elasticities between the goods at the two addresses are high enough, it would. If they are low enough, it would not. The $(1/4, 3/4)$ preemption strategy may or may not be profitable to firm 1.

Thus, the possibility raised by Judd of predatory entry in these preemptive models means that the obvious preemption strategy of locating plants at $1/4$ and $3/4$ may or may not be subgame perfect, depending on how fierce is post-entry competition. Of course, there may be other preemption strategies which are subgame perfect, even when competition is in prices. Consider, for example, the preemptive strategy of locating two plants at 0 and at 1. If competition is in prices, an entrant could induce firm 1 to abandon one of these addresses, but there may be no address for the entrant which both induces firm 1 to abandon an address and also offers the entrant positive profit in the ensuing duopoly equilibrium.[3]

9. Product diversity and economic policy

Rational economic policy requires an understanding of the welfare issues which arise in the context of differentiated products. The model using the representative consumer has the advantage of being tractable. Welfare results are easily derived from it. However, tractability in deriving incorrect results is no advantage, and we do know that in address models, whenever preferences are single peaked in (θ, p) space, aggregate consumer behavior cannot be caught by a representative consumer. Thus, it seems to us that while there may be cases for which the representative-consumer approach is appropriate, there are many problems for which an address model seems appropriate. Nothing can be learned about these problems from representative-consumer, or Chamberlinian models, since they do not capture all of the awkward facts.

Similar remarks apply to Chamberlin-style models that employ the symmetry assumption, even when they are rooted in individual taste differences, since these models appear to be inconsistent with awkward (6). So if the address model characterization of consumers' behavior captures important aspects of reality, there is no reason to believe welfare propositions derived from either of these approaches. For people interested in giving policy advice relevant to the bulk of manufacturing industries that sell differentiated goods this is a serious matter.

---

[3] In contrast to the rich set of possibilities considered in the text, Judd appears to claim that multi-address preemption is never subgame perfect. In his model, where curiously there are no addresses, just two goods, the claim is driven by his assumption that firm 1's revenue from plants at $1/4$ and $3/4$ when firm 2 also has a plant at $1/4$ is less than its revenue from one plant at $3/4$ while 2's single plant is at $1/4$. This amounts to solving the preemption issue by assumption: since predatory entry is assumed always to work, preemption is never subgame perfect.

Notice that the standard market failure associated with the divergence of price from marginal cost necessarily arises in markets for differentiated products whenever demand is not perfectly price inelastic. Market failure is a ubiquitous problem in address models with balkanization and localized competition since in free-entry equilibrium the position of each product is very much like the standard stylization of a natural monopoly. If the standard natural monopoly problem is difficult to solve in practice, the natural monopoly problem in address models is much more so since it is a pervasive problem.

In addition, the problem of optimal product diversity arises. This is, we believe, an even more difficult problem — one that, from a policy perspective, we know very little about. Our basic address model is a useful device for conveying the awkward nature of this problem since the only optimality issue is diversity. We showed in our discussion of that model that there is no general relationship between product diversity in free-entry equilibrium and optimal product diversity. However, it is clear that the diversity observed in free-entry equilibrium is unlikely to be the optimum amount. Even if the optimum diversity is a free-entry equilibrium, there are many other free-entry equilibria and no market force which pushes the equilibrium to the optimum. The awkward problem is that we do not even know the nature of the bias — whether there is likely to be too much or too little diversity in equilibrium.

If we interpret the basic model as a model of spatial competition, it is conceivable that one could discover at a modest cost all of the data necessary to determine optimal diversity. The principal difficulty concerns transport costs, the function $T(D)$ in the model. Where transport costs are out-of-pocket costs, it is not an overwhelming task to estimate the transport cost function. Where, however, $T(D)$ reflects the opportunity cost of shoppers' time, as in the retail sector, and especially where there is diversity over shoppers' opportunity costs, the task is far from trivial. There are also additional difficult issues concerning multi-purpose shopping. The point is that, even in this relatively simple environment, it is not obvious that we would recognize an optimum if we saw one. Even assuming that we could recognize one (that we could compute the optimum), the presence in any real situation of sunk capital implies that the optimal policy program which takes the market from an initial situation to the optimum is quite complex.

When we interpret the basic model as a model of differentiation in some characteristics space, we believe that we would be quite unable to recognize an optimum if we saw one. In this case $T(D)$ refers to a utility cost associated with the divergence of the characteristics of the best available good from the individual consumer's most preferred bundle of characteristics. Now we face the problem of recovering preferences from observed market behavior. In our basic model this is not an impossibly difficult task — we could, for example, imagine an experiment in which we systematically varied the price of one or more products. Provided that consumers did not play strategic games, the experiment would generate sufficient data for us to discover $T(D)$. There is, of course, no reason to believe that consumers' preferences are diverse in only one dimension, the most preferred good. In the basic model, the function $T(D)$ might very well be consumer specific. In this case, any experiment that would allow us to discover preferences would be far from trivial. It seems clear, however, that experimentation would be necessary in either case – we could not discover preferences from the data revealed in free-entry equilibrium.

The phenomenon of preemption via product proliferation has been raised as a real policy issue in an action by the U.S. Federal Trade Commission [see Schmalensee (1978]. From our perspective, the issue is whether or not this sort of preemptive activity is or is not anti-social. We can use the insights generated by Brander and Eaton (1983) to articulate, but not to answer, the question. Where prices are endogenous, the fewer the number of firms that engage in preemptive product proliferation, the higher will be the welfare losses associated with the divergence of price from marginal cost, but the greater will be actual product diversity. For example, the number of products necessary for a monopolist to preempt entry exceeds the number necessary for duopolists to preempt entry. Whether monopoly preemption is more socially desirable than some other free-entry equilibrium then depends on whether or not the added diversity associated with monopoly preemption outweighs the conventional welfare loss associated with non-competitive pricing. And so on. Thus, the question is well defined. The difficult problem concerns the discovery of consumers' preferences.

There is one exception to these disturbing results. In "large economies" equilibrium is (at least approximately) optimal when all goods are substitutes. See Hart (1979) and Jones (1987) for general results and Eaton and Wooders (1985) for results in an address model. We can illustrate what we mean by a "large economy" in the context of the simple address model we have used throughout the chapter. In that model we can create a large economy by letting the density of customers go to infinity, or by letting the product development cost, I, go to zero. With endogenous prices, prices of all firms approach marginal cost and the number of goods gets arbitrarily large in either asymptotic experiment. Hence, in the limit, every consumer is able to purchase his or her most preferred good at marginal cost. These results raise an important question: How large is large enough, and is this much "largeness" commonly – or ever – encountered empirically?

10. An historical postscript

A brief outline of some of the key points in the historical development of models of product differentiation may help to put the material discussed in this paper into perspective. Before discussing Figure 12.4, which systematizes the main points, we stress that we do not have space to give credit to all of the main

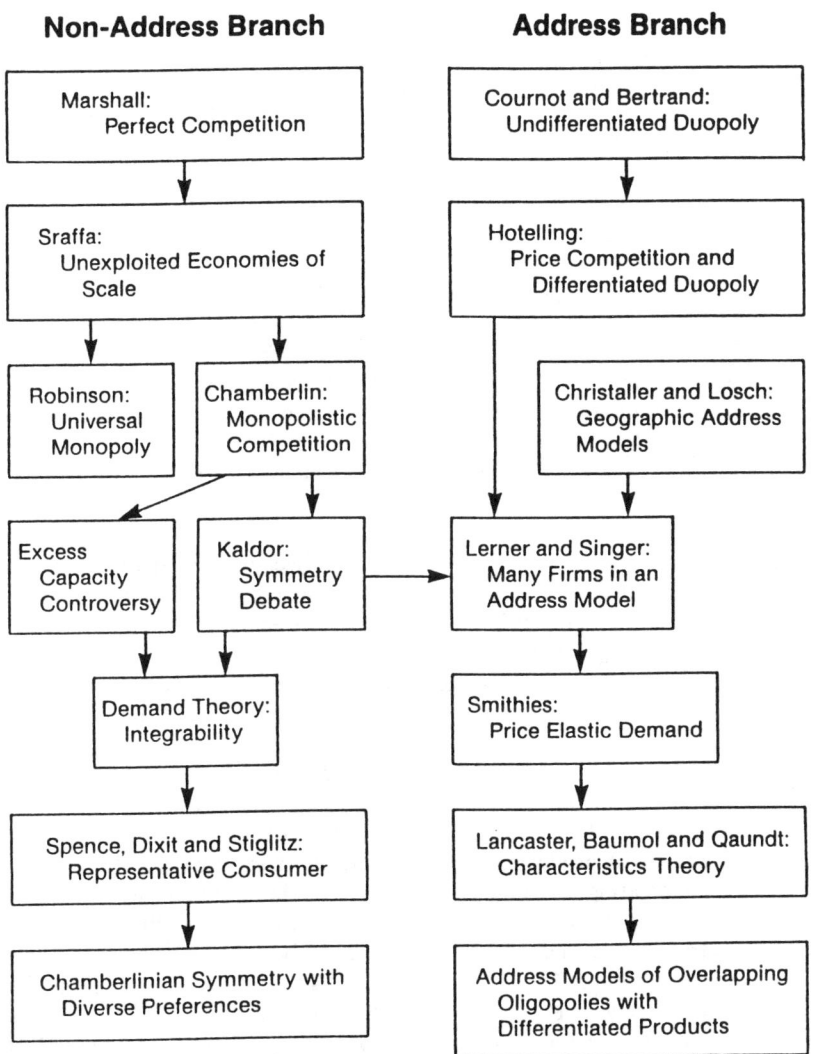

Figure 12.4. Historical perspective.

contributors. Our concern is with the flow of ideas, and we mention names only as illustrative benchmarks.

The left-hand side of the chart shows the development of the large group case of product differentiation. Shortly after the death of Alfred Marshall, Sraffa (1926) pointed out the inconsistency between the observed facts of unexploited scale economies in many manufacturing industries and the Marshallian theory of perfect competition, where all scale economies must be exhausted in long-run equilibrium.

Chamberlin (1933) and Robinson (1934) responded to Sraffa's challenge. Robinson assumed a single monopolist in each industry. Although her work greatly clarified the theory of monopoly, it proved to be a dead end as a response to Sraffa's point. Instead, the way was pointed by Chamberlin. In his theory, a large group of competitive firms, each producing one differentiated product and operating under conditions of free entry, produced an equilibrium where each firm's output was less than minimum efficient scale. The theory was a triumph in making a small amendment – differentiated products – to Marshall's theory of perfect competition, which then reconciled competitive theory with the empirical observation of unexploited economies of scale.

Ironically, the reason for its triumph soon became the greatest cause of concern about the theory. It resolved Sraffa's problem by showing that something very close to perfect competition could be consistent with the observation of unexploited scale economies. However, the presence of unexploited economies of scale, which became known as the excess capacity theorem, gave rise to innumerable controversies in response to its apparent implication of free-market inefficiency.

The controversy over the alleged adverse welfare implications of the excess capacity theorem finally faded away when it became understood that, in a society that values diversity, there is a trade-off between economizing on resources, by reducing the costs of producing existing products, and satisfying the desire for diversity, by increasing the number of products. The optimum diversity occurs when existing products are produced at points to the left of the minimum-efficient scale – therefore, "excess capacity" is *not* necessarily socially inefficient.[4]

A second, and quite different, strand of criticism of monopolistic competition was developed largely by Kaldor (1934, 1935). He attacked Chamberlin's symmetry assumption which made competition *generalized* in that, within one industry no firm had "near neighbors" who bore the main effects of any change in its behavior, and "distant" neighbors who bore smaller effects. Given symmetry, free entry would drive profits to zero (or at least to the small positive amount allowed by the integer problem). Kaldor argued that, although products at one end of the

---

[4]Bishop (1967) analyzed this issue in a Chamberlinian model. Lancaster (1979) does so in a characteristics model.

product spectrum in a given industry would be close substitutes for each other, they would be poor substitutes for those at the other end of the spectrum. He was intuitively working with an address model where goods are located in some appropriate space of characteristics. He saw competition as *localized*, even within an industry, and argued for a model of overlapping oligopolies rather than for a model of generalized intra-industry competition.[5]

Chamberlin, himself, did make a brief excursion into the area of small numbers competition and the short section on "mutual interdependence recognized" was at the time an original contribution to that theory. Furthermore, Chamberlin (1951) accepted Kaldor's arguments against the symmetry assumption. Nonetheless, his theory of large group competition had by then taken on a life of its own due to the extended and heated nature of the debates mentioned above.

By the 1960s, decreasing attention was being paid to the Chamberlinian model of monopolistic competition. Two reasons are worth mentioning. First, the realization slowly took hold that virtually all industries containing a multitude of differentiated products contained only a few firms [awkward fact (4)]. [See, for example, Markham (1964).] Thus, although the typical, real-world set of differentiated products was a large group, the typical set of competing firms was a small group. Second, growth of interest in location theory showed that localized, rather than generalized, competition was also common in many industries where firms are differentiated by their geographic location. Although, for example, there are many drugstores in a city, each has a few nearby, and many more-distant, neighbors. Here again a model of overlapping oligopolies, rather than one of symmetrically situated monopolistic competitors, seemed more appropriate.

The 1970s saw a revival of interest in all aspects of product differentiation. This was no doubt partly due to the experience of both the EEC countries after the signing of the treaty of Rome and of the GAAT participants during the Kennedy round of tariff reductions. Specialization following on these major tariff cuts among countries of roughly similar per capita incomes did not cause whole industries to close down in some countries and to expand greatly in others. Instead, in each existing industry in each country firms found product niches in which they could compete. So specialization took the form of a reduction of product lines in each country with great expansion of intra-industry, international trade. The increased production runs in each differentiated product afforded substantial reductions in unit costs. As a result the gains from specialization turned out to be substantially more than had been estimated from older constant-cost models of inter-industry specialization.

The outburst of theorizing in demand theory in the 1960s assisted the revival of interest in Chamberlin's model. Ever since the event of the "new welfare

---

[5] For a survey of all of the aspects of the debate up to 1960 – which is close to the time when the debate subsided – see Archibald (1961).

economics" in the 1940s, economists had worried about the construction of a community welfare function that could be derived from individual utility functions. In the 1960s the integrability literature showed, with standards of rigor not demanded in the 1940s, that under certain specific conditions, the community's demand behavior, and the welfare of its individuals, could be captured in a single community utility function.

In the 1970s Spence (1976a, b), and Dixit and Stiglitz (1977), developed models of monopolistic competition that used the concept of the representative consumer. A further development came with the models of Ferguson (1983), Sattinger (1984), Hart (1985) and Perloff and Salop (1985) who assumed different consumers with different tastes and then generated models of monopolistic competition that displayed the symmetry property.

To understand the development of small group competition with differentiated products we need to begin with Cournot's model of quantity competition between oligopolists producing identical products. Then came Bertrand's formulation of the alternative of price competition showing that non-cooperative behavior would drive price to marginal cost. Bertrand's critique of Cournot opened an important issue that still faces us: What conditions will favor the use of price or quantity as the strategic variable for oligopolistic competition?

The seminal article for the development of theories of competition among oligopolists producing differentiated products was Hotelling's (1929) address branch model. Address models of geographic location trace their lineage to the fundamental work of Christaller (1933) and Losch (1938). Hotelling's starting point was Bertrand's critique of Cournot. He made a crucial change of assumption by letting his duopolists compete to sell a differentiated rather than a homogeneous product.

Hotelling showed that when two competing firms were differentiated from each other, either by having different geographic locations or by producing products differentiated in some one-dimensional characteristics space, price competition could leave price high enough to cover capital costs, thus yielding a stable, long-run equilibrium. Lerner and Singer (1941) expanded Hotelling's model by increasing the number of firms beyond two. Smithies (1941) considered the consequence of altering Hotelling's restrictive demand assumption. Thirty years after its publication, however, only a modest amount of work could trace its lineage back to Hotelling's approach.

As with the other strand, a renewed interest in the address models of product differentiation was aided by developments in demand theory. The model developed by Lancaster (1966) and Quandt and Baumol (1966), in which consumers' preferences are defined over characteristics which themselves are embodied in goods, provided a structure in which the firm's decisions concerning product differentiation could be meaningfully analyzed. The following year Baumol (1967) studied a producer's optimal product design and observed that the new characteristic models provided "a promising approach to a problem that seems previously to have appeared to be intractable". Address models of competition among firms selling differentiated goods first concentrated on a proposition that had been developed from a variant of Hotelling's model, a proposition which Boulding (1966) christened the principle of minimum differentiation. [See Eaton and Lipsey (1975).] In response to that paper, Prescott and Visscher (1977) and Hay (1976) took up the issue of foresightful entry and interest quickly spread to many other issues as well.

References

Anderson, S.P., de Palma, A. and Thisse, J.F. (1988) 'A representative consumer theory of the logit model', *International Economic Review*, 29, forthcoming.
Archibald, G.C. (1961) 'Chamberlin *versus* Chicago', *Review of Economic Studies*, 29:1–28.
Archibald, G.C. and Eaton, B.C. (1988) 'Two applications of characteristics theory', in: G. Fiewel, ed., *Essays in memory of Joan Robinson*. London: MacMillan.
Archibald, G.C. and Rosenbluth, G. (1975) 'The 'new' theory of consumer demand and monopolistic competition', *Quarterly Journal of Economics*, 80:569–590.
Archibald, G.C., Eaton, B.C. and Lipsey, R.G. (1986) 'Address models of value theory', in: J.E. Stiglitz and G.F. Mathewson, eds., *New developments in the analysis of market structure*. Cambridge: MIT Press, 3–47.
Baumol, W.J. (1967) 'Calculation of optimal product and retailer characteristics: The abstract product approach', *Journal of Political Economy*, 75:674–685.
Bishop, R.L. (1967) 'Monopolistic competition and welfare economics', in: R. Kuenne, ed., *Monopolistic competitive theory: Studies in impact*. New York: Wiley, 251–263.
Bonnano, G. (1986) 'Vertical differentiation with Cournot competition', *Economic Notes*, 2:68–91.
Boulding, K. (1966) *Economic analysis*. New York: Harper.
Brander, J.A. and Eaton, J. (1984) 'Product line rivalry', *American Economic Review*, 74:323–326.
Chamberlin, E.H. (1933) *The theory of monopolistic competition*. Cambridge: Harvard University Press.
Chamberlin, E.H. (1951) 'Monopolistic competition revisited', *Economica*, 18:343–355.
Christaller, W. (1933) *Die zentralen Orte in Suddeutschland: Eine okonomisch-geographische Untersuchung uber die Gesetzmassigkeit der Verbrietung und Entwicklung der Siedlungen mit stadtischen Funktionen*. Jena: Fischer.
d'Aspremont, C., Gabszewicz, J.J. and Thisse, J.F. (1979) 'On 'Hotelling's stability in competition'', *Econometrica*, 47:1145–1150.
Deneckere, R. and Davidson, C. (1985) 'Incentives to form coalitions with Bertrand competition', *Rand Journal of Economics*, 16:473–486.
Deneckere, R. and Rothschild, M. (1986) 'Monopolistic competition and optimum preference diversity', discussion paper no. 684, Northwestern University.
Dixit, A.K. and Stiglitz, J.E. (1977) 'Monopolistic competition and optimum product diversity', *American Economic Review*, 67:297–308.
Eaton, B.C. and Lipsey, R.G. (1975) 'The principle of minimum differentiation reconsidered: Some new developments in the theory of spatial competition', *Review of Economic Studies*, 42:27–49.
Eaton, B.C. and Lipsey, R.G. (1976) 'The non-uniqueness of equilibrium in the Loschian location model', *American Economic Review*, 66:77–93.
Eaton, B.C. and Lipsey, R.G. (1978) 'Freedom of entry and the existence of pure profit', *Economic Journal*, 88:455–469.
Eaton, B.C. and Lipsey, R.G. (1979) 'The theory of market preemption: The persistence of excess capacity and monopoly in growing spatial markets', *Economica*, 46:149–158.
Eaton, B.C. and Lipsey, R.G. (1980) 'Exit barriers are entry barriers: The durability of capital as a barrier to entry', *Bell Journal of Economics*, 11:721–729.

Eaton, B.C. and Wooders, M.H. (1985) 'Sophisticated entry in a model of spatial competition', *Rand Journal of Economics*, 16:282-297.
Ferguson (1983) 'On the theory of demand for differentiated goods', University of Victoria, mimeo.
Gabszewicz, J.J. and Thisse, J.F. (1979) 'Price competition, quality and income disparities', *Journal of Economic Theory*, 20:340-359.
Gabszewicz, J.J. and Thisse, J.F. (1980) 'Entry (and exit) in a differentiated industry', *Journal of Economic Theory*, 22:327-338.
Gabszewicz, J.J. and Thisse, J. (1986) 'On the nature of competition with differentiated products', *Economic Journal*, 96:160-172.
Hart, O.D. (1979) 'Monopolistic competition in a large economy with differentiated commodities', *Review of Economic Studies*, 46:1-30.
Hart, O.D. (1985) 'Monopolistic competition in the spirit of Chamberlin: Special results', *Economic Journal*, 95:889-908.
Hay, D.A. (1976) 'Sequential entry and entry-deterring strategies in spatial competition', *Oxford Economic Papers*, 28:240-257.
Hotelling, H. (1929) 'Stability in competition', *Economic Journal*, 39:41-57.
Jones, L.E. (1987) 'The efficiency of monopolistically competition equilibria in large economies: Commodity differentiation with gross substitutes', *Journal of Economic Theory*, 41:356-391.
Judd, K.L. (1985) 'Credible spatial preemption', *Rand Journal of Economics*, 16:153-166.
Kaldor, N. (1934) 'Mrs. Robinson's 'economics of imperfect competition'', *Economica*, 1:335-341.
Kaldor, N. (1935) 'Market imperfections and excess capacity', *Economica*, 2:33-50.
Koenker, R.W. and Perry, M.K. (1981) 'Product differentiation, monopolistic competition, and public policy', *Bell Journal of Economics*, 12:217-231.
Kreps, D.M. and Scheinkman, J.A. (1983) 'Quantity precommitment and Bertrand competition yield Cournot outcomes', *Bell Journal of Economics*, 14:326-337.
Lancaster, K.J. (1966) 'A new approach to consumer theory', *Journal of Political Economy*, 74:132-157.
Lancaster, K.J. (1979) *Variety, equity, and efficiency'*. New York: Columbia University Press.
Lane, W. (1980) 'Product differentiation in a market with endogenous sequential entry', *Bell Journal of Economics*, 11:237-260.
Lerner, A. and Singer, H. (1941) 'Some notes on duopoly and spatial competition', *Journal of Political Economy*, 45:423-439.
Losch, A. (1938) 'The nature of economic regions', *Southern Economic Journal*, 5:71-78.
Markham, J.W. (1964) 'The theory of monopolistic competition after thirty years', *American Economic Review*, 54:53-55.
Novshek, W. (1980) 'Equilibrium in simple spatial (or differentiated product) models', *Journal of Economic Theory*, 22:313-326.
Perloff, J.M. and Salop, S.C. (1985) 'Equilibrium with product differentiation', *Review of Economic Studies*, 52:107-120.
Prescott, E.C. and Visscher, M. (1977) 'Sequential location among firms with foresight', *Bell Journal of Economics*, 8:378-393.
Quandt, R.E. and Baumol, W.J. (1966) 'The demand for abstract transport modes: Theory and measurement', *Journal Regional Science*, 6:13-26.
Robinson, J. (1934) *The economics of imperfect competition*. London: Macmillan.
Salant, D.J. (1986) 'Equilibrium in a spatial model of imperfect competition with sequential choice of locations and quantities', *Canadian Journal of Economics*, 19:685-715.
Salop, S. (1979) 'Monopolistic competition with outside goods', *Bell Journal of Economics*, 10:141-156.
Sattinger, M. (1984) 'Value of an additional firm in monopolistic competition', *Review of Economic Studies*, 51:321-3332.
Schmalensee, R. (1978) 'Entry deterrence in the ready-to-eat breakfast cereal industry', *Bell Journal of Economics*, 9:305-327.
Schmalensee, R. (1983) 'Econometric diagnosis of competitive localization', working paper no. 1390-83, MIT.
Shaked, A. and Sutton, J. (1982) 'Relaxing price competition through product differentiation', *Review of Economic Studies*, 49:3-13.
Shaked, A. and Sutton, J. (1983) 'Natural oligopolies', *Econometrica*, 51(5):1469-1483.

Singh, N. and Vives, X. (1984) 'Price and quantity competition in a differentiated duopoly', *Rand Journal of Economics*, 15:546–554.
Smithies, A. (1941) 'Optimum location in spatial competition', *Journal of Political Economy*, 49:423–439.
Spence, A.M. (1976a) 'Product selection, fixed costs, and monopolistic competition', *Review of Economic Studies*, 43:217–235.
Spence, A.M. (1976b) 'Product differentiation and welfare', *American Economic Review*, 66:407–414.
Sraffa, P. (1926) 'The laws of returns under competitive conditions', *Economic Journal*, 34:535–550.

[15]

B. Curtis Eaton, Richard G. Lipsey & A. Edward Safarian
Economic Growth and Policy Program
Canadian Institute for Advanced Research

The Theory of Multinational Plant Location: Agglomerations and Disagglomerations

INTRODUCTION

THIS CHAPTER, LIKE THE PREVIOUS ONE, is concerned with multinational plant location. The previous chapter considered how the decision to allocate individual investments among countries may be influenced by national differences in incentives to invest. This chapter considers the interaction among individual investments; interaction which creates tendencies for investments to cluster together in regional and/or national agglomerations. Although each chapter can be read on its own, we urge the reader to obtain some perspective on this one by beginning with the previous chapter.

As Paul Krugman notes in *Geography and Trade*, his charming and brilliant lectures on economic geography, "the most striking feature of the geography of economic activity [is its] concentration" (Krugman, p 5). In this vein, one of the most striking features of Canada is its agglomerations of economic activity.

During the debate over the Canada-U.S. Free Trade Agreement (FTA), some Canadian critics expressed concern that these agglomerations, such as are found in Toronto, throughout Southern Ontario, the industrial part of Quebec and, to a lesser extent, in the lower mainland of British Columbia, around Halifax, and a number of other centres, would be undone by the removal of the tariffs on Canada-U.S. trade. It was alleged that Canadians would revert to being "hewers of wood and drawers of water". Others argued that the broader forces of technological change are also working to dissolve agglomerations of economic activity, particularly in small open economies such as Sweden and Canada.

To address these and a number of related issues we first review the theory of agglomerations. We consider how economies of scale on the one hand, and transportation and communication costs on the other, interact to produce agglomerations. The theory provides no definitive answer to the worrying claim that free trade will unwind all or any Canadian agglomerations; theoretically, the possibility certainly exists, but history suggests the

79

probability is small. Next, we review the new technologies now coming into use. These technologies appear more likely to contribute to a growing diversity in patterns of industrial location than to the rise of a few massive agglomerations. Finally, we review the evidence on R&D conducted by MNEs — evidence which indicates there is substantial continuing concentration in the home countries. There is, however, a clear trend toward decentralization within some industries and in a number of home countries (although the pace is very slow in the case of the United States).

THE THEORY OF AGGLOMERATION

AGGLOMERATIONS ARE DRIVEN BY two potent forces: economies of scale and costs of transportation. Traditional trade theorists consider transport costs mainly in the context of convex technologies. In this context, transport costs do little more than reduce the gains from trade that would occur in a world of costless transportation. The new trade theorists, such as Brander, Grossman, Helpman, Krugman and Spencer have incorporated economies of scale and imperfect competition into trade theory. So far, however, no one — neither traditional nor new trade theorists — appears to have considered the combined forces of scale effects and transportation costs to study agglomerations. Following Krugman's 1991 lead, we turn to economic geography.

To advance the discussion one must have at least a rudimentary understanding of the implications of trade policy for the agglomeration of economic activity in Canada as well as in a world context. To ensure this, we first review what is known about economies of scale, and then look at the way in which those economies interact with transportation and communication costs to produce agglomeration. We then discuss some general features of this interaction and related processes. Finally, we turn to questions raised by trade policy where, regrettably, we can do little more than provide a conceptual framework within which they can be pondered.

ECONOMIES OF SCALE

IN THE FIRST FEW PAGES of *The Wealth of Nations*, Adam Smith establishes the foundation of our understanding of economies of scale by accounting for them in terms of specialization and the division of labour. According to Smith, specialization facilitates learning by doing; it economizes on human capital; it tends to reduce the inventory of goods in process; and finally, it promotes technical change. All but the last of these work to create static economies of scale: the last works to create what might be described as "dynamic" economies of scale. Today Smith's emphasis on specialization and the division of labour plays an important, even central, role in informal theories of the firm.

Sadly, one important strand of our understanding of economies of scale has all but disappeared in modern economics. It relates to what Eaton

& Lipsey (1993) call real capital theory (i.e., the theory of production for indivisible capital goods). It can be illustrated by Gustav Akerman's (1923) account of the durable axe. He asks: Why do we see durable axes, axes that will provide a flow of service for 25 years or more? He answers: Given a positive rate of interest, and assuming the producers of axes to be cost minimizers, one must conclude that there are economies of scale in the activities embodying the services an axe provides in a durable axe. The very existence of capital goods is evidence of economies of scale in the act of embodying productive services in durable, indivisible capital goods. Since all economic activity involves a variety of capital goods, increasing returns over some initial scale of activity would also seem to be a pervasive fact of economic life. These economies can be seen as yet another aspect of specialization and the division of labour since they involve specialization in the domain of time. Robinson Crusoe first specializes in producing and storing the services of a fishing rod (by producing a durable rod), and subsequently specializes in catching fish with the aid of the rod. Eaton & Lipsey (1993) attempt to reconstruct and reinterpret the important insights provided by Akerman, and buried by neoclassical economists.

In this broad sense then, economies of scale can be attributed to specialization and the division of labour. Moreover, such specialization inevitably involves the acquisition of both human and physical capital and, to some extent, this capital is product-specific. Both the skills and the implements that the workers wielded in Smith's famous pin factory were useful in producing pins but, one imagines, not in other economic activities. The skills constituted pin-specific human capital; the implements were pin-specific capital goods.

To determine whether a particular economic activity will be internal or external to a specific firm, and therefore whether internal or external economics exist, we must understand the basics of the modern theory of the firm. Ronald Coase (1937) provided the key insight on which the modern theory of the firm is built. He began with the simple observation that economic activity can be directly co-ordinated within the firm, or indirectly co-ordinated *via* markets, and that the boundary between the firm and the market is therefore endogenous. This boundary between internal, hands-on co-ordination, and external, arms-length co-ordination is determined by transaction costs, i.e., the costs of direct coordination and control on the one hand, and the costs of arm's length transactions on the other. Oliver Williamson, in *Markets and Hierarchies*, contributed a wealth of detail in support of Coase's research, and two key insights relevant to our purpose here. First, he noted that product- and firm-specific assets, including goods in process, special purpose capital goods, firm-specific human capital and the detailed economic know-how that is necessary to transform a bright idea into a commercially viable product (or process), create co-ordination problems that cannot be solved by arm's-length, market transactions. No supplier will produce components for

General Motors cars in the hope that GM will buy them because, once produced, the components are useful to GM and to no one else. To produce such specific components in the absence of some sort of commitment from GM (formal, as is typical in the United States, or informal, as is typical in Japan) would be folly because it puts the producer in a decidedly disadvantageous bargaining position. In the modern world of differentiated products, specific assets, specific components and specific human capital are nearly universal. In Williamson's view, the firm is an organization designed to manage the difficult co-ordination problems associated with asset specificity.

Williamson's second great contribution was to recognize that these co-ordination problems can be managed in a number of different ways, sometimes within one firm, and sometimes between firms using a variety of means to control the opportunistic behaviour that specific assets invite. As noted earlier, much of the modern theory of the MNE is based on these fundamental insights.

AGGLOMERATION

AT AN ELEMENTARY LEVEL, agglomeration is the result of two opposing forces: *economies of scale* that produce concentration; and *transportation and communication costs* that inhibit concentration. To realize economies of scale at the plant level, supplementary activities involving transportation and communication must occur: inputs (labour and materials) must be transported to the plant; output must be transported from the plant to the market; and the firm must communicate with its suppliers and customers. These supplementary activities are costly, and their cost tends to increase with distance.

To see how these forces interact to produce agglomeration, consider the problems of a planner who must choose the number and locations of plants to produce and market a fixed quantity of a final good while minimizing total costs. In this context, total costs *include* transportation and communication. For simplicity, imagine a setting in which the inputs used to produce the final good, and the demand for the final good, are uniformly distributed over a geographic area. In the solution, the number (and geographic distribution) of plants will be such that the cost savings that would be realized using one plant fewer (simultaneously optimally readjusting the locations of the remaining plants) and operating all the remaining plants a little further down the declining portion of the average cost curve, is counterbalanced by the added cost of transportation and communication entailed by the increased average distance between plants. *In this one product, partial equilibrium setting, the degree of agglomeration is determined jointly by the interaction of economies of scale at the plant level, which work to create agglomeration by encouraging fewer larger plants, and transportation and communication costs, which work to limit agglomeration by encouraging more smaller plants.* Although reality is considerably more complex than this simple example, it nevertheless illustrates one of the fundamental mechanisms of economic geography.

THEORY OF MNE PLANT LOCATION: AGGLOMERATIONS & DISAGGLOMERATIONS

To appreciate the interaction of these forces more fully, consider the above example with two modifications: 1) many manufactured products rather than one, and 2) allow individuals to choose their locations in space. Imagine, then, a one-country world in which the country's population and its natural resources are, initially, uniformly distributed and all economic activity is agricultural. Assume, too, that the geographic distribution of the country's natural resources is fixed while that of its population is endogenous. In this pristine agricultural state, all economic activity is, in effect, hand-to-mouth and perfectly localized — virtually no resources are devoted to transportation and communication.

Now introduce the production of a single manufactured good. Of course, we suppose that there are economies of scale associated with the production of this good, and that the production of the good requires product-specific capital goods, product-specific human capital, and natural resources. Notice that the specific capital, both physical and human, necessarily dictates geographic inhomogeneities in economic activity and therefore require transport of something, and, of course, the need for some sort of communication. Broadly speaking, there are two possibilities. First, the population remains geographically dispersed. This requires that natural resources, goods in process, and final goods (but not agricultural goods) must be transported from specialized worker to specialized worker, and finally to the consumer of the finished good. (This sounds very much like the "putting out" system that prevailed in England prior to the industrial revolution.) Second, the specialized workers in manufacturing themselves, and all stages of the production process become concentrated in "cities". This second possibility eliminates the transportation of goods-in-process and the final goods consumed by the workers who produce them (and live) in the city. It does, however, necessitate the transportation of agricultural goods and natural resources to the city, and some finished goods from the city to consumers in the agricultural sector.

If there is only one (or a few) manufactured good(s), and if the bulk of the population is engaged in agricultural activity, then the population may remain geographically dispersed. If more and more manufactured goods are added, and the proportion of the population engaged in non-agricultural activity increases, agglomeration becomes increasingly plausible from an efficiency standpoint. As in the one good, partial equilibrium model, the model here is also driven by the interaction of economies of scale and the costs of transportation and communication. The important additional force in the many good model concerns economies in transportation and communication that can be had if many goods are produced in the same city. Agglomeration in the same city, of the people who produce different goods, but each of whom consumes many of the goods produced in the city, eliminates the need to transport the final and intermediate goods consumed by the city dwellers. These savings in the resources devoted to transportation and communications are economies of agglomeration across different goods that are external to the individual firms producing them. As more and more goods are produced in the economy, these external agglomeration economies make agglomerations increasingly viable, but because these are external economies, the agglomeration process may be slow to start and the resulting degree and pattern of agglomeration may not be optimal.

However it begins, once begun this geographic concentration tends to feed on and reinforce itself. As each city grows, it will support the production of progressively more products and services. But the production of the additional goods and services itself contributes to yet more concentration of population, permitting yet more products to achieve the economies of scale required to bring them into production. In other words, the process of agglomeration involves positive feedback. This mechanism also involves self-reinforcing growth in both the size of the city and the range of goods produced within it.

Of course there is negative feedback as well. As was stressed at the beginning of this section, the costs of transporting raw materials to cities also tends to limit city size, because as cities get larger and fewer in number, the average distance over which raw materials are transported to the city increases. (In the example here, population is held constant, so increasing average city size entails fewer, more dispersed cities.) Similarly, the average distance manufactured goods must be transported to rural consumers increases as city size increases, which also tends to limit city size. Also, population growth itself produces a variety of all too familiar congestion effects that also tend to limit growth.

PROPERTIES OF MODELS OF URBAN AGGLOMERATION

IN THE PREVIOUS SECTION we sketched a non-linear, dynamic model of agglomeration of economic activity with two sources of non-linearity: economies of scale in the production of individual goods, and economies of agglomeration. This sort of model has recently attracted the attention of economists and researchers in the biological and physical sciences, and therefore much is known about their properties. This section includes a discussion of some of these in the context of our model of agglomeration. For a wide ranging discussion in the context of models of technical change see Silverberg (1990).

Multiple Equilibria

The most important feature of these models is multiple equilibria. Our simple model of agglomeration provides two illustrations. First, given a number of cities in equilibrium, their locations are not unique. If the entire southern Ontario agglomeration is moved east by 10 or even 100 miles, it will tend to stay put. Second, the number and sizes of urban agglomerations are not unique. If we focus on one small region, it is possible for there to be one equilibrium in which the population is very small (no agglomeration of activity) and another in which it is very large. The possibility of multiple equilibria in this sort of model is intuitive. The glue that holds urban areas together is, in essence, a complex web of positive externalities among all the economic actors in the city. The more pervasive these externalities, the stronger the forces that hold an arbitrary agglomeration of economic activity together, and the more equilibria there tend to be.

No Invisible Hand

The corollary to the proposition that multiple equilibria exist, is that there is no force guiding the economy toward some preferred equilibrium. Also, there is no reason to believe that any of the equilibria are Pareto-efficient. In other words, there is no invisible hand guiding the economy to an equilibrium with the optimal number, size(s), and locational configuration of cities. This result is also intuitive. Optimality theorems employed by economists are invariably driven by assumptions of convexity (which rule out economies of scale) and lack of external economies (which rule out economies of agglomeration). Yet, cities and regional economies exhibit pervasive non-convexities and pervasive agglomeration externalities. Clearly, standard optimality theorems have no application in this sort of economy.

Tipping

In this model, small exogenous changes or shocks can have large effects, since small shocks can tip the model from one equilibrium to another. Also, a small change in any exogenous variable, including policy variables, can lead to large changes in the equilibrium values of the endogenous variables.

History or Path Dependence

Another immediate corollary of multiple equilibria is path dependence. If current values for the model's exogenous variables are fixed, many equilibria are possible. The state of equilibrium achieved by the model is, in effect, selected by the past history of those exogenous variables.

Bygones May Last Forever

As was argued earlier, the essential stuff of economies of scale is product-specific human and non-human capital. Some of this capital is, undoubtedly, location-specific as well. For example, the stock of housing and other buildings in cities is largely location-specific, and to the extent that labour is not internationally mobile, human capital is also location-specific. Location-specific capital of this sort is another source of path dependence.

Unravelling

Path dependence has clear implications for unravelling. In our model, a pro-agglomeration policy adopted by a small region early in the process of agglomeration can have irreversible effects that survive the elimination of the policy itself.

TRADE POLICY AND DISAGGLOMERATION

SO FAR, WE HAVE ARGUED that in order to understand the geographic concentration of economic activity that exists in the world today, one must seriously consider external economies of agglomeration. These external economies are pervasive and they imply cumulative causation, the existence of multiple equilibria, and a potential role for policy to influence the process of agglomeration.

Similar results are seen with endogenous technology that creates positive feedback loops with all the potential instabilities these imply (see for example, Silverberg, 1990). These models have some cautionary messages for policy makers, even though they cannot yet be tied closely to data. Where positive feedback loops exist, because of either scale economies or endogenous technological change, small causes can have large effects that are not reversible. Enforcing the wrong policy may cause some agglomeration to unravel. Reversing the policy may not stop, let alone reverse, the unravelling. What is even more worrying, is that the absence of any strong reaction to past doses of a particular policy is no guarantee that there will not be strong reactions to small doses of that policy in future. These threshold effects can be important. For example, firms may put up with a series of small increments in the basic tax rate without responding negatively. At some critical level, however, a few leaders may decide it is time to flee and the loss of their positive external economies may lead to a more general exodus.

RAISING TARIFFS TO CREATE AGGLOMERATIONS

THE EXTENT TO WHICH Sir John A. Macdonald's National Policy of high tariffs helped to create agglomerations of economic activity has long been debated by economic historians. Three points warrant mentioning, however. First, there was a significant amount of agglomeration long before tariffs, suggesting that, although agglomerations may have been encouraged by tariffs, they were not created by them. A key reference is Mackintosh (1967), including the Preface by Dales. Second, by protecting eastern manufacturing industries, the National Policy no doubt changed the nature of the agglomerations to be more goods- and less service-oriented than they otherwise would have been. This may also have contributed to their growth, resulting in larger agglomerations than would otherwise have been the case, at least at the time. Third (and as an offsetting consideration to the second point), long-term protection of oligopolistic industries in a small market can lead to an inefficient industry structure, and hence an industry that is limited in respect of both its international competitiveness and its size. The key reference here is Eastman & Stykolt (1967). When such protected firms are subjected to increased foreign competition, as might occur because of the globalization of markets caused by falling costs of transportation and communication, their inefficiencies, and lack of technological dynamism make it difficult for them to compete. If they lose out, then the agglomerations, of which they are a significant part, will shrink.

LOWERING TARIFFS AND DISAGGLOMERATION

IF RESTRICTIVE TRADE POLICIES create agglomeration, will free trade not lead to disagglomeration? We have no definitive answer, but some theoretical and empirical evidence suggests that unravelling may not be a significant problem.

Theory highlights at least three points. First, because the unilateral introduction and subsequent unilateral removal of trade barriers can shift the economy from a small-agglomeration equilibrium to a high-agglomeration equilibrium, agglomerations created by trade barriers do not necessarily require trade barriers for their support. Second, the sunk costs associated with agglomeration produce an important lock-in effect that works against unravelling — as noted above, bygones may have influences that last forever. Third, and perhaps most importantly, the FTA is bilateral and the NAFTA is multilateral. Although foreign firms gain enhanced access to Canadian markets, Canadian firms gain enhanced access to the markets of other member countries. Hence, the direct effects on agglomeration can go either way, and may very well be neutral.

Empirical evidence also identifies three main points. First, the purpose of infant industry protection is to establish industries *that can stand up to open competition after the requisite human capital, technological know-how and infra-structure are in place.*[1] Such policies appear to have been successful in, for example, the Japanese automobile industry and many industries in the NICs.

Second, the protection provided by the National Policy and subsequent protectionist initiatives reached its peak in 1935 and has since been reduced slowly, first as a result of bilateral treaties with the United States in the 1930s and later by successive rounds of GATT-negotiated tariff reductions starting in the 1950s. The Economic Council of Canada (1983) studied the adjustments to the substantial tariff reductions instituted by the Kennedy round of GATT negotiations and found no tendency for agglomerations of economic activity to break up. The evidence up to the end of the implementation phase of the Tokyo Round cuts in 1984 is reviewed in Lipsey & Smith (1985). No one in the debate surrounding the FTA succeeded in showing good economic reasons why the removal of the final tariffs on U.S.-Canada trade would produce structurally different results from those following the major reductions of tariff protection between 1935 and 1985.

Third, well over half of the tariff cuts called for by the FTA have already been made: some tariffs were removed immediately; some were eliminated by mutual agreement of the industries involved at the end of the first and second years of the FTA; more than 50 percent of those on five- and seven-year schedules have already been removed; and 40 percent of those remaining (those on a ten-year schedule) have been removed. The preliminary evidence from the first adjustments to the FTA is not dissimilar to the evidence for adjustments to earlier tariff cuts — although there appears to be more inter-industry adjustment this time. For example, Schwanen (1993) has shown that the main job losses have been in import-competing industries, and that exports to the United States (but not to the rest of the world) have increased since tariffs began to fall under the FTA. (This includes the period of the world recession in the early 1990s.) This evidence is consistent with the success of the Canadian government's policy objective of strengthening Canadian agglomerations by transferring resources from weak, tariff-protected industries to the stronger exporting industries.

NEW TECHNOLOGIES

IN CONSIDERING THE ISSUE of the profound effect of changes in technology on agglomerations of economic activity currently being experienced throughout the world, we deal first with the rapid globalization which has mainly been caused by lowered transport costs, the greater ease and declining costs of co-ordination, and falling tariffs. We then take a brief look at the production technologies themselves.

TRANSFER COSTS AND TARIFFS

WE USE THE TERM 'TRANSFER COSTS' to mean the costs of transport and co-ordination over distance plus tariffs. All of them contribute to the costs of producing in one region for use in another. Reductions in such costs set up two opposing tendencies related to globalization.

The first tendency has already been covered in the geographic analysis of location discussed above. We determined that economies of scale in production work to increase agglomeration while transfer costs work to limit it. Lowering transfer costs (including trade barriers) has the effect of encouraging the agglomeration of those types of production that are subject to significant scale economies.

The second tendency relates to the production of intermediate goods. To put it into perspective, consider a production method that uses a *centralized assembly plant and a number of decentralized parts producers.* This method of production, still in common use today, was introduced at the end of the 19th century in response to the development and widespread use of electric motors.[2] At the beginning of the 20th century when transport costs were high, all of the parts had to be produced nearby, so a model of fully-integrated production that ignored decentralized parts production was a reasonable approximation at a national level. However, due to reductions in actual shipping costs, co-ordination costs and tariffs, what we here call 'transfer costs', have fallen dramatically over the decades. As a result, parts production has been uncoupled geographically from the assembly operation to the extent that many parts can be produced almost anywhere in the world. Simple parts requiring unskilled labour are now often produced in low-wage LDCs; parts requiring more skilled labour are often made in high-wage advanced countries. This mechanism contributes to the decentralization of economic activity.

It should be noted that there is nothing contradictory in these two forces. One exploits large scale economies in the production of one good and leads to *fewer and larger economic units*, the size of the unit being limited by transport costs. The other exploits factor price differences around the world and leads to the *decentralization* of parts production, the amount of decentralization also being limited by transport and co-ordination costs. So, tariff reductions, which constitute one part of the reduction in transfer costs, set up two opposing forces. First, they lead to decentralization (in response to geographic differences in factor costs) whenever component parts of production (either goods or services) can be separated. Second, they lead to increased agglomeration whenever there are unexploited scale economies.

New Production Methods

MODERN TECHNOLOGY AND newly developed production techniques now make it possible for manufacturers to tailor many products to individual specifications. This means that long production runs of standardized product lines are no longer necessary to achieve low costs. Nonetheless, a large overall production volume is still needed to keep a flexible factory busy doing productive work. Scope economies are important even if scale economies related to standardized product lines are becoming less so.

The new manufacturing technology is evolving with enormous speed. In their first generation, computers did what was already being done, except that they did it faster and cheaper. In subsequent generations, computer technology continues to lead to new ways to do things and new ways to conceptualize what we do. According to Goldhar (1989), new computer-integrated production in manufacturing is smaller, faster, more integrated and more flexible than anything we now have in place. It will lead to firms taking control of the market place by "deliberately truncating the product life cycle, proliferating the range and complexity of products, and fragmenting the market". In his view we can, over the next decade, confidently expect to see the development of "manufacturing process technology that reduces the economic advantage of large scale factories and makes possible a greater variety of low volume manufacturing at a single location at low cost". (p. 262)

The new technology is also accomplishing a steady reduction of the percentage of product costs accounted for by direct labour. What will matter in the future is low capital cost, effective product design and process management. This means that the competitive advantage of low-cost labour will all but disappear and (the other side of the same coin) high-cost labour locations will not necessarily be at a competitive disadvantage.

Forces that will tend to stop production from agglomerating in only a few areas include the following: i) high competition among innovating companies with home bases in all three Triad areas; ii) the need to be close to consumers of rapidly evolving products (partly because feedback from end-users to producer is critical); and iii) the localization of markets and customization of products. Flaherty assesses the outcome of these forces as follows:

> ...world-class managers will have to operate in all three major industrial centers of the Triad — Western Europe, North America and Japan and the newly industrialising countries of the Far East. The fundamental reason for this is that in these centers companies with technology and employees of comparable sophistication will simultaneously and independently be generating new products and innovations as byproducts of doing business in their local environments. By combining the three courses for improvement, mangers can almost surely achieve products and operations superior to those of companies accessing only one. Conversely, without access to the new technological directions and products emerging in each location, a company operating in only one or two of the major industrial centers could easily be blindsided when confronted with a mature, version of a technology developed elsewhere. (Flaherty, 1989, 96.)

Considerations such as those given above lead us to expect *growing diversity in patterns of industrial location*, not the rise of a few massive agglomerations with low activity elsewhere. Goldhar supports this expectation in the following words:

> We will see examples of single global scale factories with high levels of scope economies serving fragmented, but global market segments and in other situations networks of specialized focus factories contributing to a single world standard, and very likely businesses with a proliferation of locally integrated factories; all existing together in a complex global business environment. There is no 'standard solution' to the search for the 'best' way to organize manufacturing for the international market. (Goldhar, 1989, 264.)

In the circumstances, any prediction pointing toward, or away from, regional agglomeration as a result of the new technologies would be rash at this time. What is clear, however, is that the *development* of new technologies will continue to be centred in a few highly innovative centres, while the overall *use* of new technologies in production facilities will be spread over much of the world — with concentration in some being offset by dispersal in others. This is in line with much of what we know about the new technologies: they seem to be leading to increasing concentration in some fields and to "small is beautiful" developments in other fields. (Later in this study we consider a related issue — the pattern of R&D concentration in MNEs.)

The above-noted tendencies suggest that any rational basis that might currently exist for opposing the reduction of tariffs against low wage countries such as Mexico on the grounds of heavy adjustment costs in high wage countries may diminish greatly over the next decade. They also suggest that there is a potential from many countries to take part in the globalization of production. To do so it is important that these countries develop good background policies in order to be attractive to FDI rather than rely on trade restrictions to support import-competing industries.

There is also a political concern. If the rate of change and structural adjustment accelerates, any trade liberalizing agreement that is negotiated is likely to be blamed for these changes just as in Canada the FTA was blamed for the consequences of the world recession in the early 1990s.

The Geographic Location of R&D in MNE Networks

IN THIS SECTION WE CONSIDER the international allocation of R&D and, more broadly, the allocation of technological capabilities within MNEs. One of our concerns is how far this critical input is likely to remain centralized in parent firms, particularly in the aftermath of trade liberalization. Another concern is the related effects of such centralization on agglomerations of economic activity.

Research and Development

BY WAY OF BACKGROUND, we consider why many countries, especially smaller ones, continue to rely on importing technology while simultaneously trying to develop their own technologies. Making firm-specific assets available to their affiliates abroad is seen by some as the key to MNE activity. The related transfer of technology can occur in many ways, which may or may not include capital transfers. To be "transferred" successfully, however, most methods depend on contacts between specific individuals or groups. Such methods include formal research and development, informal technical exchanges involving know-how, skills development of the affiliates' personnel, knowledge embodied in products and services and the accompanying technical specifications. Much of this knowledge is tacit, and is related to continuous improvement in the production and marketing process. Partly for these reasons, and partly for proprietary and strategic reasons, much of this knowledge may not be available at an early stage or fully through markets or alliances.[3] In such instances, its importation through affiliates and the consequent spillover to local firms can cause a significant gain to national welfare.

It is not difficult to understand why national governments seek to develop technological capabilities at the same time. Innovations are centered on firms but, to some extent, they are also specific to locations. Firms draw on universities and public aspects of a country's scientific and technological capabilities. Companies (even rivals) share information at a technical level, and many local influences, such as educational systems and business and labour practices, influence the technological development paths in each location. MNEs utilize such local innovation capacities to broaden and strengthen their home-based capacities (Cantwell, 1991, p. 34).[4] Grossman & Helpman (1990) undertook formal studies of models of trade and growth where productivity gains arise not only from cross-country differences in manufacturing efficiency, but also from differences in R&D efficiency. A country may wish to develop its local technological capabilities first in order to utilize efficiently the stock of world knowledge and, second, to spur innovations that are central to growth. In both cases, developing such capabilities efficiently is recognized as a major policy challenge, particularly when the new forms of production are knowledge-intensive.

Until recently, the evidence has been that MNEs retain their R&D mainly in their home countries. What debate there was centered on the degree to which local affiliates differ from domestic firms in their propensity to undertake R&D, or go beyond simple adaptation of products and processes developed in the parent firm. There was no debate, however, on the fact that such local affiliates were generally far less R&D-intensive than their parents, especially with respect to research (R) and the innovation-related aspects of development (D).

The evidence clearly suggests that MNEs do develop most of their R&D at home, but it also shows that this depends on a variety of factors, such as the size and the technical characteristics of the home and host countries.[5] Unfortunately, analysis of this topic is severely limited by the lack of overall data on the technological and innovative capacity of firms categorized by country of ownership. We have no option but to use data on R&D and patenting, which are likely to be far more concentrated by home country than is technological capacity (as understood in the evolutionary theory of the firm). None of this, incidentally, should be confused with the *use* of technology: sectors that do not produce technology may nonetheless be highly intensive users of technology.

THEORY OF MNE PLANT LOCATION: AGGLOMERATIONS & DISAGGLOMERATIONS

MNEs in two of the three largest home countries, Japan and the United States, concentrate very high degrees of R&D within their national boundaries. Japanese MNEs are believed to have spent less than 5 percent abroad in 1989. In that same year, U.S. multinationals had only 13 per cent of their R&D abroad, a figure which had risen slowly from about 6 percent in 1966. The U.S. figure shows wide variation by country and sector, however. Virtually all of the U.S. spending abroad was in developed countries, notably countries such as Germany and the UK, both of which have a substantial technological base. Also, U.S. R&D located abroad was well above the average in some sectors, such as household appliances and drugs (UN, 1992, p. 137 and Dunning, 1993, pp. 303-304).

MNEs in most other home countries, particularly those in smaller ones, appear to do a larger proportion of their R&D abroad. It has been estimated, for example, that the R&D intensity, measured by the number of R&D workers, was about the same in German affiliates in the developed countries as in domestic German manufacturers (Dörrenbächer and Wortmann, 1991). As an example of a smaller home country, the 15 largest Swiss MNEs had almost 40 percent of their R&D abroad in 1980, (Borner, et al., 1985, p. 3). Moreover, the trend to establish R&D units abroad has been accelerating, judging by a study of 167 of the world's largest industrial firms (Pearce & Singh, 1992). Prior to 1960 these firms established only 17 percent of their new R&D units abroad. This rose to 34 percent between 1960 and 1969 and 66 percent and 63 percent respectively over the next two decades.

Before proceeding further, it is necessary to distinguish between types of R&D and laboratories. We follow Pearce (1990, Ch. 8) in noting the familiar, if imprecise, distinctions between basic, applied and developmental research. He adds a useful distinction between development that is closely related to the *innovation* of a product or process, and development that focuses on the *adaptation* of products or processes to the needs of local markets.

Pearce's studies point to significant differences in the orientation and type of R&D engaged in by subsidiaries. Three types of subsidiary R&D laboratories are identified (see also Hood & Young, 1982, cited p. 310, Dunning, 1993). *Support laboratories* are the most common type, concentrating on adaptive development of the parent's products and processes whether for the local market or for export. *Locally integrated laboratories* focus more on innovation development than on adaptation. *Internationally independent* laboratories play a specialized role within the MNE's centralized R&D program. All three types of laboratory involve communication with, and co-ordination by, the MNE network, but the second type, which implies more independence, may also require more explicit performance. Pearce goes on to note that the support laboratory is most likely to appear where the product line of the subsidiary is either a *miniature replica* of the parent's or is *rationalized* (specialized). The locally integrated laboratory suits the replica subsidiary. It also suits those where the subsidiary has won a *product mandate*. In this case the subsidiary has not only the responsibility to produce a particular line (or lines) on a regional or global basis as in the rationalized subsidiary, it must also carry out a number of headquarters functions related to these lines. The internationally integrated laboratory may have little relationship to the subsidiary's production lines, although such a laboratory often carries a certain prestige from a scientific viewpoint because there is little adaptive research involved.[6]

What determines the division of R&D between a parent company and its subsidiaries? The discussion so far suggests that strong forces favour the centralization of R&D. Those forces begin with the historic development of firm-specific advantages within the home country, followed by the accumulated R&D and know-how that go with this developed in the laboratories, production processes and supporting industries of the home base. Economies of scale and agglomeration, and reduced co-ordination problems contribute to centralization. What promotes decentralization is the need to serve local markets or take advantage of local materials, the need to utilize (or at least to monitor) local technological skills, requirements to meet government incentives or pressures, and a variety of factors related to competitive strategy. If data on know-how rather than R&D were available, the links to local production would likely be more evident. In the Pearce & Singh sample, the responding executives assigned the largest weights to various market needs in explaining the existence of subsidiary R&D units, but the technological capability of the particular country was also an important factor. Other studies have confirmed the role of these and other factors (for example, Hirschey & Caves, 1980; Dunning, 1993:307-11). A strategic factor being noted increasingly is the desire by a number of more globalized firms to locate both production and research in each of the parts of the Triad.

In the process of liberalizing trade, the roles of both local subsidiaries and Canadian-owned MNEs are changing. At present, a critical issue for subsidiaries is how far their roles will be re-defined and the extent to which that redefinition will enable them to maintain or increase their technological capacity. Eden (1991:140) has noted that in manufacturing this largely involves the sub-assembly and final-assembly types of subsidiaries, where the potential for high-level technological production exists. Trade liberalization tends to reduce the role of miniature replica subsidiaries in favour of more specialized production, distribution and servicing activities within the MNE. Along with this, support laboratory functions are also reduced (although not necessarily the capability to monitor R&D). Of course, a subsidiary may also find an enhanced role for itself in niche or small-batch production in foreign markets. The MNE may also bring its entire network to bear from time to time to solve particular problems. Nonetheless, the logic of more specialized production by the subsidiary for global markets strongly suggests that its R&D functions will diminish — unless it can find a role as a lead producer or obtain a regional or world product mandate. It may also have a role to play for historic reasons; with vertical integration or because of a merger, a subsidiary may have a significantly different product line and/or R&D focus from that of its parent and other affiliates. With restructuring pressures, however, it will still have to work hard to retain or to develop its distinction.

The rapid rise of Canadian FDI abroad over the past two decades has presented Canadian-owned MNEs and the Canadian government with a particular challenge. Canada's substantial capacity in the primary resource and processing sector has encouraged investment abroad by Canadian firms with strong marketing and other skills not closely related to R&D as conventionally measured (Niosi, 1985; Rugman, 1987). Canadian FDI in the services sector is also increasing rapidly, in part to take advantage of liberalization of entry under the Canada-U.S. Free Trade Agreement. It is not yet clear, however, whether an increase in production abroad by Canadian manufacturers will lead to further development of R&D abroad, whether through the acquisition of technology-intensive firms or the re-allocation of some Canadian capacity abroad. All of this is happening to some extent, and as Eden (1993:25) notes, some Canadian subsidiaries in the United States may very well come to dominate their Canadian parents in production and perhaps even some headquarters functions.

Similar concerns have been expressed in other home countries, both large and small, from the United States to Sweden. Policy responses, such as limiting outward FDI, run the risk of damaging the competitive power of the firms they are intended to protect. After attempting a variety of restrictions (see Safarian, 1993:194 and 367) the governments of most industrial countries appear to have concluded that the risks are too great. The related point in theory is that the competitive powers of firms and of countries are not identical. Firms draw on the resources of locations other than the home country, even as they try to maintain the characteristics of the latter.

Product Mandates

A KEY QUESTION FOR CANADIANS is: how far will MNE restructuring lead to product mandates for Canadian subsidiaries? Given a product mandate, a subsidiary is assigned regional or global responsibility for a product or product line, including all the related R&D and perhaps other functions, such as international marketing, as well. There are, however, important limits to such mandates. The subsidiary remains part of an MNE network. It continues to draw on the knowledge resources of that network, including its research and marketing skills. Also, while it may have a broader base of responsibility than a specialized subsidiary, it is still accountable to the parent for its performance. Indeed, in consideration of the risks to the parent's management in decentralizing central functions (albeit selectively by product line) the subsidiary management is likely to be under considerable pressure to perform well if it is to keep its mandate.

A number of studies have documented the difficulties with which subsidiary managements must deal in moving to such mandates. Many are ill-prepared in terms of the experience and organization necessary for strategic planning. Much depends on having a significant technological or other capacity in the subsidiary or at least the potential for one. There is also the problem of persuading a sometimes sceptical management group in the parent company to follow this course. It has been well documented that local government support has played a role in some of the better-known cases.[7] The technological competence theory provides a pessimistic view of the prospects for the development of product mandates, at least for countries lacking a high degree of technological competence with respect to production (see Cantwell, 1991 and comment by Safarian). The theory contends that MNEs will internalize the research which is central to them in strategic terms, notably in core technologies. Where they locate R&D abroad, it will be in countries that have similar levels of technological competence and with complementary technologies. Thus, technological competence is likely to remain more concentrated than competence in production and assembly.

There are several reasons for considering this view to be overly pessimistic. First, the argument may be more relevant to manufacturing than to other sectors where Canada's comparative advantage is more evident. Second, the view may be too aggregative even for manufacturing, in the sense that a country can have advantages in some sectors that support mandating, while technological opportunities may cluster in a way that benefits such a country (or some of its regions) if its investments in human capital, organization and infrastructure are such as to allow it to take advantage of these opportunities. Third, 'globalization' has been interpreted by some firms as requiring more emphasis on developing international sources of competitive advantage along with joint exploration of such possibilities. In such circumstances there should be scope for regional or global mandates as well as specialization as such.

Some of the factors that determine the scope for product mandates, as distinct from specialization, are brought out in two studies. Etemad & Dulude (1986) used patenting data to study 84 subsidiaries in Ontario and Quebec, each of which had at least one product mandate. These data suggest that subsidiaries with a capability for independent research are more likely to be part of an MNE which itself has a high technological capability. The data also suggest that such subsidiaries are also more likely to be part of a U.S.-controlled firm than one controlled overseas. Such subsidiaries are also more likely to occur when the subsidiaries and the parent firms are large in absolute terms, when the subsidiary is large relative to the parent, and when there are many subsidiaries in the global network..

Roth & Morrison (1992) analyzed these issues in the context of a set of manufacturing industries where a high degree of globalization exists. Using questionnaires involving 125 subsidiaries in six countries, including Canada, they determined that a subsidiary is more likely to have a global mandate: a) when the primary activities in the value chain are located in several countries, but the support activities (such as R&D, information systems, and management of capital) are in one site; b) when the proportion of products similar to those produced elsewhere in the MNE falls; and c) when its management, relative to the management in other subsidiaries, has expertise on issues of strategic flexibility, in contrast with expertise managing various types of interdependencies. Several other determinants often noted in the literature were not supported by their tests. These include the relative size of the subsidiary's R&D and its competency (compared to other subsidiaries), in manufacturing, R&D and marketing. This research is preliminary: finer specifications and further research may resolve some of the apparent contradictions.

There are strong pressures to maintain headquarters-type functions such as R&D in the home country. Trade liberalization and the smaller role for miniature replica subsidiaries will also tend to reduce local support laboratories. This is particularly important for a country like Canada, given the appeal of the United States as a centre for R&D and the exceptionally slow decentralization of research by U.S. multinationals. Nevertheless, the evidence clearly suggests that significant decentralization of R&D has already occurred for a number of other home countries and for some types of industries. While most formal R&D laboratories will continue to be concentrated in home countries, process developments associated with an evolutionary approach to investment still offer scope for significantly increased decentralization. The global corporation is unlikely to overlook the possibility of utilizing a key knowledge resource wherever it is located, particularly in view of the declining costs of coordinating such activities. In these circumstances, there is a role for smaller countries especially in attracting product mandates where their technological and other capabilities are attractive.

Conclusions

THE FOLLOWING SUMMARIZES the main themes of this paper and our tentative conclusions.

- Theories of agglomeration, generally, are based on the interaction between scale economies in production and transport costs. Models incorporating such forces typically display agglomeration effects, multiple equilibria, path dependency, sensitivity to small disturbances, non-reversibilities, and other characteristics that are currently attracting the attention of economists.

- These characteristics suggest that current agglomerations and comparative advantages may owe as much to past policies as to impersonal economic and physical forces. There is no doubt that policies can have large effects, and that in some countries they have had large effects. What is in doubt is whether we know enough to influence the future in predictable ways by using policies designed to create specific comparative advantages and encourage specific agglomeration.

- The extent to which protectionist policies contributed to the buildup of industrial agglomerations in Canada in the past, as they no doubt did in many of the NICs, is subject to debate. Wrenching readjustments due to such forces as the FTA, globalization and new technologies, are currently being made in the Canadian manufacturing sector. The contribution of the FTA is difficult to disentangle but there is no strong evidence that the agglomerations themselves will disappear. Path dependency, due to accumulated human and physical capital, well-developed institutions and attitudes, and more traditional sources of comparative advantage (such as climate and natural resources) suggest that it would take strong, sustained shocks to undo well-established agglomerations of Canadian industrial activity. Policy makers cannot, however, take shelter behind what is unlikely. The theory is clear in its message that thresholds can be passed, and that beyond those thresholds a cumulative unravelling of agglomerations is possible; if such a process is allowed to begin, it may be impossible to reverse it with marginal policy changes.

- The continued rapid development of the new knowledge-based technologies will have major effects on agglomerations and hence on the location of investment in countries such as Canada. The new technologies are only one of the many forces exerting pressure toward fewer and bigger agglomerations while, at the same time, pushing toward more decentralization (particularly in parts manufacturing). The net effect appears to be preserving, even enhancing, the niches available for smaller countries that have the requisite human capital to participate in the new wave of manufacturing production.

- Trade liberalization is continuing to exert pressures to centralize R&D, particularly as the role of branch plants and subsidiaries is diminished. In contrast, a decentralization of R&D seems to be occurring in some types of industry; the geographic availability of human capital, the specialized demands of local markets, and the need to have development capacity for new products near customers, are all working in this direction — with more or less force, depending on the type of product and the organization of the company producing it.

- These trends do not point to the inevitable economic decline of smaller advanced industrial countries assuming, of course, that those countries can provide good conditions for production and for R&D. Policies that provide for such conditions include those that emphasize human capital, competitive factor prices, favourable tax regimes, and attractive background conditions for international investment. The value of other, more focused, policies is still being debated. Given the strength and complexity of the forces operating, there is much to be said for a policy framework that gets the background conditions right and then lets private decisions determine specific investment and trade flows.

Endnotes

1 Modern analysis of the economics of endogenous technological change with costly and difficult diffusion due to such things as the tacitness of much technological knowledge, provides a richer analysis of infant industry tariff protection than does the text-book analysis based on the desire to import given tehcnology where the only barrier is static scale economies.
2 The size of each parts producer is influenced by its scale effects.
3 The word 'may' is used intentionally here to allow for apparent exceptions, such as Japan for a period following the Second World War.
4 These items are developed at length by the evolutionary approach to technological change (for example, see Dosi et al., 1988). Also, a number of authors have challenged Porter (1990), arguing that MNEs draw on much more than their home base for competitive power. See, for example, the 1993 special issue of *Management International Review* devoted to this theme.
5 There is a good overview of the issue in Dunning (1993, Ch. 11). See also McFetridge (ed.) 1991, especially the articles noted on p. xii. Also, two notable recent books are Pearce (1989) and Casson (1991).
6 Pearce notes that an overseas R&D facility can support functions other than those noted here, including a window on local capabilities which may be of use within the MNE group.
7 See, for example, D'Cruz (1986), Bishop & Crookell (1985), Daly & MacCharles (1986), and Rugman (1986).

Acknowledgement

GRATEFUL ACKNOWLEDGEMENT is made of helpful comments received from Rachel McCulloch, Lorraine Eden and Industry Canada staff on an earlier draft.

THEORY OF MNE PLANT LOCATION: AGGLOMERATIONS & DISAGGLOMERATIONS

BIBLIOGRAPHY

Akerman, Johan Gustev, "Realkapital und Kapitalzing: Hept I." Stockholm: Centraltryckeriet, 1923.

Borner, S. et al. "Global Structural Change and International Competition Among Industrial Firms: the Case of Switzerland." *Kyklos*, 38, (1985):77-103.

Cantwell, J. "The Theory of Technological Competence and its Application to International Production." In *Foreign Investment, Technology and Economic Growth*, The Investment Canada Research Series. Edited by D. McFetridge. Calgary: University of Calgary Press, 1991, pp. 33-67.

Cantwell, J. "A Survey of Theories of International Production." In *The Nature of the Transnational Firm*. Edited by C. N. Pitelis and R. Sugden. London: Rutledge, 1991.

Coase, Ronald. "The Nature of the Firm.", *Economica* 4, (November 1937):386-405.

D'Cruz, J. "Strategic Management of Subsidiaries." In *Managing the International Subsidiary*. Edited by Etemad and Dulude. London: Croom Helm, 1986.

Dörrenbächer, C. and M. Wortmann. "The Internationalization of Corporate Research and Development." *Intereconomics*, 26, 3, (May/June 1991):139-44.

Eastman, H.C. and S. Stykolt. *The Tariff and Competition in Canada*. Toronto: Macmillan, 1967.

Eaton, B. Curtis and Richard G. Lipsey. "Increasing Returns and All That." Discussion Paper, Department of Economics, Simon Fraser University, 1993.

Economic Council of Canada. *The Bottom Line: Technology, Trade and Income Growth*. Ottawa: Supply and Services, 1983, p. 116.

Eden, L. "Multinational Responses to Trade and Technology Changes: Implications for Canada." In *Foreign Investment, Technology and Growth*, The Investment Canada Research Series. Edited by D. McFetridge. Calgary: University of Calgary Press, 1991, pp. 133-72.

_____. "Multinationals in North America: After NAFTA," (First draft), mimeo, March 10, 1993.

Etemad, H., and L.S. Dulude (eds). *Managing the Multinational Subsidiary*, London: Croom Helm, 1986.

Flaherty, T. "International Sourcing: Beyond Catalog Shopping and Franchising." In *Managing International Manufacturing*. Edited by K. Ferdows. Amsterdam: North-Holland, 1989, p. 96.

Goldhar, J.D. "Implications of CIM for International Manufacturing." In *Managing International Manufacturing*. Edited by K. Ferdows. Amsterdam: North-Holland, 1989, p. 262.

Helpman, E. and P.R. Krugman. *Market Structure and Foreign Trade*. Cambridge, Mass: M.I.T. Press, 1985.

Hirschey, R.C. and R.E. Caves. "International Decentralization of Research and Transfer of Technology by Multinational Enterprises." Harvard University Discussion Paper 779, 1980.

Hood N. and S. Young. "U.S. Multinational R and D: Corporate Strategies and Policy Implications in the U.K." *Multinational Business*, 2, (1982):10-23.

Krugman, Paul. *Geography and Trade*. Cambridge, Mass: M.I.T. Press, 1991.

Lipsey, Richard and Murray Smith. *Taking the Initiative: Canada's Trade Options in a Turbulent World*. Toronto: C.D. Howe Institute, 1985.

Mackintosh, W.A. *The Economic Background of Dominion Provincial Relations*. Carleton Library #13. Toronto: McClelland and Stewart, 1967.

McFetridge, D.G. (ed). *Foreign Investment, Technology and Economic Growth*, The Investment Canada Research Series. Calgary: University of Calgary Press, 1991.

Niosi, J. *Canadian Multinationals*. Toronto: Between the Lines, 1985.

Pearce, R.D. and S Singh. "Internationalization of R and D Among the World's Leading Enterprises." In *Technology, Management and International Business*. Edited by O. Grandstrand et al. Chichester: John Wiley and Sons, 1992.

Pearce, R.D. *The Internationalization of Research and Development*. London: Macmillan, 1990.

Roth, K. and A.J. Morrison. "Implementing Global Strategy: Characteristics of Global Subsidiary Mandates." *Journal of International Business Studies*. Fourth Quarter, 23, 4, (1992):715-35.

Rugman, A.M. *Outward Bound: Canadian Direct Investment in the United States*. Toronto and Washington: C.D. Howe Institute and National Planning Association, 1987.

Safarian, A.E. "Direct Investment Strategies and the Canada-United States Free Trade Agreement." In *The Dynamics of North American Trade and Investment*. Edited by W. Reynolds et al. Berkley: Stanford University Press,1991a.

————. *Multinational Enterprise and Public Policy*. Aldershott: Edward Elgar Publishing, 1993, pp. 194-367.

Schwanen, Daniel "Were the Optimists Wrong on Free Trade?" Toronto: C.D. Howe Institute, Commentary No. 37, 1993.

Silverberg, Gerald. "Modeling Economic Dynamics and Technical Change." In *Technical Change and Economic Theory*. Edited by G. C. Dosi et al. London: Pinter Publishers, 1990.

United Nations. *World Investment Report: Transnational Corporations as Engineers of Growth*. New York: United Nations, 1992.

Vernon, R. "The Location of Economic Activity." In *Economic Analysis and Multinational Enterprise*. Edited by J. Dunning. London: Allen and Unwin, 1974.

Williamson, Oliver E. *Markets and Heirarchies: Analysis and Anti-Trust Implications*. Glencoe, Illinois: Free Press, 1975.

[16]

Increasing returns, indivisibility, and all that*

B. Curtis Eaton and Richard G. Lipsey

I. Introduction

Austrian economists, enquiring into the *reason d'etre* of capital goods, theorized about a two-stage production process. Robinson Crusoe first makes a capital good then uses the services of that capital good in the production of a good for his consumption. Modern firms do what Robinson Crusoe did: first they make capital goods (or have them made), then they use the services of these 'intermediate goods' to make consumers' goods. But modern theorists have not followed the lead of the Austrian School. In the one output case, for example, the modern theory of production focuses on a single-stage production function that expresses the flow of output as a function of flows of inputs. We argue that the modern suppression of the two-stage production process, which Austrians put in the forefront of their theorizing, has given rise to misunderstandings and confusions about the existence and nature of scale effects.

In this paper we return to the Austrian question and ask: Why do we see capital goods, goods that embody a stock of services, instead of pure service flows? This question leads us to explore the technology of producing individual capital goods. We use the results of this exploration to resolve a long standing puzzle relating to the theory of the firm. The puzzle concerns an apparent conflict between the pure theory of production and the empirical observation of economies of scale. On one hand, there is a strong *a priori* case for the proposition that production functions necessarily exhibit constant returns to scale. If, given input vector x, output y is the maximum output a firm can produce, then it seems natural to assume that, given input vector λx, the maximum output the firm can produce is λy. On the other hand, there is a large body of apparently contradictory evidence concerning the existence of scale economies. The most convincing evidence regarding economies of scale is the simple observation that goods are produced in firms. To a student of industrial organization, the very existence of firms is evidence that minimum efficient scale of production is positive, a result that is inconsistent with constant returns to scale. Let y^* denote minimum efficient scale. If $y^* > 0$, it is necessarily the case that $C(y^*) < 2C(y^*/2)$. Yet with constant returns to scale, fixed input prices, and perfectly divisible inputs, $C(y) = 2C(y/2)$ for all $y > 0$.

If we accept that production functions are homogeneous of degree 1, how can we account for economies of scale? One popular answer is exogenous indivisibility. See, for example, Baumol's entry in *The New Palgrave* (1987) on *indivisibilities* in which he makes the point that indivisibility gives rise to both economies of scale and scope. To put our approach in perspective, it is useful to discuss in some detail precisely how exogenous indivisibility resolves the puzzle. Suppose a certain input flow is extracted from firm specific, indivisible capital goods with the following description: each capital good provides an exogenous service flow $x' > 0$ over an exogenous infinite time horizon. Suppose too that the time invariant price of the capital good is P; then, the minimum price per unit of service flow is rP/x', where r is a time invariant interest rate. Finally, suppose that all other input flows are bought on competitive markets at time invariant prices, and that the underlying technology relating flows of inputs to the flow of output exhibits constant returns to scale. We are interested in properties of the cost function $C(y)$ that gives the minimum discounted present value of the cost of producing flow of output y over an infinite time horizon. Now, suppose we solve the cost minimization problem, ignoring the indivisibility constraint and supposing that the price per unit of the capital service in question is rP/x', and let $x^*(y)$ be the associated input demand function for capital services and $C^*(y)$ the associated cost function. Given constant returns to scale, both $x^*(y)$ and $C^*(y)$ will be proportional to y. Let y' denote the smallest output such that $x^*(y') = x'$. Output y' is the smallest output such that the indivisibility constraint is non-binding, hence $C(y') = C^*(y')$. Further, the indivisibility constraint is non-binding for any output y if and only if y is a positive integer multiple of y'. In other words,

$$C(y) = (y/y')C^*(y') = C^*(y) \quad \text{if } (y/y') \text{ is a positive integer}$$

$$C(y) > (y/y')C^*(y') = C^*(y) \quad \text{otherwise}$$

There are then economies of scale (more properly, increasing returns to outlay) up to the first point where the indivisibility constraint is non-binding, and thereafter alternating regions of diseconomies and economies of scale (or decreasing and increasing returns to outlay). We seen then that exogenous indivisibility generates the familiar scalloped shaped average cost function explored by Joseph (1938) and later by a number of authors, including Samuelson (1967). In the limit, as y gets arbitrarily large, there are approximate constant returns to outlay.

Three remarks about this exercise are in order. First, one must carefully describe the capital good one has in mind. We looked at a capital good which provided an exogenous flow of services over an exogenous, infinite time horizon. Had we chosen another sort of capital good the details of the exercise would have been different, but the general message the same. There are many possible sorts of exogenous indivisibility, but all imply increasing returns to outlay up to the first point at which the indivisibility constraint is non-binding. Second, since any capital good embodies a stock of capital services, to assess the potential for increasing returns to outlay one must look at an intertemporal production process. This is particularly true of firm specific capital goods – goods that are made to order to suit the firm's specific needs. In the above exercise, we focused on a time invariant flows of output over an infinite time horizon, but clearly there are other interesting exercises.

Finally, and most importantly, while not disputing the logic of this and related exercises, we observe that exogenous indivisibility does not adequately resolve the economies of scale puzzle for the simple reason that indivisibility is not in fact exogenous, but rather the result of conscious choice.

In this paper we conceptualize production as a two stage process. In stage one a firm specific, indivisible, capital good is produced, and in stage two a service flow from this capital good is combined with other pure flows to produce a flow of output. For clarity, we refer to the good produced in stage two as the final good. Loosely, the specific capital good produced in stage one can be thought of as the firm's plant and equipment, or plant for short. For reasons that will become clear, we assume throughout the paper that the flows of inputs used to produce a specific capital good and the other input flows used in the production of final goods are purchased on perfect markets at time invariant prices.

This two stage conception of production forces us to deal with two technologies. First, there is the familiar technology for producing the final good, that maps from flows of inputs to a flow of output of the final good; we take the position that constant returns to scale is appropriate for this technology. Then there is the unfamiliar technology for the individual capital good, or plant. This latter technology is the focus of most of our analysis, and it is here that we discover the fundamental nonconvexity that allows us to resolve the puzzle discussed above. Loosely speaking, we discover that there would be no capital goods if there were constant returns to scale in the activity of embodying a stock of services in an indivisible capital good. Much of what we have to say about this second technology applies more generally to any capital good, but for clarity we focus on firm specific capital goods.

To clarify issues we distinguish at the outset three distinct ways in which output of final goods can be changed.

Operation 1, altering the scale of input flows in stage two: We take the position that the technology for stage two of the production process, in which flows of inputs are used to produce a flow of output, exhibits constant returns to scale. This does not, however, rule out the possibility of economies of scale, since costs are determined in part by the technology for specific capital goods.

Operation 2, replication: The second operation is replication. Given a plant and a feasible production plan for the plant over time interval I, we can in principle double the flow of output at each time t in interval I by producing an exact copy of the plant and adopting its production plan. We accept that doubling output by replication doubles costs.

Operation 3, reconfiguration: In contrast to replication, reconfiguration entails the redesign or choice of a new plant, one that is optimal for the intended production plan. Suppose we are given a production plan over time interval I, and a plant that is optimal for that production plan. Given enough time, if we want to alter the flow of output in the production plan by proportion $\lambda > 0$, we can chose a new plant (or plants) that is optimal for the altered production plan. We will argue the following: (i) There is no *a priori* reason to suppose that the technology that drives reconfiguration, that is, the technology of specific capital goods, exhibits constant returns to scale. Hence, there is no reason to suppose that total costs of production entailed by reconfiguration necessarily change by proportion λ. (ii) The very existence of specific capital goods reveals a fundamental nonconvexity in the technology for such goods; we refer to this as the *fundamental nonconvexity of real capital theory*. Hence, for some production plans and some factors of proportionality $\lambda > 1$, reconfiguration entails costs that increase by less than proportion λ.

Reconfiguration of plant is meant to capture the essence of what earlier writers referred to as choice of a different technique (see Alchian (1959) for example). Clearly, reconfiguration is the economically interesting way to alter output since it permits the other options but is not restricted to them.

Our analysis is in the spirit of Gustav Akerman's (1923) analysis of the choice of durability, and Wicksell's (1934) reconstruction of Akerman's work. These works provide a clear foundation for a theory of endogenous indivisibility. Yet to our knowledge nothing has yet been built on that foundation.

We use a revealed preference approach. We observe that real capital goods have certain features – for example, it takes time to produce such goods – and we use these features in conjunction with a cost-minimizing hypothesis to derive restrictions on the technology for creating indivisible capital goods. Throughout we ignore strategic reasons for creating and holding capital goods and we assume a frictionless economy.

II. Pure capital goods

The essential feature of any capital good is that it embodies a stock of capital services. Given a particular capital good, one interesting question concerns the various ways in which the stock of embodied services can be extracted from the good. The answer to this question will, of course, depend on the capital good in question. To completely describe any capital good, one must write down all of the time profiles of capital services that can be extracted from it. Having put the matter in this way, it is clear that this descriptive task is non-trivial. We adopt a parametric approach to the problem of describing capital goods. We suppose that there are a number of classes of capital goods, and that in any one class a good can be described by specifying the values of a small number of descriptive parameters for that class. In this section, we focus on a class of capital goods that are described by just one parameter, the stock of embodied services. We call these goods pure capital goods. In the next section we look at a two parameter class of capital goods.

A *pure capital good* is one that is completely described by the stock of capital services embodied in it. Denote the stock of embodied services by S, and let s(t), $t' \le t \le t''$, denote a time profile of capital services over time interval [t',t'']. A pure capital good with embodied stock of services S can deliver any time profile of services s(t) such that

$$\int_{t'}^{t''} s(t) dt \le S \qquad (1)$$

We use the term *good* S to refer to a pure capital good with stock S of embodied capital services. Notice that a user who wanted a flow of services s(t) = 1 from t' = 0 to t'' = 100, would be indifferent between good S = 100, provided at t = 0, and a package containing good S = 75, at t = 0, and good S = 25, at t = 75. (Recall that we are ignoring possible strategic reasons for holding stocks of capital services.)

Although real capital goods that can be completely described by the stock of embodied services are rare, the Canadian arctic is littered with the 'skeletons' of one such good. A 55 gallon drum with some gasoline in it is the capital good we have in mind, and the gasoline itself the stock of embodied services. Ignoring the facts that the gasoline slowly deteriorates with age and that the size of the tap on the drum puts an upper limit on the rate of extraction, any such capital good can, for all practical purposes, be completely described by the quantity of gasoline in the drum. Storage batteries provide another example.

One revealed feature of the technology for capital goods is that it takes time to produce them. To capture this feature of the technology, we suppose that a capital good is produced using flows of n inputs over a time interval [B,T], where B is the beginning date and T the terminal date of construction. Let

$$X(t;B,T) = [x_1(t), x_2(t),\ldots, x_n(t)] \quad t \in [B,T] \qquad (2)$$

denote flows of n inputs over time interval [B,T]. For simplicity, we sometimes write $X(t)$ for $X(t;B,T)$, and we call $X(t)$ or $X(t;B,T)$ an *input bundle*. We call a pair $(S,X(t;B,T))$ a *production plan*. The production possibilities set for an indivisible capital good, Ω is the set of feasible production plans. In other words,

$$\Omega = \{S,X(t;B,T))|X(t;B,T) \text{ will produce good } S\}. \qquad (3)$$

To ensure that there is a solution to the cost minimization problem defined below, we assume that Ω is a closed set. In addition we assume that the production of good $S = 0$ requires no inputs. In other words, letting X^0 denote the input bundle in which all flows are 0 for all t, we assume that production plan $(0,X^0)$ is in Ω. We assume that all input flows used in the production of capital goods are bought on perfect markets. In addition, we assume time invariant prices, $w = (w_1,\ldots,w_n)$, and that the discount or interest rate r, is positive and time invariant.

Let $C(X(t;B,T))$ be the value at time T (the date at which construction of the capital good is completed) of input bundle $X(t;B,T)$. Then

$$C(X(t;B,T)) = \int_B^T wX(t;B,T)e^{r(T-t)}dt \qquad (4)$$

Now define $\psi(S)$ in the following way

$$\psi(S) = \min \{C(X(t;B,T))|(S,X(t;B,T)) \text{ is in } \Omega\}. \qquad (5)$$

The minimization is accomplished by choosing a starting date B and the flows of all inputs over time interval [B,T], but not a terminal date T. $\psi(S)$ is the minimum value of all the resources used to produce good S, evaluated at time T, the point in time the good is finished. Although T is exogenous, it is not an argument of $\psi(S)$ because input prices, the discount rate, and the technology are assumed to be time invariant. Notice that $\psi(0) = 0$ since $(0,X^0)$ is in Ω.

Economies of planning and coordination

One restriction on Ω is immediate. Suppose input bundle $X'(t;B',T)$ is cost minimizing for good S, and consider input bundles $X''(t;B,T)$ that satisfy the following inequality:

$$\int_B^{t'} X''(t;B,T)dt \leq \int_B^{t'} X'(t;B',T)dt \quad \forall t' \in [B',T] \tag{6}$$

with a strict inequality for some t'.[1] Clearly,

$$C(X''(t;B,T)) < C(X'(t;B',T)). \tag{7}$$

Hence, production plan $(S,X''(t;B,T))$ is not in Ω. In particular, bundles which have the same stock of services as $X'(T;B',T)$ and also satisfy inequality (6) are not in Ω. We can put this another way. The fact that it takes time to produce real capital goods is evidence of economies associated with planning and coordinating the flow of inputs. Importantly, when good S is produced over a time period that is sufficiently short, it cannot be produced at cost $\psi(S)$.

The fundamental nonconvexity

Now consider a mental experiment. Suppose at time $t = 0$, an arbitrary point in time, we actually see a pure capital good produced by a firm for its own use, good $S' > 0$, and suppose too that the firm is a cost minimizer. What can we infer about the cost function ψ and the production possibilities set Ω from the observation that $S' > 0$?

Let $s'(t)$ denote the time profile of services that the firm anticipates from good S'. Although we cannot observe the time profile itself, we can infer its existence from the fact that the firm is a cost minimizer. Ultimately, it is not the capital good itself that the firm wants to acquire, but rather the flow of services that the good will deliver. There are, of course, any number of ways the firm could acquire $s'(t)$, the desired flow of services. We get restrictions on ψ and Ω from the revealed preference argument that good S' must be no more costly than any other way of getting flow $s'(t)$.

Let t be the point in time such that the cumulative service flow extracted from the good is $S'/2$. The firm could acquire service flow $s'(t)$ by finishing a good of description $S'/2$ at $t = 0$, and another identical good at $t = t'$. The discounted cost of doing so, evaluated at $t = 0$, is $\psi(S'/2)[1+e^{-rt'}]$. Hence, by revealed preference,

$$\psi(S') \leq \psi(S'/2)[1 + e^{-rt'}] \tag{8}$$

But, when $r > 0$, $e^{-rt'} < 1$, so we get:

$$\psi(S') < 2\psi(S'/2). \tag{9}$$

Since $\psi(0) = 0$, this experiment reveals a nonconvexity in $\psi(S)$, one manifestation of the fundamental nonconvexity for pure capital goods.

The nonconvexity in $\psi(S)$ can be traced to a corresponding nonconvexity in the production possibilities set Ω. Let $X'(t)$ denote the cost minimizing input bundle for good S'. Inequality (9) implies that production plan $(S'/2,X'(t)/2)$ is not in Ω. Yet $(S'/2,X'(t)/2)$ is a convex combination of $(0,X^0)$ and $(S',X'(t))$ both of which are in Ω. Hence, Ω is not a convex set.

The same sort of revealed preference argument can be constructed to support the following:

$$\psi(S') < I\psi(S'/I) \quad \forall \text{ positive integers } I > 1. \tag{10}$$

Hence, $(S'/I,X'(t)/I)$ is not in Ω, although it is a convex combination of production plans that are in Ω, another manifestation of the fundamental nonconvexity.

There is another way to put the point. Assume for purposes of argument that Ω is convex. Then, whenever $(S,X(t))$ is in Ω, so also is $(S/2,X(t)/2)$. But this implies that the left side of (8) is strictly greater than the right side, so long as $r > 0$. In words, Ω convex and $r > 0$ imply that $S > 0$ is inconsistent with cost minimization. Hence, given a positive interest rate and cost minimizing firms, the very existence of pure capital goods requires that we drop the assumption that Ω is convex.

In setting out this mental experiment we supposed for simplicity that the firm produced good S' for its own use. It is trivial to extend the experiment to encompass the case in which the firm produces the capital good, not for its own use, but for sale. To do so, think of the firm as selling not good S', but the service flow $s'(t)$. If the firm chooses to provide $s'(t)$ by producing good S', we are led by the same route to the same conclusions: necessarily, $\psi(S)$ is not a convex function, nor is Ω a convex set. We refer to the nonconvexities we have outlined as manifestations of a *fundamental nonconvexity* because the very existence of good $S > 0$, in combination with rationality and stationarity assumptions, dictates the existence of a nonconvexity.

The returns to scale controversy
To put this result in context of the controversy concerning returns to scale, it is useful to rewrite the technology P in a way that looks like a standard production function. Define the function $G(X(t;B,T))$ as follows:

$$G(X(t;B,T)) = \begin{array}{l}\text{maximum stock of capital services that can be}\\\text{embodied in an indivisible capital good, given input}\\\text{bundle } X(t;B,T)\end{array} \tag{11}$$

The fundamental nonconvexity implies that $G(X(t;B,T))$ exhibits increasing returns to scale for at least some input bundles: clearly, $G(X'(t)) = S'$, while $(S'/2,X'(T)/2)$ not in Ω implies that $G(X'(t)/2) < S'/2$; hence $G(X'(t)) > 2G(X'(t)/2$. This appears to violate the proposition that we accepted for production of final goods: the proposition that production functions exhibit constant returns to scale (are homogeneous of degree 1). But, $G(X(t;B,T))$ is not, in the usual sense of the term, a production function since a change in the input bundle result in a charge in the description of the indivisible good that is produced, not in a charge in the quantity produced of a good of fixed description. The function $G(X(t;B,T))$ gives us the maximum quantity of capital services that can be produced, given that the services are embodied in one capital good. If we start with input bundle X(t;B,T) and use it to produce a good with G(X(t;B,T)) units of embodied services, when we double the input bundle we are not replicating what we initially did, rather we are producing quite a different capital good, one with a stock of embodied services equal to G(2X(t;B,T). Hence, there is no *a priori* reason to think that G(X(t;B,T)) should be homogeneous of degree 1.

Economies of scale
So far we have argued two points about pure capital goods. (i) There is no *a priori* reason to think that Ω is a convex set. (ii) Were we to see such a good, we would be forced to infer that Ω is not a convex set. Now we want to argue that the fundamental nonconvexity necessary to account for the existence of pure capital goods implies economies of scale in the production of the final good, even though the underlying technology for producing final goods exhibits constant returns to scale.

Since a pure capital good embodies a stock of capital services, to show economies of scale in the production of final goods that use the services provided by a pure capital good, we must consider the production of a stock of final goods as well. But we want to employ the familiar constant returns to scale flow production function for final goods. Hence, we are forced to look at some sort of intertemporal production plan for final goods. The choice of a specific intertemporal production plan is, of course, arbitrary. We choose to look at a production plan in which a constant flow of the final good is produced over an infinite time horizon because this production plan is what one would expect in a state of intertemporal equilibrium for the economy as a whole. It will be clear, we hope, that the points we make are not driven by this choice.

We imagine a situation in which a flow of output y (of good Y) is produced using a flow of labor, n, and a flow of capital services, s, according to the following production function:[2]

$$y = f(n,s) \qquad (12)$$

We assume that f(n,s) is homogeneous of degree 1 in (n,s) and that both inputs are essential. Let V(y) be the discounted cost of producing flow of output y over an infinite time horizon. We want to show that when the firm uses pure capital goods to produce the required flow of capital services,

$$V(ay) < aV(y) \quad \forall \, a > 1, y > 0 \qquad (13)$$

In other words, we want to show that when pure capital goods are used to produce capital flows that are inputs into the production of good Y, there are universal increasing returns to outlay, or universal economies of scale, even though the production function for good Y exhibits constant returns to scale.

The first thing we need to note is that a cost-minimizing firm will never have more than one capital good at any point in time. Suppose, for purposes of argument, that it had two capital goods over some interval of time. Whatever the intended time profile of capital services to be derived from them, the firm could create the same flow by exhausting the first capital good, and only then finishing the production of the second. And, so long as the interest rate is positive, this reduces the present value of the firm's costs at any point in time. The firm will produce the flow of output y by purchasing a time invariant flow of labor n, and by producing an infinite series of capital goods of description S every S/s periods to create a time invariant flow of capital services s. Let w denote a time invariant wage rate, W the present discounted value of w over an infinite time horizon, and C(s;S) the discounted cost of obtaining a time invariant flow of capital services s over an infinite horizon by producing capital goods of description S every S/s periods. Clearly,

$$C(s;S) = \psi(S)/[1 - e^{-r\tau}] \quad \tau = S/s. \tag{14}$$

The function C(s;S) has the following properties.

$$\begin{aligned} &C_1(s;S) > 0 \quad \forall\, s > 0 \\ &C_{11}(s;S) > 0 \quad \forall\, s > 0 \\ &\lim s \to \infty\ C_1(s;S) = \psi(S)/(rS) \\ &\lim s \to \infty\ C(s;S)/s = \psi(S)/(rS) \\ &\lim s \to 0\ C_1(s;S) = 0 \\ &C(as;S) < aC(s;S) \quad \forall\, a > 1,\, s > 0,\, S > 0 \end{aligned} \tag{15}$$

The functions C(s;S) and C(s;S)/s are illustrated in Figures 1 and 2.

The firm's cost minimizing problem is then to choose s, n, and S to minimize nW + C(s;S), subject to the constraint that it produce flow of output y. So define V(y) as follows:

$$V(y) = \min\{nW + C(s;S) \mid y = f(n,s)\}. \tag{16}$$

Now consider an arbitrary positive flow of output, y' > 0, and let s', n', and S' denote the associated cost minimizing values of the endogenous variables. The following inequalities establish that there are universal economies of scale in the production of good Y.

$$V(ay') < aWn' + C(as';S') < aWn' + aC(s';S') = aV(y') \quad \forall\, a > 1 \tag{17}$$

The first inequality follows from the fact that flows (an', as') will produce ay', but are not the cost minimizing flows, and the second from the fact that C(as;S) < aC(s;S), for a > 1.

In the introduction we showed for one sort of capital good just how exogenous indivisibility causes economies of scale, and argued that despite this fact, economies of scale in the real world are not explained by exogenous indivisibility. It is useful to review this line of reasoning for pure capital goods. Notice first that the last line of (15) is sufficient to establish the result that exogenous indivisibility of a pure capital good implies universal economies of scale in the production of any

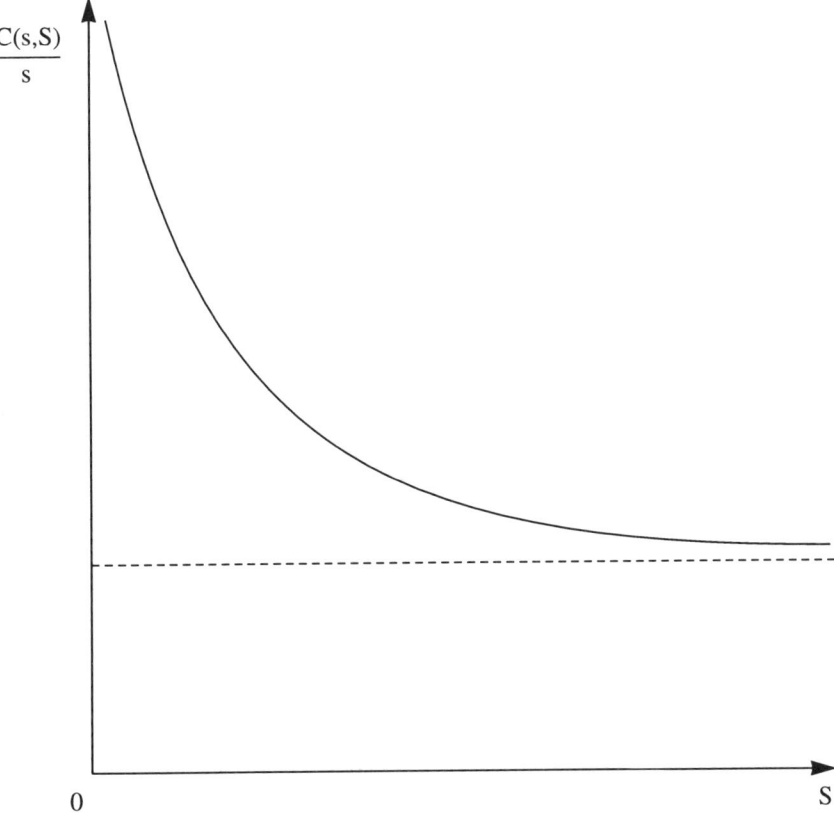

Figure 1

final good that uses as an input the services of the pure capital good, even though the flow production function for the final good is homogeneous of degree 1. Now suppose we see an indivisible pure capital good used in the production of some final good. We will also see economies of scale in the production of the final good for the reasons laid out above. Can we attribute the economies of scale to the observed indivisibility? Only if the indivisibility is truly exogenous. If it is endogenous, both the economies of scale and the observed indivisibility are manifestations of a common cause, the fundamental nonconvexity identified above. Clearly then, the mere association of indivisible capital goods and economies of scale does not allow us to explain the second by the first. Further, our casual empiricism leads us to the view that the vast bulk of the indivisibilities we in fact see are engineered – are endogenous – and hence that the observed correlation of indivisibility and economies of scale reflects a deeper common cause.

Economies of scope
We can also show that the fundamental nonconvexity necessary to account for the existence of pure capital goods implies economies of scope even in situations

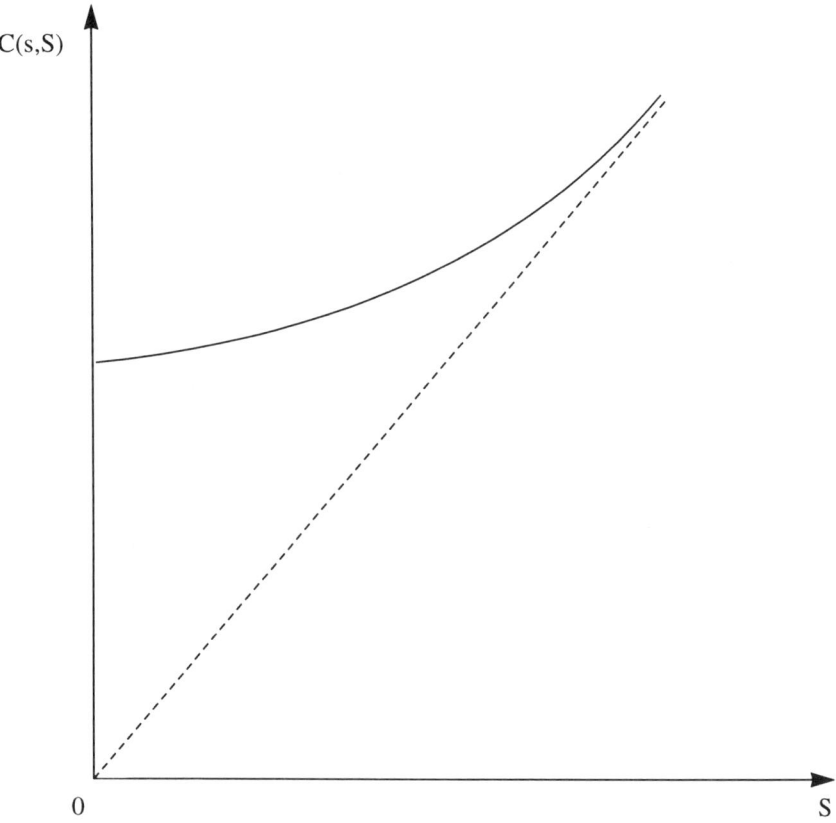

Figure 2

where there is no jointness in production. Suppose that the production functions for two final goods are homogeneous of degree 1 in all inputs, and that the service of a firm specific, pure capital good is an essential input. Now imagine producing arbitrary constant flows of the two goods, y_1 and y_2, over an infinite time horizon. We want to show the following:

$$V_1(y_1) + V_2(y_2) > V(y_1, y_2) \tag{18}$$

where $V_i(y_i)$ is the discounted present cost of producing y_i using dedicated capital goods to provide the flows of capital services, and $V(y_1, y_2)$ is the discounted present cost of producing both flows of goods using dual purpose capital goods to provide the flows of capital services. Notice that in writing this joint cost function we are not assuming that the capital service is a joint input, only that in any small time interval the flows of the capital service needed to produce the flows of output are extracted from the same capital good.

Let (n_1, s_1) and (n_2, s_2) denote cost minimizing flows of capital services and labor when the goods are produced using dedicated capital goods, and let S_1 and S_2

denote the cost minimizing stocks of capital services embodied in the dedicated capital goods. With no loss of generality, assume that $s_1 \leq s_2$. The following inequalities are easily established:

$$C(s_2;S_2)/s_2 > C(s_1;S_2)/s_1 > C(s_1;S_1)/s_1 \tag{19}$$

Therefore,

$$C(s_2;S_2) > (s_2/s_1)C(s_1;S_1) \tag{20}$$

Using this result we get

$$C(s_1;S_1) + C(s_2;S_2) > [1 + s_2/s_1]C(s_1;S_1) \tag{21}$$

Further

$$(1 + s_2/s_1)C(s_1;S_1) > C(s_1(1 + s_2/s_1);S_1) = C(s_1 + s_2;S_1) \tag{22}$$

Therefore,

$$C(s_1;S_1) + C(s_2;S_2) > C(s_1 + s_2;S_1) \tag{23}$$

The following inequalities then establish the economies of scope result.

$$V_1(y_1) + V_2(y_2) = W(n_1 + n_2) + C(s_1;S_1) + C(s_2;S_2) > W(n_1 + n_2) \\ + C(s_1 + s_2;S_1) > V(y_1+y_2) \tag{24}$$

The first inequality follows from (23) and the second from the fact that S_1 is not the cost minimizing description of the dual purpose capital good.

The universal economies of scale and scope associated with pure capital goods arise because there is no upper bound on the rate at which services can be extracted from such a good. As production of the final goods that use these capital services increases without limit, the lifetime of each successive unit of capital decreases without limit and hence the amount, and cost, of waiting approaches zero. This effect is not necessarily found with more complex types of capital goods. In the next section we consider another class of capital goods that require two parameters for their description.

III. Flow-constrained capital goods

In this section we focus on the class of what we call *flow-constrained* capital goods. A flow-constrained capital good can be completely described by its durability D and the maximum rate at which services can be extracted from it, R.

We use three gross features of real, flow-constrained capital goods to impose restrictions on the technology: a capital good is durable (D > 0); it provides a maximum service flow that is bounded away from 0 (R >> 0); it takes time to produce a capital good. We want to find necessary conditions on the technology for producing such goods that are implied by these awkward facts.

As in the preceding section, let X(t;B,T) denote flows of n inputs over a time interval beginning at time B and terminating at time T. Let ((R,D),X(t;B,T)) denote the production plan 'produce good (R,D) using input bundle X(t;B,T)'. The production possibilities set for a flow constrained capital good, Ω, is then defined as follows.

$$\Omega = \{((R,D),X(t;B,T))|X(t;B,T) \text{ will produce good } (R,D)\} \tag{25}$$

We assume that Ω is a closed set, that the production plans $((R,0),X^0)$ $(R \geq 0)$ and $((0,D),X^0)(D \geq 0)$ are in Ω, that all input flows are bought on perfect markets at time invariant prices, and that the discount rate, r, is positive and time invariant. As above, let C(X(t;B,T)) be the value at time T of input bundle X(t;B,T).

Now define $\psi(R,D)$ in the following way.

$$\psi(R,D) = \min \{C(X(t;B,T))|((R,D),X(t;B,T)) \text{ is in } \Omega\} \tag{26}$$

The minimization is accomplished by choosing a beginning date B, but not a terminal date T, and flow of all inputs over time interval [B,T]. Given the stationarity assumptions we have made, even though it is exogenous, T is not an argument of $\psi(R,D)$.

The fundamental nonconvexity
Now consider a mental experiment analogous to the one in the previous section. Suppose we observe capital good (R',D') constructed over time interval [B',T] for which R' > 0, and T > B'. Let X'(t;B',T) denote the cost minimizing input bundle. What can we infer about $\psi(R,D)$ and Ω?

Remarks in the previous section regarding economies of planning and coordination are directly applicable to flow constrained capital goods, indeed to any capital goods that are not produced instantaneously.

Clearly, there is a nonconvexity in C(R,D) with respect to durability. Any flow of capital services s(t) that good (R',D') can deliver can be replicated by producing two identical goods of description (R',D'/2) completing one of them at time T and the other at time T + D'/2. Then, using the revealed preference argument and the assumption that r > 0, we get:

$$\psi(R',D') \leq \psi(R',D'/2)[1 + e^{-r'D/2}] < 2\psi(R',D'/2) \tag{27}$$

The very existence of durable capital goods is then evidence of a fundamental nonconvexity in cost as a function of durability. This is, to us, the basic point of Akerman's (1923) work.

Similarly, any flow of capital services s(t) that good (R',D') can deliver can be replicated by producing two identical goods of description (R'/2,D') completing both at time T. Hence,

$$\psi(R',D') \leq 2\psi(R'/2,D') \tag{28}$$

We can get a strong inequality, and hence a nonconvexity of $\psi(R,D)$ with respect to R, if we assume that firms place a positive value on flexibility. That is, if two capital goods of description $(R'/2,D')$ are more flexible than one of description (R',D'), and if the firm values flexibility, we can infer a strong inequality from the fact that the firm chooses (R',D')

$$\psi(R',D') < 2\psi(R'/2,D') \tag{29}$$

Clearly, these nonconvexities in the cost function for good (R,D) reflect corresponding nonconvexities in the production possibilities set.

Economies of scale and scope
In the case of pure capital goods we found universal economies of scale and scope because the per unit cost of capital services was a strictly decreasing function of the service flow. Therefore, to consider economies of scale and scope for flow constrained capital goods, define AC(R) as follows:

$$AC(R) = \min \{\psi(R,D)/[R(1 - e^{-rD})]\}. \tag{30}$$

The minimization is with respect D, and we denote the minimizing value of D by $\Delta(R)$. AC(R) is the minimized per unit cost of obtaining flow of services R over an infinite horizon from a series of identical capital goods of description $(R,\Delta(R))$, produced every $\Delta(R)$ periods.

It is possible, though clearly not necessary, that $\psi(aR,D) < a\psi(R,D)$ for all $a > 1$, $R > 0$, and $D > 0$. In this case AC(R) is a decreasing function of R for all $R > 0$, and there are universal economies of scale and scope with flow constrained capital goods, just as there are with pure capital goods. And for the same reason: the per unit cost of capital services decreases as the flow of services increases.

To go further, we need more specific empirical knowledge. To show where this might take us, assume (as seems likely to be the case empirically) that a well-defined minimum of AC(R) with respect to R exists, and let R^* denote the minimizing value. In this case, when the firm wants a service flow that is large relative to R^*, it will use many capital goods simultaneously. Although the (minimized) per unit cost of capital services attains the value $AC(R^*)$ only for flows that are integer multiples of R^*, as R gets arbitrarily large, the divergence of per unit costs from $AC(R^*)$ approaches zero.

If capital goods are firm specific as we have assumed, or if there are significant transaction costs driven by the indivisibility of the capital goods, we then have economies of scale and/or scope up to the point where the firm is using R^* units of the capital service. Beyond that point there are alternating regions of diseconomies and economies of scale as the firm's use of the capital input increases.

In contrast, if capital services are generic inputs (as opposed to firm specific inputs), then we can imagine an approximately perfectly competitive market for capital services, so long as quantity demanded is large relative to R^*. Alternatively if all firms use a flow of services that is large relative to R^*, and if there are many such firms, we can imagine an approximately competitive market for goods of description $(R^*, \Delta(R^*))$.

IV. Concluding comments

There is a long tradition in which it is argued that the phenomenon of economies of scale in the production of final goods is caused by exogenous indivisibilities in firm specific capital goods. This argument is appealing for two reasons. First, as a matter of logic, exogenous indivisibility does imply economies of scale up to the first point at which the indivisibility constraint is non-binding. Second, as an empirical matter, indivisibilities are clearly associated with economies of scale. We reject this explanation, and instead argue that indivisibility and increasing returns are joint manifestations of what we call the fundamental nonconvexity of real capital theory.

The key point in our argument is an empirical observation: Indivisibility is not exogenous, but is rather a matter of economic choice. Any man-made capital good that we have seen can be designed to be more or less durable, can be designed to provide a larger or a smaller flow of services, can be designed to be more or less portable, and so on for a large number of economically relevant descriptors. There are, we would argue, very few exogenously indivisible capital goods. Hence, increasing returns cannot be caused by exogenous indivisibility.

The key question in our argument is this: What causes indivisibility? The straightforward answer is that the mere existence of such endogenous or designed indivisibility reveals a nonconvexity in the technology for producing individual capital goods. Loosely speaking, for firms to choose to create capital goods, it must be the case that there are increasing returns in the activity of embodying a stock of capital services in an indivisible capital good. Put the other way round, if there were constant returns in this activity, no firm would choose to create indivisible capital goods. Then, the indivisibilities that we actually observe and the increasing returns that are invariably associated with them are seen to be joint manifestations of this fundamental nonconvexity.

To say more, one must develop a deeper empirical understanding of the fundamental nonconvexity. One must understand the physical principles that govern how goods can be made to be more or less durable, the physical principles that govern how they can be made to deliver a larger or smaller flow of services, and so on.

We have assumed throughout that the input flows used to produce capital goods were purchased on perfect capital markets. We did so in order to argue that the mere existence of capital goods implied a fundamental nonconvexity in cost as a function of the stock of services embodied in an indivisible capital good, and therefore in the underlying production possibilities set. Of course, in most real situations, many of the input flows used to produce capital goods are themselves derived from capital goods. This raises a number of interesting issues and possibilities that we have not yet tackled.

Notes

* We first stated the outline of the basic argument in this paper in Archibald, Eaton, and Lipsey (1986). We wish to acknowledge helpful comments on the present paper from many colleagues, including John Chant, Jeffrey Church, Steve Easton, Richard Harris, Elhanan Helpman, Robert Jones, Nate Rosenberg, Ed Safarian, Nicolas Schmitt and those who attended seminars where the paper was presented at Flinders University, Simon Fraser University, University of Tasmania, and meetings of the Economic Growth and Policy Group in May of 1992 and of The Canadian Economics Association in June of 1992.

1. The integration is over each $x_i(t)$, and the inequality holds for all n integrals.
2. It is trivial but unenlightening to extend the following analysis to the case where n and s are vectors of inputs.

References

Akerman, J.G. (1923), *Realkapital und kapitalzins: heft I*. Stockholm: Centraltryckeriet.
Alchian, A. (1959), 'Costs and output', in: M. Abramovitz (ed.), *The allocation of resources*, Palo Alto: Stanford University Press.
Archibald, G.C., Eaton, B.C., and Lipsey, R.G. (1986), 'Address models of value theory', in: J.E. Stiglitz and G.F. Mathewson (eds), *New developments in the analysis of market structure*. Cambridge: MIT Press, 3–47.
Baumol, W.J. (1987), 'Indivisibilities', in J. Eatwell, M. Milgate, and P. Newman (eds), *The new palgrave, a dictionary of economics, volume 2*. London: The Macmillan Press Limited, 793–95.
Joseph, M.F.W. (1938), 'A discontinuous cost curve and the tendency to increasing returns', *Economic Journal*, **43**, 390–93.
Samuelson, P.A. (1967), 'The Monopolistic Competition Revolution', in R.E. Kuenne (ed.), *Monopolistic Competition Theory: Studies in Impact. Essays in Honour of Edward H. Chamberlin* New York: John Wiley.
Wicksell, K. (1934), 'Real capital and interest: Dr. Gustav Akerman's "realkapital und kapitalzins"', Appendix 2(a) of K. Wicksell, *Lectures on political economy*, London: Routledge & Kegan Paul.

Name index

Akerman, G. 274, 299
Alao, N. 167
Alchian, A. 297
Anderson, S. 234
Archibald, G. 106, 186, 192, 194, 204–5, 219, 237, 239, 254
Arrow, K. 42–5, 48

Bacon, R. 121, 131
Bain, J. 155
Baumol, W. 184, 186, 202, 217–18, 245, 265, 268
Beckman, M. 33–4, 37, 91
Beckmann, M. 135
Berry, B. 120
Bertrand, J. 236, 259, 265, 268
Bonanno, G. 257
Borner, S. 286
Boulding, K. 1, 13, 119, 269
Brander, J. 260, 264, 273
Bucklin, P. 120

Cantwell, J. 285, 289
Caves, R. 152, 154, 287
Chamberlin, E. 91, 177–8, 183–4, 194–5, 209, 220, 231–2, 234, 236, 252, 262, 265–7
Christaller, W. 166–8, 265, 268
Clark, W. 120
Coase, R. 274
Cournot, A. 147, 156, 159, 163, 207–8, 232–3, 257, 259, 265, 268

d'Aspremont, C. 205, 258–9
Dacey, M. 167
Dales, J. 279
Dasgupta, P. 205
Davidson, C. 258
Debreu, G. 42–5, 48
Deneckere, R. 235, 258
Devletoglou, N. 141
Dixit, A. 145–6, 154–6, 164, 186, 194, 196, 203–4, 206, 208–9, 231, 234, 265, 268
Donaldson, D. 142
Dorfman, R. 186
Dörrenbächer, C. 286
Dulude, L. 289
Dunning 286–7

Eastman, H. 280
Eaton, B. 52–7, 62, 64, 68–70, 74, 86, 90–92, 96, 113, 115, 119, 128, 142, 145, 154–5, 162, 176, 186, 198, 203–6, 210, 214–15, 220, 237, 239, 248–9, 251–4, 260–61, 264, 269, 273–4
Eddington, A. 184
Eden, L. 287–8
Etemad, H. 289

Ferguson, C. 234, 268
Fetter, F. 134–5, 142
Flaherty, T. 283
Foster, J. 129
Fox, K. 142

Gabszewicz, J. 205, 211, 252, 255, 258–9
Garrison, L. 120
Gee, J. 86–8, 90–92
Gilbert, R. 205, 213
Goldhar, J. 282–3
Golledge, R. 120
Gorman, W. 183
Grace, H. 32
Grossman, G. 273, 285

Hand, Judge Learned 109
Hart, O. 216, 234, 264, 268
Hay, D. 213, 245, 269
Helpman, E. 273, 285
Hicks, J. 42–3, 79
Hirschey, R. 287
Holton, R. 120
Hood, N. 286
Hotelling, H. 1, 3, 13, 20, 62–3, 92, 112, 119–20, 126, 128–9, 132, 186, 205, 231, 259, 265, 268–9
Hyson, C. 134–5, 142
Hyson, W. 134–5, 142

Jones, L. 264
Joseph, M. 297
Judd, K. 261

Kaldor, N. 47, 91, 94–5, 177, 183, 219, 253, 265–7
Kennedy 267
Keynes, J. 46, 62

Koenker, R. 232
Kreps, D. 259
Krugman, P. 272–3
Kumar, T. 142

Lancaster, K. 183–4, 186, 192–3, 218–19, 238–9, 242, 254, 265, 268
Lane, W. 210, 213, 241
Lav, M. 37
Lerner, A. 91, 119, 265, 268
Lipsey, R. 52–7, 62, 64, 68–70, 74, 86, 90–92, 96, 113, 119, 128, 145, 154–5, 162, 176, 186, 198, 203–6, 210, 214–15, 220, 237, 248–9, 251, 254, 260–61, 269, 274, 280
Lösch, A. 14, 16, 17, 24, 26, 39, 40, 120, 142, 166, 168, 186, 265, 268

Macdonald, J. 279
Mackintosh, W. 279
Markham, J. 267
Marshall, A. 42, 265–6
Mills, E. 37
Morrison, A. 289
Myrdal, G. 56

Nash, J. 25, 147, 206, 208, 214, 251–2
Nash, D. 135
Nelson, R. 120
Newbery, D. 205
Niosi, J. 288
Novshek, W. 205, 210, 251

Panzar, J. 217
Pearce, R. 286–7
Puloff, J. 186, 195–6, 234, 268
Perry, M. 232
Porter, M. 120, 130, 152, 154
Prescott, E. 186, 203–4, 213, 215, 245–7, 269

Quandt, R. 184, 265, 268

Robinson, J. 265–6
Rogers, A. 120
Rosenbluth, G. 106, 186, 192, 194, 204–5, 219, 237, 254
Roth, K. 289
Rothschild, M. 130, 235
Rothschild, R. 213

Rugman, A. 288
Rushton, G. 120

Safarian, A. 288–9
Salant, D. 258
Salop, S. 68, 186, 195–6, 203, 205, 218, 234, 242, 251, 268
Samuelson, P. 297
Sattinger, M. 234, 268
Scheinkman, J. 259
Schelling, T. 145, 147, 154–6, 204, 206
Schmalensee, R. 68, 106, 145, 203–4, 213, 218, 254, 260–61, 264
Schwanen, D. 281
Shaked, A. 92, 186, 211, 255
Shapiro, C. 258
Silverberg, G. 277, 279
Singer, H. 91, 119, 265, 268
Singh, N. 259
Singh, S. 286–7
Smith, A. 47, 273–4
Smith, M. 280
Smithies, A. 91, 112, 119, 265
Spence, A. 145–6, 154, 186, 194, 196, 204, 209, 231–3, 265, 268
Spencer, B. 273
Sraffa, P. 265–6
Steiner, P. 186
Stigler, G. 217
Stiglitz, J. 186, 194, 196, 209, 231, 234, 264, 268
Stykolt, S. 280
Sutton, J. 186, 211, 255

Thisse, J. 205, 211, 252, 255, 258–9

Visscher, M. 186, 203–4, 213, 215, 245–7, 269
Vives, X. 259
von Stackelberg, H. 157, 160–61, 163
von Thünen, J. 83

Wicksell, K. 299
Williamson, O. 274–5
Willig, R. 217
Wooders, M. 252–3, 264
Wortmann, M. 286

Young, S. 286

Economists of the Twentieth Century

Monetarism and Macroeconomic Policy
Thomas Mayer

Studies in Fiscal Federalism
Wallace E. Oates

The World Economy in Perspective
Essays in International Trade and European Integration
Herbert Giersch

Towards a New Economics
Critical Essays on Ecology, Distribution and Other Themes
Kenneth E. Boulding

Studies in Positive and Normative Economics
Martin J. Bailey

The Collected Essays of Richard E. Quandt (2 volumes)
Richard E. Quandt

International Trade Theory and Policy
Selected Essays of W. Max Corden
W. Max Corden

Organization and Technology in Capitalist Development
William Lazonick

Studies in Human Capital
Collected Essays of Jacob Mincer, Volume 1
Jacob Mincer

Studies in Labor Supply
Collected Essays of Jacob Mincer, Volume 2
Jacob Mincer

Macroeconomics and Economic Policy
The Selected Essays of Assar Lindbeck Volume I
Assar Lindbeck

The Welfare State
The Selected Essays of Assar Lindbeck Volume II
Assar Lindbeck

Classical Economics, Public Expenditure and Growth
Walter Eltis

Money, Interest Rates and Inflation
Frederic S. Mishkin

The Public Choice Approach to Politics
Dennis C. Mueller

The Liberal Economic Order
Volume I Essays on International Economics
Volume II Money, Cycles and Related Themes
Gottfried Haberler
Edited by Anthony Y.C. Koo

Economic Growth and Business Cycles
Prices and the Process of Cyclical Development
Paolo Sylos Labini

International Adjustment, Money and Trade
Theory and Measurement for Economic Policy Volume I
Herbert G. Grubel

International Capital and Service Flows
Theory and Measurement for Economic Policy Volume II
Herbert G. Grubel

Unintended Effects of Government Policies
Theory and Measurement for Economic Policy Volume III
Herbert G. Grubel

The Economics of Competitive Enterprise
Selected Essays of P.W.S. Andrews
Edited by Frederic S. Lee and Peter E. Earl

The Repressed Economy
Causes, Consequences, Reform
Deepak Lal

Economic Theory and Market Socialism
Selected Essays of Oskar Lange
Edited by Tadeusz Kowalik

Trade, Development and Political Economy
Selected Essays of Ronald Findlay
Ronald Findlay

General Equilibrium Theory
The Collected Essays of Takashi Negishi Volume I
Takashi Negishi

The History of Economics
The Collected Essays of Takashi Negishi Volume II
Takashi Negishi

Studies in Econometric Theory
The Collected Essays of Takeshi Amemiya
Takeshi Amemiya

Exchange Rates and the Monetary System
Selected Essays of Peter B. Kenen
Peter B. Kenen

Econometric Methods and Applications
(2 volumes)
G.S. Maddala

National Accounting and Economic Theory
The Collected Papers of Dan Usher, Volume I
Dan Usher

Welfare Economics and Public Finance
The Collected Papers of Dan Usher, Volume II
Dan Usher

Economic Theory and Capitalist Society
The Selected Essays of Shigeto Tsuru, Volume I
Shigeto Tsuru

Methodology, Money and the Firm
The Collected Essays of D.P. O'Brien
(2 volumes)
D.P. O'Brien

Economic Theory and Financial Policy
The Selected Essays of Jacques J. Polak
(2 volumes)
Jacques J. Polak

Sturdy Econometrics
Edward E. Leamer

The Emergence of Economic Ideas
Essays in the History of Economics
Nathan Rosenberg

Productivity Change, Public Goods and Transaction Costs
Essays at the Boundaries of Microeconomics
Yoram Barzel

Reflections on Economic Development
The Selected Essays of Michael P. Todaro
Michael P. Todaro

The Economic Development of Modern Japan
The Selected Essays of Shigeto Tsuru
Volume II
Shigeto Tsuru

Money, Credit and Policy
Allan H. Meltzer

Macroeconomics and Monetary Theory
The Selected Essays of Meghnad Desai
Volume I
Meghnad Desai

Poverty, Famine and Economic Development
The Selected Essays of Meghnad Desai
Volume II
Meghnad Desai

Explaining the Economic Performance of Nations
Essays in Time and Space
Angus Maddison

Economic Doctrine and Method
Selected Papers of R.W. Clower
Robert W. Clower

Economic Theory and Reality
Selected Essays on their Disparities and Reconciliation
Tibor Scitovsky

Doing Economic Research
Essays on the Applied Methodology of Economics
Thomas Mayer

Institutions and Development Strategies
The Selected Essays of Irma Adelman
Volume I
Irma Adelman

Dynamics and Income Distribution
The Selected Essays of Irma Adelman
Volume II
Irma Adelman

The Economics of Growth and Development
Selected Essays of A.P. Thirlwall
A.P. Thirlwall

Theoretical and Applied Econometrics
The Selected Papers of Phoebus J. Dhrymes
Phoebus J. Dhrymes

Innovation, Technology and the Economy
The Selected Essays of Edwin Mansfield
(2 volumes)
Edwin Mansfield

Economic Theory and Policy in Context
The Selected Essays of R.D. Collison Black
R.D. Collison Black

Location Economics
Theoretical Underpinnings and Applications
Melvin L. Greenhut

Spatial Microeconomics
Theoretical Underpinnings and Applications
Melvin L. Greenhut

Capitalism, Socialism and Post-Keynesianism
Selected Essays of G.C. Harcourt
G.C. Harcourt

Time Series Analysis and Macroeconometric Modelling
The Collected Papers of Kenneth F. Wallis
Kenneth F. Wallis

Foundations of Modern Econometrics
The Selected Essays of Ragnar Frisch
(2 volumes)
Edited by Olav Bjerkholt

Growth, the Environment and the Distribution of Incomes
Essays by a Sceptical Optimist
Wilfred Beckerman

The Economics of Environmental Regulation
Wallace E. Oates

Econometrics, Macroeconomics and Economic Policy
Selected Papers of Carl F. Christ
Carl F. Christ

Strategic Approaches to the International Economy
Selected Essays of Koichi Hamada
Koichi Hamada

Economic Analysis and Political Ideology
The Selected Essays of Karl Brunner
Volume One
Edited by Thomas Lys

Growth Theory and Technical Change
The Selected Essays of Ryuzo Sato
Volume One
Ryuzo Sato

Industrialization, Inequality and Economic Growth
Jeffrey G. Williamson

Economic Theory and Public Decisions
Selected Essays of Robert Dorfman
Robert Dorfman

The Logic of Action One
Method, Money and the Austrian School
Murray N. Rothbard

The Logic of Action Two
Applications and Criticism from the Austrian School
Murray N. Rothbard

Bayesian Analysis in Econometrics and Statistics
The Zellner View and Papers
Arnold Zellner

On the Foundations of Monopolistic Competition and Economic Geography
The Selected Essays of B. Curtis Eaton and Richard G. Lipsey
B. Curtis Eaton and Richard G. Lipsey

Microeconomics, Growth and Political Economy
The Selected Essays of Richard G. Lipsey
Volume One
Richard G. Lipsey

Macroeconomic Theory and Policy
The Selected Essays of Richard G. Lipsey
Volume Two
Richard G. Lipsey

Employment, Labor Unions and Wages
The Collected Essays of Orley Ashenfelter
Volume One
Edited by Kevin F. Hallock

Education, Training and Discrimination
The Collected Essays of Orley Ashenfelter
Volume Two
Edited by Kevin F. Hallock

Economic Institutions and the Demand and Supply of Labour
The Collected Essays of Orley Ashenfelter
Volume Three
Edited by Kevin F. Hallock

Monetary Theory and Monetary Policy
The Selected Essays of Karl Brunner
Volume Two
Edited by Thomas Lys

Macroeconomic Issues from a Keynesian Perspective
Selected Essays of A.P. Thirlwall
Volume Two
A.P. Thirlwall

Economics Against the Grain Volume One
Microeconomics, Industrial Organization and Related Themes
Julian L. Simon

Economics Against the Grain Volume Two
Population Economics, Natural Resources and Related Themes
Julian L. Simon

Money and Macroeconomics
The Selected Essays of David Laidler
David Laidler